FRAN TAYLOR

COMPANY MAN

COMPANY MAN

The Rise and Fall of Corporate Life

Anthony Sampson

TIMES
BUSINESS

RANDOM HOUSE

This work was originally published
in the United Kingdom by HarperCollins
Publishers, London.

Library of Congress Cataloging-in-Publication Data
Sampson, Anthony.
Company man: the rise and fall of corporate life/Anthony
Sampson.
p. cm.
Includes bibliographical references (p.   ) and index.
ISBN 0-8129-2631-5 (alk. paper)
1. Corporate culture.   2. Organizational behavior.   I. Title.
HD58.7.S258   1996
302.3'5—dc20   95-34536

Manufactured in the United States of America on acid-free paper
24689753
First U.S. Edition

Contents

Acknowledgements

IN THE CONCEPTION and creation of this book I am specially grateful to Richard Johnson, my editor at HarperCollins, and my longtime agent Michael Sissons, who saw the point and scope of it from its origins and encouraged me through the dark days of its mid-career. I also owe much, as in many previous books, to my friend and constant adviser Robin Denniston who has kept his sharp eye on unnecessary verbiage. My long-suffering assistant Carla Shimeld has seen it through more than usual recastings and drafts with extraordinary patience and care. My wife Sally has reassured me and helped me on our travels together, and both she and my daughter Katie have contributed ideas and sources. For contacts and suggestions in Japan I am specially grateful to my friend Takashi Kakuma of Shogakukan, to my agent Tom Mori and to my old colleague and publisher Shigeki Hijino of TBS Britannica.

In my researches and interviews I am indebted to more people in three continents than I can mention, but I am specially appreciative of the following: Percy Barnevik, Asa Briggs, Mourik Broekman, Rhiannon Chapman, Paul Coombes, Howard Davis, Francis Duffy, Ronald Dworkin, Nigel Dyck-hoff, Keisuke Fujino, Brian Gannon, Sir James Goldsmith, Sir Owen Green, Professor Charles Handy, Lord Hanson, Randolph Harrison, Sir John Harvey-Jones, Christopher Haskins, John Heiman, Robert Heller, Sir Bryan Henderson, Masuhiko Hirobuchi, Eric Hobsbawm, Michael Hodges, Sir Christopher Hogg, Sir Peter Holmes, Nigel Humphreys, Spencer Hyman, Isao Inoue, Masataka Itoh, Sir Martin Jacomb, Francis Jago, Tom Jago, Charles Jencks, John Jones, Guy de Jonquiere, Nobumitsu Kagami, Jonathan King, Mikio Kitano, Yuriko Koike, Takaaki Kojima, Sir Kit McMahon, John Manser, Thomas Mullins, Peter Newton, Masahiro Oga, Hiroshi Ota, Sir Geoffrey Owen, Sir Michael Perry, Peter Pugh, Charles Raw, Sir Richard Rogers, Alastair Ross Goobey, Peter Rowlinson, Garry Runciman, David Sainsbury, Professor Arthur Schlesinger, Professor Kenneth Simmonds, David Simon, George Soros, Hideya Taida, Geoffrey Tudor, Louis Turner, Stanley Weiss, Nicholas Wolfers.

Introduction

Read more novels and fewer business books.
Relationships are really all there is.

TOM PETERS

I have always been curious about the life and role of company man. I was born in the company town of Billingham in north-east England, where my father was a research scientist with the biggest British chemical corporation, Imperial Chemical Industries. At home he seemed silent and withdrawn. Later as a schoolboy in London, I was taken to visit him in the splendid new corporate palace on the Thames: walking through the great nickel doors and up the automatic elevator I found a far more masterful person behind a huge desk in an imposing office with an obedient secretary and a magic teleprinter. It seemed a picture of permanence and grandeur to which I could never aspire.

I remained fascinated as a child by the daily life that went on in the great office buildings which I glimpsed through the windows, and in the great new American skyscrapers which were overshadowing each other as symbols of the growing corporate powers which were encircling the world. As their inhabitants swarmed into the elevators every morning they seemed to be joining in obscure rituals up in the clouds, quite cut off from ordinary mortals; and despite the occasional Hollywood movie I could never imagine what people really did inside them or what they all said to each other.

Later as a journalist and writer I began trying to investigate the workings of power – first in Britain, then in Europe and America. I had the opportunity to penetrate behind the corporate façades, to ask chairmen and secretaries what they were up to, and to understand more of their motives and viewpoints. When I wrote successive books about multinational corporations – including oil companies, arms companies and airlines – I found myself sharing some of the ordeals

xi

of their nomadic managers as I flew between anonymous hotels and attended conferences, banquets and conventions in windowless halls. As an irreverent loner with no badge of identity I was conscious, like other outsiders, of the intense commitment and self-containment of these separate worlds; but I was often struck by the strength of individual spirits and ambitions which co-existed with corporate loyalties. In the eighties I also became intrigued by the quite different make-up of the financial entrepreneurs whom I got to know, like Sir James Goldsmith, George Soros and Richard Branson, who were part of the new explosion of money round the globe – which I looked at in a television series, *The Midas Touch*. And on several visits to Tokyo, working alongside Japanese executives, I saw something of the more collective and unified attitudes of Asian company men, who were beginning to challenge Western ideas. By the nineties, when I came back into Western corporate territory, the ground seemed to be shifting underfoot: the big companies were rethinking all their assumptions, and the rivalry between Asian and Western capitalism was becoming a central theme of contemporary world history.

Reading novels and watching plays and films, I had always been puzzled that they had so little to say about the office life and company politics which provided the daily background to middle-class families like my own, and which seemed much more relevant than the parliamentary games and party-politics. Novelists and historians had regarded company people as a race apart, much further apart than lawyers, doctors or Members of Parliament, even than generals or admirals. Yet they were now really at the centre of society, with a confidence based on apparently secure employment, and on recognised achievement. As economic competition took over from military conflict company man was as much a potential national hero as the commander, while his social influence was everywhere. His habits and preferences were changing the lifestyles of cities and suburbs; his conferences and entertainments determined the design of hotels and restaurants; his travels decided the air routes; his language and priorities permeated politics, public service and even academia. The title 'executive' became the password into the promised new world of markets and prosperity.

With this curiosity and vantage-point I had long wanted to write a social history of company man which would try to connect him with the broader historical and literary context. My ambition was revived by the corporate dramas of the nineties, and the contests between America, Europe and Asia which revealed all the vulnerabilities and insecurities of the protagonists.

So in this book I set out to trace the story of company men – and later company women – as social rather than economic beings. I try to depict them, not just as actors in company histories, nor as 'humanware' alongside software and hardware, but as individuals in the round who have always faced difficult and changing relationships with their employers, and between their offices and homes. I make much use of writers and outside observers who have provided insights and sidelights into human predicaments which have been too often ignored by management experts, and obscured by mechanical structures and attitudes. And I give special attention to the recurring tension between the human spirit and the machines which it has created: the theme which has kept returning in different forms since the Industrial Revolution, and which has reached a new phase in the age of computers.

In covering such a wide geographical canvas, I have not tried to provide a comprehensive history. I do not attempt to furnish an economic analysis, or to describe the development of unions, industrial disputes or strikes. I have concentrated on the changing character of middle-class company man, picking out the phases and episodes which seem most significant and enlightening, and providing close-ups of a few big companies which have provided models and fore-runners for others: including General Motors and IBM in America, Shell and ICI in Britain, and Toyota and Sony in Japan.

I first take a glimpse into the future, visiting the weird frontier of innovation in north-west America, where young entrepreneurs and computer programmers are developing new species of company people between the forests and the mountains. I then flash back through history to show how the modern corporation and office life first emerged out of the chartered company and the family firm in the nineteenth century, and how the 'organisation man' was established by the mid-twentieth century as apparently permanent and indispensable.

In the second half of the book I describe how successive shocks battered the confidence of Western executives and forced them to rethink their theories of management and their role in society. Raiders took over and broke up established giants; Asian competitors arrived with their more harmonious attitudes; computers took over from middle-managers; career women challenged men's egos, clubs and jobs; companies pared themselves down into leaner headquarters, with temp managers and short-contract consultants. The remaining company people were pressed to become more agile, and to control their own destiny; which might ultimately be to lose their job. The office-building which had been the fixed centre of social life appeared to be dissolving into a placeless network of tele-commuters, mobile telephones, databanks and electronic mail. But while conventional company people were insecure as never before, the corporate chiefs were more powerful than ever, and better-paid even when they failed; thus creating a new kind of class structure.

This transformation provides I believe one of the most extraordinary elements in the history of the late twentieth century, which is still working itself through; and I hope I may have been able to shed some light on it in the midst of the fray.

ANTHONY SAMPSON
London, November 1994

COMPANY MAN

CHAPTER ONE

Frontier City

We feel the machine slipping from our hands
As if someone else were steering;
If we see light at the end of the tunnel
It's the light of the oncoming train.

ROBERT LOWELL, 'Since 1939', 1977

The enemy of the market is not ideology but the
engineer.

J.K. GALBRAITH,
The New Industrial State, 1967

The north-west coastline of America has been a frontier for successive new kinds of company man ever since the early nineteenth century,
when the Hudson's Bay Company first sent out a group of outcasts,
whom they called 'the very scum of the earth', to buy furs. They
were followed by loggers and timber-merchants who cut down the
enormous forests along the bays round Seattle and shipped logs to
build new towns in California; and then by the traders, bankers and
camp-followers who arrived in Seattle after 1897, when it became
the main port for the Alaskan gold-rush.

The forests remained the chief source of wealth; and in 1900
Frederick Weyerhaeuser bought nearly a million acres of forest,
which was to be the basis of the huge Weyerhaeuser timber corporation, still based outside Seattle. But in 1916 William Boeing, having
made a timber fortune in the north-west, launched a small aircraft
business in Seattle which was to become the city's biggest source of
prosperity, and the biggest aerospace company in the world. In the
late twentieth century the Seattle lifestyle began to attract new kinds
of young company people, who depended on brainpower rather than
natural resources, and who were developing computer software,

3

bio-tech, cellular phones and Nintendo games. They were creating new kinds of companies – not huge engineered organisations like Boeing, but shapeless organisms like amoebae or jellyfish: fast-changing alliances of people who might at any time regroup themselves and set up their own businesses. The most innovative were the most insecure, as they confronted the kind of uncertainties which had faced Bill Boeing sixty years before. And Seattle became an artistic frontier, too, with a vigorous youth-culture, and one of the highest proportions of under-thirty-fives of any city in America. It had countless cinemas, fish restaurants and sportscars, bookshops and above all music clubs. It was the home of Kurt Cobain and the rock group Nirvana, and the birthplace of 'grunge' – the style of tattered trousers and ragged dresses, of rich kids trying to look poor, and of music sounding 'like a zoo on fire'.

The forests, the mountains and the ocean still dominate Seattle, with its sea-mists, lakes, islands and bays which look like Norwegian fjords. Every morning an odd mix of commuters from the surrounding islands stream onto the ferries: some looking like Nordic fishermen in beards and sailors' caps, others like student dropouts in T-shirts and sneakers. As the boat chugs across the water the dawn sun lights up the glittering skyscrapers; young commuters bring out laptops, cellular phones and computer journals, and as the boat docks on the pier they stride into downtown Seattle and disappear into the office blocks. But there's a tension between the natural beauty and the pressures of technology. 'For my generation it's a hard combination,' a Seattle banker in his fifties told me. 'One foot in the environment, one in business. We can live on the island, in a beautiful house among the trees. But all the time we're being wired up and linked to new technologies – with faxes, computers and e-mail – which cut us off from the nature around us.'

Seattle people have their own kind of weirdness, which was popularised by David Lynch's cult TV serial *Twin Peaks*, partly set in hotels in the nearby mountains, which became a new tourist attraction. Serial killers have been strangely attracted to this coastline, and studies have suggested a high incidence of madness and suicides. But Seattle people still seem much saner and soberer than Southern Californians, many of whom come north as refugees from riots and crazy philosophies. They are not obsessed by each new fad, and they welcome both clean new industries and campaigning environmentalists, or 'tree huggers'. The wild beauty of the north-west, with its forests and mountains, seems in total contrast to the disciplined mechanical world of the offices, computers and factory-sites which have been cleared from the virgin landscape. And it underlines the contrast between the individual spirit and the machines which have circumscribed it – as is revealed in different ways by Seattle's two biggest corporations.

EDUCATING THE BOEINGITES

A few miles north of Seattle, the freeway towards Canada runs close to a high white wall, three-quarters of a mile long, interrupted only by six vast blue-grey gates which look like a giant's garage doors. Behind them is one of the wonders of the modern world, the biggest factory on earth. It was first built in 1967, when bulldozers cleared a whole forest to make way for a structure big enough to contain a row of Jumbo Jets, the brand-new Boeing 747s. Now it has been enlarged to make room for the new wonder, the Boeing 777.

Behind those great gates lies a roofed city, with its own micro-climate and weather, where 8,000 people are working in surroundings as cut off from the outside world as a film studio or a theme park. Inside the life seems as normal and settled as a country town. There is a railway line and a main street along which pass cars and bicycles, past vending-machines, first-aid stations and garbage-wagons looking for parking space ('Do not park Dumpster here'). From ground level the activities look quite homely and commonplace. In one section, like a rag-trade factory, women are sewing together long electric wires. In another, men are fitting cables into a Jumbo: what they call 'stuffing the bird'. In another, wings are racked like slices of bread in a toaster, waiting to be fitted to planes. At a higher level a man is sitting on the hump of a Jumbo, picking rivets from a cardboard box and drilling them into the plates. In another section are full-sized mock-ups of the planes, which show how all the wires, pipes and bulkheads fit together.

It is only from the walkways above that you can see the full scale of the roofed city: a vista of Jumbos taking shape, accumulating their wings, tails and fittings until they are ready to be rolled out through the great doors onto the airfield to be tested, painted and flown off to join the air fleets of the world.

But the routine is less settled than it looks. In one corner a more elegant plane, covered in shiny green vinyl, has been detached from the rest, with a more ordered space around it: the brand-new Boeing 777, which stands out as the latest triumph of the engineers. The engineers had no mock-up for this plane. Its real mastermind was a sophisticated computer programme called Catia, which showed in three-dimensional detail how all the separate components would fit together. And Catia also compelled the engineers to fit together. 'We found that the computer was really a communications tool,' said one Boeing man. 'The computers forced engineers to co-operate to prevent them spitting out incompatible plans.' The Boeing factory, behind all its apparent order, became a battleground of changing human relationships. It was a painful experience, for Boeingites have always been a very separate, confident species: most of them have spent their adult lifetimes with Boeing, living in Boeing suburbs, belonging to Boeing clubs – even a club for the occult – and playing golf with other Boeingites.

Over eight decades Seattle watched the tiny business grow into the world's biggest aircraft company, providing tens of thousands of jobs and repeatedly breaking new engineering frontiers. By the end of the Second World War it was turning out a bomber every hour. By 1960 it was producing the 707, the first regular passenger jet; by 1967 it was making the 747, the first wide-bodied jet.

Seattle could never forget Boeing: it was surrounded by four air-fields full of Boeing planes, and it was so dependent on Boeing's donations to city projects that it kept them secret. No politician could ignore 'the great gorilla': the most famous local Senator, 'Scoop' Jackson, whose house is now a monument, was known as 'the Senator for Boeing'.

The Boeing engineers had their ups and downs. After the worst cutbacks, in 1970, some of them took to driving taxis. People joked about 'Boeing, Boeing, Gone', and suggested that the last person to leave Seattle should turn off the lights. But Boeing recovered to ride high on the boom of the eighties, and it faced none of the humiliations that beset General Motors or IBM: its engineers were still winning battles on the leading edge of aerospace, while auto-engineers had fallen back. Even the unions could not blame Boeing for the cyclical downturns, and they praised its management. 'We work hand-in-hand with Boeing,' said Connie Kelliher, the spokesperson of the Machinist's Union in Seattle. 'It's survived much better than other aerospace companies like Lockheed or McDonnell. We only become adversarial when we negotiate wages.' But by the late eighties even the Boeing engineers were having to emerge from their proud specialisation and rethink their whole approach to their work. There was no outward crisis: Boeing was at the top of the business cycle, with full orders for Jumbos. But the new chairman, Frank Shrontz, a lawyer who had worked in the Pentagon, was concerned that the European Airbus was catching up with Boeing's technology and undercutting its prices. At the same time Boeing was hiring large numbers of young managers and workers, who resented the autocratic company hierarchy. 'There was a one-way flow,' as one of those recruits told me. 'It was a culture struggle between the old guard and the newcomers who wanted to be involved in decisions. You could sum up the argument in one word: communications.'

This was a shock to Boeing's top managers. 'As a young man I'd stood in line to work overtime. I'd often work seven days a week,' said Larry McKean, the director of human resources. 'Suddenly the new employees were challenging authority, complaining about the eight layers of managers, and wanting empowerment. They had new values – but we still had the old management.'

Shrontz realised that Boeing had to pay more attention to its employees, and that there was something wrong with the company's management. Like many other battered bosses, he looked to Japan, sending his top executives to tour the most successful Japanese plants. They were amazed at what they saw. They came back to Seattle insisting that they did not want to make Boeing Japanese, but they began slowly to introduce Japanese methods – to reduce inventories, to speed up production, to connect with customers, and above all to motivate their own people.

The hardest part was to teach managers how to manage change. The heads of divisions could make the connections, but the real problem was making 16,000 managers connect. 'A lot of them weren't interested,' said McKean. 'They said, "I don't ask people – I tell 'em what to do."' Boeing eased these managers out gradually, allowing them to retire early with grace, and remained relatively paternalistic. Their top people visited Jack Welch, the boss of General Electric (see Chapter 14), who had fired hundreds of managers, and decided they could not be so ruthless. But Welch persuaded them that people must be taught to 'control their own destiny', and they followed his system of making managers assess their peers. 'At first I thought it was bullshit,' said McKean, 'but it really works. You *can* teach people to control their own destiny.'

The engineers were the hardest of all to convince. At first 'they rolled their eyes and hoped it would all go away'. 'We had always talked about breaking down the barriers,' said McKean, 'but the engineers were very specialised and cut off, even from other engineers: their managers really managed things, not people. One senior engineer had worked for thirty-five years without going on the factory floor. There was a Berlin Wall between them and the others: they just threw stuff over the top, and expected the marketers to sell it. We had to bring the engineers closer to people. But we couldn't turn Boeing upside down overnight; we had to empower people, to teach them how to think.'

Why had it taken so long to accept something which now seems so obvious: that people work better when they are consulted and treated as adults? Almost fifty years ago Edwards Deming, the American prophet of quality, had lectured in Seattle about how workers must be given responsibility for their own products; but he had been ignored in America, and his ideas were only accepted in Japan. Why had Boeing been so slow, I asked McKean. He paused and said sadly, 'Trust. We monitored them, supervised them, told them when to go to the bathroom. We didn't trust our own people.'

Boeing is only one dramatic example of the realisation that swept through many Western companies towards the end of the twentieth century: that they had not just slipped back in efficiency and productivity, but had failed to connect with the human beings on whom they depended. The machines had overwhelmed the men.

HUMANISING THE MICROSOFTIES

Much more far-reaching changes were emerging from another part of Seattle, from the headquarters of the Microsoft corporation. Microsoft had grown up not from massive engineering projects, but from inside the brain of a young Seattle computer-freak, Bill Gates, the son of a local corporate lawyer who in a few years had turned it into one of the biggest corporations in the world. The Boeing people, despite their experience with computers, were baffled by the young intruders. 'They're a lot of oddballs, those Microsoft people,' said Larry McKean; he thought his chairman had never properly met Bill Gates. One Boeing man, Mike Hallman, had defected to Microsoft to become their president in 1990, and had tried to broaden Microsoft's horizons and relationships; they had found him too laid-back and unaggressive, and eased him out after two years. But Microsoft had more thrilling prospects than Boeing; and it was initiating more revolutionary changes in the relationship between people and machines.

There is nothing industrial about lunching at Microsoft. Along Microsoft Way, among the forests outside Seattle, there is no tower block, no main gate, no sign of security guards: there are only groups of uniformly low white buildings, each with wide green-glassed windows, surrounded by pines and azaleas growing close to the walls, and by car-parks full of foreign cars. It looks like a private university or an expensive sanatorium. I was directed to one of the buildings, where I tapped out my name onto a computer. My young host soon appeared, and drove me in his untidy little car across the campus to the big central building containing the restaurant. The path across the lawn was embedded with metal slabs like tombstones commemorating Microsoft's main achievements over the last twenty years, beginning with 'Basic', the programme which first opened up the personal computer. Another slab had the slogan: 'EVERY TIME A PRODUCT SHIPS IT TAKES US ONE STEP CLOSER TO THE VISION: A COMPUTER ON EVERY DESK AND IN EVERY HOME.'

Inside, the cheerful cafeteria was full of young employees looking like a gathering of cosmopolitan graduate students transplanted into a vacation project. They had every kind of face and accent – Chinese, Japanese, Indian, and several who were unmistakably British. They were lining up for a range of cheap ethnic dishes, including excellent Thai chicken and rice; there were free soft drinks, in the Microsoft tradition, but no alcohol.

The Microsofties all had the same casual look. Many of them wore T-shirts, pullovers, jeans and trainers. They were nearly all young – the average age of the company's employees is thirty-two – and almost half were women, looking as confident and relaxed as the men. Few of the men conformed to the stock picture of the computer-nerd – pebble-glasses, awkward movements and pens in their outside pockets – but they all seemed addicted to their work, and many were overweight.

The campus was designed to encourage an open-air life, with sportsfields and a nature walk through the woods, but the walk was clearly not much trodden, and the rural setting seemed at odds with the intensive atmosphere: sometimes teams became so engrossed in a project that they worked all night, or slept briefly in bedrooms provided on the campus. It all seemed to have the excitement of a wartime project; and over lunch one Microsoftie compared it to the British intelligence centre at Bletchley in the Second World War – where his own father had worked – which brought brilliant young academics together to break German codes.

Inside, the Microsoft buildings were austere, with small, plain cubicles all the same size, wired up for a computer and telephone equipped with voice-mail and electronic mail. E-mail is the favoured means of communication, and Microsoft have developed their own system, which they insist is a critical part of their corporate democ-racy, for it allows any employee to communicate direct with the boss, while also providing a social bulletin board which links up Micro-softies with common interests in sport, chess or movies. But the democracy has its limitations and controls: the management have been worried about employees using their computers to pursue their own business projects, and have installed programmes which can monitor them. And the limitations of voice-mail and e-mail become clear to anyone trying to communicate with Microsoft from the outside world; its own chief 'communicator', Marty Taucher, is pronounced Talker but is known to journalists as 'Non-talker'.

The austere collegiate culture will be even more emphatic when a new campus is built on a neighbouring site. It has been designed by a leading architect in Seattle, who showed me a model. It looks more like a monastery than a campus, with formal traditional buildings and small windows, built round a 'Commons' with a tower and a cloister which will be the centre for communal activities. The architect enthused over the medieval unity, the monkish cells and the gardens which were designed to provide 'blow-off space' where Microsofties could gain inspiration like meditative friars.

On the campus there is nothing to suggest that hundreds of the employees are millionaires, and that a handful are worth over $100 million. 'Most of them don't have time to think about it,' one employee told me. 'Not many take the money and run,' I was assured by the human resources manager Susan Voeller, a veteran of all of six years in the company. 'There's no real connection between the success of Microsoft stock and the rate of attrition. We're not surprised by the commitment. We hire people with a lot of drive.' But the rest of Seattle, I found, is puzzled and disconcerted by so many young multi-millionaires who don't seem to know how to spend their fortunes. 'When I sit down to discuss plans with them,' said the architect, 'I keep remembering that they're so rich. I can't help thinking: "Where did *I* go wrong?"'

Bill Gates, the billionaire chairman, encourages a casual, egalitarian style. 'They cultivate the youth-culture image,' said Paul Andrews, his biographer. 'They're trying to maintain the start-up mode.' 'We're setting an example of letting people work as they want,' said Susan Voeller. As I left the campus I noticed four dark suits and ties, but they turned out to belong to Japanese vendors.

But Microsoft also encourage an intense competitiveness and pursuit of profits. 'They're not interested in your clothes, your style, or when and how you work: you can work at home all the time,' said one Microsoftie. 'But they're sure interested in what you produce. They review your progress twice a year, with marks from one to five. Four means exceptional; one means you're out.' All Microsofties are repeatedly compared to their peers, and Bill Gates is more like a headmaster or supervisor than a tycoon: to be questioned by him is like a final university examination. But behind that discipline is the ultimate motivation of profit, maintained by granting generous stock-options. As I was told: 'It's like a return to raw nineteenth-century capitalism.'

The relentless pursuit of profits arouses criticism, or jealousy, from the computer heartland Silicon Valley, down in California; particularly from Apple, who see Microsoft as their chief competitor. 'Their recruitment is based on greed,' said Frank O'Mahoney, the 'corporate mouthpiece' of Apple in Cupertino. 'They live, eat and sleep with each other.' 'Seattle doesn't have the same constant mobility as Silicon Valley,' said Paul Saffo of the Institute of the Future in San Francisco, whose wife was a co-founder of Aldus, a rival software company. 'Microsoft has a corrupting effect on Seattle, and they're too dependent on Bill Gates. If they lost Gates they'd be in free fall.' Susan Voeller insists that Seattle is more liveable than California, with safer neighbourhoods; but she concedes that there's some disadvantage in not being in Silicon Valley where Microsoft would have fifty similar companies nearby.

Bill Gates, it is said, chose Seattle not so much because it was his home town, as because the constant rain encouraged hard work. 'Nothing quite cools the ardour as much as steady rain,' says Peter Drucker, the veteran management guru who lives in California. 'It keeps people indoors. But I'm told that Microsoft has a lot of office romances.'

Behind all the austere dedication is the personality of Bill Gates, who dominates Microsoft with the combination of mathematical brilliance and commercial ruthlessness which made him realise he could control a revolutionary new means of communication. He often compares himself to Henry Ford, who had the same vision: Ford had his moment of truth when he saw a copy of *The American Machinist* which explained how to build a gasoline engine, and exclaimed: 'a barrel of money was to be made in it'. Gates had his moment in January 1975, as an undergraduate at Harvard, when he read about the Altair computer and realised that he could make a fortune by devising a standard programme for a mass-produced version – which became 'Basic'. Gates, like Ford, was obsessed by his mission and his company: when he chose girlfriends, and eventually his wife, he chose them from inside Microsoft. And, like Ford, he wanted to control the world – not through machines, but through programmes which were substitutes for the human mind: 'Well, someday they're gonna unravel this,' he once said, 'and we'll actually be able to put people onto chips.'

Microsoft remained very cut off from the traditional life of Seattle. Its campus seems a world away from the Rainier Club, a classical building tucked between shiny skyscrapers in downtown Seattle which is the traditional meeting-place for old money. At lunch there I saw no sign of Microsoftie members, who were anyway (my banker host assured me) reluctant to put on ties. 'Microsoft are caught up in their own social world and their own e-mail,' he explained. 'The first time I became aware of them was at a Harvard Reunion at the Four Seasons Hotel. We were just about to sit down to dinner when five young men came in wearing T-shirts saying MICROSOFT AT HAR-VARD. It was then that I realised what was going to hit Seattle.'

The old rich were even more shocked when they learnt that the misfits from Microsoft had bigger fortunes than theirs, and that young William Gates was the richest man in America. His parents, Bill and Mary, became pillars of many local causes, but their billionaire son remained notably absent from good works, and explained that he was not yet 'in the philanthropic mode'. Bill Gates has since made some generous gifts, including several million dollars to Seattle University on its magnificent campus overlooking the sea. He has also contrib-uted to the daring new Seattle Art Museum designed by Robert Venturi, which displays the names of its benefactors in its entry hall, including BILL AND MARY GATES, followed by MR WILLIAM H. GATES III. Other Microsoft multi-millionaires have been more adventurously and visibly generous: one has endowed a Jimi Hendrix museum, another is restoring the old Paramount Theatre. But there are still billions waiting to be spent, and the Microsofties still keep their distance, while the old Seattlans keep asking: When will they start spending their money?

The Microsofties are masters of their own digital universe; but they find great difficulties in connecting with broader communications, as is obvious from a glance at any software manual, with its language incomprehensible to outsiders. Bill Gates himself was always a boy-wonder, with a precocious talent for arithmetic which he developed to the neglect of wider interests and experience. But now Microsoft faces a challenge which requires a much broader understanding: to be one of the controllers of the 'Information Highway' which can link up homes across the world with data-banks, entertainment and communications along the telephone wires. And this requires the kind of 'usability' which is outside the Microsofties' experience. As one Microsoft document describes the problem: 'An emphasis on a holistic approach to usability in which it is integrated into all parts of the product development process is new to the software industry.'

Microsofties are having, in fact, to connect up with a world of ordinary human emotions and relationships which have little to do with digits. Already they have been recruiting much more literary, wide-ranging people, including journalists, publishers and even poets, to help them grapple with their future opportunities. 'The programmers don't actually read poetry, but they respect it,' said one of the newcomers. 'It's the first place where I haven't had to disguise that I'm interested in poetry.' But the Microsofties still face a great psychological leap, to escape from their obsessive campus into the wider culture of the outside world, and the thoughts and needs of ordinary customers.

Ever since the Industrial Revolution there have been recurring worries about the disconnection between men and machines, between families and corporations, between organic growth and mechanical structures, between fragmentation and unity. 'It is the Age of Machinery, in every outward and inward sense of that term,' lamented Thomas Carlyle in 1838. At the end of the nineteenth century Henry Adams – the grandson and great-grandson of American presidents – warned that 'The multiplicity of unity had steadily increased, was increasing, and threatened to increase beyond reason.' The next century saw new technologies and mass-production creating far greater specialisations; while prophets speculated about machines dehumanising society and overwhelming the human spirit. In 1950 Norbert Wiener, the mathematician who invented cybernetics, warned of the dangers of the new computing machines: 'The mechanical control of man cannot succeed unless we know man's built-in purposes, and why we want to control him.' Ten years later, just before he went to work for Boeing, the young writer Thomas Pynchon, inspired by reading Adams and Wiener, wrote an enigmatic short story, 'Entropy', which gave his own picture of disintegration 'from ordered individuality to a kind of chaos'.

Big corporations were themselves beginning to look more like machines, and the 'organisation men' appeared as the agents of conformity, with their commitment to scientific management, their intricate pyramids, layers and interfaces. But by the 1980s the top-heavy Western companies, with their 'scientific' management, were being humiliated by the more agile Japanese; while the computer was seen as an agent for liberation as well as conformity. A new generation was looking towards more intimate relationships and teams, to the kind of basic enterprise with which companies began, and questioning the whole nature of the company itself.

CHAPTER TWO

John Company

The idea of the company, of a group of individuals sharing commercial responsibility, has never been easy to define or understand. In the Middle Ages nearly all business was conducted by individuals trading with each other at fairs, or selling goods or services to their governments; some of them developed into family firms. During the Crusades, merchants had to collaborate to share the costs and risks of their ventures abroad, and in the Italian city-states maritime firms began to call themselves *compagnie*, whose members 'took bread' with each other (*cum-panis*). In sixteenth-century Britain the Merchant Adventurers sold cloth to the Low Countries under the strict discipline of a corporation which had its own government and legal entity, which allowed it to survive its members and become a permanent body.

The forerunners of today's corporations were the merchant companies which grew up in north-west Europe in the seventeenth century, supported by governments which granted them monopolies in return for taxes. The long voyages by the Muscovy Company to Russia, or by the Levant Company to the Middle East, were too expensive for any single investor to finance, so they joined together in 'joint-stock companies' which became increasingly effective; after first financing only individual voyages, they became self-perpetuating by issuing shares which could be bought or sold – thus stimulating the first stock exchanges, in place of traditional business gambling. But there were obvious worries about the diminished responsibility of directors, compared to partners whose own money was directly at risk. Directors, as Adam Smith warned, 'being the managers rather of other people's money than of their own, it cannot well be expected that they should watch over it with the same anxious vigilance with which the partners in a private co-partnery frequently watch over their own'.

Lawyers were also worried about the legal character of a corporation as an 'artificial person'. As the seventeenth-century jurist Sir Edward Coke pronounced: 'They cannot commit treason, nor be outlawed nor excommunicated, for they have no souls.' His words were echoed by the Lord Chancellor Lord Thurlow in the next century: 'Corporations have neither bodies to be punished, nor souls to be condemned, they therefore do as they like.' The essayist William Hazlitt, taking Coke's judgment as his text, put it more vividly in 1824: 'Corporate bodies are more corrupt and profligate than individuals, because they have more power to do mischief, and are less amenable to disgrace or punishment. They feel neither shame, remorse, gratitude, nor goodwill.' And Hazlitt brilliantly defined the dangers in the evolution of corporate man:

> The claims of an undefined humanity sit looser and looser upon him, at the same time that he draws the bonds of his new engagements closer and tighter about him. He loses sight, by degrees, of all common sense and feeling in the petty squabbles, intrigues, feuds, and airs, of affected importance to which he has made himself accessory.

THE INDIA HOUSE

The most far-reaching corporation was the British East India Company, which for two and a half centuries provided a unique commercial continuity and a model for other businesses. It was chartered by Queen Elizabeth I in 1600, for merchants financing expeditions to India, and soon became a permanent joint-stock company, with an interval in the eighteenth century after which it emerged as a 'new' company. It overtook its once dominant rival, the Dutch East India Company, which expired on the last day of the eighteenth century, while itself becoming more multinational, with much of its stock owned by Dutch and other foreigners. And it outlasted its ambitious French rival which was revived in 1719 as a *'compagnie perpetuelle'* heavily backed by the state, but collapsed fifty years later. The French company has a vivid memorial in the Breton port of Port

Louis where it was founded, with a charming museum showing its influence over the whole region. The British company is sadly uncommemorated, swallowed up by the Foreign Office; but at its peak its cultural as well as commercial influence was pervasive. It was nicknamed 'John Company' (like the Dutch company, which sometimes called itself 'Jan Compagnie' – an imaginary potentate who could impress Indians who did not understand the idea of joint ownership). The British company bewildered many Englishmen too: it was an intricate combination of interests, including ship-owners, traders and private buccaneers loosely held together by a board of directors – a confusing arrangement with some resemblances to the modern Lloyd's of London. Both employees and investors liked to personify the Company through its chairman, which could lead to dangerous misunderstandings.

The London headquarters of the Company acquired its own hierarchy of examiners and clerks, distinct from the owners. At first it was run from the private mansion of its Governor, Sir Christopher Clitherow, but in 1729 it moved into its own special 'India House'. This was virtually the first commercial office-building, with a public hall and committee-room 'scarce inferior to anything of the like nature in the City'. In 1800 it moved into a much grander building with a 200-foot frontage and six columns supporting a magnificent pediment.

The India House radiated a sense of permanence, but like so many future grand corporate headquarters it represented a company already in decline and forgetful of its original purpose, to make profits. By the nineteenth century it appeared almost as a sovereign state which had seen lesser nations come and go. It had acquired its own army and was administering much of India. But it relied on its royal charter for its monopoly, while its diminishing profits depended not on India but on tea from China. It had allowed the most profitable part of the China trade, the sale of opium, to be taken over by a separate company, set up by William Jardine, a former surgeon on East India ships, who co-founded the company which survives today as Jardine Matheson; while the free port of Singapore was set up by another ex-servant of John Company, Stamford Raffles. The East India Company continued to administer the subcontinent, without much profit, until the Indian Mutiny in 1857, when the British government took over, and the Company was dissolved after 259 years.

Over its long life the East India Company had built up a tradition of loyal company men, including writers and scholars who could thrive in their jobs without being cut off from intellectual activity, and who provided vivid glimpses of early office life. In 1819 the Company boldly recruited three administrators who combined original thinking with dedicated service: Edward Strachey, a retired Bengal judge; the novelist Thomas Love Peacock; and the Scots philosopher James Mill, who had just published his authoritative *History of British India*. Mill continued his academic work, including his classic *Elements of Political Economy* (1821), and helped to originate London University; but he was also a dedicated company man. 'The business, though laborious enough,' he explained, 'is to me highly interesting. It is the very essence of the internal government of sixty million people with whom I have to deal.'

In 1823 Mill was joined by his more famous son John Stuart Mill who became his assistant and stayed with the Company for thirty-five years, until it was abolished. Like his father, he saw no difficulty in working for the Company while pursuing his studies: he was kept in the office only from ten till four, and he wrote much of his great works, *System of Logic* and *Principles of Political Economy*, in office hours. He preferred office-work to journalism as a means of subsistence for 'anyone qualified to accomplish anything in the higher departments of literature or thought', and explained in his autobiography that he

> found office duties an actual rest from the other mental occupations which I have carried on simultaneously with them. They were sufficiently intellectual not to be a distasteful drudgery, without being such as to cause any strain upon the mental powers of a person used to abstract thought, or to the labour of careful literary composition.

Thomas Love Peacock, who worked for the Company at the same time as James and John Stuart Mill, was more famous for his satirical novels; but this did not prevent a successful career in business. He commemorated his duties, which began with a sumptuous breakfast at ten and ended at four, in a poem on office life:

> From ten to eleven, ate a breakfast for seven:
> From eleven to noon, to begin 'twas too soon;
> From twelve to one, asked 'What's to be done?'
> From one to two, found nothing to do;
> From two to three began to foresee
> That from three to four would be a damned bore.

But Peacock was a 'model man of business' and an innovator. He succeeded in speeding up the delivery of mails to India, which then went only twice a year by sail round the Cape of Good Hope, by planning steamships – his 'iron chickens' – which by navigating the Euphrates could provide deliveries once a month. He was loyal to the Company, and his literary friend Leigh Hunt complained to Shelley about his 'new Oriental grandeur, his Brahminical learning, and his inevitable tendencies to be one of the corrupt'. But Shelley himself, just before he died, asked Peacock about a possible job in India 'at the court of a native prince'. Peacock became quite a grand figure in the Company: the clerks saw their chief only when he arrived and 'was ushered to his office with great ceremony by the uniformed messengers who stood at the outer door'. But his devotion to the business did not stop him writing his best book, *Crotchet Castle* (1831), or restrain his satire: he wrote a long poem attacking banknotes and Scots economists, 'The Paper Money Lyrics', which he circulated among his office colleagues.

The first real chronicler of office life was a mere accounts clerk, the essayist Charles Lamb, who joined the East India Company at the age of seventeen in 1792. Leigh Hunt described him as 'dressed with a Quaker-like plainness'; and Thomas de Quincey recalled visiting Lamb in the India House in 1804. He was shown to a large room where six 'quill-driving gentlemen' were working behind a railing. Lamb was sitting on a stool so high that he had to descend gradually, like a horseman dismounting.

Lamb remained a humble clerk, without the privileges of Peacock or Mill, but he achieved his own kind of immortality through his descriptions of the office in his essays and letters: he was the first fully-documented company man. His six-hour day was hardly burdensome, and not very strict. When he was reproved for arriving late, he replied that he made up for it by leaving early. But, after twenty years of this, he saw his life slipping away. In 1815 he wrote to his friend William Wordsworth:

> Confusion blast all mercantile transactions, all traffick, exchange of commodities, intercourse between nations, all the consequent civilisation and wealth and amity and link of society, and getting rid of prejudices, and knowledge of the face of the globe – and rot the very fires of the forest that look so romantic alive, and die into desks.

Soon afterwards Lamb's workload diminished and his salary doubled, but he still believed his life was wasting away. 'Thirty years have I served the Philistines,' he wrote to Wordsworth in 1822, 'and my neck is not subdued to the yoke. You don't know how wearisome it is to breathe the air of four pent walls without relief day after day.' When Lamb retired due to ill-health in 1825, with a pension of two-thirds of his salary, 'it was like passing out of time into Eternity. Every year to be as long as three.'

How much more would Lamb have achieved if he had been liberated earlier? He described eloquently and frequently the constraints of the office, which cut him off from the countryside he loved, imposing 'that dry drudgery at the desk's dead wood'. Yet he showed little sign of becoming a major poet; his real monuments are his essays, of which some of the most delightful describe office life with humour and intimacy.

MANAGERS AND RAILWAYS

Outside the big companies, the character of the 'man of business' or the 'business man' emerged more emphatically during the Industrial Revolution. Mrs Craik's novel *John Halifax, Gentleman* (1857), set in the early nineteenth century, graphically describes a steam-engine first being used in place of a water-mill: 'a soul had been put into that wonderful creature of man's making, that inert mass of wood and metal, mysteriously combined. The monster was alive!' The novel tells the story of John Halifax, a poor lad who becomes a master-tanner and marries the boss's daughter, living in a large house which is never really divorced from the stinking tannery or the mill. Halifax 'possessed to the full that "business" faculty, so frequently despised, but which, out of very ordinary material, often makes a clever man; and without which the cleverest man alive can never be altogether a great man'.

It was not till the mid-nineteenth century that the concept of the business manager began to appear as an agent, operating between the owners and the workers. In Mrs Gaskell's great novel *North and South* (1854–55), the 'masters' clash directly with the 'men'. The mill-owner Tom Thornton is in direct control of his workers and confronts them personally when they strike. His house is in the shadow of the mill: 'As for the continual murmur of the work-people,' says his mother, 'it disturbs me no more than the humming of a hive of bees.' When Thornton has to close his mill because of the losses caused by the strike, he applies for a job under another owner which would give him 'the opportunity of cultivating some intercourse with the hands beyond the mere "cash nexus"'. He explains that

> no mere institutions, however wise, and however much thought may have been required to organise and arrange them, can attach class to class as they should be attached, unless the working out of such institutions brings the individuals of the different classes into actual personal contact. Such intercourse is the very breath of life.

The increase in the size of companies as a result of the Industrial Revolution removed the owners from direct control over the work-force, while their homes became grander and more detached from the sources of their wealth. In the eighteenth century the merchant was likely to live next door to his warehouse or his counting-house; but the new man of business, the 'manager', began to emerge in the space between merchants and clerks, keeping his distance from both.

Charles Dickens's novel *Dombey and Son*, published in 1848, gives a unique picture of this new kind of manager. The domineering Paul

Dombey has his offices around the corner from the East India House in the midst of the City of London, while his own home – the 'Home Department' of his business – is well removed, in 'a tall, dark, dreadfully genteel street' near Portland Place, where he can impress his business friends. Dombey is preparing his son to succeed him, but the sensitive boy dies, and Dombey delegates much of the business to James Carker, who works 'in a little chamber like a bath-room, opening from the passage outside Mr Dombey's door'. Carker the Manager (as Dickens calls him) is a man of about forty, 'always closely buttoned up and tightly dressed', with bright, smiling teeth. He is not a partner, but receives a percentage of the profits, which he has invested to become a rich man. He lives in a house of refinement and luxury with soft cushions and thick, noiseless carpets, in the green and wooded country near Norwood in South London, from which he commutes on horseback to the City. He manipulates his staff and flatters Dombey who treats him as his 'confidential agent'. Carker oversees the counting-house 'with lynx-eyed vigilance': after the clerks have gone home he 'would explore the mysteries of books and papers, with the patient progress of a man dissecting the minutest nerves and fibres of his subject'.

When Carker elopes with Dombey's second wife, Dombey discovers he has hopelessly mismanaged the business, creating 'a labyrinth of which only he has held the clue'. Dombey pursues Carker with relentless vengeance to France and back to England: Carker, half-crazed, falls in front of a train and is killed. Dombey in his fury neglects his business, which goes bankrupt, and the accountants move in, making free 'with the great mysteries, the Books'. Dombey declines into morbid isolation until he is miraculously reconciled with his daughter, repents his former obsession with money, and ends up playing happily with his grandson.

Carker is the forerunner of the modern company man, the manager with interests quite distinct from the owner's who can take over control as the family weakens. And in the background of Dickens's novel is a menacing new force: the relentless spread of the railroads through the country, representing destruction and death, but also irreversible change. A boy, called Biler after an engine-boiler, shows the resourcefulness of a new age; a London village is ruthlessly uprooted to make way for the tracks; Carker is killed by a train. And the railways were already introducing a new kind of company man who had to manage an unprecedented scale of operations, first across the country, then across the world.

Throughout Europe small family businesses were being undermined by the new pace and scale of industry. Thomas Mann's novel *Buddenbrooks*, published in 1901, describes the slow decline of a German family business in the nineteenth century. The founder's grandson, Senator Thomas Buddenbrook, builds a magnificent new mansion but celebrates the firm's centenary with deep unease, outmanoeuvred by tougher rivals and bewildered by the new world of railways and customs unions. The old family home is sold to his deadly rival, his son is too weak to succeed, and the Senator dies young, leaving the firm to be liquidated and the new mansion to be sold to an elderly spinster. As in so many novels and plays, the grand family house is the symbol, first of material success, then of decline; and Mann quotes the proverb 'When the house is finished, death comes.'

The hectic growth of the railways in Britain called for rapid and complex new organisations with a sense of punctuality and discipline which were quite foreign to most of the country. For the first few years the railways provided a wonderful means of escape for criminals and fugitives, until the telegraph lines arrived in the 1850s to provide still faster communications which could apprehend them at their destination. In *North and South* the villain escapes on a train and his pursuer curses himself afterwards for not realising that the telegraph could have caught up with him.

The only real precedent for the huge railway companies was the army, and they naturally devised uniforms for their porters and other workers – who came mainly from agricultural labour and domestic service, and continued to be officially called 'servants'. For their managers they turned to retired army officers, and majors and captains ran many of the chief companies, including Captain O'Brien of the North-Eastern, Captain Lawes of the Lancashire and Yorkshire, and Captain Coddington of the Caledonian.

The master-manager in the new hierarchy was the stationmaster, influenced by the army quartermaster or the mill master, but ruling a much more disciplined world, responsible for punctuality, safety and obedience from his staff, often operating a long way from headquarters. The stationmaster in his top hat was a new figure of authority: he was, as the author of *Our Iron Roads* described him in 1883, 'the captain in command of all the human and steam forces that aggregate around that little world-microcosm in the railway cosmos called a station'.

The nerve-centres of the railways were the London termini. Euston station became the headquarters of the biggest company in Britain, the London and North-Western Railway, which linked London, Birmingham and the north-west. It had a huge hall eighty feet high, with a statue of George Stephenson and a grand staircase leading to a gallery decorated with sculptures of industry and science, round which were the boardroom and chief managers' offices. Inside the biggest was the general manager, Captain Mark Huish, who never became a director, but was a pioneer manager who 'devised methods of management and control necessary to the conduct of his employer's business'.

The railways, after the first turbulent years of speculation and fraud, brought a sense of respectability to business activities, and many public figures became involved in their workings. Lord Salisbury, the future Prime Minister, was chairman of the Great Eastern Railway from 1868 to 1872: he refused a high salary but took the job very seriously. Sir Edward Grey, later Foreign Secretary, became a director of the North-Eastern Railway in 1898, after he had gone into opposition, and was later chairman. He loved the practical problems of the organisation compared to politics: 'One can sit with one's feet on the ground instead of standing on one's head hurraying with one's hands, which is about all one can do in opposition.'

The transformation of commerce by the railways was only made possible by the development of joint-stock companies which enabled thousands of small investors to finance them. The introduction of limited liability protected investors from bankruptcy, and effectively separated the managers from the owners – the Carkers from the Dombeys – and gave company men much greater independence. In Britain the Act of 1855 began to make limited liability the norm, stipulating that every such company's name should end with the word 'Limited'.

The early results were not encouraging, as many of the new companies went bankrupt. But the joint-stock companies became much safer investments and greatly increased the role of the professional manager: as Henry Fawcett wrote in 1863, 'In a joint-stock company, all depends on the manager or agent.'

The limited companies which boomed through Europe in the mid-nineteenth century were quite new kinds of institution which cut across the traditional powers of government. As Peter Drucker has described it:

> This new 'corporation', this new 'Société Anonyme', this new 'Aktiengesellschaft', could not be explained away as a *reform*, which is how the new army, the new university, the new hospital presented themselves. It clearly was a genuine innovation . . . It was the first new autonomous institution in hundreds of years, the first to create a power centre that was within society yet independent of the central government of the national state.

Railways laid the basis for large-scale industry, with their layers of managers, including engineers, technicians and administrators of whole railway towns which had sprung up alongside the junctions and workshops. They were like permanent armies, providing strict discipline for the careful maintenance and timekeeping which was essential to avoid disasters. Everywhere they built up elaborate social systems, mythologies and hierarchies, heavily influenced by their country's military traditions. Emile Zola's novel *La Bête Humaine* (1890) brilliantly describes the microcosm of a French railway company and station - 'this little world of employees tied to a clockwork existence by the uniform sequence of regulation hours', and the intense emotional involvements, down to the engine-driver in love with his engine. The murder of a railway official on a train undermines the whole company: 'spreading upwards through the complicated mechanism and dislocating the vast machine of railway organisation, even upsetting the top administration'.

In the German empire the nationalised railways and postal service could provide, said the sociologist Werner Sombart, 'three-quarters of a million men who stood stiff at attention when their superior spoke to them'. In Prussia railway employees were legally military reservists: stationmasters and signalmen stood rigid as a train passed, as if it were an inspecting general. The European railways were easily imbued with national pride and rivalries. Continental termini like the Gare de l'Est in Paris had statues depicting the European capitals, and the wagons-lits proclaimed the internationalism of the *Grands Expresses Européens*; but each country's railway companies were deeply influenced by the growing spirit of nationalism.

AMERICAN DESPOTS

In the United States the impact of the railroads was still more abrupt and far-reaching. At the end of the eighteenth century the great majority of Americans were farmers living in their farmhouses, and most manufacturers were artisans living close to their shops, if not above them. The American business man began to emerge as a separate species in the mid-nineteenth century, a more self-conscious leader than his European equivalent, boosting his local community or city, and often becoming the centre of his society: Daniel Boorstin describes him as 'a peculiarly American type of community maker and community leader'. When the railroads stretched across the American continent, they transformed the scale of activity and undermined local businesses even more drastically than in Europe. They were less influenced by military models and were financed almost entirely from private funds, in contrast to Continental Europe where governments provided most of the finance. They quickly established a new pattern of business. The early American corporations were chartered by the state, to undertake specific projects like building canals; but the railroad age saw independent corporations which soon began to challenge the state, with their own legal status. 'The corporation came to be regarded by the courts as if it were a person,' as the historian Joseph Furnas puts it. 'It can contract debts, sue debtors, buy and sell. Investors may buy pieces of it – like promoters taking pieces of a prizefighter.'

The corporations soon appeared as a serious threat to the American tradition of individualism. Already in 1869 Charles Francis Adams, who had witnessed the ferocious battles to control the railroads, was warning that modern society had created a class of artificial beings who bid fair soon to be the masters of their creator. It is but a very few years since the existence of a corporation controlling a few millions of dollars was regarded as a subject of grave apprehension, and now this country already contains single organisations which wield a power represented by thousands of millions . . . they are already establishing despotisms which no spasmodic popular effort will be able to shake off. Everywhere, and at all times, however, they illustrate the truth of the old maxim of the common law, that corporations have no souls.

Many contemporary observers saw the railroads as introducing a new tyranny dominated by a few unscrupulous owners such as Commodore Vanderbilt, the railroad king who especially alarmed Adams. 'The individual will hereafter be engrafted on the Corporation – and democracy running its course, and resulting in imperialism; and Vanderbilt is but the precursor of a class of men who will wield within the State a power created by the State, but too great to control.'

The problems of the individual businessman in the new corporate age form the background of the novel by William Dean Howells, *The Rise of Silas Lapham*, published in 1885. Lapham has built up a paint business which he personally runs from his office, with the help of an array of book-keepers, an office boy and a typewriter girl. He and his wife Perses live simply, in keeping with their own rough-hewn Puritan morality, which is occasionally overridden by commercial pressures. The Laphams become socially ambitious, and build a pretentious mansion: 'Money is to the fore now,' says their leisured Bostonian neighbour Bromfield Corey: 'It is the romance, the poetry of our age.' Lapham's business is undermined by competition from younger rivals who can transport paint much more cheaply from West Virginia, while his once-valuable mill is at the mercy of a railroad. He has a chance to recoup by selling the mill to a group of Englishmen, but he soon realises that they are acting on behalf of shareholders for whom they care nothing: they represent the 'potential immorality which regards common property as common prey'. Lapham refuses to sell the mill, and faces bankruptcy.

By the 1880s the great American trusts in coal, iron, steel and oil had solidified the power of a handful of entrepreneurs. As Theodore

Dreiser described them in *The Titan*: 'There was growing up a feeling that at the top there was a set of giants – Titans – who, without heart or soul, and without any understanding or sympathy with the condition of the rank and file, were setting forth to chain and enslave them.'

At that time entrepreneurs or financiers were largely regarded as being outside society – as was suggested by the use of two foreign words to describe them. In Britain Trollope's great novel *The Way We Live Now* (1875) depicted the French financier Augustus Melmotte – a man with 'a wonderful look of power about his mouth and chin' – and his American partner Hamilton K. Fisker as villains corrupting the British aristocracy with their mastery of international deals and the new telegraph (a story remarkably similar to Robert Maxwell's a century later). In America the financier was seen as hardly a fit subject for novelists or historians, but the Chicago novelist Henry Fuller, a bank clerk's son who described the business world in *The Cliff Dwellers* and *With the Procession* (see next chapter), insisted that the American genius 'is expressing itself with great fluency, volume, eloquence – in its own way in its own field: politics, finance and invention'. Theodore Dreiser gave full credit to Fuller in *The Financier* (1912) and *The Titan* (1914), the first great business novels, based on the life of the financier Charles Yerkes who had made a fortune from Chicago street railways and the London Underground. Dreiser gave his financier Frank Cowperwood a heroic status, as an artist comparable to other creative geniuses: 'Finance is an art. And it represents the operations of the subtlest of the intellectuals and of the egoists.' He explored his hero's genius with open admiration: 'It was a powerful mind, turning, like a vast searchlight, into many a dark corner; but it was not sufficiently disinterested to search the ultimate dark.' He interspersed Cowperwood's business deals with his seductions, adultery and successive marriages which showed the same driving ambition and duplicity. And he compared him to the brilliant fish the Black Grouper, or Mycteroperca, which can adapt its colours to any surroundings: 'You cannot look at it long without feeling that you are witnessing something spectral and unnatural, so brilliant is its power to deceive ... What would you say was the intention of the overruling intelligent, constructive force which gives to Mycteroperca this ability?'

But no single owner could hope for long to control the vast and complex new corporations, and the major investors soon had to delegate responsibility to professional managers. The first simple railroads were run personally by a superintendent, like a textile mill; but as the lines interlocked a succession of crashes soon made clear the need for organised systems. The Western Railroad between Worcester and Albany, according to the business historian Alfred Chandler, was the first to define a careful internal organisational structure, with two middle-managers and two top managers. By the 1880s the huge increase in traffic and connections had forced all the big railroads to build up a professional management, including accounting systems which revolutionised book-keeping, to co-ordinate the movements of goods and passengers. As the biggest railroads stretched across the continent, weaker companies went bankrupt and many investors were ruined, but managers became more secure and professionalised. By the end of the century the big railroads were limiting competition, which allowed them to establish bureaucracies, with promotion depending on seniority. They were already moving away from 'finance capitalism' towards a new 'managerial capitalism'.

The railroads provided the means and the models for the concentrations of industry that followed, and other entrepreneurs adopted their systems of management. Andrew Carnegie had worked as an executive on the Pennsylvania Railroad before he built up his massive steelworks in Pittsburgh, and he adopted a similar management structure with the help of a general manager, William Shinn, who had also worked for the Pennsylvania company.

In the last two decades of the nineteenth century a succession of inventions were transformed into giant corporations stretching across America. Many of these companies were to survive through the next century, still based on the same products. In Pittsburgh Henry John Heinz adopted the new continuous process of canning foods, while in Philadelphia Joseph Campbell and the Dorrance family began canning soups. In Cincinnati William Procter and James Gamble, who had accidentally discovered a soap which floated, built a model plant to sell it across the United States. In Rochester George Eastman patented his 'Kodak' camera for amateurs. In Chicago Gustavus Swift began using refrigerated railcars. Also in Chicago William Wrigley developed his chewing-gum into a national network. In Atlanta Asa

30

Candler set up plants for his new drink Coca-Cola, while in St Louis Adolphus Busch perfected his light beer Budweiser, followed by Michelob, which he began distributing and advertising nationally.

By the end of the century the American business world of fifty years earlier was almost unrecognisable. Henry Adams, writing in 1905, described how 'All New York was demanding new men, and all the new forces, condensed into corporations, were demanding a new type of man – a man with ten times the endurance, energy, will and mind of the old type – for whom they were ready to pay millions at sight.'

Before long the masters of these new forces were not so much the individual financiers and inventors who had first unleashed them, as the emerging company men who knew how to operate inside them, and to impose their own will over the new structures.

CONFUCIUS AND THE KITCHEN

Western managers and engineers were extending their railroads and factories across the world, through Asia and Latin America, but they saw them as the achievement of white people only: a few observant visitors, however, realised that the new spirit was also stirring in others. When Rudyard Kipling paid his second visit to Japan in 1892 he recorded: 'In Tokyo live the steadily-diminishing staff of Europeans employed by the Emperor as engineers, railway experts, professors in the colleges and so forth. Before many years they will all be dispensed with, and the country will set forth among the nations alone and in its own responsibility.'

In Japan the corporation was a sudden and revolutionary force, for the arrival of Western influence and technology coincided with the dismantling of the feudal system after the young Emperor Meiji came to power in 1868. The hundreds of family merchant houses which had enjoyed local monopolies could not survive the collapse of feudalism and the inrush of technology, but the tradition of family responsibility set a pattern for later corporations. The Meiji government, having seen the success of private enterprise in the West, avoided direct involvement in industry and sought to encourage Japanese entrepreneurs, who came from the same kind of educated elite as the government. It was, as Michio Morishima describes it, the world's first successful privatisation, resulting in the creation of the *zaibatsu* trading groups which were to dominate Japanese industry for most of the next century.

The most effective Japanese innovator was Eiichi Shibusawa, the son of a rich farmer who gave him a samurai education, who had learnt some of the secrets of European industry on a visit to France. He was surprised to see a banker given the same respect as a colonel, and returned to Japan convinced that the joint-stock company was the key to modernisation. He joined the Ministry of Finance, where he opposed the pressures of militarism and bureaucracy, and left to become a banker, rising to be president of the first bank, the Dai Ichi, which wielded a powerful influence over joint-stock companies. Shibusawa decided that the Japanese could successfully co-operate and pool their resources, unlike the Chinese who remained individualists within their families (a tradition which Mao Tse-tung was later determined to uproot, but which survived powerfully among the overseas Chinese). He was determined 'to build modern enterprises with the abacus and the Analects of Confucius'.

The former Japanese ruling class, the samurai, had lost their old role as warriors, and much of their income and status: they even had to cut off their top-knots and wear Western clothes. But the corporations gave them a new opportunity. The old merchant class of family businesses had become complacent. They had been despised by the samurai for their 'unspeakable business of buying and selling' – as Confucius said, 'Gentlemen keep clear of the kitchen.' But the more ambitious samurai found a new role in establishing companies with the help of the lump sums which had compensated them for the loss of their military jobs; and Shibusawa and others were convinced that the old Confucian ideals could be transferred to modern business. The best-educated samurai were channelled into businesses which needed superior skills. 'The role of samurai families in founding Japan's modern business class can hardly be exaggerated,' wrote the historian Yasuzo Horie.

The great Japanese trading companies each began with their own links with government. Yataro Iwasaki, a peasant's son, built up a coastal shipping business with the help of government subsidies and expanded into insurance and warehousing. He coined the name Mitsubishi ('three diamonds') in 1873 for his family holding company. His ships had a virtual monopoly, which aroused competition from rivals including Mitsui, which had its own strong links to government and compared itself to the British East India Company. The two firms fought an epic fare-cutting battle until, in 1884, Mitsubishi eventually won control of a combined company, NYK (Japan Shipping), while Mitsui became increasingly powerful in other industries.

As the Japanese joint-stock companies issued more shares they became less dependent on the founding families, but they maintained the principle of 'familism' which gave them a firmer identity than Western companies, and a stronger hold over their employees. Yanosuke Iwasaki, who took over Mitsubishi from his elder brother, explained: 'Although this enterprise calls itself a company and has company structure, in reality it is entirely a family enterprise.' Everything in the company was 'exclusively the responsibility of the president'. As in the West, the first burst of individualist entrepreneurs soon gave way to professional managers; company offices, shops and government departments became the training grounds of Westernised 'salarymen', dedicated to their company's services and promised life-time employment. And over the next century Japanese employees were more content than Americans to accept collective activity, endorsed by Confucian principles. As Rodney Clark puts it: 'In Japan there could be unqualified approval for the hard-working, stable, gregarious, sociologically-conscious fledgling manager, fresh from his law or commerce course. In America even today memories of pristine individualism unsettle the collective ideal.'

Japanese managers from the start were better educated than the Americans or British: by 1920 46 per cent of Japanese business leaders had been to university. The traditional Japanese business or shop (*shoten*), run by masters without Western education, was overshadowed by the Western-style company (*kaisha*), which required educated professional managers who understood Western methods.

The biggest groups looked to Tokyo University (established in 1877) and its new rivals for their managers, which began a tradition of the 'old boy network' as at Oxbridge in Britain, but with more commercial motivation. By 1926 'the business world was already dominated by university graduates and was unworkable without them'.

These company men, working their technological wonders in a separate world, were more cut off from the rest of society than their American or European counterparts. Tokyo was being transformed from a 'Low City' to a 'High City': three- or four-storey buildings emerged between the little wooden houses, including the Mitsui Bank in Nihonbashi and the Mitsui Club with its wide verandahs and colonnades. Mitsubishi bought a meadow near the Imperial Palace and built rows of ornate brick buildings which they called 'Londontown' – the site of today's Marunouchi district. Kintaro Hattori, the founder of the Seiko watch company, built a factory in Tokyo in 1885 which became one of the world's leading watchmaking centres, and later bought a building on the main Ginza crossroads where he built the Hattori tower, a symbol of Ginza ever since. The Mitsui (later Mitsukoshi) dry-goods shop turned into an imposing department store, glittering with illuminations from electricity which turned shadowy Tokyo into a city of light. Electric light became a symbol of the Japanese industrial revolution, and the foundation of huge corporations. In Tokyo an inventive samurai, Ichisuke Fujioka, developed an arc lamp which provided the first electric light in Japan; his factory turned into the Tokyo Electric Company which later merged with a firm in Shibaura to become the Tokyo Shibaura company, later known as Toshiba. In Osaka in 1918 a young technician, Konosuke Matsushita, set up his own electricity company which was to become a global giant, including the huge range of Panasonic products as well as Hollywood films.

The Japanese company man was determined to overtake and outdo his American rivals. To many Western visitors he appeared obsessed with imitation and excessively obedient to his company. The American writer Lafcadio Hearn insisted in 1904 that Japan could not give enough freedom to individuals to compete effectively in the world market-place: 'While Japan continues to think and to act by groups, even by groups of industrial companies, so long she must always continue incapable of her best.'

But the power of corporations was now changing the nature of society across the world, and Americans and Europeans were facing their own problems in confronting the growing scale of business.

CHAPTER THREE

Individuals versus Corporations

Capitalist societies start as sandpiles and end up as
girdered structures.

ROBERT HEILBRONER,
Twenty-First Century Capitalism, 1993

In 1905 the novelist Henry James returned with some apprehension
to his native America, after twenty years in Europe. When his ship
docked at Manhattan he was astonished by 'The huge jagged city
. . . looking at the sky in the manner of some colossal hair-comb
turned upward and so deprived of half its teeth that the others, at their
uneven intervals, count doubly as sharp spikes.' The new skyscrapers
looked 'like extravagant pins in a cushion already overplanted'. Wandering inside one of the tall buildings he was overwhelmed by the
intensity of 'each of these huge constructed and compressed communities, throbbing, through its myriad arteries and pores, with a
single passion, even as a complicated watch throbs with the one
purpose of telling you the hour and the minute'.

James had always kept aloof from business: his grandfather had
made a fortune of $3 million from canals and other investments but
his descendants, as Henry James put it, 'were never in a single case
. . . for two generations guilty of a stroke of business'. His novels are
full of very rich men the source of whose fortunes are obscure, like
Adam Verver, the art collector in *The Golden Bowl* (1904), who made
his money out of the 'American City'. James's dread of commerce
was increased by his return to the United States, where he kept
seeing the unmitigated 'business man's face' – in contrast to the
much finer texture of women's faces with 'their less commercialised,
distinctly more generalised, physiognomic character'. He was awed by
the unrestrained power of money that emanated from the skyscrapers,

35

'Nowhere else does pecuniary power so beat its wings in the void,' and wished he could listen to the human note within it; he lamented that this was 'a line of research closed to me, alas, by my fatally uninitiated state'.

More down-to-earth American novelists were determined to explore and explain the social effects of the new scale of business; but most disliked what they saw. *The Jungle*, written in 1906 by the young Upton Sinclair, gives vivid descriptions of the slaughter-houses and meatpackers of Chicago, describing the wretched conditions of the workers, and the diseased animals, the rotting beef, poisoned rats, and even human remains which went into canned food. 'What *Uncle Tom's Cabin* did for the black slaves,' Jack London told Sinclair, '*The Jungle* has a large chance to do for the white slaves of today.' But the American public, to Sinclair's disappointment, were much more shocked by their adulterated food than by the social conditions. 'I aimed at the public's heart,' he wrote later, 'and by accident I hit it in the stomach.' And the big American food companies, with the exception of Heinz, resisted the clamour for government regulation for clean food which followed Sinclair's book.

British writers were still more separated from the growing big businesses. Only a few authors since Charles Lamb – like Kenneth Grahame, who was Secretary of the Bank of England for ten years until 1908, when he wrote *The Wind in the Willows* – had combined creative activity with a commercial career. In 1890 the young poet Walter de la Mare found a job with the Anglo-American Oil Company, which had recently been set up in London by Standard Oil, where he laboured as a junior clerk from 9 a.m. to 6.30 p.m. After eighteen years he found working for the 'American tradesmen' unbearable when a new boss, a 'snuffy little man made of black bread' arrived to impose economies which included giving de la Mare the job of two people. Luckily his poet-patron Sir Henry Newbolt got him a grant of £200 a year which enabled him to resign in 1908. De la Mare's managing director John Usmer responded coolly that 'A company like ours is a poor place for anyone to be in who is at all ambitious,' and that only salesmen had real prospects – an ungracious reply, de la Mare thought, from 'the richest monopoly in the world'. Looking back on his business career, the poet could not recall the smallest passage or character sketch in his writing which was inspired by his time in the company.

The humorist P.G. Wodehouse was more revealing about business organisation, though full of nostalgia for country-house life. After leaving school he spent two unhappy years in London working at the Hongkong and Shanghai Bank, which he described in an early novel, *Psmith in the City* (1910). The hero, Psmith, is a bumptious young cricketer just out of Eton, whose father makes him work in the New Asiatic Bank; Psmith's manager, Bickersdyke, is a short, stout man with 'a hard, thin-lipped mouth, half hidden by a rather ragged moustache', who has already committed the sin of disturbing a cricket match. Once in the bank 'Psmith, the individual, ceases to exist, and there springs into being Psmith, the cog in the wheel of the New Asiatic Bank'. He is dispirited by his ordeals in Fixed Deposits, Forwards Bills and the Cash Department: 'Most people look on the cashier of a bank as a sort of human slot-machine,' says his friend Mike. But after Psmith has successfully demoralised Mr Bickersdyke at his club he is allowed by his father to go to Cambridge, assuring Mike that 'the bank was no place for us'.

Writers everywhere reacted with bewilderment and fear to the new scale of corporate business; but the impact was far more drastic in the United States, where it transformed politics. 'We are in the presence of a new organisation of society. Our life has broken away from the past,' said the future President Woodrow Wilson in 1912.

You know what happens when you are the servant of a corporation. You have in no instance access to the men who are really determining the policy of the corporation. If the corporation is doing the things it ought not to do, you really have no voice in the matter and must obey the orders, and you have oftentimes with deep mortification to co-operate in the doing of things which you know are against the public interest. Your individuality is swallowed up in the individuality and purpose of a great organisation . . .

The truth is, we are all caught up in a great economic system which is heartless. The modern corporation is not engaged in business as an individual. When we deal with it, we deal with an impersonal element, an immaterial piece of society.

European visitors to America were struck by the tension between the individual and the corporation. In 1904 the German sociologist Max Weber watched the seething crowds from the middle of Brooklyn Bridge: a panorama of mass transportation and noisy motion. He saw the skyscrapers as fortresses of capital, which reminded him of 'the old pictures of the towers of Bologna and Florence'. And he contrasted these towering bulks of capitalism with the tiny homes of American college professors: 'Among these masses, all individualism becomes expensive, whether it is in housing or eating. Thus, the home of Professor Hervey, of the German department of Columbia University, is surely a doll's house with tiny little rooms, with toilet and bath facilities in the same room (as is almost always the case).'

When the young novelist H.G. Wells visited New York in 1906 he noticed how 'happy returning natives greet the great pillars of business by name, the Saint Paul building, the World, the Manhattan tower'. He was fascinated by the beautiful and well-organised interiors of the office buildings: 'To step into them from the street is to step up fifty years in the scale of civilisation,' and he visited a factory in New York State which was 'like the interior of a well-made clock'. But watching the Manhattan crowds he realised: 'The individuals count for nothing, they are clerks and stenographers, shopmen, shop-girls, workers of innumerable types, black-coated men, hat and blouse girls, shabby and cheaply-clad persons . . . the distinctive effect is the mass, the black torrent, rippled with unmeaning faces, the great, the unprecedented multitudinousness of the thing, the inhuman force of it all.'

Wells saw the threat to individual freedom as the crucial issue in the emerging America: 'That steady trend towards concentration under the individualistic rules, until individual competition becomes disheartened and hopeless, is the essential form of the economic and social process in America as I see it now, and it has become the cardinal topic of thought and discussion in the American mind.'

The domination of big business was symbolised by the skyscraper, which conveyed an awesome concentration of activity in contrast to the variety of low buildings around it. In Chicago, the first home of skyscrapers, the sixteen-storey Monadock office building in 1891 was, said the architect Louis Sullivan, 'an amazing cliff of brickwork rising sheer and stark, with a subtlety of line and surface, a direct singleness of purpose, that gave one the thrill of romance'. And the steel-girder buildings which followed it redefined 'this amazing city of steel and iron', as Theodore Dreiser called Chicago in the 1890s.

Both companies and their architects were determined to disprove the prevalent belief that commercial buildings could not be graceful, as they competed with ever-taller towers. In 1908 the Singer Tower in New York designed by Ernest Flagg became the world's tallest building for eighteen months, only to be overshadowed by the head-quarters of Metropolitan Life, the insurance company which then employed 30,000 people – which still stands at the end of Madison Avenue. Four years later the Woolworth Tower, full of lawyers and businessmen, became the peak of commercial grandeur with its Gothic pinnacles 792 feet above the street. It was called 'the cathedral of trade', though its architect Cass Gilbert insisted that it was modelled on town halls in Flanders. It was Gilbert who finally over-came the prejudice, the journalist Mark Sullivan wrote, that business buildings could not be made beautiful.

Skyscrapers and big corporations grew up together, and the build-ings dramatised the separateness and stratification of the new com-mercial power. In Chicago Theodore Dreiser was amused to see how the press, pulpit and officials licked the boots of the new business magnates, who behaved 'as though the life of a great and forceful metropolis depended on them alone'. And Dreiser's novel *Sister Carrie* describes New York in the early 1890s through the eyes of George Hurstwood, the ex-manager of a Chicago saloon who has come to be 'a great believer in the strength of corporations'. 'He began to see as one sees a city with a wall about it. Men were posted at the gates. You could not get in. Those inside did not care to come out to see who you were. They were so merry inside there that all those outside were forgotten, and he was on the outside.'

The buildings and the corporations looked inhuman and anony-mous, but their first character was established by individual entrepre-neurs who understood how to build up new kinds of organisations, based on railroads, city managements or the reformed US Army. They constructed hierarchies of engineers, middle-managers and accountants to connect up the complex systems, allocating resources and co-ordinating distribution and selling. They left their imprint on their corporations for most of the rest of the century, confirming the words of Ralph Waldo Emerson back in 1841: 'An institution is the lengthened shadow of one man.'

Three men established structures which were to influence industrial society throughout the world. John D. Rockefeller, Henry Ford and Thomas Watson created their own systems in critical areas – business organisation, assembly lines and salesmanship – which turned out not only mass products, but mass-produced company men.

THE STANDARD OIL COLLAR

The most awesome symbol of the new scale of business was the headquarters of Standard Oil at 26 Broadway, 'the most famous business address in the world', a massive structure of fifteen storeys which represented a legendary power.

> Solid as a prison, towering as a steeple, its cold and forbidding façade seems to rebuke the heedless levity of the passing crowd, and frown on the frivolity of the stray sunbeams which in the late afternoon play around its impassive cornices. Men point to its stern portals, glance quickly up at the rows of unwinking windows, nudge each other, and hurry onward, as the Spaniards used to do when going to the offices of the Inquisition.

Thomas Lawson, who wrote that description in 1906, was a veteran banker and broker who had worked with Standard Oil (later Esso, now Exxon) from the inside. He was awe-struck by the 'Private Thing', the separate identity of a corporation 'which comprehends, but exists independently of, its legalised functions'; and his racy book *Frenzied Finance* (1906) provided a unique insight into Standard Oil's workings.

Inside the building, Standard Oil had established its own elaborate rituals and formalities: while the employees rushed between offices, the heads of the Trust moved with dignity. 'When the secretary of the Standard Oil Company goes from the third to the fourth floor,' wrote a contemporary newspaperman, 'he puts on his hat and makes the journey as though performing a ceremonious call.' On the eleventh floor H.H. Rogers presided over his elegant mahogany office, the 'sanctum sanctorum', decorated with framed letters from Abraham Lincoln, Ulysses S. Grant and Mark Twain. All the most important schemes had to 'go upstairs' for decisions by the partners who every day at 11 a.m. sat round the table in the big room on the fifteenth floor, where 'views are exchanged, policies talked over, republics and empires made and unmade'. The partners' shrewdness was legendary, even among rival tycoons: 'I never came into contact with any class of men so smart and able as they are in their business,' said the railway king William Vanderbilt.

Standard Oil had been created by John D. Rockefeller in 1883, when he formed the trust to control the huge majority of the United States' oil supplies. He had succeeded in turning a wild and cut-throat business, subject to alternate gluts and shortages, into a highly-organised industry, run from a centralised headquarters. And he rightly saw himself as the father of big business: 'This movement was the origin of the whole system of modern economic administration. It has revolutionised the way of doing business all over the world.'

But though Rockefeller remained the biggest single shareholder, he had retired at fifty to devote himself to philanthropy, and Standard Oil was taken over by an executive committee of nine trustees, ruling over a network of staff departments. They were all rich men in their own right, who had built up their own oil businesses before merging with Rockefeller. Many developed other interests: Henry Flagler, who was in the whiskey business before he became Rockefeller's closest associate, made another fortune developing Florida; H.H. Rogers, who ran Standard's pipelines and natural gas, gambled on the stock market and became the patron of writers including Mark Twain.

But Rockefeller's successor as the boss of Standard Oil was totally dedicated to the oil business. A tough little Irishman, John D. Archbold, 'the Napoleon of Oil', concealed his ruthless pursuit of profits behind a laughing style: 'He would make up his mind with one flash of his dark snapping eyes, and then was smiling again.' He sauntered down the hallways whistling hymns, but enforced a cold and punctilious style: executives always wore coats and ties, and never used first names in the office. And as Thomas Lawson described it, the first rule was that '"Every 'Standard Oil' man must wear the 'Standard

Oil' collar." This collar is riveted on to each one as he is taken into "the band", and can only be removed with the head of the wearer.'

The monopoly power of the big trusts soon came under fierce attack, and in 1890 the Sherman Anti-Trust Act was passed to limit them. Standard Oil reformed itself to avoid a break-up, and in 1899 created a holding company to maintain control. But the courts still pursued it, and in 1911 came a historic judgment of the Supreme Court, which found that 'the very genius for commercial development and organisation ... soon begat an intent and purpose to exclude others'. Standard Oil was forced to dissolve itself into components based on each state, and the biggest component, Standard Oil of New Jersey, became the leader, rather than the controller, of the industry.

The break-up turned out a blessing in disguise for the shareholders: it released new executives for dynamic marketing and technical improvements. 'The young fellows,' said one senior manager, 'were given the chance for which they had been chafing.' Profits soon increased: a year after the break-up most of the components had doubled the value of their shares. The founding families no longer dominated the companies: in 1913 New Jersey's legal counsel reported that the Rockefellers 'have absolutely retired, and are simply receiving their dividends and voting at the annual meetings'. But the iron structure remained, as Rockefeller had predicted: 'The day of combination is here to stay. Individualism has gone, never to return.'

SCIENTIFIC MANAGERS

In manufacturing industries the individual was facing a more inhuman enemy, in the shape of mechanical processes which threatened to turn man into a machine. They were often unfairly blamed on Frederick Winslow Taylor, the engineer who developed the idea of 'scientific management', which came to be called Taylorism. Contemporary writers liked to depict Taylor as a fanatic of timekeeping and obsessive control. John Dos Passos described his death in 1915: 'The night-nurse heard him winding his watch; on the morning of his fifty-ninth birthday, when the nurse went into his room to look at him at four thirty, he was dead with a watch in his hand.'

In fact Taylor was much more humane than most manufacturing bosses, and he was much concerned with harmony at the work-place, like later Japanese industrialists. In his classic *Principles of Scientific Management*, published in 1911, he argued that workers and bosses should have more equal responsibilities, and that workers should be encouraged to suggest improvements – which today sounds very Japanese. He insisted that managers – a word he disliked – must study the workers' characters to help them advance, and become the servants of the workers, not their masters. Scientific management, he told Congress in 1912, 'is not holding a stopwatch to a man'. He called for 'a complete mental revolution' which must be 'equally complete on the part of those on the management's side'. His champion today, Peter Drucker, claims that Taylor 'had as much impact as Marx or Freud'. Like those two he was a much more original (and readable) thinker than most of his followers.

But Taylor inevitably became associated with the assembly lines which followed him, with the mechanisation of men and the lack of human communication – particularly in factories where foreign workers spoke little English. Taylor's insistence on separating each task made factory-work a deadening experience, which was not to be relieved till half a century later, when Japanese ideas provided alternatives. His methods for speeding up production were inevitably exploited by employers with no interest in their workers' character or welfare.

The new breed of managers had no intention of becoming the servants of the workers. They were preoccupied with establishing their own status and security, and they saw scientific management as the source of their authority against the more arbitrary and intuitive rule of the entrepreneurs. 'On their claims to hold the keys to efficiency,' wrote Rosabeth Moss Kanter, 'and to know the "one best way" to organise work, managers provided a basis for their ever-extending role.' But in the process the manager lost much of his initiative, and the very word 'manager' became associated less with the enterprise of the early political or theatrical managers, and more with a fixed place in a large machine.

THE LIMITS OF FORDISM

It was Henry Ford who was responsible for the most thorough sub-
jugation of men to machines. His achievement rested on his mass-
production of cars, in his Rouge River plant near Detroit which
became the world's biggest company town. But the result was the
mass-production of both workers and managers, stamping a conformity which later came close to undermining the American car industry.

Ford originally had some genuine idealism. He was ahead of his
time as an equal-rights employer, giving opportunities to blacks,
women and handicapped workers. He loved nature, particularly birds,
and wished that all workers could take long summer holidays. 'Power
and machinery, money and goods,' he wrote in his memoirs, 'are
useful only as they set us free to live.' He insisted that his first
duty was to provide service, rather than profits, and said, 'There is
something sacred about a big business which provides a living for
hundreds and thousands of families.' He was an enemy of bureaucracy, and he laid into management hierarchies – like some radical
reformers seventy years later. When the company was faced with
bankruptcy in 1920 he fired half the office staff of 1,000, and sold
off desks, typewriters, telephones and even pencil sharpeners. When
his son Edsel commissioned a new building for the firm's accountants
and salesmen, he fired all the accountants and ripped up their offices,
before Edsel reinstated them. Henry Ford warned that great administration buildings could easily end up as tombs. He hated organisation
charts, titles and management meetings: 'There is no bent of mind
more dangerous than that which is sometimes described as "genius
for organisation".' He saw managers, like machines, as periodically
needing replacement: 'Sometimes it is the men "higher up" who
most need revamping – and they themselves are always the last to
recognise it.'

But Ford knew that his system was dehumanising, and he did little
to soften it. 'A great business is really too big to be human. It grows
so large as to supplant the personality of the man.' Looking back
twenty-five years after he set up his company, he recognised that
'The modern worker finds himself part of an organisation which

leaves him little initiative.' He insisted that 'the work and the work alone controls us'. He did not believe in the 'glad hand', the professionalised 'personal touch' or the 'human element', and he distrusted personal relations: 'It is not necessary for people to love each other in order to work together. Too much good fellowship may indeed be a very bad thing, for it may lead to one man trying to cover up the faults of another.'

The more eccentric Ford became (like many autocrats later), the more he demanded conformity. He played his top managers against each other to make them insecure, and fired them if they became too powerful. He lost most of his senior managers, including James Couzens, his original right-hand man, and William Knudsen, his production expert, who moved to General Motors. His last henchman, Harry Bennett, was a thuggish ex-sailor who roughed up union bosses and enjoyed dealing with the Mafia. Below the top, Ford insisted on yes-men: as his cars were all black, his managers were all grey.

Fordism, as his method came to be called, marked the extreme of the command system, the industrial counterpart to political dictatorships in Germany and Russia, providing cheap, efficient products by dictating to both the worker and the consumer. But in a prosperous democracy it sowed the seeds of its own destruction, as consumers inevitably looked for more choice – which rival companies could offer. It is all the more remarkable that the Ford company has survived as a major industrial force at the end of the century. The name Ford entered mythology, in Communist Russia as well as the West, as a symbol both of man's mastery and of his enslavement. When the Mexican communist artist Diego Rivera was commissioned by Henry Ford's son Edsel to decorate the Detroit Institute of Arts he was thrilled by the scale of the Rouge River plant, and painted huge murals which heroically portrayed all the power of men and machines. 'Marx made theory, Lenin applied it,' Rivera explained, 'and Henry Ford made the work of the socialist state possible.' But Ford also provided a new vision of hell: an underworld dedicated to homogenising not only goods, but tastes, ideas and education. Aldous Huxley's satirical novel *Brave New World*, published in 1932, was set in 'the year of our Ford 632': children with names like Lenina, Benito, Morgana, Mond and Marx are indoctrinated into a system where capitalists and communists have merged to enforce total conformity. Their masters make the sign of T, swear 'Oh, Ford' and remind students that 'history is bunk'. A clock-tower called Big Henry proclaims the hours with golden trumpets playing synthetic music and a loud bass voice singing 'Ford, Ford, Ford'.

The most devastating critique of Fordism was much more light-hearted: Charlie Chaplin's film *Modern Times* (1936), has the subtitle 'A story of industry, or individual independence – humanity crusading in the pursuit of happiness.' In a few sequences of slapstick Chaplin appears as a worker at the Electron Steel Corporation, desperately trying to keep pace with the assembly line, twitching in rhythm, and spied on even when smoking in the lavatory. The boss experiments with an automatic feeding machine which goes wild, splashing a pie into Chaplin's face. Chaplin is caught up in the giant cogs of a machine, dances with oilcans, becomes involved in a communist march, and goes to jail before finding success and happiness as a singer in a restaurant with Paulette Godard. The whimsical farce provided a more potent warning about the dangers of mass-production than all the management experts.

For Ford's success was achieved at a terrible cost in individual initiative, and it effectively destroyed the tradition of skilled craftsmen dedicated to their customers, which had been the pride of most industries in the previous century. The undermining had begun long before Ford, in many industries: the great Homestead steel mills strike in Pittsburgh in 1892, which Henry Clay Frick brutally suppressed, was the last stand of the old craftsmen against cheap labour hired by the steelmasters. But Ford's assembly line forced both workers and customers into its discipline, and broke the link between the two, which had been crucial to quality. Adam Smith wrote in 1776: 'The real and effectual discipline which is exercised over a workman is not that of his corporation, but that of his customers.' Ford left no room for any craftsmen or contact with customers. In the words of a report by the Massachusetts Institute of Technology in 1989:

The triumph of this system was so complete that other patterns of production were virtually wiped out. There was little room left in the economy for a craft tradition, with less-hierarchical work organisations and the direct participation of skilled workers in production decisions, or for other means of serving smaller segments of the market.

The conformity of the managers and the destruction of the crafts perpetuated a system which left little room for flexibility, pride in quality or sensitivity to changing tastes. It was left to the Japanese, who had never obliterated their craft tradition, to devise a more imaginative system of mass-production after the Second World War which could provide more scope for both workers and customers (see Chapter 11). When the global market-place opened up in the 1970s and customers became more discriminating, the American car managers remained trapped in mass-thinking as well as mass-production until they were almost too late to respond to the Japanese challenge.

REGIMENTING THE SALESMEN

The spread of mass-production regimented other occupations that depended on industry, including suppliers, agents, brokers and, above all, salesmen. The travelling peddler had a picturesque history, from the medieval mountebank selling elixirs at fairs to the Victorian commercial traveller showing his samples at coaching inns. In America in the mid-nineteenth century the wholesalers, who were the dominant entrepreneurs, began employing 'drummers' or 'greeters' who met retailers in hotels or saloons in the city market-places. But the big corporations required more disciplined salesmen. By the 1880s the drummer was a recognisable figure on the railroads – well-dressed, extrovert, heavy-drinking and promiscuous, combining outward self-confidence and adventurousness with an insecurity which often turned to alcoholism. One of them was Charles Drouet in Theodore Dreiser's novel *Sister Carrie*, set in Chicago in 1889:

His suit was of a striped and crossed pattern of brown wool, new at that time, but since become more familiar as a business suit. The low crotch of the vest revealed a stiff shirt bosom of white and pink stripes. From his coat sleeves protruded a pair of linen cuffs of the same pattern, fastened with large gold-plate

47

buttons, set with the common yellow agates known as 'cat's eyes'. His fingers bore several rings – one, the ever-enduring heavy seal – and from his vest dangled a neat gold watch-chain, from which was suspended the secret insignia of the Order of Elks.

The new captains of industry needed stricter control over these individualists to establish their products across the continent; and at the turn of the century John Henry Patterson in Dayton, Ohio, a 'violent, vengeful, genius', began developing techniques which were to earn him the title of 'the father of modern salesmanship'. He was building up the National Cash Register company, 'the Cash', into a near-monopoly of machines which were becoming indispensable to shop-keepers; and he trained an army of salesmen in the arts of persuasion, cajoling and denigrating rivals. Patterson knew how to strip down his salesman's personality, then to make him totally dependent, and then to reassure him with enveloping paternalism, promising him the riches and security which a monopoly could afford. The ego-breaking technique owed something to the army training camp, but more to the missionary. The itinerant preacher, zealously converting the sceptical heathen and promising eternal salvation, was trans-muted into the salesman clinching a deal by promising worldly security.

Among Patterson's trainees was an ambitious, puritanical young man called Tom Watson, the son of an immigrant Scots-Irish farmer, who became the most successful salesman in the region. Patterson entrusted Watson with an illicit assignment: to set up a new, ostensibly independent, company to compete with the Cash's rivals, discover their secrets, undermine them and then buy them up cheaply. Watson pursued this knock-out strategy until the victims eventually took the case to the Federal Government, as a flagrant restraint of trade. In 1912 thirty men from the Cash, including Patterson and Watson, were indicted for restraint of trade and maintaining a monopoly, by a prosecutor who compared their methods to Mexican bandits. Watson and Patterson were sentenced to a year in jail, then granted bail and allowed to appeal; the case was endlessly postponed.

Soon afterwards Watson was fired by Patterson, and was left with a young wife and no money. But he was now an experienced salesman while business machinery was booming. Charles Flint, a prominent trust-organiser and arms dealer, had put together a combine called the Computer-Tabulating-Recording Company (CTR), which included a punch-card system which had been used for the 1890 census. Watson persuaded Flint to appoint him chief executive, with 5 per cent of the profits. He applied Patterson's techniques to motivating salesmen with the promise of a growing market for office equipment. He knew, as Ford did not, how to inspire the loyalty of his managers, and promised lifetime security in return for total commitment. His company, under its new name of International Business Machines (IBM), was to transform the world of communications and computers; but its success was based less on its technical mastery than on understanding how to organise salesmen. The striped suit, linen cuffs and gold watch-chain of Charles Drouet in 1889 had given way to the uniform white shirts and dark suits of the IBM salesmen.

THE VISIBLE HAND

The new patterns of company men, whether in oil, cars or office machines, were already set before the First World War, and the war massively strengthened the corporate powers, making their managers more important as their own planning merged into the military planning. After the United States joined the war in April 1917, the government took over control of the railway and telegraph systems and provided huge orders for arms and ships to create its own emergency fleet. Businessmen transferred to the armed forces and to government, to help build up an unprecedented war machine, with centralised production and distribution which played a decisive role in the Allied victory. The corporations which in peacetime had seemed so menacing to individual freedoms now emerged as the essential means of defence against foreign tyranny; and many of their products became the life-blood of democracy. The oil companies turned from bogeys to heroes as they supplied their precious fluid: Standard Oil of New Jersey boasted that they supplied a quarter of the entire oil of the Allies. Just after the Armistice Lord Curzon, who had served in the

British War Cabinet, told a petroleum conference that 'the Allied cause had floated to victory upon a wave of oil'.

By the end of the war the shape of the twentieth-century business corporation was established, and the nineteenth-century structures of American business were almost unrecognisable. 'The American businessman of 1840,' wrote the historian Alfred Chandler, 'would find the environment of fifteenth-century Italy more familiar than that of his own nation seventy years later.' The gradual, organic growth of family firms and local industries had given way to the mechanical structures of the railroads, the trusts and the assembly lines, each with their layers of managers constructed like scaffolding. And the company men appeared much less at the mercy of unpredictable conditions of trade than family owners like Silas Lapham: they were controlling much of the market, and developing the trade. As Thorstein Veblen described them as early as 1904:

> Instead of investing in the goods as they pass between producer and consumer, as the merchant does, the business man now invests in the processes of industry; and instead of staking his values on the dimly foreseen conjunctures of the seasons and the acts of God, he turns to the conjunctures arising from the interplay of the industrial processes, which are in great measure under the control of business men.

Their power challenged Adam Smith's theory of free enterprise, by which the 'invisible hand' achieved the division of labour, and balanced supply and demand. The managers played a very visible hand, as they planned and co-ordinated specialised products for mass markets. As Alfred Chandler wrote in his classic study of business *The Visible Hand*: 'Modern business enterprise became a viable institution only after the visible hand of management proved to be more efficient than the invisible hand of market forces.'

But the worries of individuals confronting corporations on both sides of the Atlantic would not go away. For the new industrial structures were increasingly cut off from the societies and customers for whom they operated, and repeatedly vulnerable to autocrats and despots. And the company men were establishing a self-contained office life with many of the diseases of bureaucracy, which cut them off from the normal understanding of human relationships and behaviour – at a cost which became clearer as the century rolled on.

CHAPTER FOUR

The Machine and the Maiden

Not as priest or soldier or judge does youth seek honour today, but as a man of offices. The business subaltern, charming and gallant as the jungle-gallopers of Kipling, drills files, not of troops, but of correspondence.

SINCLAIR LEWIS, *The Job*, 1916

In the mid-nineteenth century the new company men were establishing their own working habitat, based on an emphatically masculine culture, which would resist any competition or threat from company women. Most Victorian offices were exclusively male, and little more than extensions of the master's own study, where a few clerks sat or stood at high desks in an 'outer office'. The typical clerk had lost status since the days of Charles Lamb, and Dickens described his downtrodden life in 1836–37 in *Sketches by Boz*:

> the dingy little back office into which he walks every morning, hanging his hat on the same peg, and placing his legs beneath the same desk: first, taking off that black coat which lasts the year through, and putting on one which did duty last year, and which he keeps in his desk to save the other. There he sits till five o'clock, working on, all day, as regularly as the dial over the mantel-piece, whose loud ticking is as monotonous as his whole existence.

Armies of office workers were employed as copyists or scriveners to transcribe legal documents all day; a deathly existence eerily described in Herman Melville's short story 'Bartleby' in 1853. Bartleby is a pallid, forlorn young scrivener who comes to work for a lawyer in Wall Street and then begins living in the office, refusing to leave until he is removed to prison, where he dies, leaving no clues about his past life except a rumour that he had worked for the Dead Letter Office in Washington, where scriveners copied letters which were then consigned in cartloads to be burnt.

Most industrial offices were part of the factory itself. As late as 1890 William Lever was running his soap company at Port Sunlight near Liverpool from his office in the centre of the building; it was 'raised above the level of the surrounding offices, and had walls of glass. From here he could survey the activities of the staff. Practically the whole of the business was carried in his head and was directed by verbal instruction.' It was not till the beginnings of cost-accounting and scientific management at the end of the nineteenth century that managers could begin working out their projects away from the factory. As David Landes put it, 'The office was beginning, but only beginning, to dominate the shop.'

But already by the mid-nineteenth century commercial businesses, particularly insurance and banking, were moving into imposing buildings in the big cities. In London in 1849 Sun Insurance, the world's oldest insurance company, occupied a new kind of purpose-built headquarters with the style of a fashionable mansion. Thirty years later the Prudential, the giant of life-assurance which already handled seven million policies, began constructing its Gothic castle in Holborn where it still stands. By the end of the century the city-centres in Europe and America were being defined by the 'temples of commerce' – like the Met. Tower in New York – with their own disciplined communities inside them.

The bleakness of office-life, and the longing to escape it, became a recurring theme for popular writers. The British novelist Shan Bullock wrote *Mr Ruby Jumps the Traces*, set in 1902, about a clerk in London dreaming of travelling abroad. 'The big crowded room wherein he sat, so bare and business-like, with its floor covering of brown linoleum, its painted walls, its litter of papers and vouchers and account-books on high desks and shelves and tables, with its pervading atmosphere of stale tobacco, dust and stuffiness.' Looking at the ships on the Thames bound for distant places, he is suddenly impelled to take a trip to Gibraltar; but he soon returns to the constraints of the family and office.

Sinclair Lewis's first novel, *Our Mr Wrenn*, set in New York in

1910, is about a sales-entry clerk in the Souvenir Company. 'He was always bending over bills and columns of figures at a desk behind the stock-room. He was a meek little bachelor – a person of inconspicuous blue ready-made suits, and a small unsuccessful moustache.' He is dominated by his boss, Mortimer R. Guilfogle, but eventually determines to lead his own life: 'Old Goglefogle didn't consider him; why should be consider the firm?' Having inherited a thousand dollars, he resigns, to find himself bewildered by his independence two weeks later: 'All proper persons were at work of a week-day afternoon.' He sails to Europe, but after confusing adventures sails back to Manhattan with relief, to see again 'the vast pile of New York skyscrapers, standing in a mist like an enormous burned forest'. Between the Met. Tower and the Times he notices the good old 'Souvenir Company Office'.

The new skyscrapers provided a much more self-contained work-style than the low office-buildings around them. Most early skyscrapers were speculative buildings, with corridors leading into small separate offices which were leased to individuals. The Chicago writer Henry Fuller, in his 1893 novel *The Cliff-Dwellers*, describes life in the fictional eighteen-storey Clifton building, which contained four thousand people. It included bankers, brokers and realtors, with a supporting army of clerks, stenographers, janitors and scrub-women, complete with a barber-shop, cigar-store, ten elevators, four big boilers in the basement and a restaurant at the top. The shops and wide corridors between the offices, like miniature streets, provided their own social life, and Fuller's story revolves around the skyscraper for, as he explains: 'the Clifton aims to be complete within itself, and it will be unnecessary for us to go afield either far or frequently during the present simple succession of brief episodes in the lives of the Cliff-dwellers'.

But skyscrapers were soon being commissioned by big corporations, reflecting and reinforcing their rigid disciplines. Already by 1904 the Larkin building in Buffalo, designed by the young Frank Lloyd Wright, provided a prototype for a corporate skyscraper, to provide maximum supervision and discipline of hundreds of women mail-order clerks in a factory atmosphere in keeping with the principles of Taylorism – including seats designed to provide the minimum of movement.

THE WOMEN ARRIVE

It was the arrival of women in the offices which was the beginning of the real social revolution. For most of the nineteenth century middle-class women lived lives far removed from any office or factory. Unmarried daughters awaited suitable husbands, to provide family life and financial security. If they failed they might become governesses, teachers or companions; only if they were desperate or disgraced would they work in an office, let alone a factory, like Lily Bart in Edith Wharton's novel *The House of Mirth* who became a seamstress before taking an overdose of chloral.

But already by the 1880s some middle-class women were entering commercial activity, and enterprising employers were opening up new escape-routes from the home, with jobs ranging from shop assistants to saleswomen to book-keepers. George Gissing's novel *In the Year of Jubilee*, set in London in 1887, describes women beginning to work in 'houses of business'. 'Now we have women of title starting as milliners and modistes,' says the fashionable Mrs Damerel, 'and soon it will be quite a common thing to see one's friends behind the counter.' The heroine Nancy Lord, left with a baby and without a husband, contemplates becoming a governess or even somebody's secretary: 'That sounded pleasant, but very ambitious: a sense of incompetency chilled her. In an office, in a shop, who would dream of giving her an engagement?' Eventually she gets a job working for a 'dress-supply association' set up by a woman friend who needs 'someone ladylike to sit and answer questions' – a job Nancy thoroughly despises: 'I advise fools about the fashions, and exhibit myself as a walking fashion-plate.'

In the United States ambitious girls could leave their small towns to try their luck in the big industrial cities, with some hazards. In Theodore Dreiser's novel *Sister Carrie* the young heroine arrives in Chicago in 1889 to find magnificent buildings, with plate-glass windows on the ground floors, each occupied by a company or a new department store:

> The casual wanderer could see as he passed a polished array of office fixtures, much frosted glass, clerks hard at work, and

genteel business men in 'nobby' suits and clean linen lounging about or sitting in groups. Polished brass or nickel signs at the square stone entrances announced the firm and the nature of the business in rather neat and reserved terms. The entire metropolitan centre possessed a high and mighty air calculated to overawe and abash the common applicant, and to make the gulf between poverty and success seem both wide and deep.

Carrie searches for a ladylike job, only to find herself confronting the harsh demands of mass-production: 'the machine and the maiden'. She has no skills and eventually gets a job in a shoe-factory punching eyeholes in leather shoes, until she is liberated by men-friends who transport her into a world of high living and eventual success in the theatre.

By the turn of the century two inventions were beginning to transform the opportunities for women in offices. The first, the typewriter, was invented by a Pennsylvania journalist, Christopher Sholes, who sold the patent to the Remington arms company who offered their first machines in 1873. Employers soon found that women excelled as 'typewriters' – which at first described the typist as well as the machine. Women were already used to take down shorthand as 'stenographers', but now they were much more in demand than men: in 1887 a London newspaper recorded that women 'beat them altogether as type-writers'. Frank Cowperwood, the hero of Dreiser's *The Titan*, employs in the late 1870s a pretty Polish girl, Antoinette, to work as his new typewriter. They soon have an affair: he becomes more interested in her, 'wondering at the amazing, transforming power of the American atmosphere'.

In Bernard Shaw's play *Candida* in 1895 the typist Proserpine Garnett is 'a brisk little woman of about thirty, of the lower middle class, neatly but cheaply dressed in a black merino skirt and a blouse, rather pert and quick of speech'. She works for a clergyman, clattering away at her machine and fiercely protecting it from curious visitors: 'You've been meddling with my typewriter, Mr Marchbanks ... I suppose you thought it was a sort of barrel-organ.' She can use the machine as a kind of weapon, typing 'with clattering asperity' and shifting her paper carriage 'with a defiant bang'. But she plays no more serious role in the drama than the traditional cheeky maid.

Attractive typists soon found new social horizons away from the constraints of their homes, and began to be seen as a threat to marital peace. Already by 1895 a British book on *How to Get Married* reported that 'the marriage of the type-writer and her employer is so frequent that it has passed into a joke'. In the same year in America Silas Lapham, the hero of William Dean Howells's novel, employs a beautiful 'type-writer girl', Zerrilla Dewey, who has 'the air of unmerited wrong habitual with so many pretty women who have to work for a living'. Mrs Lapham, who used to help her husband in the business, is vexed to find Zerrilla in the office, with her hat and handbag hung in the corner next to her husband's coat: 'She forgot how much she had left herself out of his business life.'

In the fast-changing social world of New York or Chicago shorthand-typing could provide ambitious girls with easy access to rich bosses. In *The Cliff-Dwellers* Cornelia McNabb promotes herself from waitress to type-writer girl inside the Clifton skyscraper, studying the social columns of the newspapers and typing for the financier Brainard: 'He gives her letters every day. She corrects his mistakes,' observes Brainard's daughter Abbie; and before long Cornelia is engaged to Brainard's son.

A very few typists were transported into a world of undreamt-of riches. In Detroit Evangeline Côté joined the stenographic department of the Ford motor company in 1909 as a pretty, bright-eyed girl of sixteen: three years later she was running the stenographic department. She caught the eye of Henry Ford who asked her to work late in his office and often drove her home. She married one of Ford's aides, John Dahlinger, and six years later had a son, whom many people thought was fathered by Ford. In any case, he gave her a palatial mansion, a farm, a holiday estate and a flying boat.

The telephone, which was to open up the companies more subtly to women, had far wider repercussions, which are still today transforming or subverting office-life. In America its advance was rapid: four years after the first telephoned message in 1876 there were already 54,000 receivers. The telephone soon allowed managers to separate themselves further from the factories. As one historian of the telephone described it: 'Head office, in a smart quarter of town, could have its own character, unrelated to the less appealing aspects of the business elsewhere.' Chicago, where the fire of 1871 had razed the old commercial centre, became the world capital of telephones, which rang through the new skyscrapers. They enabled all large organisations to become more centralised: 'The telephone has been to centralisation of government,' wrote Hugh Thomas, 'what the loud-speaker has been to the mass orator.' And they gave special scope for entrepreneurs to extend their control and speculation: in 1910 the financier E.H. Harriman was reported to have a hundred telephones in his mansion, sixty of them long-distance.

The telephone widened the contrast with business styles across the Atlantic, where Europeans were much more resistant to this new threat to their privacy. British businessmen, even stockbrokers, resisted the noisy instrument or banished it to the basement or the lavatory. 'With the new instrument hanging over his desk,' complained *The Times*, 'the merchant or the banker will be liable to perpetual interruptions from telephonists who will begin with some such phrase as "Oh, by the bye".'

The future playwright Bernard Shaw actually worked briefly for the Edison telephone company in London in 1879, trying to persuade householders to allow wires across their roofs. He discovered that 'it was a telephone of such stentorian efficiency that it bellowed your most private communications all over the house'. Shaw exploited his experience in his early novel *The Irrational Knot* (1880), whose hero, an Irish-American electrician, describes how telephones, typewriters and electricity are beginning to intrude on aristocratic leisure. Even playwrights in Europe, who later found the telephone invaluable to their stagecraft, were slow to welcome it. Strindberg first introduced it to the stage in *The Father* in 1887, and frequently used it thereafter; though he was inclined to treat it as a morbid symbol of sinister influences.

But the most far-reaching social consequence of the telephone was to bring thousands of women into offices. Thomas A. Watson, the assistant of the inventor Alexander Graham Bell, observed how the telephone could paralyse the most eloquent men, and recalled a prominent lawyer who could only reply after a long pause, 'Rig a jig-jig and away we go.' But women were much more fluent, and proved invaluable in the telephone exchanges. The first woman operator in Boston in 1878 was followed by a procession who found switchboards more respectable and protected work-places than saloons or billiard halls, and who were more decorative than male operators: the President of Bell Canada was fascinated by the graceful movements of the women operators, who reminded him of 'my grandmother playing a harp'. Even in Tokyo, where public telephones were introduced in 1889, the exchanges provided new opportunities for the daughters of impoverished middle-class families.

By the twentieth century women with their machines were making the office more exciting and professionalised, an alternative to home which could be a relief for wives as well as husbands. 'A man who has no office to go to – I don't care who he is – is a trial of which you can have no conception,' says Marion, the adventurous heroine of Shaw's *The Irrational Knot*. Between 1861 and 1911 the number of male clerical workers in Britain multiplied by five, but women clerks multiplied by 500. A book by Mostyn Bird on *Women at Work* in Britain in 1911 described the change in London streets over only ten years:

> In the morning, at nightfall and in the luncheon hour women pour in and out of every block of office buildings in numbers that rival men. Early trains are crowded with them, and they mingle in the home-ward bound streams of the evening. The City is no longer the man's domain, the woman's footing there is now assured and is a commonplace of mercantile life. Even Government Office and banks, those two most conservative institutions, now employ a certain number of women clerks.

Offices allowed many girls to escape from dominating mothers and stifling homes, into a much more matter-of-fact and rational atmosphere. But they had their own narrow limits. The new jobs were cleaner and more genteel than manufacturing or domestic service, but the typist had little independence, and her job could be regarded as even more servile. As Mostyn Bird emphasised:

> She is at the service of the mind, the wits, of her employer ... Her own ideas upon the subject she deals with are of no consequence whatever; her personality has far less influence upon her work than that of the domestic servant. It is a curious mechanical service, this, both of memory and of tapping fingers.

The stenographer has to listen with attention and transcribe with accuracy into shorthand or with her typewriter, the ideas of her employer; while her own must be non-existent.

But she already had a chance, at least in theory, to be trained to become a manager:

In the merchant's office she can get an insight into business methods, in the counting-house she can learn practical book-keeping, either of which will be of immense value if she is called to manage a small business of her own or for an employer. A humble position behind a typewriter in some editorial or publishing office has often been the first stepping-stone to independent journalism, and even to an Editor's chair.

In social life, the female secretary could be welcome: 'Women secretaries are increasingly in demand for public men, business men, both at home and in their private offices.' The presentable secretary enjoyed a prestige above that of a mere clerk, with a social as well as a professional role, and she was expected to spend much of her salary on clothes: 'Her afternoon and party frocks must be sufficiently fashionable though not conspicuous,' says Mostyn Bird. 'Her style of dress must not be of the kind to render her distinguishable as "the secretary" in her smart surroundings, although she need not aim at rivalling the extravagance of Society women.'

By the time of the First World War women had become indispensable to most big offices. In 1900 the American *Ladies' Home Journal* was urging women to stay out of offices, but by 1916 the magazine was 'glorifying the feminine traits of stenographers; their ability to radiate sympathetic interest, agreeableness, courtesy'. Many secretaries or stenographers were better-educated and more intelligent than their bosses. Sinclair Lewis's Mr Wrenn had to dictate to 'an efficient, intolerant young woman, who wrote down his halting words as though they were examples of bad English she wanted to show to her friends, and waited for the next word with cynical amusement'. But most secretaries concealed their superiority, and devoted their talents to furthering their bosses' ambitions. An efficient secretary came to be seen as an 'office wife' who could also tend to her boss's domestic needs, competing with the home wife for his attention. Secretaries were often younger, prettier and more admiring than wives: second marriages became a recurring pattern.

The most evocative picture of the problems of early office woman is Sinclair Lewis's third novel *The Job* (1916), whose heroine is Una Golden, a lively girl who leaves her small town in Pennsylvania to become a stenographer in New York in 1905: 'In this fumbling school, she was beginning to feel the theory of efficiency, the ideal of Big Business.' She finds a job with the *Motor and Gas Gazette*, where she first beholds 'the drama and romance of the office world':

A world is this whose noblest vista is composed of desks and typewriters, filing-cases and insurance calendars, telephones, and the bald heads of men who believe dreams to be idiotic. Here, no galleon breasts the sky-line; no explorer in evening clothes makes love to an heiress. Here ride no rollicking cow-boys, nor heroes of the great European war. It is a world whose crises you cannot comprehend unless you have learned that the difference between a 2-A pencil and a 2-B pencil is at least equal to the contrast between London and Tibet; unless you understand why a normally self-controlled young woman may have a week of tragic discomfort because she is using a billing-machine instead of a typewriter. The shifting of the water-cooler from the front office to the packing-room may be an epochal event to a copyist who apparently has no human existence beyond bending over a clacking typewriter, who seems to have no home, no family, no loves; in whom all pride and wonder of life and all transforming drama seem to be satisfied by the possession of a new V-necked blouse.

After being crossed in love Una survives all the tyrannies of office work – time-clocks, efficiency experts, competing women – but craves domestic life and marries a hard-drinking salesman. He soon loses his job and resents his dependence on her income: 'You women that have been in business simply ain't fit to be married. You think you're too good to help a man.' She walks out on him and returns to business as a confidential secretary; after two years of marriage 'the office world was of the loftiest dignity'. She enjoys the office Christmas party, the village atmosphere, and learns about society from a worldly saleswoman whose father was a friend of Henry James. She begins selling real estate, becomes a sales-manager and eventually runs a group of hotels. She meets up again with her first love in the office world who asks her to marry him, but she remains pulled by both lives: "I will keep my job – if I've had this world of offices wished on to me, at least I'll conquer it, and give my clerks a decent time," the business woman meditated.'

All women who entered offices had first to accept their masculine values, and leave their femininity at home. At the beginning of the century Henry Adams, observing the intensity of the new business life, was saddened by the failure of the American woman to create her own society, and by the American man's failure to respect feminine values as he became engrossed by the new machines. 'He could not run his machine and a woman too; he must leave her, even though his wife, to find her own way, and all the world saw her trying to find her way by imitating him.'

EUROPEAN BUREAUCRATS

Europeans, with their aristocratic and military traditions and more settled communities, were less ready than Americans to accept the values and styles of the new businessmen. But the earlier social structures – the country estate, the regiment or the cathedral close – were beginning to fade, and the old patterns were re-emerging in new disguises within company headquarters. German military ranks were transmuted into the hierarchies of the *Gesellschaft*. French administrators from the Napoleonic *grandes écoles* moved into railways or electricity. And the British style of country-house life was recreated in the new company buildings which were often designed to look like the mansions of the aristocracy. The great hall became the front office, the grand staircase became the directors' lift, the footmen became chauffeurs; while the sub-classes of housekeepers, nannies, governesses, companions or housemaids were recreated in the new layers of office managers, personnel officers, private secretaries or tea ladies.

Office life was still depicted by novelists as soulless, inhuman or merely absurd, but most middle-class people were beginning to accept it as the most normal way of life: a centre of activity as natural as the farmhouse, the church or the barracks a century earlier. And the home itself was beginning to yield to the office as the centre of the community. The German industrialist Walther Rathenau, looking back on the changes before World War I, described how 'The workshop and the office were divorced from the home; the working hours grew longer; the business man, the official employee, and the man of learning, began to spend the whole day away from the dwelling; the entire community of the household was broken up.'

But the big business organisations which were growing up in the European cities were far more impersonal and incomprehensible than the earlier hierarchies of the church or the army. The orders and regulations of the *sociétés anonymes* were passed up and down the pyramids, with no single person being clearly responsible. They could create a nightmare of persecution, as was most terrifyingly described by a sensitive young insurance clerk in Prague. Franz Kafka's novels convey his own private sense of persecution in rarefied symbolised terms; but his eloquent letters provide the most haunting accounts of the constraints of office life.

In Prague in 1907 Kafka joined his first employer, the Italian insurance company Assicurazioni Generali, which had been founded in Trieste in 1831 and was operating across Europe – as it still does today. He worked in an imposing palace in Wenceslas Square, with a ponderous doorway, statues and a globe on top. He studied insurance conscientiously but drearily, working eight to nine hours a day including Saturday. 'If my troubles previously walked on their feet, they're now, aptly, walking on their hands.'

I'm not complaining about the work so much as the swampy viscosity of time. The fact is that office-hours can't be divided up: even during the last half-hour the pressure of the eight hours can be felt just as much as during the first. It's like a train journey that goes on overnight; finally, dispirited, you no longer think either about the labour of the engine or about the scenery, hilly or flat, but you blame everything on your watch, which you hold constantly in the palm of your hand.

After nine months Kafka moved to the Workmen's Accident Insurance Institute for the Kingdom of Bohemia, in a massive Prague building with a porter with a huge beard at the entrance who intimidated workers coming to apply for compensation. Kafka took an insurance course, wrote reports about car insurance and defended the institute against detractors: his boss reported that he 'combines constant interest in all memoranda with very great zeal', and said that the department would collapse without him.

But Kafka was seeing the office in funereal terms. From his desk he watched a kind of bier which moved through the corridors carrying files and documents. 'Each time it passed,' he told his girlfriend Felice, 'I thought it was highly suitable for me, was waiting for me.' Some years later he worked for two hours a day in a market garden, to recover from the deadly office work. 'The only true hell,' he told Felice, 'is there in the office, I no longer fear any other.' After fourteen years he left the office for ever. 'Kafka came and went as quietly as a mouse,' said the office cleaner. A colleague was told to take away the 'rubbish' on his desk – a slender glass vase holding two pencils and a penholder, and a blue-and-gold teacup and saucer from which he drank his milk. But for the rest of the century his private imagination was to acquire a universal dimension, conveying all the horrors of anonymous bureaucracy overwhelming the individual with its impenetrable power.

CHAPTER FIVE

Managers and Despots

This world, which has never before been ready to
accept universally any of the universal faiths offered
for its salvation, is apparently prepared to embrace
the religion of science and technology without reser-
vation.

DAVID LANDES, *The Unbound Prometheus* (1969)

The emerging corporations of the early twentieth century were still
confusing entities with an uncertain legitimacy. The original founders
and owners were yielding control to the company men, who were
establishing scientific systems of management; while the thousands
of small shareholders, the theoretical owners, were powerless to intervene. But the bigger the corporation, the more it needed decisive
leadership, and decisions were constantly pushed upwards, towards
a peak. And company men on both sides of the Atlantic were in
danger from autocrats who were out of control.

The businessman himself was rapidly extending his influence after
the First World War, as a pillar of society; most of all in America.
As Sinclair Lewis had described him in 1916: 'No longer does the
business man thank the better classes for permitting him to make
and distribute bread and motor-cars and books. No longer does he
crawl to the church to buy pardon for usury. Business is being recognised – and is recognising itself – as ruler of the world.'

American businessmen were establishing their own social networks
and influence, encouraged by clubs with branches in each city, holding weekly lunches: the Rotary Club, for instance, founded in 1905,
had 150,000 members by 1930. Companies were increasingly taking
over from the churches as the chief social network. 'Business itself
was regarded with a new veneration,' wrote the historian Frederick
Allen, looking back on the twenties. 'Once it had been considered

65

less dignified and distinguished than the learned professions, but now people thought they praised a clergyman highly when they called him a good business man.'

High-flying salesmen saw the Bible as their text-book and Christ as their prophet. Fred F. French, the New York builder, quoted the slogan 'Knock and it shall be opened unto you' by 'the greatest Human-nature Expert that ever lived'. The Metropolitan Casualty Insurance Company explained that 'Moses was one of the greatest salesmen and real-estate promoters that ever lived.' Bruce Barton, co-founder of the advertising agency BBDO, wrote a book about Jesus, *The Man Nobody Knows*, which described how he had 'picked up twelve men from the bottom rank of business and forged them into an organisation that conquered the world'.

European intellectuals observed the new breed of businessmen with amazement. G.K. Chesterton described them after visiting America in 1922: 'They sit about in groups with Red-Indian gravity, as if passing the pipe of peace; though, in fact, most of them are smoking cigars and some of them are eating cigars ... I fancy that all those hard-featured faces, in spectacles and shaven jaws, do look rather alike, because they all like to make their faces hard.'

On a more practical level business managers became more professionalised and seriously trained. Colleges organised courses and gave degree-credits for commercial subjects including advertising, marketing and even stenography. Business schools proliferated, providing courses in industrial organisation: the Wharton School in 1881 had been followed by the Harvard Business School 1908, and a host of imitators. The new profession of management consultants was developing from engineering experts. In 1921 the consultants Day & Zimmerman advised General Motors on their internal reorganisation: four years later one of their partners, James O. McKinsey, set up his own firm of management consultants which was to become the most famous in the world.

During the seven-year boom of the twenties it was the entrepreneurs and financiers who set the pace and achieved glory as the providers of unparalleled prosperity. But the Great Crash of 1929 undermined the investment which supported them, discredited their dealings, and devastated production and jobs. The Depression of the thirties put much more emphasis on the managers, who had to look for new markets and products to survive; while the newer industries including airlines, radio and telephones called for skilled engineers who were opening up the new communications.

The Crash turned many managers and engineers against the political and economic system which had produced it, and they began to look for alternatives, in which they would play key roles. Already in 1921 Thorstein Veblen had predicted that engineers would assert themselves against owners, and 'disallow that large absentee ownership that goes to make the vested interests and to unmake the industrial system'. Veblen's ideas were developed by Howard Scott, an eccentric engineer who warned that growing productivity would create permanent unemployment: the industrial age had 'turned upon its masters to destroy it'. Scott wanted to create a technocracy, giving control to the experts, and replacing money based on gold with new units based on energy, to be called ergs and joules. The Depression gave a sudden boost to Scott's technocracy, and for a short time his meetings attracted big crowds – until he revealed his lack of any serious political plan, and the movement died out. But the overcapacity and underproduction of the Depression led many captains of industry to accept the need for central economic planning, and to look for agreements and cartels to protect and stabilise their own markets.

The trend towards cartels and planning encouraged autocrats at the top; while the fear of unemployment made company men more dependent on them and grateful for any kind of work. In all three of the industries we have looked at – in oil, cars and business machines – the chief companies came to be dominated by single leaders.

STANDARD OIL: DOMINATION AND TREASON

Standard Oil of New Jersey, though no longer controlled by the Rockefellers, was still run as a kind of fiefdom; and in 1917 it appointed a new chairman, Walter Teagle, a hereditary oilman whose father had competed with Rockefeller before selling out to him. Teagle provided a bridge between the first generation of owners and the later professional managers. Though himself the product of nepotism, he told executives not to engage relatives to work with them, but to refer them to other departments. 'The first duty of an executive is to provide for continuity of efficient management,' he told them in 1929. 'No executive has fulfilled his duty until he has trained his successor.' But he himself dominated the company without much thought about a successor. He repeatedly reorganised it, delegated powers to specialists, and divided it into separate divisions – one of the first companies to do so – while maintaining his personal hold. Like Henry Ford he detested organisation charts and manuals, kept lawyers out of the main board, and took care that the key decisions would not be made by a committee. He kept aloof from the senior company men, mostly petroleum engineers who had climbed 'up the pipeline'. He took three months' holiday a year for hunting and fishing, giving orders from his estate. He employed his own private spy, James Flanagan, and established a friendship with President Roosevelt. When he met with his global rivals – Deterding, Gulbenkian and Cadman – to carve up the control of the world's oil, to prevent overproduction and price-wars, he did not confide in his underlings.

But Teagle lacked political sensitivity. After Hitler had come to power he extended a secret deal with the German chemical cartel IG Farben which gave them a precious patent for aviation fuel, in exchange for patents in synthetic rubber which were crucial to the Nazi war-machine; and Standard Oil's scientists continued to supply valuable information to the Germans after the invasion of Europe. The next year Thurman Arnold, the anti-trust chief in Washington, charged Standard Oil with restrictive agreements and fiercely attacked Teagle who became confused and ineffective, and appealed to Roosevelt in vain: soon afterwards Senator Harry S Truman took up the attack, even accusing Standard Oil of treason. The charges were overstated: as Thurman Arnold had explained, 'What these people were trying to do was to look at the war as a transitory phenomenon and at business as a kind of permanent thing.' But Teagle never recovered: he resigned, nervous and fumbling, before the end of his term in 1942. His board were determined to avoid future autocrats.

GENERAL MOTORS:
CENTRALISED DECENTRALISATION

It was the auto industry which faced the greatest problems of organisation, and which was to provide the model of professional management for others, in the shape of General Motors. It was influenced by the old chemical company run by the duPont family who had established a gunpowder company in Delaware in 1801 and retained control through the nineteenth century. They expanded into other products including plastics, and introduced professional managers and well-organised divisions; while the family retained their influence, partly by marrying off their daughters to the top executives. After the First World War the chairman, Pierre duPont, saw a chance to move into the automobile industry through the ailing General Motors.

GM had been put together by a brilliant loner, William Durant, but the recession of 1920 left the company with growing debts and huge stocks of unsold cars, which forced him to yield control. DuPont bought 36 per cent of the stock, and delegated the task of reorganisation to a master-manager, Alfred P. Sloan. It was Henry Ford's stubborn autocracy, and refusal to give customers a choice, which gave Sloan his opportunity. He had been brought up in the early auto age, with the instincts not of an inventor like Ford, but of a consumer who longed to own a car: 'I wanted one but couldn't afford it.' He became an electrical engineer at MIT but never lost his awareness of the customer. As he explained: 'Any rigidity by an automobile manufacturer, no matter how large or how well established, is severely penalised in the market.'

Sloan presented his policy as the opposite of Ford's: 'A car for every purse and purpose.' He set up five separate divisions making ranges of automobiles classified by price, and devised an almost opposite management system to Ford's: decentralised, strictly defined and self-perpetuating. The long-term survival of General Motors, he explained, 'depends upon its being operated in both the spirit and the substance of decentralisation'; and he wanted a happy medium between the extremes of pure centralisation and pure decentralisation.

But he still required a powerful centre: he replaced Durant's tiny base with a massive headquarters, where strong general executives presided over large staffs of accountants and advisers, ruled by an executive committee of ten members headed by duPont as chairman and Sloan as president. The board concentrated on long-term planning and allocating resources, leaving day-to-day management to line staff and financial divisions. This was basically a military system going back to the Prussian army of the early nineteenth century, with the general's HQ delegating to the field commanders. But it was far more complex, and to resolve the rivalries of the three divisions Sloan set up a 'multidivisional' structure, with a network of committees. Over forty years the system was to be copied by many other big companies in Europe as well as America, and it originated the committee-type of company man who was skilled in teamwork and compromise.

Sloan was chief executive for twenty-three years, and became the hero of professional managers, as General Motors overtook Ford to become the world's biggest auto company. It became the chief symbol of American efficiency and prosperity, admired by Democrat politicians as much as Republicans. In the election of 1928 John J. Raskob, the chairman of General Motors' finance committee, became chairman of the Democratic National Committee, and moved the Democratic headquarters to the GM building in New York – 'an ideally bullish address' – to reassure voters.

It was not until fifty years later that the full weakness of the GM system became apparent. It was a model of mechanical structure, as opposed to organic growth. As Sloan put it, it was 'designed as an objective organisation, as distinguished from the type that gets lost in the subjectivity of personalities'. He warned that it was 'not the appropriate organisation for purely intuitive executives, but it provides a favourable environment for capable and rational men'. But Sloan's own decisions and choice of men were often intuitive, and he knew that he wielded great personal power: 'Decentralisation or not, an industrial corporation is not the mildest form of organisation in society. I never minimised the administrative power of the chief executive.' So long as the boss was a decisive genius like Sloan, the system could work. But without strong leadership it degenerated into mediocrity, impersonality turned into irresponsibility, and it developed a rigidity which (as Sloan warned) 'is severely penalised'.

IBM: THE LIMITS TO THINKING

Thomas Watson was turning his young IBM company into a more advanced model of paternal dependence, with a more dedicated kind of company man. As Peter Drucker described him: 'He created in the 1930s the social organisation and the work community of the post-industrial society.' In the small town of Endicott, in New York State, Watson was training a highly-disciplined force of salesmen and managers to extend his near-monopoly of punch-cards, and creating a modernised kind of company town.

Endicott already had a famous shoe-factory owned by George Johnson, an idealist who believed in industrial democracy and who lived close to his workers, concerning himself with their personal problems. He had 25,000 employees to whom he sought to give a sense of belonging and purpose. His company, Endicott-Johnson, became famous for employing impoverished Eastern Europeans: arriving at Ellis Island, their only English words (it was said) were 'Which way E-J?' The visitor to Endicott can still see evidence of Johnson's reputation, commemorated by two arches across Main Street which proclaim: 'Gateway to the Square Deal Towns: erected by EJ Workers'.

Thomas Watson learnt from Johnson's paternalism, but imposed a much more puritanical and disciplined regime. His managers and salesmen wore dark suits and white shirts, did not drink and had signs on their desks saying THINK. The contrast with the shoe-workers was extreme – as described by the writer Robert Manning, who was brought up nearby:

> The street might as well have been a wall, dividing as it did class from class. At quitting time each working day the shoe-workers in their dark shirts, ravelled sweaters or team jackets, and scuffed brogues marched down their side of the street, making for nearby bowling alleys and corner saloons where they'd dally a bit before going home. As they walked, some of the E-J workers looked across at the white-collar IBM employees in their sombre suits and ties or neatly tailored dresses, and chanted, 'While you're thinkin', we're drinkin'!'

71

The slogan THINK emphasised the superior, scientific character of IBM man; but it was in blatant contradiction to the demands for total loyalty to the company. 'Loyalty saves the wear and tear,' Watson told his employees, 'of making daily decisions as to what is best to do.' IBM-ers were to become caricatures of loyal company men, immortalised in their company songs in praise of Watson, reminiscent of later Japanese company songs:

> We're here to cheer each pioneer
> And also proudly boast
> Of that 'man of men' our friend and guiding hand.
> The name of T.J. Watson means a courage none can stem:
> And we feel honoured to be here to toast the 'IBM'.

Tom Watson's son, who would soon be groomed for the succession, was embarrassed by the excesses of his father's paternalism, particularly when he commissioned an IBM symphony; but he went along with it. As he later recollected:

> Magazine cartoonists used to make fun of these signs, and IBM's critics thought they were ridiculous: how could anyone really *think* in a company that was such a one-man show? But to everybody inside, the message was crystal clear: you would sell more machines, and advance faster, if you used your head.
>
> I used to marvel at how willingly new employees embraced the company spirit. As far as I could tell, nobody made fun of the slogans and songs. Times were different then, and I suppose being earnest didn't seem as corny in 1937 as it does today. And of course jobs were awfully hard to come by in the 1930s, so people would put up with a lot.

And Watson was a master-salesman, who learnt from his own harsh experience as a hustler that his men needed both strict motivation and rewards. 'I want my IBM salesmen to be people to whom their wives and their children can look up,' he told Peter Drucker in 1939. He instilled an evangelical zeal for hard work and discipline: 'The man who utilises every minute of every hour becomes a bigger, better being every minute.' He set salesmen strict targets which entitled them to the banquets of the 100 Per Cent Club, which interspersed pep-talks and praise with lavish hospitality. The IBM extravaganzas culminated in IBM Day in 1940 when 10,000 employees in special trains converged on the New York World's Fair. And Watson himself was amply rewarded, as he pushed up IBM's profits through the Depression. Roosevelt's New Deal in the 1930s brought a surge of government orders for machines to implement the new social security system, and the federal government became IBM's biggest customer. By 1934 Watson's own salary (with his share of profits) was the biggest in the United States, ahead of top entertainers like Will Rogers and Janet Gaynor and other industrialists including Sloan.

Watson had brilliantly succeeded in forging his modernised company man, who could master the expanding technology, and sell it with commitment, rewarded by lifetime security. But the paternalism in his company towns was based on personal autocracy, and on a dependence and conformity which could not, in the end, keep pace with the technology it had helped to unleash.

LEVER: RULING BY FEAR

The British had inherited their own tradition of paternalism and company loyalty, descended partly from landed estates or the chartered corporations including the East India Company, and partly from the more benign owners of industry. Families like the Wedgwoods, the Cadburys and the Rowntrees had established model factories and villages to house their employees with a sense of responsibility handed down from father to son.

Giant combines were slower to develop, while the British government controlled many new industries including telephones, broadcasting and much of the oil (through British Petroleum). But the big corporations showed the same tendency towards dominating leadership, reinforced by the European pattern of cartels. Three great companies, Unilever, Shell and ICI, took shape as models of management engaged in world trade. The first two were Anglo-Dutch, and the third was strongly influenced by German origins, but all were associated with Britain's national purpose. And while they each built up elaborate systems, committees and teams of professional managers, they were each vulnerable to domination by an autocrat.

The British side of Unilever had originated with the Victorian soap king William Lever, who had built up his soap company in Port Sunlight outside Liverpool, and ruled it through personal command. He expanded rashly into new areas, from African trading to fish-shops; when he faced losses in 1920 he fired managers with deliberate ruthlessness, to intimidate the rest. 'Now what has produced the efficiency since 1921?' he asked three years later, and explained that it had been done by 'combing out inefficient men, and too highly paid men, elderly men, and men past their work steadily for the last three years, and I am confident that this has produced a state of "fear" in the minds of the remainder that if they were not efficient their turn would come next'.

Lever died in 1925, leaving a leaderless and near-bankrupt empire facing tougher competition from America and Europe. Five years later Lever Brothers merged with the Dutch Margarine Unie to form the giant Unilever, with an Anglo-Dutch board under the chairmanship of Lever's former accountant from Cooper Brothers, D'Arcy Cooper. It was only then that professional managers became more effective, operating from the new building on the Thames at Blackfriars which remains its headquarters today. But Unilever was still caught between its centre and its periphery, as it still is. At first Cooper tried to centralise everything until (as one Canadian executive complained), 'You had to cable London before you went to the bathroom.' Then they devised a carefully decentralised structure, with almost autonomous companies in each country, which became a kind of model for Europe. But Unilever was facing growing competition from Procter & Gamble from its concentrated headquarters in Cincinnati; and the tension between the centre and the provinces would never be resolved.

ICI: 'THEY CAN'T DO WITHOUT ME!'

A more lasting dictatorship was the great chemical combine Imperial Chemical Industries, created in 1926 with intensely patriotic ambitions as a counter to the German cartel IG Farben, which had just united the leading chemical companies including BASF, Bayer, Agfa and Hoechst. ICI linked two powerful tycoons: Alfred Mond (later Lord Melchett), who talked with a thick German accent into his waistcoat, had taken over the Brunner Mond chemical business from his father, and was dedicated to industrial relations and 'rationalisation' – the adjustment of supply to demand. Harry McGowan was a Glaswegian ex-office boy who had gained control of Nobel Industries, which he expanded from dynamite into broader investments and alliances abroad, notably with duPont. The two tycoons planned the merger on the SS *Aquitania* on 26 October 1926, on Cunard paper. They chose the name ICI with deliberate ambition – 'Imperial in aspect, imperial in name' – with the firm belief that 'the Empire would be Great Britain's economic salvation'. McGowan, as he told Mond, could not believe the theory that competition was essential to efficiency.

The chemical combine was determined to build up a unique body of managers to fulfil its imperial purpose, organised on military lines: it established a central staff department, run first by a major-general, then by a naval captain, and employees who were veterans of the First World War (like my father) were encouraged to call themselves 'Major' or 'Colonel'. Public schools were invited to send bright boys to a selection committee endorsed by the headmasters of Eton, Harrow and Winchester, and ICI perpetuated the old British distinction between 'the professions', including lawyers, accountants and chemists, and 'trade', including engineers and commercial men. Their Cheshire country house, Winnington Hall, which provided the grand social centre, had an exclusive membership which favoured Oxford graduates and accountants. ICI became famous for its paternalism and security, and its record of scientific research; but it betrayed the weaknesses of giant size and monopoly. Melchett himself had warned, when attacking socialist ideas, that 'it is quite impossible to control any industry beyond a certain magnitude'; and ICI was too protected to be commercially realistic. Its great new Nitrogen plant at Billingham-on-Tees (where I was born) was a model company town, admired by intellectuals as well as scientists: 'Artistically, Billingham is near perfect,' wrote Aldous Huxley after visiting it in 1931: 'In its own kind it is a magnificent poem.' But commercially it was a white elephant, based on imperial markets which never materialised.

Outwardly ICI was a pillar of imperial science: in 1928 it opened its resplendent new building on the Thames, with its elaborate nickel doors and statues of scientists and the chairman. But inwardly – as the company historian revealed forty years later – McGowan was a reckless speculator who was using his company's investments to support his own gambles. In 1937, just after McGowan became a peer, his co-directors discovered that he was on the verge of personal bankruptcy. They tried to oust him in favour of his deputy, Lord Melchett, who then had a heart attack. McGowan remained in command, with a slightly lower salary and with some supervision from a new management board, but still firmly in charge. As he told his dentist: 'They can't do without me!'

SHELL'S DICTATOR

The third of the great combines, Royal Dutch Shell, came under the control of a uniquely powerful dictator despite a formidable elite of professional managers. The Shell oil company had been set up by Marcus Samuel in 1898 as an offshoot of his trading business, to buy oil from Russia; with his brother Sam he ran the whole business with a group of clerks. In 1901 they were joined by Robert Waley-Cohen, a Cambridge graduate from another rich Jewish family, who began recruiting future managers for Shell, which was merged with Royal Dutch in 1906. Waley-Cohen's father had helped to establish the Cambridge University Appointments Board – the first of its kind – and young Robert was inspired by the Raj in India to believe that British graduates provided ideal managers, dedicated and incorruptible. He opposed the notion that business was not a fit career for gentlemen; and resisting pressure from Samuel's friends and relations he selected scores of Cambridge graduates sent by the board. Shell executives acquired the status of a kind of para-diplomatic corps (some of them were connected with the British secret service), but better-paid. Waley-Cohen, like Lord Melchett, was a strong advocate of 'rationalisation', and did not want his valuable managers to 'spend their lives in cancelling out one another's activities in mutual competition'. Rationalisation depended on

industry having the kind of men who 'exemplified the native characteristics of the British race'. The Shell managers did indeed become
the elite among British company men, with a style and confidence of
their own: in many Asian capitals the Shell representative competed
with the British Ambassador in grandeur.

But Shell's patriotism was not quite what it seemed; the merger
in 1906 had given 60 per cent of the shares to Royal Dutch, whose
chairman Henri Deterding had become increasingly despotic and
anti-British. The British Foreign Office was privately worried: 'Sir
Henri's word is law,' wrote a British diplomat in 1927. 'He can bind
the Board of Shell without their knowledge and consent.' By the
1930s, when Deterding was in his seventies, his dictatorship was
more dangerous; for he was entranced by Hitler, and also by a German secretary who became his third wife. In 1935 he negotiated with
the Nazis to give them a year's oil reserves on credit. After he was
eased out of Shell in late 1936 he retired to Germany and became
closer to the Nazis: when he died in 1939 Hitler and Goering both
sent wreaths to his funeral, and the Nazis tried to use his shares to
gain control of Shell's global network – which was forestalled by a
swift redistribution of shares.

Deterding's defection caused a deep trauma in Shell's corporate
psyche. His bust was removed from the company's headquarters in
The Hague, and the official history still remains unwritten. Shell,
like Esso, was determined not to repeat the mistake; thereafter it was
ruled by a committee of directors who were retired at sixty.

THE GERMAN HELL

The problem of industrial dictatorships was more serious within Germany, which provided its own warning to other countries. Since the
hectic industrialisation of the mid-nineteenth century the benign
business families like Thomas Mann's Buddenbrooks had rapidly
given way to dominating industrialists who imposed mechanical
systems based on military hierarchies. Werner Siemens, the co-
founder of the great electrical company, warned his brother Charles
in 1856 to toughen his attitudes: 'Always be determined and

unscrupulous. That in so large a concern is called for. Once begin to be considerate of private interests and you will fall into a morass of demands and intrigues.'

In 1915 the German sociologist Werner Sombart was concerned about the exemption of the modern businessman from personal judgements within a big company: 'You pass no judgement on his personal conduct, which is governed by other principles. Indeed, the firm may not have an individual head at all. It may be an impersonal limited company, the directors of which change from time to time. Their personal morality stands in no relationship to the business. The "name" of the business is all that matters . . .'

The powerful new dynasties, like the Siemens and the Krupps, saw themselves more confidently than the British, as entrusted with long-term responsibilities which were less vulnerable to the short-term pressures of the joint-stock company. The German predicament was passionately discussed by Walther Rathenau, the Jewish business-man-philosopher whose father Emil had founded the electrical giant AEG (Allgemeine Elektrizitaet Gesellschaft) which became a model of large-scale organisation, much admired by Lenin among others. Walther became his father's right-hand man and by 1909 he was on the board of eighty-four big companies: he described how 'three hundred men, all acquainted with each other, control the economic destiny of the Continent'. But Walther had a much more spiritual and questioning attitude than his father, and was intellectually repelled by the mechanistic world of the great companies: 'Never in the history of man has any system of ideas so uniformly dominated such a stupendous number of people as the mechanistic.' He was worried by the impersonal character of the joint-stock company:

> The de-individualisation of ownership simultaneously implies the objectification of the thing owned. The claims to ownership are subdivided in such a fashion, and are so mobile, that the enterprise assumes an independent life, as if it belonged to no one; it takes an objective existence . . . the enterprise becomes transformed . . . into an institution which resembles the state.

Rathenau, enjoying his own luxurious lifestyle, became increasingly alarmed by the impact of mass-industry on individual freedom.

'Mechanisation as a mass organisation requires human energy, not in units, but in streams,' he wrote in the middle of the First World War. 'All the slaves who built the pyramids of the Pharaohs would not suffice even as a corps of toolmakers for a modern lord.' But he never achieved the political influence he sought after the war: in 1921 he gave up the presidency of AEG to become Minister of Reconstruction and later Foreign Minister. But his moderation and internationalism infuriated the Right, and in June 1922 he was assassinated.

After the First World War German companies remained much influenced by army discipline. Many senior managers retained their militarism, and deliberately recruited old regimental colleagues. 'The immediate guardians of military spirit in industrial offices after 1918 were demobilised officers in the preferred position of personnel director,' wrote Hans Speier. 'Next to them was the staff of academic adjutants, who carried the *esprit de corps* of their fraternities into the firms. They also disseminated their spirit as alumni by recommending and preferring members of their fraternities for appointments to vacant positions.'

It was hardly surprising that expressionist writers and artists associated factories and science with the forces of darkness. In 1926 the film-maker Fritz Lang produced his spectacular silent film *Metropolis*, influenced by his visit to Manhattan two years before, which gave a fearful vision of industry and the future. The 'Lord of Metropolis' rules in luxury over a gigantic underground factory, full of cogs, jets, boilers and giant clocks, to which armies of workers march from their subterranean city. The foreman uncovers a workers' revolt led by the passionate Maria; a mad scientist makes a robot in Maria's image to spread confusion among the workers, who set about destroying their own homes and reducing the city to ruins. The masters dance in evening dress while the world below collapses. 'There can be no understanding between the hands and the brain,' says Maria, 'unless the heart acts as mediator.' The melodrama seemed silly to many contemporaries including H.G. Wells; but Hitler wanted Lang to work for him – before Lang fled to America. And the horrific images of *Metropolis* expressed fears about the brutality of the German industrial system which were to be justified.

Hitler bullied, cajoled and flattered German industrialists to

79

underpin his war machine. Most of the great names of German industry, including IG Farben, Thyssen and the Deutsche Bank were persuaded to finance his election campaign in 1933; a few held out, including Siemens, AEG and initially Krupp, the most powerful company of all. But soon they all rallied round and Krupp became Hitler's most valuable industrial ally: their factories at Essen became his arsenal, their salesmen his spies, and their executives interlocked with the SS. Krupp became hardly distinguishable from an army, with the same sense of purpose, the strict levels of command and the fear in the background. In return Krupp could extend their arms empire through occupied Europe and work their factories with slaves from the East; while in 1943 Hitler promulgated the notorious Lex Krupp which allowed the dynasty to rule the company in perpetuity. After Hitler's defeat the Nuremberg trials found Alfried Krupp guilty of war crimes and sent him to jail. Post-war German industrialists reacted heavily against Hitler's cult of leadership, the *Führerprinzip*, and embraced new systems of industrial democracy and supervisory boards introduced by the wartime Allies. The Krupp family entered into myth as a doomed dynasty of tyrants and perverts, caricatured in Visconti's 1969 film *The Damned*.

But the more worrying flaw in German wartime industry was not so much the dictatorship of the bosses as the acceptance of it by tens of thousands of ordinary managers who organised atrocities – slave labour, exterminations and constant betrayal of each other – as if they were quite normal: what Hannah Arendt called 'the banality of evil'. The abdication of personal responsibility gave a new horror to the old principle that the corporation had no soul. The danger went much wider than Nazi Germany: it was the living-out of the Kafkaesque nightmare, of anonymous bureaucracy taken over by evil forces, and the real lesson was that company man could not abdicate his own moral responsibility. As C.S. Lewis put it:

> I live in the Managerial Age, in a world of 'Admin'. The greatest evil is not now done in those sordid 'dens of crime' that Dickens loved to paint. It is not done even in concentration camps and labour camps. In those we see its final result. But it is conceived and ordered (moved, seconded, carried and minuted) in clean, carpeted, warmed and well-lighted offices, by quiet men with

white collars and cut fingernails and smooth-shaven cheeks who do not need to raise their voices. Hence, naturally enough, my symbol for Hell is something like the bureaucracy of a police state or the offices of a thoroughly nasty business concern.

CHAPTER SIX

The Airless Cage

Authors and actors and artists and such
Never know nothing, and never know much . . .
People Who Do Things exceed my endurance;
God, for a man who solicits insurance!

DOROTHY PARKER, 'Bohemia'

The centres of the growing corporate power were the office-buildings, with their own values and assumptions. They were becoming communities in their own right, detracting still further from the earlier centres: whether the extended family, the church or the farm. They were not commemorated by novelists with the same zeal that Trollope had brought to the church, or Dickens to the law. They were much more cut off from the lives of women, children and families, as they imposed their scientific structures on the human drama; and their conformity gave less scope for creativity. But they were becoming the core of twentieth-century middle-class life.

By the 1920s the standard American office was becoming still less like a study and more like a machine. The single small office with the name on the glass door and the loyal secretary inside remained a stereotype, immortalised by Raymond Chandler and Humphrey Bogart. But insurance offices, banks and accountants were creating their own self-contained blocks in the cities, cut off from traditional communities. The First World War had given a new impetus to mechanisation, with adding machines, tabulators, addressing machines as well as typewriters. By 1909 the new American profession of 'office managers' had formed their own National Association inspired by Frederick Taylor's theories.

The new business values were satirised in Sinclair Lewis's novel *Babbitt* in 1922, which soon established the word Babbitt in the language, defined in the Oxford Dictionary as 'a type of materialistic, self-complacent business man conforming to the standards of his set'. Babbitt is a forty-six-year-old real-estate dealer who is promoting the new word realtor ('sounds more like a reg'lar profession'). He lives in the mid-west town of Zenith among austere towers of steel and cement and limestone, 'sturdy as cliffs and delicate as silver rods. They are neither citadels nor churches, but frankly and beautifully office-buildings.'

When Babbitt looks out from his house he can see one of the tall new buildings: 'He beheld the tower as a temple spire of the religion of business, a faith passionate, exalted, surpassing common men.' His own Reeves building is a village in itself:

> The little unknown people who inhabited the Reeves building corridors – elevator-runners, starter, engineers, superintendent, and the doubtful-looking lame man who conducted the news and cigar stand – were in no way city-dwellers. They were rustics, living in a constricted valley, interested only in one another and in The Building. Their Main Street was the entrance hall, with its stone floor, severe marble ceiling, and the inner windows of the shops.

Babbitt's identity revolves round the office. His spectacles have 'huge, circular, frameless lenses of the very best glass; the ear-pieces were thin bars of gold. In them he was the modern businessman; one who gave orders to clerks and drove a car and played occasional golf and was scholarly in regard to Salesmanship.' His pockets contain a modern loose-leaf notebook, a fountain pen, a silver pencil, a watch-chain with a gold penknife, silver cigar-cutter, seven keys and a good watch. His office is his pirate-ship, while his car is 'poetry and tragedy, love and heroism'.

Babbitt is proud of the orthodoxy: 'It's here in Zenith, the home for manly men and womanly women and bright kids, that you find the largest proportion of these Regular Guys, and that's what sets it in a class by itself.' Then he suddenly rebels with a surge of liberalism, sympathy for strikers and an affair with a dangerous widow. He beholds 'his way of life as incredibly mechanical. Mechanical business – a brisk selling of badly-built houses. Mechanical religion – a dry, hard church, shut off from the real life of the streets, inhumanly respectable as a top-hat. Mechanical golf and dinner-parties and bridge and conversation.' He antagonises his business colleagues and refuses to join the Good Citizens' League. But when his wife has an operation he realises the charm of the Good Fellows, joins the League and wins back the affection of his friends.

The new mechanised office life was anathema to creative Americans, including the veterans who came back from the First World War. John Dos Passos, the son of a corporate lawyer, wrote novels which expressed the dissolving dream of individual enterprise. In *The Big Money* (1936) a wartime air ace, Charley Anderson, returns to America to sell light aircraft equipped with his own inventions. He speculates in the stock-market, intrigues in Washington and is lured to Detroit where he marries a banker's daughter and becomes a vice-president of an aircraft corporation. But at heart he remains a restless individualist, and goes off with an actress and dies after racing a train to a level-crossing.

In 1920 Henry Miller, a would-be writer of twenty-nine, became employment manager of the Western Union telegraph messenger service in New York. At first he took his job seriously, working from eight to six. He worried about turning down gallant war veterans and put a sign on his desk: 'Do Not Abandon Hope All Ye Who Enter Here'. He wrote a 'Proposed Solution to the Messenger Problem' which recommended that 'the Company must make the boy feel that he is more than a mere cog in the wheel'. And he defied the company's racist policies by hiring Jews, blacks and Indians, and even ex-convicts. But he became more rebellious as the company began enforcing a more military discipline: when they moved him into a new office in the Flatiron Building he felt he 'was in an airless cage now, surrounded by infernal contraptions that buzzed and rang and gleamed'. He despised his own power over the messengers, 'exasperated to think that human beings could beg so ignominiously for such a thing as a job'. His new girlfriend June Smith urged him to write full-time, and after five years he suddenly left Western Union without bothering to pick up his wages, whispering to himself, 'My own master absolute.' Later in *Tropic of Capricorn* (1939) he described the inhuman conditions at the 'Cosmodemonic Telegraph Company': 'I want to prevent as many men as possible from pretending that they have to do this or that because they must earn a living. *It is not true.*'

The world of business organisation, of accounting, engineering or factory management, was moving still further away from the experience of individualists and writers. John O'Hara, who had worked as an evaluating engineer, portrayed the hero of *Butterfield 8* in 1935 as an engineer who had been to Yale and the Harvard Business School before becoming branch manager of a manufacturing plant which his grandfather had founded. 'He would disclaim any real knowledge of engineering, frankly and sometimes a little sadly, but this had a disarming effect on real engineers: they would think here is a guy who is just like a kid the way he wants to be an engineer and he might have made a good one.'

Most novelists avoided describing company life, even if they knew something about it. Scott Fitzgerald's father had run a small furniture business which failed; in 1898 he became a salesman for the soap company Procter & Gamble in Buffalo and Syracuse, but he was fired when Scott was aged eleven. It had a traumatic effect on the boy: 'He came home that evening an old man, a completely broken man,' he wrote later. His father wanted Scott to go into business, but his mother had enough money to send him to Princeton, which provided the material for his first novel.

Advertising was the industry which most required creative talent, and which attracted needy writers or poets; but many of them despised it for its corruption of truth and debasement of standards. Harry Pulham, the hero of J.P. Marquand's best-known novel, *H.M. Pulham Esquire* (1940), comes from a conventional Boston-and-Harvard family. 'Grandpapa Pulham made hooks and eyes in Methuen for ladies' dresses, darling,' his mother tells him, 'and you must never be ashamed that he made such useful things.' After Harvard Harry amazes his father by joining an advertising agency in New York: 'Advertising!' says the family servant: 'What a thing now for a gentleman to do.' Harry enjoys the pretty girls and the comedy of campaigns for Coza soap, and falls in love with an ambitious and enterprising copywriter. But he marries a conventional wife and retreats back into Boston life as an investment counsellor, entertaining old Harvard friends. He dislikes modern novels about farmers in the Dust Bowl or travelling salesmen. Looking back on his dull married life he reflects: 'I have lived, on the whole, the only sort of life for which I was really fitted.'

A seedier advertising office emerges from the British detective writer Dorothy L. Sayers, who worked creatively at Benson's agency before publishing her *Murder Must Advertise* in 1933. Her hero Lord Peter Wimsey takes a job at Pym's agency in order to solve the murder of one its employees. He disguises himself as a vacuous copywriter, a 'Wooster in horn-rims', and enjoys the frolics of other Oxford men devising comic slogans and outrageous lies about adulterated food or bogus cures. 'I think this is an awfully immoral job of ours,' says Wimsey at one point, but a colleague explains: 'By forcing the damn-fool public to pay twice over – once to have its food emasculated and once to have the vitality put back again – we keep the wheels of commerce turning and give employment to thousands, including you and me.' Like other rich men Wimsey had never before paid attention to advertisements:

> He had never realised the enormous commercial importance of the comparatively poor. Not on the wealthy, who buy only what they want when they want it, was the vast superstructure of industry founded and built up, but on those who, aching for a luxury beyond their reach and for a leisure for ever denied them, could be bullied or wheedled into spending their few hardly won shillings on whatever might give them, if only for a moment, a leisured and luxurious illusion.

Wimsey enters into the game, devising a campaign for Whifflets cigarettes which pushes up sales by 500 per cent. But when he discovers that the agency is being used by a sinister dope-ring, he is not much surprised: 'As far as I can make out, all advertisers are dope-merchants.'

Office life was not abhorrent to all writers. Poets in particular, who could only compose for short periods, were often quite content with the secure routine, and like John Stuart Mill they could find their duties 'an actual rest from the other mental occupations'.

The American poet Wallace Stevens worked for thirty-nine years from 1916 for Hartford Accident in Connecticut as a lawyer specialising in surety claims, rising to be vice-president. His colleagues could not understand his poems – when one asked him for a clue he replied: 'Oh, forget it. You're much too literal-minded!' Stevens worried that being a poet would tarnish his reputation 'among the Babbitts of business', and asked his wife to keep it secret: 'There is something absurd about all this writing of verses ... you see, my habits are positively lady-like.' He had almost opposite personalities at work and at home. In the office he was a daunting figure, mastering his files and cases, happily immersed in paperwork. 'He finds it difficult sometimes to distinguish himself from the papers he handles,' he wrote of himself in 1938, 'and comes almost to believe that he and his papers constitute a single creature, consisting principally of hands and eyes: lots of hands and lots of eyes.' But at home his wife domi-nated him. His manservant John Rogers (who later became a pro-fessor of black history) recalled: 'Wallace was such a giant of a man, and she was just a little person. If she called or wanted something, his response was fantastic.'

T.S. Eliot was also quite content with office life. He was hired by Lloyds Bank in London in 1917 to work in the Colonial and Foreign Department, on the basis of being a linguist (though he only spoke French and Dante's Italian). It was routine work, tabulating and inter-preting the balance sheets of foreign banks, and Eliot sometimes complained about it; but in fact he was fascinated by 'the science of money', and seemed reassured by the rigour of business life, as if, wrote his biographer Peter Ackroyd, 'he needed the discipline, or protection, of a "proper" occupation before he could feel at ease with his own creative instincts'. When the critic I.A. Richards visited him in 1918 he found him in a basement 'stooping, very like a dark bird in a feeder, over a big table covered with all sorts and sizes of foreign correspondence'. Eliot began writing poetry again when he joined the bank, and published his first volume of poems, including 'The Love Song of J. Alfred Prufrock', four months later. His nine years at the bank were (says Ackroyd) 'arguably the most important years in his creative life. The man who wrote *The Waste Land* was a man behind his desk, a bank official indistinguishable from other such officials except perhaps for the absolute decorum of his dress, arriving at 9.30 and leaving at 5.30.'

But few British novelists had practical experience of offices or factories. Henry Green was a full-time businessman who inherited his father's engineering business in the Midlands, and one of his novels, *Living* (1929), is about factory life. His writer friends marvelled at his combining the two activities; but in fact he turned out to be a hopeless manager, and ended his years as an alcoholic.

OFFICE VERSUS HOME

Women saw offices with quite different eyes, for the work-places remained a male-dominated world, with their standardised, semi-military trappings of green filing-cabinets and dark wooden desks. Like army barracks they were the opposite of homely, and women could easily come to regard them as alien territory, which required either surrender or constant resistance. The tension between office and home became a recurring theme in everyday life, and the subject of novels and films like *Take a Letter Darling*, *Wife or Secretary* and *After Hours*.

But for unmarried women the office could become a substitute for a home, or the harsh alternative to a romantic marriage. The heroine of Booth Tarkington's American novel *Alice Adams* (1921) is the vivacious daughter of a downtrodden clerk. She looks with dread at Fincke's Business College, imagining the hideous obscurity within, 'as dreary and as permanent as death'. She visualises 'pretty girls turned into withered creatures as they worked at typing-machines; old maids "taking dictation" from men with double chins'. Alice is attracted to an eligible young man; but her father starts a glue factory which ends in disaster, her brother is disgraced and she is left with no prospects. She walks through the portal of Fincke's and up the dark steps, reminded of a French romance whose heroine is deserted by a faithless lover and takes the veil.

Lively young women began to look to the office to provide not only an income but an escape from their parents, which gave them growing social acceptance. 'But it's interesting mommer,' says Janey Williams in Dos Passos's novel *The Forty-Second Parallel* (1930), when her mother bewails the fact that she has to work as a stenographer. 'In your day it wasn't considered ladylike, it was thought to be demeaning. But it isn't now.'

And on both sides of the Atlantic the office was opening up opportunities for both matrimony and a career which were reflected by
romantic fiction. Arnold Bennett's sentimental novel *Lilian* (1922)
tells the story of a pretty 'typewriting girl' in an agency in Mayfair
surrounded by the office Underwoods 'ammunitioned with paper', the
day-book, night-book, ledger and bill-forms, 'where every machine
amounted to an individuality, and was loved or hated and shamelessly
intrigued for or against'. Lilian is spotted by the company's handsome
owner Felix Grig, who falls in love with her and takes her to the
Riviera, where she is determined to 'lose the typewriting girl in the
woman of the world'. He makes her pregnant, marries her, and then
dies. In the end she takes over the firm and the team of typists: 'She
was the most romantic figure that those girls had ever seen; she was
all picture-paper serials and cinema films rolled together and come
to life and reality.'

But the British still saw office life more bleakly than the Americans, more associated with failure. George Orwell's Mr Bowling in
Coming up for Air (1939) describes his lifetime in an insurance
office:

> Well, I got the job, and, as I said earlier, the job got me. I've
> been with the Flying Salamander close on eighteen years. I
> started off in the office, but now I'm what's known as an Inspec-
> tor, or, when there's reason to sound particularly impressive, a
> Representative . . .
> When I look back I realise that my active life, if I ever had
> one, ended when I was sixteen. Everything that really matters
> happened to me before that date . . . Well, they say that happy
> people have no histories, and neither do the blokes who work
> in insurance offices.

J.B. Priestley wrote his novel *Angel Pavement*, published in 1930,
about a dingy City office which sells veneer and inlays for furniture,
struggling to keep up with foreign competition. The young office-
workers appear to be 'shedding a part of themselves, and that the
most valuable part, leaving it behind, somewhere near the street door'.
Only the obsessive cashier Mr Smeeth feels that 'his days at the office
were filled with important and exciting events'. The secretary Lilian

Matfield appears to nurse 'some huge, some overwhelming grievance against life', and despises her sloppy and feeble boss Mr Dersingham. The office is suddenly transformed by the arrival of James Golspie, an extrovert entrepreneur from the Baltic, who finds cheaper sources for veneers and saves the business from collapse. He brings a new excitement and flirts with Miss Matfield who is thrilled by his brigandish style; but after a few months he despairs of the British and sails off to South America: 'They're half dead, most of 'em – half dead. No dash. No guts. I want a place where everybody's alive.'

Yet the life of the secretary was not necessarily as demeaning as men liked to depict it. The novelist and poet Stevie Smith spent thirty years as a secretary, most of them for Sir Neville Pearson, the chairman of a publishing house for whom she did routine tasks including shopping for his wife. In 1935 she wrote her first novel, typing it partly in the office on the yellow paper used for carbon copies: she called it *Novel on Yellow Paper*. It is about a secretary called Pompey Casmilus who lives in the suburbs, and works contentedly for her boss Sir Phoebus. Both are quietly reassured by the dull routine of office life: 'The great link between us two is the happy way we both get quickly bored.' 'I love Sir Phoebus, at this moment, I love him with a deep and grateful love. He is the only man with whom I have consistently (I think, perhaps he does not) behaved myself, as a willing donkey, as a happy equable creature, blandly and happily performing its duties.'

But the intimate small office was giving way to more mechanical organisations which discouraged emotional entanglements, and fought shy of creativity. The dread of writers, from Wodehouse to Henry Miller, of being 'cogs in the wheels', was becoming more widely justified. And while factories were looking more like offices, offices were becoming more like factories. As the sociologist C. Wright Mills described them in 1953:

As skyscrapers replace rows of small shops, so offices replace free markets. Each office within the skyscraper is a segment of the enormous file, a part of the symbol factory that produces the billion slips of paper that gear modern society into its daily shape. From the executive's suite to the factory yard, the paper webwork is spun; a thousand rules you never made and don't know about are applied to you by a thousand people you have not met and never will.

CHAPTER SEVEN

Organisation People

> If America ever destroyed its genius it would be by
> intensifying the social virtues at the expense of
> others, by making the individual come to regard him-
> self as a hostage to prevailing opinion, by creating,
> in sum, a tyranny of the majority.
>
> ALEXIS DE TOCQUEVILLE, *Democracy in America*

The Second World War reinforced the big corporation as a permanent institution, accepted as a new kind of economic and social entity.
'Less than ten years ago it still seemed to be a vital issue of American
politics whether to have Big Business or not,' wrote Peter Drucker
in 1946. 'Today the very question is meaningless if not frivolous.'
He saw the large mass-production plant as the social reality, 'our
representative institution, which has to carry the burden of our
dreams'. The war had given both American and British businessmen
much more confidence and legitimacy after their unpopularity during
the Depression. They moved in and out of government service, planning, reorganising and advising the armed forces on management, as
they had in the previous war, but on a much larger scale. They built
up whole new cities, dedicated to the war effort, and helped to bring
back full employment for the first time since the Great Crash, with
a sense of common purpose and achievement. In America they
achieved an industrial 'miracle' – the precursor of all the post-war
miracles – with undreamt-of levels of production. But they had not
learnt the full lesson. The miracle was the result of mobilising people,
rather than resources, and of motivating them with a sense of involvement. After the war the companies soon lost much of the spirit of
co-operation and flexibility. The managers fell back into mechanical
attitudes, separating themselves from the workers and imposing their
rules without consultation.

In theory there was a greater sense of democracy. The war against Hitler had caused a revulsion against any acceptance of dictatorship or arbitrary rule, in industry as much as in politics, and had encouraged emphasis on participation and committees. And after Hitler companies as well as governments felt themselves challenged by the communist and socialist alternatives to prove themselves to be democratic institutions which looked after their people. But the war had also brought the corporations closer to military systems and planning with their own systems of command and control. And as they became involved in the Cold War against the communist bloc, their structures showed more resemblance to the bureaucracies and apparatchiks with which they were competing.

American companies had been influenced not only by the huge military orders but by the disciplines that went with them, including long-term planning and logistics; and after the war many companies looked to generals and admirals to become directors or chairmen. 'The management cadre itself is being rationalised into military-like shape,' wrote the radical critic C. Wright Mills in 1953: 'In fact some of the very best ideas for business management have come from men of high military experience – the "bureaucrats" about whom businessmen complained so during the war.' Industrial managers – including many ex-officers – copied military systems for appraising or promoting their staff, and adopted the psychological tests which the army had developed to sort out and classify hordes of untested and variegated recruits. Company men became closer to military men, who could remain valuable contacts to further their business. The immediate demobilisation brought a collapse of orders, as it had twenty-seven years before, which confronted the huge arms and aviation industries with potential disaster. But the communist menace and the Korean war were to provide a new and continuing surge of orders, bringing unprecedented security to the defence industries. The prime contractors for the federal government during wartime remained the same companies during the Cold War. The 'military-industrial complex', as President Eisenhower (or his speech-writer) first called it in 1961, became a lasting alliance as the Pentagon worked closely with a handful of companies including 'the Generals' – General Motors, General Electric and General Dynamics. The arms companies preached individual free enterprise, but they all knew

93

they depended on the state for their survival. Lockheed man in Burbank competed with McDonnell man in St Louis, but the rules and the prizes were set in Washington.

And the concentration of power continued as the biggest companies took over a still larger share of the American economy in the fifties and sixties. In 1947 two hundred industrial companies held 47 per cent of the total corporate manufacturing assets; by 1963 they held 56 per cent; by 1968 they held 61 per cent. They were accustomed to proclaiming their power by their skyscrapers in their company cities: the Gulf skyscraper in Pittsburgh, the Texaco tower in Houston, the Reynolds building in Winston-Salem. Now their contest for glory was focusing on Manhattan, where they competed in splendour along Park Avenue or Sixth Avenue like the Venetian *palazzi* along the Grand Canal. But the most elegant towers were not usually the result of corporate committees, but of determined individuals: like the Seagram building commissioned by the chairman's wife, or the Lever building commissioned by the maverick boss Charles Luckman – who was soon afterwards fired. Most of the post-war skyscrapers, like the Exxon or Citibank towers, appeared as safely anonymous as the company men who controlled them.

MANAGERIAL REVOLUTION

The technical owners of big companies, the shareholders, were now mostly the 'institutions', the pension funds and insurance companies, who were usually unwilling to intervene. 'A policy of nonaction by the institutions,' wrote Adolf Berle, the lawyer-politician who first analysed corporate ownership, 'means that the directors and managements of the corporations whose stock they hold become increasingly self-appointed and unchallengeable; while it continues, it freezes absolute power in the corporate managements.'

In 1940 James Burnham, a lapsed Trotskyist, had spelt out the political and social implications of the changing ownership in his book *The Managerial Revolution*, the title of which became a catch-phrase. He described the transition 'from the type of society which we have called capitalist or bourgeois to a type of society which we have called "managerial"'; and analysed how the new managers were taking over as the ruling class in both capitalist and communist countries. He argued that 'The capitalists, the ruling class of modern society, are losing control, that the social structure which placed them in the position of ruling class is being transformed, not tomorrow, but now, as we watch. In the new structure, when its foundations are completed, there will be no capitalists.'

Capitalists appeared to be disappearing out of sight while the very word went out of fashion. The managerial image of the corporation was reflected at annual general meetings which were increasingly publicised and prearranged with elaborate public relations. The chairman would proclaim unanimous decisions, and announce new directors chosen by the existing officers. Increasingly a few dissident individual shareholders would try to embarrass or frustrate the corporate plans; but they could not sway the big shareholders, the pension funds and insurance companies who usually preferred the status quo. The lack of accountability was denounced by a former vice-president of General Electric, T.K. Quinn, who wrote a book, *Giant Business*, in 1953: 'We had then, in effect, a huge economic state governed by non-elected, self-perpetuating officers and directors – the direct opposite of the democratic method.'

The managers fortified their kingdom to perpetuate themselves and reinforce their promotion and security. 'Management development' became the new fashion, and by 1955 half the big American companies had special programmes to develop managers, ostensibly to ensure the continuity of the company, but primarily to perpetuate the managerial class.

Not surprisingly the new generation of bosses were less enterprising than their predecessors. In 1950 Mabel Newcomer analysed the backgrounds of chief executives of companies with assets of more than $75 million, and found that the typical boss was a Republican Episcopalian aged sixty-one, expecting to retire at seventy. He owned less than 0.1 per cent of his company's stock, and he had never practised independently or had a business of his own, as his father was more likely to have done. Faster-growing companies were more varied: their typical chief had wider experience, was less likely to be a lawyer or engineer, and reached the top five years younger. Newcomer was not worried by the signs of bureaucratisation among established companies: 'Any loss of imagination and daring appears to be offset by a more scientific approach to the problem of production and by more planning and research.'

But the disappearance of the owners left doubts about where responsibility really lay. The managers, who were responsible to each other, were naturally reluctant to take risks which might damage their promotion and prospects. The literary scholar Edmund Wilson had defined capitalist society as 'a vast system of passing the buck'; and the sociologist C. Wright Mills developed the charge: 'All managers are "middle-managers" who are not organised in such a manner as to allow them to assume collective responsibility.' The identity of the corporation he found much more baffling: 'the capitalist spirit has been bureaucratised and the enterprise fetishised ... The name of the firm is all that matters and this name does not rest upon the personal quality of its head; it rests upon the business routine and the careful administration of appropriate publicity.'

Some businessmen as well as their critics were worrying about the conformity of the new company men. 'What became of the independent spirit?' asked the educationalist Clark Kerr in *Fortune* magazine in July 1953; he urged individuals to develop their own self-protection to avoid 'total involvement in any organisation'. His concern was part of a wider fear that Americans were losing their 'inner-directed' individual sense of purpose, and becoming preoccupied with pleasing each other, or being 'other-directed'. The phrases were invented by the lawyer-sociologist David Riesman in his book *The Lonely Crowd*, first published in 1950. He described how businessmen since the era of Henry Ford had basically changed: from grappling with the impersonal challenges of the frontier, with 'the hardness of material', to concentrating on their relations with colleagues. The change, he warned, had weakened the companies' interest in their products. Successful masters of their trades, whether machine-tool men, doctors or journalists, could only earn more money if they became desk administrators cut off from their craft, and played down their old skill. 'If one is successful in one's craft, one is forced to leave it.'

Post-war idealism had stirred up resentments against conformity, as it had a quarter of a century earlier. These were summed up in Sloan Wilson's popular novel *The Man in the Gray Flannel Suit* – still more popular after Gregory Peck played the hero in the film (1956).

The book told the story of Tom Rath, a war veteran filled with guilt about killing people and leaving his illegitimate child in Italy. He tries to find a job in New York which will maintain his integrity and the respect of his idealistic wife. Instead he is hired to write speeches he doesn't believe in for a single-minded broadcasting tycoon; but he realises 'I want to eat, and so, like a half million other guys in gray flannel suits, I'll always pretend to agree, until I get big enough to be honest without being hurt.' His entrepreneurial boss respects Tom's integrity and befriends him, with a warmth and optimistic energy. Tom tells his wife:

> I really don't know what I was looking for when I got back from the war, but it seemed as though all I could see was a lot of bright young men in gray flannel suits rushing around New York in a frantic parade to nowhere. They seemed to me to be pursuing neither ideals nor happiness – they were pursuing a routine. For a long while I thought I was on the sidelines watching that parade, and it was quite a shock to glance down and see that I too was wearing a gray flannel suit.

In 1956 a young editor of *Fortune*, William H. Whyte, produced his book *Organisation Man*, which provided sociological evidence for the growing conformity of American company men. Whyte was not worried by the 'surface uniformities' like grey flannel suits, but by a deeper-seated change, away from the traditional American Protestant ethic, towards a new 'social ethic' which subjugated the individual to the group – a change which seemed to hark back to an earlier sense of belonging, as in the Middle Ages. He traced this social conformity through schools, universities and office hierarchies, all the way out to suburbia. He conducted detailed interviews in the company suburb of Park Forest, Illinois, where he found families conditioned to become part of larger groups, dedicated to 'inconspicuous consumption' and to producing 'organisation children'. Whyte warned that the social ethic was dangerously static and self-destructive, an obstacle to American innovation and scientific discovery. He offered no easy solution – 'The conflict between individual and society has always involved dilemma' – but he called for the organisation man to fight the organisation.

The Organisation Man in his Grey Flannel Suit soon entered business mythology, obliging many executives to profess that they were in fact individuals. In 1959 the chairman of duPont, Crawford Greenewalt – a wide-ranging scholar who was writing a definitive study of the humming-bird – delivered lectures contradicting the belief that big companies were conformist: he did not himself own a single grey flannel suit. He complained that the American business-man had been 'neglected by the historian, scorned by the literateur, and snubbed by the social critic'. He admitted that the colourful pioneers like Rockefeller or J. Pierpoint Morgan had been succeeded by 'somewhat austere and anonymous institutions', and that individual effort had gradually merged into group effort. He was also concerned about some signs of dehumanisation: he found it 'offensive to human dignity to rely upon psychological-testing bureaucrats in forming our personal judgements'. But he was not worried about the loss of individuality: 'The more effective an executive, the more his own identity and personality blend into the background of his organ-isation.' And he rather confirmed Whyte's contention that companies were harking back to the one-ness of the Middle Ages. 'Teams of labourers built the pyramids and teams of craftsmen the medieval cathedrals. Now, for the first time, however, management itself has become a team effort with group direction, group initiative, and group responsibility.'

The critique of company man was developed further by the jour-nalist Vance Packard, who first made his name with *The Hidden Persuaders* (1957), which first publicised subliminal advertising. In *The Status Seekers* in 1959 he described how big corporations had created a new national class structure by constructing layers of man-agement and status which were almost as rigid as ranks in the army or the civil service: they had devised intricate varieties of status through the size of offices, desks or cars, while they imposed their corporate hierarchies on local communities more effectively as Ameri-can families were becoming more mobile. The United States, Packard complained, was 'still desperately trying to adjust to the growth of vast bureaucratic institutions'. He returned to the attack four years later in *The Pyramid Climbers* which criticised companies' inter-ference with employees. 'Private bureaucracies have recently become more intrusive in their personal demands on the individual at the managerial level,' he reported, 'and more manipulative toward that individual.'

ESSO'S INSULATION

Most big American corporations were now run by professional managers who were increasingly constrained by committees and by worries about their public image. The oil companies were much less bold than at the time of their buccaneering origins, and the biggest, Standard Oil of New Jersey, or Esso, was specially nervous after Walter Teagle was accused of treason in 1942 – creating a turmoil which (said the company history) had 'all but shattered' the morale of the board. Their new chairman, Frank Abrams, an ex-refinery manager, was worried about the company's insulation from society. 'Millions of people in this country and elsewhere are in a very real sense looking over our shoulders as we discuss and deliberate,' he told his colleagues in 1946. Three years later he wondered whether businessmen understood that 'the social order of things in this country has undergone a fundamental change', or whether 'we are blinded by the way we live'. He and his colleagues, he explained, 'come from very modest beginnings . . . but we haven't maintained our ties with the folks from whom we came'.

Esso's chief executive Eugene Holman – who remained in that position for sixteen years until 1960 – was a geologist who made long-term plans for staff as well as oil, and designed a programme for 'developing reserves of key personnel comparable to the reserves of physical assets' (this was part of the trend towards calling people 'human resources'). But the Esso managers, like other oilmen, continued to lack broad experience outside the refineries. After the war Esso moved profitably into the Middle East, joining the consortia of companies in Saudi Arabia and Iran, but with little political understanding; and a later chairman, Monroe Rathbone, was responsible in 1960 for the rash decision to reduce the oil price which precipitated the formation of OPEC.

GENERAL MOTORS' COMMITTEES

General Motors was more than ever the archetypal giant corporation, which had proved its management skills in the war, when it employed half a million people. Alfred Sloan, the architect of its decentralised structure, had moved up in 1937 from chief executive to chairman, which he remained for the next twenty years, retiring at the age of eighty. In 1941 Charles Wilson had taken over as president until in 1953 President Eisenhower made him secretary of defence, which enabled him to push through new American highways, ostensibly for defence, which provided an opportunity for the auto industry. His twin careers symbolised the closeness between GM and government, summed up in his much-misquoted phrase: 'For years [he actually said] I thought what was good for our country was good for General Motors, and vice-versa.'

But GM had failed to humanise its model of management. Its wartime achievements had been based on recruiting inexperienced workers, and on the shortage of managers which allowed those workers to take responsibility. When Peter Drucker was asked to write his own report on GM he strongly advised that it developed the ideas of responsible workers and self-governing plants. Charles Wilson welcomed the prospect and began a dialogue with workers by asking them to write reports on 'My Job and Why I Like It'. But the unions opposed this, threatening a strike, while Sloan as chairman rejected any idea of responsible workers. Both sides preferred the traditional division: 'Managers manage and workers work'. Drucker's report in 1946, in the form of his book *Concept of the Corporation*, argued that labour should be regarded as a resource, not a cost, and that big corporations had a special responsibility to society. He prophetically warned of the limitations of isolated executives and the parochialism of the 'military mind'.

The book infuriated GM's managers including Sloan, who then decided to write his own book (see Chapter 5). But Drucker's ideas were quickly taken up by other corporations including Ford and General Electric, and his book was quickly translated in Japan, where it had a major influence on corporations including Toyota.

Sloan and Wilson were succeeded by unimaginative chairmen – James Roche, Richard Gerstenberg, Thomas Murphy – who seemed almost indistinguishable to the outsider's eye: they had all come from small mid-west towns, risen up through the GM committees, and held conventional Republican views. They perpetuated Sloan's structure, without questioning its human needs. Yet General Motors was still seen as a model of how to run big business, through collective decisions and committees. As one executive described it:

> The committees are the company, and one of the ways you rise in the company is by being a committee man – preferably secretary of one of the committees. The people who succeed at GM generally come into the company very early, at low-level jobs. They don't have big ideas about rising to the top. They stick with the company, and eventually a few make it. To the outsider they're not very impressive. They're not very interesting as people. They tend to talk in platitudes. All they know is the automobile industry.

IBM'S TAME DUCKS

Already by the sixties IBM was overtaking GM as a model for large-scale organisation and motivation, with its gleaming new plants at Endicott, its research laboratories and its armies of ambitious salesmen. Thomas Watson had taken full advantage of the explosion of computer technology and the demand for information, and he had the imagination to make close links with universities, which gave IBM its breakthroughs into computers. The IBM buildings adopted the style of campuses rather than factories: the new white headquarters at Armonk evoked a Zen-like calm with a Japanese garden in the middle, and an egalitarian atmosphere. When I was taken to lunch at the canteen I queued up behind the chairman. Watson insisted that IBM's most important belief was its 'respect for the individual', and he praised its 'wild ducks'. He took the metaphor from a Kierkegaard story which described how tamed ducks get fat and lazy and cannot rejoin the wild flock. 'You can make wild ducks tame,' said

Watson, 'but you can never make tame ducks wild again. And in IBM we try not to tame them.'

But IBM was full of tame ducks. It was still imposing a strict uniformity on its company men in their white shirts and dark suits which contradicted its academic aspirations and its slogan 'THINK'. The novelist Peter de Vries told a story about a company executive who takes the instruction literally, giving him so many philosophical doubts that he is fired. 'If I'm ever confronted with a sign telling me to think, I'll damn well think twice before I do.'

After Watson died in 1956 he was succeeded by his son Thomas Watson Junior, a more humane and sensitive boss who was sceptical of the personality cult. He modified the company's extreme centralisation, adopting the line-and-staff system of General Motors and others, and appointed a management team of about twenty men. But the rapid development of technology still called for bold central decisions, including the massive 360 computer which was reckoned to have cost more to develop than the atom bomb. And IBM was ruthlessly wielding its monopoly power to try to destroy smaller and more agile new rivals, like Control Data who were developing faster supercomputers – which produced new evidence for an anti-trust suit. When Watson retired after a heart attack in 1970 IBM still appeared unassailable, with a unique record of growth and profits. But it was already beginning to miss out on the wave of young creativity in computers and software.

THE TECHNOSTRUCTURE

In the 1950s and sixties American corporations appeared to many economists as permanent, autonomous powers at the heart of society: what Kenneth Galbraith called *The New Industrial State* in his book in 1966. Galbraith described how committees of managers, engineers and specialists organised 'the technostructure', and how the vast producing organisation 'reaches forward to control the markets it is presumed to serve and, beyond, to bend the customer to its needs'. The corporations, he explained, bamboozled consumers to buy their products through their advertising, while persuading academia through their grants to turn out tame organisation men. The whole structure depended on maintaining profits, but the industrial system had adapted to the technostructure to ensure that big corporations did not lose money. In 1964 the largest hundred companies in America had all made profits; even in the mild recession of 1957 none had made a loss. 'The power remains securely with the technostructure as long as earnings are large enough to make accustomed payments to the stockholders and provide a supply of savings for reinvestment.'

Galbraith, like other commentators, saw the big companies with all their faults as social as well as economic necessities, which could maintain their profits and finance their future research and development by controlling prices within their oligopolies. The consumers might complain about being bamboozled and lacking real choice, but they had no alternative providers. The big corporations appeared to need their layers of management and their technostructure to achieve their mastery. Few critics noticed or worried that large numbers of company men were not productively employed. It was not until the surge of international competition in the seventies that the companies realised they were making the wrong products with the wrong people.

Chairmen on their side were becoming less interested in maximising their profits, and were talking – with varying degrees of candour – about their responsibilities and duties to society, whether to education, the community, or political goals. In return they expected society to accommodate itself to their own purposes. They saw their corporations as becoming more closely integrated into society. Some past critics of corporate greed welcomed this change of heart; others saw it as a worrying extension of their control. As Adolf Berle put it: 'Our ancestors feared that corporations had no conscience. We are treated to the colder, more modern fear that, perhaps, they do.'

It was left to comedies and satires to point out that corporations were very far from the rational, profit-minded organisations that economists depicted; and that, like armies, they developed their own corruptions and rackets when they were not challenged by serious rivals.

The most memorable picture of office life was Billy Wilder's film *The Apartment* (1960), in which Jack Lemmon plays the part of a bewildered young executive of an insurance company in New York: 'There may be a lot of employees here, but we're one big happy family.' The staff work in a vast open-plan with rows of desks, exchanging corporate jargon ('Premium-wise and billing-wise we are 18 per cent of last year October-wise'); but the senior executives work in glass-panelled rooms protected by their secretaries, busy with sexual intrigue. The hero lends the key to his apartment to his superiors for their affairs, after which he is promoted to assistant director, with privileges including lunch in the executive dining room, a panelled office and the precious key to the executive washroom. But he finally rejects the corporate corruption. 'I've decided to become a *mensch* – you know what that means? – a human being,' he tells his elevator girl Miss Kubelik (Shirley Maclaine), who drunkenly mutters: 'That's the way it crumbles, cookie-wise.'

The popular guides to business achievement were satirised in the musical *How to Succeed in Business Without Really Trying* – inspired by a book by Shepherd Mead, and turned into a film in 1967. The hero begins as a window-cleaner peering into an office building until he discovers a guide to success, which advises him how to choose his company: 'Make sure it's large enough so that no one knows what anyone else is doing.' He penetrates the corporation, full of conspiring executives in straw hats detached from any serious production: 'What the hell's a factory?' Flirtatious secretaries begin their day with a well-organised manicure, hairdressing and make-up followed by a coffee-break. Executives sing the refrain: 'I play it the company way. Wherever the company puts me, there I stay.' The hero follows the guide's precepts: never take a risk, always put the blame on somebody else, steal other people's ideas. He begins in the mailroom but is rapidly promoted by flattering the boss and his bird-brained girl-friend. He pretends to come from the boss's own university Old Ivy, but has to admit that he was only the window-cleaner; whereupon the chairman, about to retire, reveals that he too began as a window-cleaner, and triumphantly appoints him as his successor.

As big companies became more bureaucratised and anonymous, they appeared still more as the enemies of creativity and individuality. Joseph Heller, who had worked in advertising before writing *Catch-22*, described in his 1974 novel *Something Happened* life in an automobile casualty insurance company, supposedly run by twelve old men: but 'Nobody is sure anymore who really runs the company,' says the hero. The company is kept going by fear: 'Just about everybody in the company is afraid of somebody else in the company.'

The novelist Kurt Vonnegut, who once worked for General Electric, later described the company's annual summer meeting as an 'orgy of morale building – through team athletics, group sings, bonfires and skyrockets, bawdy entertainment, free whiskey and cigars'. And he wrote a short story about a young journalist who goes to work in a huge industrial works. He is resentfully inducted into the system of ratings – for appearance, loyalty or promptness – and told about the salary curve and the quarter-century club for company veterans. Then a wild deer is discovered in the labs, and surrounded by company police. The hero unwires the fence to let it escape into the woods, and then follows himself.

It was the benevolence of corporations which was most frequently criticised, rather than the ruthlessness which had made them hated before the war. Alan Harrington's book *Life in the Crystal Palace* (1959), which took its title from Dostoevsky's *Notes from Underground*, described his three years with a big corporation in suburbia, caught up in a benign labyrinth from which the company men could never escape. 'We are not worried about our jobs, about the future,' says one of them, 'about much of anything.' Despite all the company's talk about free enterprise, Harrington found it more like a state bureaucracy from which no one could be fired. 'Every so often I hear my seniors at the corporation inveigh against socialism, and it seems strange. I think that our company resembles nothing so much as a private socialist system.' When his account was published many of his ex-colleagues agreed with it. But it was not until much later that critics became aware of the more fundamental resemblance between corporations and socialist bureaucracies: that they both depended on commands from the top which prevented initiatives and ideas from the bottom.

CHAPTER EIGHT

Families versus Bureaucrats

In Europe after the Second World War, British companies appeared to have a long lead over their rivals on the devastated Continent. But the victors' triumph was won at the expense of commercial realism. They remained trapped in their military glory and industrial systems, while the vanquished were compelled to start from scratch, and think again. And the Continental business families re-emerged with their control and motivation revived by the challenges of war, reasserting their continuity and will to survive with more dedication than the British dynasties.

British company men were seen as secondary to the wartime achievement, while military leaders were brought into industry despite their lack of experience. General Sir Brian Robertson took over British Railways, Air Marshal Sholto Douglas commanded British European Airways, General Weeks commanded Vickers, General Sir Ian Jacob chaired the BBC, Lord Portal chaired British Match. Other big companies were chaired by imperial grandees with little industrial experience, like Lord Knollys at Vickers or Sir John Hanbury-Williams at Courtaulds.

Many big companies were still chaired or controlled by descendants of the founding families: including Wedgwood, Pilkington, Cadburys, Bowater and the Quaker families of Barclays Bank. A few – like the Sainsburys, the Swires, the Sieffs of Marks & Spencer or the Keswicks of Jardine Matheson – retained the ancestral energy. But many family companies suffered from an amateurism at the top which discouraged professional managers.

British company men, confronting a Labour government in 1945, were embarrassed to talk about profits and saw themselves as an industrial civil service; some were almost indistinguishable from the staff of nationalised industries. 'In a culture of being rather than doing,' wrote the management consultant Alastair Mant, 'the industrial managers have remained obsessed with the status rather than the *actions* of the professional classes.' The layers of managers, the annual increments, the fine distinctions between office carpeting and company cars, were all much influenced by the military and Whitehall. 'The basic fact is the large corporation,' wrote the Labour intellectual Anthony Crosland in 1956, 'facing fundamentally similar problems, and acting in fundamentally the same way, whether publicly or privately owned.' Crosland later poured contempt on 'the other-directed organisation men of Shell and ICI . . . Jelly-fish where their predecessors were masterful, they are slaves to their public relations departments, constantly nervous lest some action may provoke a parliamentary question, frowns in the Board of Trade, trouble with the unions, or criticism in the press.'

But the industrial headquarters appeared confident enough, determined to assert their status and grandeur in an insecure world. The competition for splendour was comically evident in the electrical companies, which reached a crisis in the sixties. Lord Chandos, an aristocratic wartime minister, was seen as the prince of business: he ruled Associated Electrical Industries from his palatial suite overlooking Buckingham Palace, with a fine dining room and a legendary cellar, while his own country mansion Trafalgar House was subsidised by the company. Lord Nelson (known as 'Half-Nelson'), the hereditary chairman of the rival English Electric, commissioned an extravagant pile on the site of the Gaiety Theatre in Aldwych, furnished like a miniature Versailles. By 1968 both companies had been swallowed up by General Electric, which was to be run by Arnold Weinstock for the next quarter-century from a gloomy little office-block in Mayfair. The fate of the business palaces corroborates Professor Parkinson's law about headquarters: 'A perfection of planned layout is achieved only by institutions on the point of collapse.' This was a variant of the proverb in Thomas Mann's *Buddenbrooks*: 'When the house is finished, death comes.'

Gradually British companies began to accept transatlantic management ideas, encouraged by the Anglo-American Council on Productivity set up in 1948 which sent teams of managers and union leaders to America, and by American companies including Esso, General Motors and IBM which were expanding in Britain. Faced with a shortage of labour and a long boom, British managers looked more seriously at Taylorism and time-and-motion study, which they had long resisted. The stopwatch remained a bogey for union leaders, brilliantly caricatured in the film *I'm All Right Jack*, directed by John Boulting in 1959, in which a factory is brought to a halt by the arrival of a naïve young graduate and a man with a stopwatch. Nigel Balchin's 1953 novel *Sundry Creditors* – a rare fictional insight into industry – describes a friendly but inefficient family factory, whose old chairman talks about workers as human beings, in the process of being taken over by a tough corporation whose managers are amazed by its senti- mental loyalties: 'To marry sheet metal, and form an emotional alli- ance with a press shop!' They insist on applying time-studies to the workers in order to rationalise the rates, to the horror of the factory manager: 'But you couldn't do that here. Not have somebody standing over the men clicking a watch.'

The eager young company men with their conformity and brand-names were a favourite butt for intellectual writers like John Betjeman, himself the descendant of a Victorian family firm which invented a tea-trolley:

> I am a young executive. No cuffs than mine are cleaner;
> I have a Slimline brief-case and I use the firm's Cortina.

The provincial lives of company men were gloomily portrayed in the novels of Roy Fuller, who later became Professor of Poetry at Oxford. He had spent much of his life as a solicitor in the Woolwich Building Society, surprised later that he had 'faced the plod' when his heart was not in it. In Fuller's novel *A Father's Comedy* (1961) the hero works in a large public authority, chaired by an ex-union leader, where he aspires to become company secretary, with a knighthood and social acclaim. In *Image of a Society* (1956), Fuller describes the enclosed world of a North Country building society whose executives intrigue over promotion and garage-space, dreading retirement. The solicitor hero Philip Witt, with literary ambitions, worries about keep- ing his real self in an unconnected compartment: was it now 'a hope- lessly debased alloy'? He has a chance to escape from the treadmill through an affair with his boss's passionate wife, but he cannot escape his own self-constraints. His plodding rival wins out through patient devotion which makes the hero reflect: 'Here was an organisation that helped to preserve the community, brought stability and thrift into the lives of many to whom those qualities might otherwise have remained alien, and for itself made only such profit as was consonant with preserving its existence indefinitely.'

SHELL AND ICI

Provincial industries and old family firms were a world away from the big corporations we have observed, which were having to compete globally – and were becoming models for others. Shell and Unilever (which reappears in Chapter 10) were both compelled as Anglo-Dutch companies to be international at the top; and they had developed balancing systems of professional management.

Shell were determined to avoid autocrats after the trauma of Deterding's dictatorship. After the war they were run by a committee of Seven Men under a chairman who had to achieve a consensus; and they sidelined their most forceful director, Felix Guépin, who was in Deterding's mould. In 1957 they chose as chairman John Loudon who was a merchant prince more than a buccaneer: he was the son of a former chairman, from a grand Dutch family, but like most Dutch he retained a strong commercial realism. He was also a natural diplomat who believed in decentralisation, and reorganised Shell with the help of McKinseys into an elaborate pyramid which left the Seven Men free for the major decisions. Shell set a pattern for sensitive diplomacy – which it needed, for much of its oil came from the developing world, and it had been taken by surprise when the Mexican government nationalised its valuable oilfields in 1938. Shell responded with a global programme of 'regionalisation', promoting Asian or African managers to conciliate nationalist movements, and becoming more subtle in dealing with post-war anti-colonialism than its rivals, BP and Exxon. But it created a still more complex bureaucracy, with a network of co-ordinators co-ordinating other co-ordinators to hold together their five hundred separate Shells across the world, controlled from the conspicuous new Shell Centre in London which appropriately looked down on the Houses of Parliament.

The 'Shellocrats' were the most loyal and confident of all company men, carefully selected from universities, rigorously trained, highly-paid – and expected to go to the ends of the earth, with their wives. Some believed they had been deliberately uprooted to ensure that they had only one loyalty, and certainly Shell men gave a remarkable commitment. 'I wish they wouldn't talk about oil as if it was a faith,' one complained to me: 'Anyone would think it was a church.'

ICI was almost equally concerned with loyalty and professional management, but it lacked the international challenge of Shell. It, too, was determined to avoid autocrats. When the imperious Lord McGowan retired in 1950, after twenty years as chairman, he was followed by other self-made Scots, who were much more committee-minded; but they were slow to catch up with critical new trends, like oil competing with coal, and the leadership alternated uneasily between scientists and businessmen. Lord Fleck, who became chairman in 1953, was a distinguished scientist with the style of a boffin rather than a businessman, who took a patient attitude to ICI's research (my father ran its pure research centre at the time). In 1960 the board chose a chairman almost opposite in character, the ex-tax inspector Sir Paul Chambers, who reacted more swiftly to European competition and expanded petrochemicals and fibres. But he antagonised the scientists and eventually overreached himself with a hostile bid for the rival giant Courtaulds, which only succeeded in arousing its fierce opposition.

ICI was still seen as a model for industrial management, intelligent and benign: some of its directors went on to revamp other industries, as Lord Beeching reorganised British Rail. ICI recruited 5 per cent of Britain's annual output of graduates, including the cream of the chemists. But with its heavy protection it wasted much of its talent, and was far less dynamic than the German companies which had first precipitated its own merger in 1926. The German combine IG Farben was broken up after the war into three of its original components – Bayer, BASF and Hoechst – which rapidly benefited from competition and the release of new energies (like Standard Oil four decades earlier), and twenty years later each was bigger than ICI. The board of ICI had considered splitting the company in 1950, but eventually only offloaded its metals subsidiary IMI. They may have forgotten Lord Melchett's warning: 'It is quite impossible to control any industry beyond a certain magnitude.'

THE CONTINENT REVIVES

In the post-war years many British company men were ex-officers who were inclined to bask in military glory, and confuse it with commercial supremacy, taking for granted their markets abroad. They found it hard to comprehend that individual motivation and skills were more important than material wealth, and were astonished by the succession of Continental 'miracles' emerging from the ruins. The recovery was indeed an extraordinary demonstration of will-power: as a naval officer in post-war Hamburg, I saw with disbelief the first Volkswagens emerging from the destruction.

Businessmen on the Continent had been through far more devastating wartime experiences than the British: their nations defeated, their factories commandeered or destroyed, their security undermined. But chaos and insecurity brought much greater realism and urgency, and they knew they must manufacture and export to survive. German managers soon proved once again that human resources were more important than physical resources. By the mid-fifties dynamic companies were reasserting themselves from the rubble with all the more enterprise because (like the Japanese) they got no support from a military-industrial complex, while the wartime Allies had helped to clear the dead wood for new growth. The Allies had been determined to punish Hitler's commercial accomplices, and sentenced Alfried Krupp to twelve years in prison for using slave labour. Only three years later he was released, and regained ownership of his company, which was determined to maintain its empire based on steel and coal. But it expanded too rapidly and eventually in 1967 the banks foreclosed: Alfried's son gave up his rights to the business, and Krupps became an ordinary corporation with bankers and economists on the board, moving into space, aircraft and nuclear reactors with very limited success.

The new generation of German company men had all the advantages of starting again. Their uncluttered offices in rectangular blocks

symbolised a more functional attitude than the British pseudo-
mansions, without hang-ups about class, and with a more defined
sense of command. But they also had the advantage of a system
of supervisory boards, including union representatives – which the
post-war Allies had encouraged – which overcame some of the resentment from workers and limited the scope for autocrats.

Many of the old business dynasties reasserted their ownership, while rich new families emerged. The Thyssens, who had
first introduced Hitler to big business, owned 30 per cent of the
biggest steel group in Europe, run from an elegant skyscraper in
Düsseldorf. The Flick family owned 40 per cent of Daimler-Benz,
and the Quandt family took over control of the rival BMW in 1960.
The Henkels, the soap-kings of Düsseldorf, rejoined their battles
with Unilever and Procter's. At their best, the German families were
able to give a long-term direction and decisiveness at the very top,
while encouraging their company men to become more professionalised and profit-minded than the British, without their aristocratic
pretensions.

FAMILY FIEFS

Throughout most of Europe families retained more control over
business than in Britain or America, giving employees a sense of
identity and continuity which attracted all the more loyalty in the
discontinuity of the post-war politics.

Family firms, it is worth remembering, had a much older history
than governments or nations. The oldest of all is reputed to be the
Hoshi hotel, a traditional Japanese inn which claims to have been
founded in the year 718, and is now said to be managed by the
forty-sixth generation. But Europe has many family companies which
date back over more than four centuries, including the Italian Antinori
wine company (founded in 1385) and Beretta firearms (1526); and a
cluster of alcohol businesses set up in the sixteenth and seventeenth
centuries, such as Hugel in France (1639) and Codorniu in Spain
(1551). Most of them concentrate on one product, and wine families
show a unique survival-rate despite the risks of alcoholism: vineyards

require special skills and dedicated communities, and inspire a devotion to the product which is the secret of continuous success:

> I wonder often what the vintners buy
> One half so precious as the stuff they sell.

The British have a few family companies over three hundred years old, whose owners meet in their own Tercentenarians Club, including Richard Durtnell of Durtnell's building company in Kent (1591), Christopher Hoare of Hoare's Bank (1672), and Richard Early of the blanket firm in Witney – who all avoided the temptations of too-rapid growth. But the oldest British institutions are the charities like hospitals, colleges or schools, which have retained a fixed purpose and manageable size, outliving all their founding families. Most British commercial families lost their will or ability to run a business after the second generation, or have been defeated by the problem of succession – like Dombey and Son.

On the Continent there were many more continuous family firms: the sons, grandsons and great-grandsons of the founders were more likely to remain committed to the business than in Britain, less attracted by country estates or gentlemanly pursuits. Economists and historians continued to argue that the British post-war decline was the result of ineluctable economic forces; but the British commercial dynamic clearly suffered from the loss of family motivation.

Sweden, which remained neutral, came out of the war with the most powerful business dynasties: in 1968 fifteen families – headed by the Wallenbergs, Brostroems, Kempes and Bonniers – controlled a fifth of the country's private industry. But in the war-torn countries the continuity of the families was more important; and powerful families like the Brenninkmeyers (who control C&A in Britain) were soon able to re-establish their holds.

ITALY UNDER FIAT

It was families rather than governments that were the key to the recovery of Italy, which provided the most unexpected of European miracles – astonishing the British and Americans, who still believed that Catholics lacked the commercial discipline which could only come from 'the Protestant ethic'. Many old Italian families, like the shipping families of Genoa, had maintained a continuous commitment to business for centuries. And by the late fifties new Italian companies were making the most spectacular inroads into the newly-formed Common Market, headed by entrepreneurs with the kind of drive which had almost disappeared from Britain. They dominated their company towns with a paternalism which attracted the loyalty of managers and workers who were pouring in to the towns from the farms.

The most all-embracing was Fiat in Turin, which was more like a kingdom than a company, and which provided a kind of caricature of family power. In 1899 Giovanni Agnelli, a young cavalry officer fascinated by the new automobiles, set up a company which he developed into an industrial empire he dominated for forty-five years, playing in with every regime. He picked his key managers as he walked round his factories, delegating huge responsibilities while maintaining firm control. Before he died he summoned his twenty-three-year-old grandson Gianni and told him: 'You are the only one in the family whom I trust, and you must assume your responsibilities.' Young Gianni, then a restless playboy, left Fiat in charge of its chief executive Professor Valletta, but in 1966 he took full command, joined by his brother Umberto. He was an unashamed hereditary capitalist, and talked about his huge empire with a throwaway confidence, as if he had no fears about losing it.

'I am what Italians call a *campanilista*,' he said. 'I identify with the *campanile*, the bell-tower of the village ... I have always tried to ensure that Turin is the decision-making centre.' Fiat had its own training-college, sports grounds and entertainment centres, and later took over Turin's main paper *La Stampa*, and its football team Juventus, which was Agnelli's obsession. He saw his involvement as totally different from the American tradition. 'I would never make a decision which might be damaging to Turin's local administration. A Texan capitalist couldn't care less about local government, he couldn't care less about the federal government.'

Agnelli was proud of his family's continuity: while General Motors might change its boss every three or four years, he ran Fiat for twenty-eight years. 'I have never compared myself to my managers,' he said in 1983, 'although I have made some big financial decisions on my own, and decided on new investments, I have never involved myself in managerial decisions.' He saw himself above the petty controls of government: he contributed to most political parties, while his managers made their own deals with Rome. But Fiat's corruption, and protection from imports, made it dangerously vulnerable to the exposures of the nineties (see Chapter 20).

PATERNALISTS AND BUREAUCRATS

Below the families, the company men on the Continent were more influenced than the British by American professional management. Europeans set up their own business schools modelled on Harvard's analytical systems and case studies, beginning with INSEAD, set up at Fontainebleau in 1959. Social idealists hoped that the new managerial class would come from very diverse backgrounds, but most of them turned out to come from the old professional, administrative or military families of the traditional European bourgeoisie. 'So marked was the middle-class origin of the new managerial class,' wrote Michael Postan in 1966, 'that hardly any recent sociological study of industry fails to bring it out.' They emerged from a limited class whether in Social Democrat Scandinavia or Catholic conservative Italy, and they grafted themselves naturally onto the nineteenth-century lifestyle, with formal entertainments, semi-military protocol, and imposing headquarters.

The German entrepreneurial class harked back to an earlier age of stable structures after the post-war chaos. As the sociologist Ralf Dahrendorf described them in 1965: 'At the top of German enterprises, self-made men and first-generation entrepreneurs have become the exception; the overwhelming number of leading entrepreneurs were born into the upper class, grew up in families of entrepreneurs or professional people, and studied in universities, generally law or technical disciplines. Circulation is almost as rare in entrepreneurial positions as it is in the Catholic Church.'

As the first energy and fluidity of the European miracles subsided in the mid-sixties, the structures tended to harden again into a formal bureaucracy – which British and Americans had always seen as a French or European disease: 'That Continental nuisance called bureaucracy,' as Thomas Carlyle had described it in 1872. The earlier bureaucrats had grown up within the state power of absolute monarchies, but their attitudes soon spread into private industry, reinforced by the confidence of 'technocrats' with sophisticated engineering and financial skills who saw themselves as indispensable to large-scale management. In France the Napoleonic elites educated by the *grandes écoles* had been modernised and extended to provide technocrats for both public and private industry.

It was a state of mind as much as a structure. European intellectuals enjoyed looking down on the stratification of company bureaucrats, but they too were trapped in compartments. Michel Crozier, the French sociologist who made a pioneering study of bureaucracy, conducted his own comparative survey of the attitudes of employees and supervisors in six insurance companies whom he saw as 'the best symbols of the men and women who inhabit the "little boxes" of our popular folklore'. But Crozier came to think that 'in the process of our intellectual development we have all become men in boxes'.

> Young people will have to discover, as some of us did in the late fifties, that organisational life has some advantages for us imperfect human beings ... Mass culture and mass society, it seems, cannot condition persons directly. They condition them only through the games persons play, in which they use the circumstances of their lives to differentiate themselves from the silliness of these games; but one must admit that they have always existed.

Both the Continental bureaucratic style and the family paternalism had emerged from a quite different business tradition to the Americans or British. The different versions of capitalism (see Chapter 20) would never have been lumped together if they had not all been confronting the same enemy of communism. The big Continental companies were much less influenced by shareholders, much more by banks or the state; and their executives and directors were more inclined to see themselves as serving the community, their own employees, or their nation. Their commitments gave advantages in long-term thinking and stability but drawbacks in lack of flexibility and risk-taking. As Agnelli of Fiat described it: 'The US is a country where capitalism today remains more adventurous than anywhere else. In Europe it's much more "established", more settled. In America it's more creative . . . Our European societies are more "set in their ways", the areas in which a man can make independent decisions are much smaller, we are hedged in.'

The Europeans exported their concepts of company towns, with all their paternalism, through the developing world, where they provided strongholds of security and comparative prosperity which attracted the unemployed from miles around. The Asian or African manager or 'comprador' in an international company enjoyed a prestige which separated him from local businessmen. Haresh, the hero of Vikram Seth's novel *A Suitable Boy*, set in India in the 1950s,

had often wondered why people made such a fuss about the young man from Imperial Tobacco or Shell or some other foreign firm which was based in the town or travelling through, not realising that for a mere trader such a member of the comprador classes was a man important beyond his years; he could dispense and revoke agencies, he could make or break one's fortune. He invariably travelled around in a car with a chauffeur, and a car with a chauffeur in a small town was a great thing.

Seth's novel graphically describes the multinational Bata shoe company (which he calls Praha) controlled by the Czech Bata family which founded it in 1894, established shoe factories all round the world and has run them from Canada since the Second World War. Haresh visits the Praha compound outside Calcutta and sees

The endless rows of workers' houses; the offices and cinema; the green palm trees lining the road and the intensely green playing fields; the great, walled factory – the wall itself painted in neat segments advertising the latest lines of Praha footwear; the officers' colony (almost exclusively Czech) hidden behind even higher walls; all these were seen by Haresh through the discomfort and greyness of a hot, wet morning.

Haresh gets a job with the company, and is allowed to live inside the officers' colony. When his prospective bride Lata visits the compound she is worried by the stench and crudity of the tannery, but her mother is impressed by the officers' club and decides that the colony would be 'the ideal place to bring up her grandsons'.

Today, the real Bata company is still run by the founder's grandson Thomas Bata, with a strong 'common culture' but with many non-Czechs running local branches, and without the certainty of lifetime employment: 'Today's economic conditions make such policies unworkable.'

RUSSIA'S INVISIBLE EMPIRES

The Russian victors were the least able to cope with peacetime industry in a fast-changing world, without any entrepreneurial families, and with a vast bureaucracy. Their managers confused military with commercial success far more than the British; while the autocratic communist structure and ideology both prevented them from understanding the realities of world competition and denied them their own freedom.

Huge company towns had been the basis of Russian industry, some originating from encampments set up by foreign entrepreneurs in the nineteenth century. Khrushchev was brought up in the mining town of Yuzovka, named after a Welshman called Hughes who built its ironworks in 1869: 'I worked at a factory owned by Germans, at pits owned by Frenchmen, and at a chemical plant owned by Belgians.' After the revolution the great Ford plants in Michigan and the German electrical plants of AEG inspired Lenin in his definition of communism: 'Soviet power plus electrification of the whole country.' Company towns became more dominant as Stalin became obsessed with heavy industry: without commercial constraints or competition the huge factories became far less manageable than their Western equivalents. In Leningrad, across the river from the palaces, domes and spires, a vast industrial complex grew up with 100,000 workers in a single plant, overshadowing the grim blocks of apartments where they lived. Here, more than in any Western city, workers were living out Fritz Lang's nightmare of *Metropolis*, in their segregated underworld.

But the post-war idea of the 'managerial revolution' gave young managers hopes of liberation; for it promised political as well as administrative autonomy. The communist bosses, like some rich capitalists in the West, owned industries they could not control or understand; and they were finding the 'commanding heights' less commanding than they looked. Managers on both sides of the iron curtain – all concerned with rational planning, autonomy and continuity – felt the same need to assert themselves against their nominal bosses, and enjoyed high status as the masters of industrial growth. When the American management expert David Granick studied communist industrialists in the late fifties he was struck by the resemblances as much as the contrasts with the West: 'The industrial manager is kingpin in both the two giant economies,' he wrote in *The Red Executive* in 1960, 'while he holds a much more modest role of esteem in Britain.' Granick saw communist managers as securely entrenched. 'Well trained, well disciplined, politically conscious and active, the Red Executive seems a figure permanently established in the seats of the mighty.'

As the Moscow planners changed their policies, the factory became more crucial for maintaining some continuity: 'It has been the only stable structure in all of Soviet industry,' wrote Granick. As the Moscow command system became more obviously inefficient, individual factory-managers pressed with some effect for greater autonomy, and in 1957 Khrushchev appeared to move towards more decentralisation, to weaken the industrial empires. But the Party bosses could still block innovations which threatened them; and without a free market their autonomy was strictly limited, for the state still fixed their prices. The battles between the factories and the centre remained unresolved: 'The Russians are still fighting the age-old administrative battle to maintain central control.'

The structures remained very military, with fixed ranks and steady promotion which was jeopardised by risk-taking. One American military attaché described the rules as 'Don't buck the system, don't make any waves, don't go looking for extra work, don't push for reforms because that means changing the way of doing things: just cover your ass.' In fact, he reflected, not unlike the US Army.

The Soviet army benefited more from competition than did consumer industries. Military priorities overrode others, and the army could make demands that the consumer could not. The military sector, said the Polish-American lawyer Samuel Pisar, was 'the only sector of the Soviet economy which operates like a market economy, in the sense that the customers pull out of the economic mechanism the kinds of weaponry that they want'. The military could be strikingly competitive, as they showed when they launched the first Sputnik in 1957. But that triumph misled the West about the effectiveness of other Soviet sectors.

In most industries the potential innovator in the Soviet Union faced more daunting obstacles than anyone in General Motors; his predicament was vividly conveyed by Vladimir Dudintsev in his novel *Not By Bread Alone*, first published in 1956, a few months after Khrushchev had proclaimed the end of Stalinism in his speech to the 20th Party Congress. The hero is a lone inventor, Lapotkin, who devises a new machine for casting pipes in a remote factory complex, or *kombinat*, in Siberia. The manager Drozdov obstructs him and warns: 'The lone wolf is out of date. Our new machines are the fruit of collective thought.' Lapotkin then goes to Moscow where he is opposed by entrenched institutes, pompous scientists and the self-engrossed Ministry: 'Like an enormous ship, the Ministry was running full speed before the wind; all the seamen were conscientiously standing their watches; no one wanted to be bothered with the hare-brained project of a machine for the casting of iron pipes, a project not included in any plan.'

Lapotkin is prosecuted for giving away official secrets and sentenced to a labour camp, while a few brave allies pursue his plan, successfully build the machine and get him released. But the bureaucrats remain inside their fortresses, approving an inferior machine. 'Now at last I see the "invisible empire" of bureaucracy,' says Lapotkin: 'Besides myself only those who are its citizens can see it.'

Dudintsev's exposure of Russian bureaucracy created a furore in the Soviet Union and a success in the West which embarrassed the author: 'We speak boldly and honestly about our deficiencies and our difficulties,' he explained to Western readers, 'because they are the birth-pangs of a new world in which there is no injustice.' The new Soviet world was never born; but the bureaucratic nightmare was more universal than Westerners liked to think. Western company men had been developing their own invisible empires whose limitations would only emerge in the glare of world competition.

CHAPTER NINE

Revolt

The relationship between the individual and the corporation in the post-war decades was still uneasy. By the sixties company men were being fiercely denounced in virtually all Western countries by radical students, as warmongers, racists, liars or polluters. It became part of a much wider rebellion against universities, governments and Western society in general, which eventually led to wild excesses, lost its popular following and provoked a right-wing reaction. But the revolt marked a watershed – the end of the consensus between corporations and society.

It was in America that the movement, like most post-war movements, began. Company men had an early warning in 1964, when a single spectacular abuse of corporate power revealed the arrogance and isolation of General Motors. A crusading young lawyer, Ralph Nader, had been investigating the poor safety records of the newest cars, particularly of General Motors' new Convair, which he analysed in a sensational book, *Unsafe at Any Speed*. General Motors, with staggering crudity, responded by hiring a detective agency to investigate Nader's background, including his sex life. Nader soon discovered this, and reported it to a Senate sub-committee which was studying his complaints about safety. The Senators summoned General Motors officials to explain, including the President James M. Roche, who apologised but did not reveal the murky details of the investigations. The evidence which then emerged showed the gulf between private and corporate morality. General Motors' lawyer Eileen Murphy explained how she rather admired 'Ralphie-boy', but saw the investigation as a professional challenge: 'That's one thing in General Motors. You just press a button and you get what you want.' She approached a Washington attorney and ex-FBI agent, Michael Danner, who in turn hired a detective to pursue Nader. 'He seems to be a bit of a nut or some kind of screwball,' Danner explained. GM wanted to get something on him 'to get him out of their hair and to shut him up'.

'I am responsible for my actions,' Nader wrote, 'but who is responsible for those of General Motors?' He later sued the company for invasion of privacy, and was paid $425,000 in compensation – which helped him to finance a bevy of idealistic young lawyers and helpers, 'Nader's raiders', who were inspired by his example to pursue further abuses of corporate power. Nader was never anti-capitalist: he was determined to rectify capitalism to make it serve the consumer, an attitude ahead of his time. And he had shown up the folly of General Motors' self-absorption. 'A GM willing to accept that big business is indeed "affected with the public interest",' wrote Peter Drucker later, 'would not have made the crucial mistake of hiring detectives to investigate Ralph Nader.'

Nader's crusade was only one symptom of a wider suspicion of corporate behaviour and values, at a time when big companies were getting still bigger. During the twenty-one years from 1948 to 1969 the twenty largest industrial corporations in the US increased their control of all manufacturing assets from 48 to 58 per cent. This concentration was hastened by a new wave of mergers which had been encouraged by the Vietnam boom. The financial operators behind them were immigrants and outsiders – including James Ling, Charles Bluhdorn, Tex Thornton, Saul Steinberg and Harold Geneen – who were not inhibited by links with the old industrial establishment and were prepared to push their power to its limits. By building up their share prices they bought other companies to create 'conglomerates' with a wide range of businesses which further centralised the control of industry. Leading Democrat politicians warned of the dangers: 'In this society of ours,' said Senator Hart of the Senate Anti-Trust Committee, 'we depend on diffusion of power as the best means of achieving political democracy.' But the anti-trust movement had become less effective since the beginning of the century, and most of the new concentrations were allowed.

The conglomerators proclaimed the theory of 'synergy' – a word first applied to combinations of drugs – which argued that the performance after a merger was greater than the sum of its parts: in shorthand, '2+2=5'. Company men dreaded that the mergers would be followed by large-scale sackings: *Welcome to our Conglomerate – You're Fired!* was the title of a book by Isidore Barmash. In fact conglomerates were surprisingly ineffective in reducing workforces, while they required more expensive financial controls: even costlier when they went abroad (see Chapter 10). The financial managers were still further removed from the products – which exacerbated the weakness of mature industries.

The conglomerates added to the bureaucracy of business, but once again humorists were more perceptive than economists. Mock-serious laws and principles had originated in post-war Britain, where Stephen Potter had written satirical books about *Gamesmanship*, *Lifemanship* and *One-Upmanship*. In 1957 Professor C. Northcote Parkinson first promulgated his famous Law in *The Economist* which explained that 'Work expands so as to fill the time available for its completion.' In 1969 Dr Laurence Peter and Raymond Hull, paying tribute to Potter and Parkinson, published *The Peter Principle*, which held that 'In a hierarchy every employee tends to rise to his level of incompetence.' But the most trenchant attack on big companies came from a successful entrepreneur, Robert Townsend, who had built up the Avis rent-a-car business before it was taken over by the conglomerate ITT in 1965. ('If you have a good company,' he advised afterwards, 'don't sell out to a conglomerate.') Townsend used his experience to write *Up the Organisation*, which claimed that big companies were based on the false assumptions that people hate work, need to be driven and dislike responsibility: 'For the last two hundred years we've been using the Catholic Church and Caesar's legions as our patterns for creating organisations.' He offered drastic remedies for gigantism: do without personal secretaries, abolish organisation charts, fire the whole advertising and purchasing departments, don't hire graduates from the Harvard Business School. 'If the chief executive doesn't retire gracefully after five or six years – throw the rascal out.' Townsend's successor at Avis, Bud Morrow, discounted his tips. 'You couldn't save a company, or run it, with his methods,' he told me in 1972. 'Townie's not an administrator – he's not consistent enough – he's an artist. He didn't need a secretary, because he used other people's: my secretary typed his book for him.'

The humorists, though popular, had little impact on the corporate chiefs, who were still subject to laws of expansion and mediocrity.

The conglomerators could continue to satisfy their shareholders while their share prices stayed high in the boom. It was not until profits collapsed in the slump of the mid-seventies that their basic fallacies began to come to light.

The assumption that people hate work was already worrying some businessmen in the sixties, influenced by earlier psychological theories, through the science of 'neo-human relations'. Frederick Herzberg, who was a consultant for AT&T, preached 'job enrichment' and individual self-development. Douglas McGregor rejected 'Theory X', which assumed that workers had to be coerced and punished in order to work, and replaced it with 'Theory Y', which allowed people to enjoy work with managers who could motivate and inspire them. Abraham Maslow, who experimented in a California electronics factory, promoted 'Theory Z', which insisted that workers needed secure structures and a sense of direction to maintain high standards and goals.

Many companies adopted programmes for 'organisational development' designed to increase productivity by making employees happier. Chief executives began sending their managers to 'team-building' courses to give them 'sensitivity training' to make them understand each other and communicate more easily. The notions of group analysis and therapy, which had originated with experiments in far-out California, were adapted to hard-headed decision-making in profit-seeking companies. Silent and self-reliant executives were compelled to bare their secret thoughts and hear what their colleagues thought of them, or to play nursery games to re-establish the openness they had lost in their youth. But there were often cross purposes in this team-building. While the academic psychologists saw themselves as enriching people's jobs, senior managers were often more interested in manipulating their juniors to safeguard themselves – much as they had re-interpreted Taylorism earlier in the century. 'Being the customer who paid the bill,' wrote one British consultant, 'the managers were quite capable of dispensing with the more egalitarian and more humanistic aspects of the OD package with which they did not agree.'

The Europeans were more sceptical about psychological theories, whether X, Y or Z, but several big companies in the sixties began sending their senior managers to team-building courses and 'T-groups': I remember one Shell friend asking himself round urgently for a drink, at the end of a gruelling T-group when his colleagues for the first time had told him about his shortcomings. The Europeans, with their irony and divided loyalties, took team-building less seriously than Americans, and preferred to show their detachment by joking, their traditional form of bonding. Yet many European companies were to turn again to team-building courses in the nineties.

STUDENTS

The attempts to humanise the big corporations were not enough to attract a new generation of students, who rejected the corporations' social benefits and saw them as wrecking the environment, oppressing minorities and manipulating demand through advertising and sponsorship. They were much less afraid of unemployment than their parents, and disillusioned with materialism and dependence on the 'consumer society'. As their favourite philosopher Herbert Marcuse explained it: 'The people recognise themselves in their commodities; they find their soul in their automobile, hi-fi set, split-level home, kitchen equipment.' The students dreaded being trapped in corporate life, and looked to alternative lifestyles and values to give meaning to their existence. The more rebellious were fascinated by the idea of a counter-culture totally liberated from industrial pressures, and allowing the human mind to expand creatively – with new adventures in sex, drugs and communal living – a vision of escape which was perpetuated in Dennis Hopper's film *Easy Rider* in 1969.

The students' main concern was the Vietnam war which threatened them with the draft, and their first target was the American government. But they saw the big companies as the accomplices and beneficiaries of the war. They blamed IBM for computerised bombing, and Dow Chemicals for napalm, which burned its victims alive. The military-industrial complex acquired a more sinister meaning, personified by Robert McNamara, the Secretary of Defense, with his powerful frame, rimless glasses, swept-back hair and mastery of logistics. McNamara was an appropriate bogey. He had moved easily between big business and big government: he had first shown his analytical skills in the wartime air force, then as one of the 'whizz-kids' who revived the Ford motor company after 1945. In the Pentagon after 1960 he applied all his energy to rationalising the armed forces, and escalating the Vietnam war, until he belatedly realised that bombing could not win it, and left to join the World Bank, where he attacked poverty as single-mindedly as he had attacked Vietnam. He was the ultimate manager. 'The real threat to democracy,' he wrote in 1968, 'comes, not from overmanagement, but from undermanagement. To undermanage reality is not to keep free. It is simply to let some force other than reason shape reality.' To the young rebels that was anathema: 'It is to level life down to a standstill of so-called living,' wrote Theodore Roszak, 'that technical expertise can cope with.' McNamara never acknowledged the dangers of the military-industrial complex which he had once headed; but he represented all the young fears of big business linked to big government, commissioning evil in 'clean, carpeted, warm and well-lighted offices'.

The American students rallied against the Vietnam war which overshadowed their immediate careers; but they were also revolting against the whole nature of industrial society and work, at a time of relatively full employment – paradoxically increased by the war itself. Both students and workers felt more able to drop out, change bosses or not turn up for their jobs; and the big auto companies were confronting much more absenteeism and bad workmanship from young workers who hated their conditions. General Motors set up a highly automated new plant at Lordstown in Ohio, designed to attract young workers who would not tolerate Detroit; but the employees felt even more dehumanised by the automation, and in spring 1972 they organised a strike which set back the managers further. In fact General Motors, like the other car companies, had done nothing to improve the human relations and involvement in their plants, which the Japanese were already achieving. The automation at Lordstown was simply extending the mechanical model, which was anathema to both workers and students.

The broad attack on industrial society spread from America to Europe, to set off a quick succession of student revolts, with apparently spontaneous combustion. The European students were not directly threatened by Vietnam, but like the Americans they were bored by the monotony of business and offices after the years of prosperity, and no longer worried by unemployment; and the

Americans lit their fuse. The revolts often began with protests against the universities, which were easy targets, and then spread to a wider denunciation of materialism and social repression.

Researching a book about Europe at the time, I watched the industrial scene being transformed. In late 1967 I was being shown round the model car plants of Renault by confident managers who explained about the five-week holidays and the three-course cuisine in the canteens. A few months later Renault was the prime target of the radical students trying to persuade workers to bring industry to a halt; and in May 1968 I visited the great Renault factory in Paris to find it at a standstill, occupied by its workers. In the next months factories everywhere seemed to be threatened. In Lyons the workers at the Berliet truck-factory revolted, rearranging the giant letters above the factory to spell LIBERTÉ. In Germany, a group of workers rebelled at the Daimler-Benz car-plant in Mannheim, and at the Hoechst chemicals works outside Frankfurt. The most theatrical protest was in Italy, in the 'hot autumn' of 1969, when workers at the Fiat factory in Turin actually burned cars in protest against 'the tyranny of the assembly line'.

The workers' discontent had more economic significance than the students' protests; for they were part of a 'worldwide wage explosion' which marked the end of the post-war consensus. 'After twenty years, a new generation had become adult,' wrote the historian Eric Hobsbawm, 'for whom the inter-war experience – mass unemployment, insecurity, stable or falling prices – were history and not part of experience.' But the dramatic revolts in the factories proved short-lived, for workers rarely shared the students' anti-materialism: 'For the workers, the car is a fetish,' the French student leader Daniel Cohn-Bendit complained later. In France Presidents de Gaulle and Pompidou first appeared to give way to the protesters and conceded large wage increases: but de Gaulle soon reimposed his authority after ensuring his military backing.

But the European company men were in shock, having failed beforehand to detect the pent-up fury; and they knew that the problem lay more with the managers than the workers. Revisiting the Continent in the aftermath, I realised how much the revolts had shaken up managements' attitudes. In Turin Fiat had acquired a sudden new openness and informality, as their young public-relations women made fun of their own company. The chairman Gianni Agnelli explained his own concern about the appalling workers' conditions – 'Would you like to see the nastiest jobs in the whole factory?' And even he had doubts about the future of the car: 'In the most highly motorised countries a slow rejection process is taking place.'

In Sweden, ruled by a social-democratic consensus, the revolt had come as a special shock to bosses who prided themselves on their close relations with students: a survey by their research body SNS showed only a quarter of the students wanting to join private companies. In the summer of 1969 Swedish chairmen held a conference at Tylosand to discuss the crisis with student critics and others including myself. With apparent humility they listened to ferocious attacks on their repressive attitudes, materialism and autocracy; and discussed how to make their companies acceptable. In the following years Volvo and other Swedish companies took the lead in developing new teamwork to escape the monotony of the assembly line.

In Britain the revolt had been much less fiery: the students were more privileged, more distrustful of ideas, and had already been liberated culturally, after the 'Swinging Sixties' had debunked the old Establishment. When Cohn-Bendit tried to whip up the London School of Economics he was met with apathy and scepticism. But even British students fiercely attacked big companies and their links with academia, most notably at the new University of Warwick. The more far-seeing companies took note. Shell was one of the most sensitive, and they exposed their managers to student critics at seminars in their country club. But they still rejected the more rebellious and unconventional potential recruits, in favour of duller conformists. The rejection of rebels, followed by the cutbacks in recruiting in the seventies, was to cost Shell and other companies dearly two decades later when that generation reached the top. 'After 1968 we didn't get the best graduates,' their personnel director explained to me in 1993. 'We were too arrogant, and didn't understand the attitude shift. We didn't just lose the oddballs, we lost some of the clever mainstream graduates. We're suffering the results now.'

The failure of Western companies to attract the best students during the 'decade of disgust' was all the more serious in the face of the coming challenge from Japan: in the words of Charles

Hampden-Turner and Fons Trompenaars, in their book *The Seven Cultures of Capitalism*:

> At precisely the time that the Japanese economy was growing at 8 to 10 per cent per annum, students in North America and much of Western Europe withdrew their allegiance from commerce en masse, most especially the members of elite educational institutions, in favour of the social challenges described by Presidents Kennedy and Johnson. What this 'decade of disgust' cost the economies is still to be calculated, since those who dropped out might now be leading major corporations.

By the mid-seventies the student revolt had spent itself across the West. With mounting unemployment graduates were more anxious to get jobs of any kind. The anti-materialism gave way to a new wave of consumerism, as young people became walking posters, advertising beer, holiday resorts or luxury products on their T-shirts or car-stickers. The counter-culture which had peaked in the early seventies subsided into rural enclaves: into isolated hippie communes in California or English villages where groups of families pursued the good life. The recession of the mid-seventies, accelerated by the oil crisis, turned out to mark the end of the quarter-century of the post-war boom in the West – a century after the long Victorian boom. And the student revolt, as Hobsbawm put it, 'served as a warning, a sort of memento mori to a generation that half believed it had solved the problems of Western society for good'.

Conservative businessmen could watch with relief as graduates once again eagerly competed for jobs; and they observed how the student revolt had been discredited by fanatics and anarchists, by the Weathermen in America, the Baader-Meinhof gang in Germany or the Red Brigade in Italy, who provoked a new toughness from their governments and a right-wing political backlash.

But the revolt was always cultural as much as political, more like a new romantic movement than a serious revolution. Most of the rebels were not so much anti-capitalist as opposed to authoritarian attitudes and the mechanical controls of the new industrial society – summed up by the credit-cards' 'Do not bend, fold or mutilate'. Their revolt was another chapter in the history of the individuals' battle against the mechanical organisation. As the veteran American judge William O. Douglas warned in 1970: 'The search of the youth today is for ways and means to make the machine – and the vast bureaucracy of the corporation state and of government that runs that machine – the servant of man. That is the revolution that is coming.'

Many of their fears were expressed in Charles Reich's book *The Greening of America* in 1970, which depicted a corporate state whose government was allied with companies and uncontrolled technology, creating an artificial culture and meaningless work. The state and the corporations were turning America into a vast anti-community, Reich warned, stripping the family of its functions, and causing a tragic loss of self. Reich traced three phases in self-awareness. In Consciousness 1 the unrestrained competition of the robber barons led to the social chaos of the Depression. In Consciousness 2, beginning with the New Deal and consolidated after the Second World War, the individual was sacrificed to mass industry and organisation for the supposed common good, but with a fearful loss of identity: 'What looks like a man is only a representation of a man who does what the organisation requires.' But in Consciousness 3 a new generation was emerging in the late sixties, betrayed by the loss of humanity and the horrors of the Vietnam war, but determined to recover their inner selves and to choose their own way of life, dress and language: 'The individual is liberated, and the power of choice is now his.'

The choice was not as wide as it looked from the dress and the language. Many of the new generation started their own companies, without losing their unconventional style: they showed that 'hip capitalism' could work without the conformism of the fifties. Others slipped into corporate life, contributing an extra creativity. But most of them lost their idealism. In the early seventies Michael Maccoby, a psychoanalyst from Harvard, interviewed and tested 250 successful executives in twelve major companies, with a special focus on two high-tech multinationals. He identified four types: the 'craftsman', the 'jungle fighter', the 'company man' – like Whyte's organisation man – and the 'gamesman', who became his special study: the dynamic, risk-taking executive who enjoys change and wants to influence its course – within the corporate context. The new high-tech industries including computers were producing highly competitive gamesmen, who reconciled their individuality with their teams and company goals – but often at the cost of dampened passion, emotional castration and depression. The gamesman was not highly moral: he might pollute the environment or intrude on privacy, and he looked to others to set the rules of the game. Maccoby sadly summed up: 'Given our socio-economic system, with its stimulation of greed, its orientation to control and predictability, its valuation of power and prestige above justice and creative human development, these fair-minded gamesmen may be as good as we can expect from corporate leaders.'

The rebels, of course, did not achieve the political liberation they hoped for, but the opposite. By the early seventies conservative governments had been returned in Washington and London. The most lasting achievement of the French students had been the dis-crediting of the 'Obsolete Communism' of the French Communist Party, which lost much of its intellectual support.

By the eighties the radical attack on the post-war consensus in both America and Europe had shifted to the Right, as the neo-capitalists attacked the state, not for its authoritarian oppression, but for its high taxes, welfare spending and interference with free enterprise. The new Right, as one historian put it, 'put to use some of the anti-bureaucratic, anti-statist, libertarian discourse of the 1960s and, standing it on its head, attempted to turn it into a populist-style capitalistic politic'. Company men, as we will see, had more to fear from the Right than the Left.

But European corporations were never so complacent again after their battering from the students – many of whom were the children of company men. And two powerful movements which originated in the sixties were to gather momentum until they changed the whole context of corporate thinking.

The Greens, though they had deeper roots, owed much to the student rebels: in Germany Dany Cohn-Bendit had supported the environmentalists, while Rudi Dutschke helped to found the Green Party which was launched (just after he died) in 1980. The original protests against chemical pollution or oil-spills extended into much broader sustained campaigns across the West which were to compel all major corporations to have their own environmental officers and to drastically rethink new plants, ships and pipelines.

The women's liberation movement began partly in protest against the male domination of the student groups. In Germany the women members of the radical SDS (Sozialistischer Deutscher Studenten- bund) rebelled to form their own Women's Action Council who pelted the men with tomatoes and insisted that the leaders should discuss orgasms as well as class struggle. In America women broke away from *their* SDS (Students for a Democratic Society) in indignation: 'SDS was absolutely the most sexist place I've ever been,' said one of them, Barbara Haber. Militant women eventually became more forceful than men in self-expression and self-awareness; and women's liberation produced a cohort of executives in communi- cations, who helped to transform office attitudes (see Chapter 19).

Within business itself the revolts had released new energies and creativity; and in America they were the seedbed for the new com- puter revolution (see Chapter 13). The mainframe computer had first been developed with the help of the military-industrial complex, and helped to reinforce large-scale organisations. But the young computer engineers and programmers, who developed mini-computers in the seventies and personal computers in the eighties, grew out of the massive disillusion with Vietnam and big-company conformity. Most of them were aggressively capitalist, single-minded in their jobs and little interested in wider self-expression. But they were react- ing against their parents' assumptions about conventional business, and without the questioning of the sixties they would never have happened.

The spirit of the sixty-eighters or *soixante-huitards* lived on in Europe and America, not only in communes and workshops, but in more commercial creative innovations which appeared in shops, restaurants, architecture and marketing. Young businessmen with more open attitudes were able to channel their energy into new work- styles and markets for natural foods, environmentally-friendly prod- ucts or ethnic clothes. Hip entrepreneurs in flowery shirts proved as money-minded as white-shirted company men, while giving staff more personal freedom, which became crucial to entertainment and communication industries. And the shrewdest operators knew how to connect up a rebellious youth culture with the discipline of large-scale organisations.

AIRLINES AND BRANSON

The airlines provided a special challenge for new thinking, to attract the millions of young tourists, particularly in the competitive trans-atlantic market. In 1977 Freddie Laker, a daring showman who had been operating British charter flights, began flying his 'Skytrain' across the Atlantic, offering cheap flights with 'no frills' and much razzamatazz. But when the big airlines cut their own fares he was soon overextended and bankrupted four years later. Then in 1981 a young American financier, Donald Burr, started his 'People Express' which again cut transatlantic fares and service to the bone. Burr was a more serious capitalist innovator, confronting established airlines like Pan Am which were hopelessly overstaffed. 'To compete seri-ously,' he told me, 'you need *alignment* between the individual and the enterprise'; and he gave both responsibilities and shares to his young employees. He ran the airline with the kind of informality advocated in *Up the Organisation* – without a secretary or an office – and for a time it was a romantic success: teenagers flocked to the planes, air hostesses became millionaires. But Burr could not resist overexpanding and challenging the giants; and People collapsed.

It was left to a more surprising Englishman to launch a successful popular airline, and to provide a new role model combining youthful panache with commercial discipline. Richard Branson had begun as a boy-wonder of the sixties: I first met him when at sixteen he came to ask advice about starting a magazine called *Student*. He had a breezy, innocent style but turned out to have the rare ingredients of a true entrepreneur: he had left school early, ignored all the rules and had unlimited self-confidence backed by an ambitious mother. He was soon cultivating the image of a fun-loving and classless hippie, with a pirate beard and shapeless sweaters, living and working from a barge where he seemed to have no cares in the world. But he was really a single-minded workaholic with a financial ambition encour-aged by his public school, Stowe, which was a breeding-ground for showmen and entrepreneurs. After Branson's magazine collapsed he started his Virgin record company where he made shrewd contracts with outlandish stars, from Boy George to the Sex Pistols, and learnt how to motivate a young staff through responsibility and glamour more than money.

When he started his Virgin airline in 1984 it seemed a rash and surprising switch: 'I decided there must be room for another airline when I spent two days trying to get through to People Express,' he told me on his barge. 'That was the sum of my market research.' But he was also influenced by his mother, who had been a pioneer air hostess, and he knew that airlines needed showmanship to put 'bums on seats'. Flying on the maiden voyage I first realised Branson's mastery of publicity, as he endlessly relaunched the jumbo with champagne for the cameras, filled the plane with pop stars and celebs, and dressed himself as an airline pilot in the cabin. He could transform an ordinary 747 into a glamour-object which could attract both tourists and eager staff; and he also brought imagination and innovation, including video films and a new 'upper class', into a workaday unimaginative business. He made the most of playing David challenging the Goliath of British Airways, like his predecessor Freddie Laker but more shrewdly, and when BA used dirty tricks against Virgin he sued them with deadly publicity.

Branson's exhibitionism alarmed conventional bankers and many colleagues: Sir James Goldsmith did not forgive him for pushing him into the pool of his Mexican castle. But he proved more cautious and more lasting than most other hyped heroes of the eighties, like Ronson, Ratner, Halpern and Nadir. When he made Virgin a public company in 1988 it was shunned by many big funds, and the share price was depressed when he made a risky transatlantic balloon trip. He decided that 'Being an entrepreneur and the chairman of a public company just doesn't mix,' and bought back the shares after two years. But he then sold his music business, with a personal profit of £400m, and concentrated on expanding his airline.

Branson anticipated later ideas about management leadership. He used his famous face to give a sense of unity and personality to all his businesses, and his casual style as camouflage for his astute dealings. He knew how to harness creativity to commercial toughness: his commercial director Paul Griffiths had a degree in music, and his personnel director Nick Potts began as an opera singer. Potts insisted that empowerment, which became the buzz-word of the nineties, 'typically exists naturally with youth, vigour and smallness in organisations'. But Branson's real breakthrough was in connecting up the fantasies of the sixties with the hard-headed commercial realities of the next decades.

CHAPTER TEN

Multinational Men

By the early sixties a new species of company man was evolving in the West with migratory habits which had been unpredictable twenty years earlier. He could fly non-stop across the Atlantic in seven hours; he could stay in a foreign country for only one night, at a hotel which looked indistinguishable from its counterpart at home; he could talk to his home office or his wife without delay by a direct-dial telephone. He was more widely travelled than any earlier businessman voyaging by steamships and railroads. He was beginning to see the free world as a single unit – like the student rebels who shouted 'Down with Borders!'

But compared to those slower travellers, he had corresponding limitations. His real experience of other countries was much more limited; he was more insulated from their inhabitants; and the further he travelled, the more he was dependent on his company. Sometimes he could not be sure where his ultimate loyalty lay: with his nation or his company? And his alternative source of security, his home and his family, was hard to combine with the constant uprooting. While the earlier wives of army officers, sea-captains or traders had recognised status and structures as they awaited their husbands' return, the wives of the jet-travellers could be more confused about where they really belonged.

There was nothing new about international businessmen: in the eighteenth century the officers of the East India Company sailed to bases halfway across the world, on behalf of shareholders in Holland and Portugal as well as Britain. In the nineteenth century Singer, based in New York, had their biggest sewing-machine plant in Scotland, while Standard Oil had subsidiaries in China and the Swede Alfred Nobel built factories across Europe to make dynamite. By 1907 Royal Dutch-Shell was jointly owned by Dutch and British.

Henry Ford set up a factory in Manchester in 1911, and already saw business defying world frontiers.

But these earlier businessmen were all subject to sea-changes, and had to adapt to local conditions if they were to survive, while the new multinational men with their jet planes and telephones were able to provide an unparalleled uniformity very quickly. When the new European Common Market was formed in 1956 American businessmen took advantage of it with a speed and directness which amazed and amused the Europeans, as they flew between Paris, France and Rome, Italy, as unaware of different languages and customs as the high-speed tourists of the 1969 film *If it's Tuesday, this Must be Belgium*. They assumed Western Europe was a single continental market-place like their own. 'The Americans keep talking about something called Southern Europe,' Agnelli of Fiat complained to me. They thought they could sell the same product everywhere without national differences; and they were often proved right.

The jet-travellers ignored warnings about dislocation. In the early jet age some company doctors still insisted that executives should take a day off after a long flight, to avoid the disorientation of jet-lag; and some companies encouraged transatlantic travellers to return by sea to re-orientate themselves. By the seventies most businessmen took the acceleration of travel for granted: many kept their watch set to their home-time, and went straight from a transatlantic night-flight to a meeting. But they inevitably became still more detached from the lives of more earthbound people, including their customers. And they could not speed up their normal human activities – of thinking, reading or sleeping.

The global lifestyle of businessmen inevitably had great limitations, as I realised when I tried to follow their workings: flying constantly in Jumbos across the time-zones, moving from one L-shaped hotel room to another, with a dwindling sense of time or place. The habit of constant movement could become an end in itself: as J. Kenneth Galbraith remarked, it was easy to confuse movement with thought. The self-contained world of hotels and airports began to appear as the reality, while the hinterland beyond the perimeters seemed unreal (one airline boss even designed his drawing room like the front of a 747, to make himself feel at home). The airport lounges had become the social equivalent of the nineteenth-century coaching inn, the meeting-place for constant travellers at the crossroads – but with no rooted people to provide local atmosphere or values.

Many of these new nomads were not surprisingly bewildered about their relationship with the nations to which they were flying. In the sixties many company chiefs looked to a new world order in which nationalism would wither away under some kind of supranational authority. 'The world's political structures are completely obsolete,' said Jacques Maisonrouge, the Frenchman who became head of IBM World Trade Corporation and a model for the new global man. 'The political boundaries of nation-states are too narrow and constricted to define the scope and sweep of modern business,' said William I. Spencer, president of First National City Corporation. Some chairmen foresaw a truly supranational existence. Tom Clausen, the president of Bank of America, himself earthbound in California, looked forward to 'an international corporation that has shed all national identity'. Carl A. Gerstacker, chairman of Dow Chemicals, was even rasher: 'I have long dreamed of buying an island owned by no nation and of establishing the world headquarters of the Dow company on the truly neutral ground of such an island, beholden to no nation or society.' He was offered the Minerva atoll near Fiji, but turned it down as having too conservative a vision: 'They're just fed up with government.' Gerstacker went on to speculate on 'anational' corporations which would have directors from varied origins and residences: 'in a sense junior counterparts of the United Nations Security Council'. His remarks embarrassed a later chairman, Paul Orrefice, who explained in 1983 that Gerstacker really meant that Dow hoped to do business 'the same way all over the world'.

The global rhetoric concealed much humbug. Most American companies abroad remained firmly controlled by American citizens, influenced by American foreign policy and defence contracts. The furthest-flung European companies could be the most 'ethnocentric': like the airlines, or like Nestlé, the Swiss food giant whose directors all had to be Swiss citizens. But the most dynamic American multinationals were undoubtedly beginning to break down national distinctions: they were much more meritocratic, less class-bound or family-bound than national companies in Europe, and their European managers found more scope for promotion outside their own country where they could escape from its constraints. They mixed up

nationalities more thoroughly than earlier world bodies like the
Catholic Church, the Red Cross or the Foreign Legion. The global
corporation, claimed Aurelio Peccei, a director of Fiat, with some
justification, 'is the most powerful agent for the internationalisation
of society'.

The corporations did more to integrate the new Europe than the
idealists of the European Community; for by cross-posting nationalities – a Dutchman in Britain, a Frenchman in America, a German
in France – they created more genuinely anational systems than the
'Eurocrats' in Brussels. The biggest, including General Motors, Ford,
IBM and ITT, created networks of European subsidiaries which
could interchange both parts and people. Jean Monnet, the founder
of the Community, had foreseen that the process of free trade and
harmonisation would gradually lock the nations together in a mesh
of common interests; but the multinationals forced the pace by
extending their corporate loyalty beyond frontiers. When I made this
point in a speech in Paris in 1969 I was alarmed to notice Monnet
himself (whom I knew and admired) in the audience; but he said
afterwards that he agreed with me.

These new company men were beginning to appear as 'world managers'. As Richard J. Barnet and Ronald G. Miller described them
in 1974 in their book *Global Reach*, they were 'the first in history with
the organisation, technology, money, and ideology to make a credible
try at managing the world as an integrated unit'. National governments watched their power with growing ambivalence. On the one
hand they held the keys to critical new exports and technologies,
backed by larger resources than any government: their motto, wrote
Andrew Shonfield, seemed to be 'Anything you can do, we can do
better.' On the other hand they were challenging areas of national
sovereignty and evading national controls, including effective taxation,
while the most ambitious were beginning to pursue their own foreign
policies.

The multinationals appeared impregnable behind their castle walls
which could repel local invaders. Like armies they closed their ranks
to enforce secrecy and loyalty when faced with disclosure, and reacted
with crude punishments – as had earlier giants including Standard
Oil, which imposed its own 'Standard Oil collar' (see Chapter 3), or
General Motors when it persecuted Ralph Nader. There were very

few whistle-blowers when they abused their powers, even when hundreds of employees knew about it. The conformity was alarming to outsiders: when the Dow chemical company was producing the deadly herbicide Agent Orange, they faced no whistle-blowers, one lawyer complained, 'because nobody believes there is anything to blow the whistle on'. Only a rare political assault from Washington could provide an occasional glimpse of corporate workings through Congressional hearings.

Europeans had an even stronger tradition of company secrecy, with more severe penalties for breaking it. The most terrifying example was the case of Stanley Adams, who worked for the Swiss pharmaceuticals company Hoffman-La Roche in Basel and revealed to the European Community in Brussels that they were breaking the rules by eliminating competition. Under Swiss law Adams was arrested, jailed and effectively ruined. It was a warning, as Roche intended, to any future whistle-blower. 'I wonder if there aren't other individuals,' Adams said at the end of his own account of his ordeal, 'who have followed their consciences but, unlike me, have never been heard of again.' Adams was a violent man, and his persecution further isolated and destabilised him: some years later he was charged with trying to murder his second wife and sentenced to jail.

By the late sixties there was a rash of warnings about the escalating powers of the multinationals. In 1968 Professor Howard Perlmutter of the Wharton School, a fashionable guru, predicted that by 1985 two to three hundred companies would dominate the world's industrial output. Commentators predicted a major confrontation with the weakened nation-states. 'As the role and influence of international companies increases,' wrote Christopher Tugendhat in 1971, 'their tensions with governments will become worse.' Hugh Stephenson predicted *The Coming Clash* in 1972: 'When the history of the late twentieth century is written, it will surely be said that it was the operations of industry that did more than anything else to undermine the overwhelming dominance of the nation-state over the condition of man for the last three centuries.'

The giant companies appeared increasingly awesome and mysterious. The names of IBM, ITT, Ford and Mobil shone out above the city-centres and airport highways like symbols of invading powers. Their prominence made them convenient scapegoats, like Standard

Oil a century earlier, for all the frustrations and worries of local citizens who became more anxious and bewildered after the oil-shocks of the seventies. The American resentment was brilliantly caricatured by the film *Network* in 1976, written by Paddy Chayevsky and directed by Sidney Lumet, against a background of rising oil-prices, Arab wealth and humiliation in the West. The hero Howard Beale, a television commentator, complains on screen: 'I don't know what to do about the depression and the inflation and the Russians and the crime in the streets.' He becomes a national hero when he asks all his viewers to stick their heads out of their windows and yell: 'I'm as mad as hell and I'm not going to take it any more!' But eventually his boss puts him down with a tirade about the new economic realities:

> You get up on your little twenty-one-inch screen and howl about America and democracy. There is no America. There is no democracy. There is only IBM and ITT and AT & T and duPont, Dow and Union Carbide, Exxon. Those are the nations of the world today . . . We no longer live in a world of nations and ideologies, Mr Beale. The world is a college of corporations, inexorably determined by the immutable by-laws of business. The world is a business, Mr Beale. It has been since man crawled out of the slime.

THE GENEEN MACHINE

Of these new global bogeys, it was ITT which became the most notorious. ITT was the biggest of the new conglomerates in America which had gobbled up hundreds of companies in the sixties. It had grown into a far-flung multinational with a fierce system of financial controls and a heavy political clout to bully governments, particularly its own. And it soon became the focus of fears about the unaccountability of multinational men.

ITT looked very American; but it was really an unusual case of a company which had always been an outsider with no real roots and was born on an offshore island (the kind of origin Gerstacker of Dow might have dreamt of). Its birthplace was in Puerto Rico in 1920, where a young Danish-French sugar-broker, Sosthenes Behn, had acquired a tiny telephone business as a bad debt and began to turn it into an international company with a name which deliberately resembled the established AT&T. Behn built up an 'international system' in Latin America and Europe by playing in with local dictators, including Franco in Spain and Hitler in Germany. He was all things to all men: ITT's German companies, which included a share in Focke-Wulf bombers, became crucial to the Nazi war machine, but when Hitler was defeated ITT successfully claimed compensation for the destruction of the Focke-Wulf plants by Allied bombers.

After Behn died in 1957 the ITT board was in disarray, and following a worried interim they chose another autocrat, Harold Geneen, as chairman. Geneen was an owlish accountant, much less charismatic than Behn, but with the same buccaneering instinct concealed behind his spectacles. He was determined to diversify ITT, ostensibly to balance the uncertain future of telephones, but basically to extend his own power. Having boosted the share price, he raided a succession of companies ranging from Avis rent-a-car to Levitt houses to Rayonnier forests to Continental Baking to Sheraton Hotels. By 1970 ITT had four hundred separate companies operating in seventy different countries, providing a worrying political leverage: next year a Congress report on conglomerates warned that ITT 'has created a virtually self-contained corporate structure that exists and acts outside the scope of any of the countries in which it provides services'.

Geneen required intense dedication and obedience from his managers: when I interviewed him in Brussels in 1972 he seemed like a gnome in a fairy-tale, spinning threads into gold and weaving spells over his underlings. He devised a 'Geneen machine' which took accounting systems to new extremes, to control and motivate his company men – who were made still more dependent by constant uprooting and travel. Every month a Boeing 707 flew ITT executives from New York to Brussels for a crucial international meeting. When I managed to infiltrate one I saw them sitting round a huge horseshoe-shaped table in a darkened room, confronting the impassive figure of Geneen. A big screen displayed the statistics about each subsidiary, while a sharp arrow would pause at a significant figure – a major loss, or serious discrepancy – and Geneen would coldly question the manager in charge, and if necessary humiliate him. It was a terrifying ordeal which made some managers physically sick. But it provided the control that Geneen demanded, to inspect any overspending, excess commitments or mistakes: 'I want no surprises.'

ITT-ers were much-admired managers: they earned higher salaries and gained more experience than elsewhere, and other corporations were beginning to follow their techniques. But Geneen was a control-freak, with a regime based on fear and domination which demanded total priority over family and community and which left a wake of breakdowns and divorces. When I asked one ex-ITT manager why he had resigned he replied: 'I want to rejoin the human race.'

Geneen's ambition overreached itself when he tried to control governments, first in America, then abroad. In 1969 a new anti-trust chief in Washington, Richard McLaren, was determined to stop the economic concentration, and tried to move against ITT, which had just made its biggest acquisition, the venerable Hartford insurance company (where the poet Wallace Stevens had worked). Geneen fought back, mobilising his lobbyists and pledging $400,000 for the Republicans to hold their convention in San Diego. Soon afterwards an anti-trust settlement was announced which allowed ITT to keep Hartford, but then a document came to light from ITT's chief lobbyist, Dita Beard, which clearly suggested a link with the pledge. ITT's apparent bribe became a new gift to the Democrats in the scandal-time of Watergate. A Senate committee took it up, without proving a direct link but exposing Geneen's relentless use of his lobbying power. 'Have we reached a point in our society,' asked Senator Hart, 'where there has been permitted to develop a private concentration of power which, because of the enormity of their reach, makes impossible the application of public policy to them?'

ITT intervened much more rashly in Chile, to execute its own foreign policy. Geneen was worried that the Chile telephone company, his biggest business in Latin America, would be nationalised if the communist leader Salvador Allende came to power. He looked to the CIA for help through one of his directors, John McCone, a former CIA chief. Geneen suggested, as he recalled later: 'Don't you think we ought to get together with a plan and we'll put money in?' He promised a million dollars to help stop Allende. Henry Kissinger, then Secretary of State, turned down the offer while pursuing his own plans to stop Allende; but ITT's men in Chile kept closely in touch with the CIA men on the ground. When Allende was nevertheless elected and went ahead with nationalising the telephones Geneen switched his efforts to gaining compensation. Then in March 1972 ITT's correspondence was leaked, revealing the company's close workings with the CIA and causing a furore in Washington and Chile. Much later the Securities and Exchange Commission (SEC) revealed that ITT had spent a total of $8.7 million on illegal activities round the world, in countries including Indonesia, Iran, the Philippines, Algeria, Mexico, Italy and Turkey.

ITT was never the same again: its international credibility was battered by the scandals, while in the following recession its acquisitions were looking much less profitable. In two years its share price, damaged by the 'scandal discount', went down from $80 to $12. Geneen's autocracy was becoming a liability, but he was hard to unseat: in 1977 he was pushed upstairs to become chairman under a less assertive chief executive, Lyman Hamilton, who began selling off subsidiaries. Two years later Geneen fought back, had Hamilton fired and succeeded by his new favourite Rand Araskog – a coldly efficient Swedish-American without imperial pretensions. Geneen finally retired in 1980, to run his own investment company. Araskog continued selling off ITT's ragbag of companies, to concentrate on the high-tech communications about which it knew most – and which showed the most scope for growth. Without Geneen's obsessive ambition, the business empire made little sense. The components proved to be worth more as separate entities, and ITT began 'deconglomerating'.

The intricate structure of the Geneen Machine proved to be the extreme case of the centralised multinational conglomerate, and showed its unworkability. The ITT-ers trained by Geneen were remarkable financial controllers, with extraordinary discipline; but it was simply not practicable to rule such a wide empire with such lack of human trust and creativity, and such expensive supervision. Without the zeal at the centre and the fear at the periphery, the empire fell apart.

The ITT scandals had provoked American Senators to form an

unique investigatory body: the Sub-Committee on Multinational Corporations. It was chaired by Senator Frank Church, an eloquent populist from Idaho who was already wary of multinationals and who could now find out how they really worked, with the help of subpoena powers and a resourceful chief counsel, Jerome Levinson. It was their investigation of ITT which revealed how Geneen ruthlessly deployed his lobbyists, spies and public-relations staff to extend his interests; and their volumes of evidence provided unprecedented documentation about how a global company could mobilise its executives to exploit its political power.

Other multinationals were now also vulnerable. After the energy crisis of 1973 showed up the West's desperate dependence on Arab oil, many politicians began to doubt the ultimate loyalties of oilmen, whether in Britain or America: 'We must re-examine the premise that what's good for the oil companies is good for the US,' said Senator Church. His committee recorded with copious detail the diplomatic role of the 'Seven Sisters', the giant oil companies who had pursued their own foreign policy in the Middle East with a short-sightedness which had precipitated the formation of OPEC and encouraged a fool's paradise of cheap oil. They had become truly 'world managers' as they negotiated with sheikhdoms and princes, with occasional prompting and support from their governments.

The Watergate scandal meanwhile was uncovering details of secret corporate gifts to the Republican Party and others, and bribes by two aerospace companies, Northrop and Lockheed, gave the Church Committee the chance to penetrate the most secretive of all company men, the international arms salesmen. Thousands of subpoenaed documents revealed how they had bribed world dignitaries – including Prince Bernhard of the Netherlands, who was then compelled for a time to resign all public positions, and Kakuei Tanaka, the Japanese premier who later resigned. But they also revealed the predicament of the salesmen, who were frantically seeking orders to maintain their factories with a fierce loyalty to their corporation: sitting in their hotel rooms, worrying lest others were outbidding them, and using shady agents to slip behind the 'black curtain' and promise that cash payments would clinch the deal. The further they roamed abroad, the more anxiously they depended on their masters back home.

In the long wake of Watergate the Church Committee could uncover company secrets more thoroughly than any investigation since the Second World War. The clouds lifted to reveal first the foothills, then the peaks of American corporate power, with the authentic details of subpoenaed documents and evidence under oath. The view did not remain clear for long. In 1975 Church turned his searchlight on the international banks, to discover whether their huge deposits of Arab money might be used to influence foreign policy. But the top bankers refused to reveal their individual deposits, and flew to Washington to try to stop the hearings. The senators were already becoming more cautious as American voters became preoccupied by their economic crisis and overseas competition. Soon afterwards the Church Committee was disbanded. The reports of investigating journalists were also dwindling in the new patriotic atmosphere; corporate executives were becoming more discreet, and had taken to shredding incriminating documents, while new American laws were tougher on corporate corruption. The clouds returned, and the view disappeared.

EUROPEANS V AMERICANS

The Europeans in the sixties had depicted multinationals as an American phenomenon. This was misleading, for many European companies, particularly British and Dutch, had huge subsidiaries in the United States. But the Americans were more visible, both because of their rapid expansion and because they imposed a more uniform style on their overseas companies – as typified by Geneen, who liked to see the initials ITT wherever he went. The European giants, accustomed to wide national differences in their home continent, were more discreet in dealing with foreign countries and delegated more power to local managers. When the European Community was created in 1956, allowing freer exchange of goods across national frontiers, each product manager saw himself as expert in his own people's habits and tastes in foods, drinks, clothes or scents: brands which might look the same, like instant coffee, margarine or soup, had subtly different flavours in each country. But many companies faced a shock when confronted with Americans who realised that foreigners could be persuaded by massive advertising and promotion to share their own tastes.

The classic battle was between the two soap-and-detergent giants. Unilever, the Anglo-Dutch combine based in Rotterdam and London, had prided itself on a delicate balance between global head-quarters and local managers. An advertisement for recruits in 1961 summed up the approach:

AVIS UNILEVERENSIS (MANAGERIALIS)

Plumage: highly variegated. Habits: too numerous to list. Habi-tat: the world. Distinctive characteristics: a high flyer. The birds who run Unilever come in many shapes and sizes . . .

Unilever man relished the fine distinctions of local tastes, like the shades of colour in their powder Omo. But the formation of the European Community provoked a massive invasion of Europe by Procter & Gamble, the old soap company based in Cincinnati who had already beaten back Unilever's assaults on their American terri-tory. Procter's highly-trained marketers – the 'Proctoids' as they came to be called – had no respect for national differences: they launched the same products, like Daz or Tide, into European countries with the same formulae, and with the same aggressive salesmanship to launch them into the shops and burgeoning supermarkets, while Unilever's national managers were dazed by the blitzkrieg. Eventually Unilever had to appoint super-managers, discreetly called co-ordinators, to supervise their separate products on a global scale, which inevitably made the company more centralised, like Procter's.

In later years the rival giants kept changing shape, centralising and decentralising in different areas. Unilever still benefited from sensi-tive local managers, particularly in the developing world: it could introduce new ideas and products from the periphery – like Timotei, which began as a failed deodorant in Finland and was developed into a global shampoo. But the opening-up of the single European market in 1992 pressed Unilever to become more centralised in Europe, while Procter's were giving more scope to their company men abroad to take note of local differences. By the mid-nineties competition had made them much more alike, until (as one Unilever director put it) there was 'hardly a cigarette paper between them'.

But back in the late sixties many Europeans were alarmed by the growing power of American multinationals, as they outstripped or bought up competitors. Their fears were focused and magnified in 1967 by Jean-Jacques Servan Schreiber, the French financier-politician who then owned the weekly *L'Express*. He promoted with panache his sensational book *The American Challenge* which accurately depicted a new era after Vietnam when military wars would be replaced by duels for technology: 'Now we are beginning to discover what was concealed by twenty years of colonial wars, wars that dominated our thoughts and our behaviour; the confrontation of civilisations will now take place in the battlefield of technology, science and management.'

Servan-Schreiber believed the Americans had mastered the tools of reason, in science, organisation and management, while European managers were still hindered by irrational traditions, by family firms, by reliance on flair rather than systematic thought. He saw American economic power turning into political power, as the corporate bosses pulled the levers of strategy and technology. They were already conquering space exploration and supersonic travel, but Europe could respond to the American challenge by training young people for information systems, whose importance the Americans did not yet realise.

The challenge alarmed and excited the Europeans, particularly the French, just when their Concorde seemed threatened by American plans for supersonic planes. But the apparent crisis really marked the peak of American influence in Europe. By the seventies investment was already moving in the opposite direction, encouraged by the challenge and the collapse of the dollar. European multinationals began buying up American companies on the cheap, sometimes with disastrous consequences as they moved into businesses they did not understand. British American Tobacco bought American stores, including Saks Fifth Avenue, Gimbels and Marshall Fields, which proved less profitable than they looked, while Imperial Tobacco bought Howard Johnson roadside restaurants at an exorbitant price. By the mid-eighties the Americans were beginning to complain about growing foreign ownership and control – particularly from Japan, a challenge which Servan-Schreiber did not foresee.

THE WORLD MANAGERS

By the eighties, European and American multinationals were competing with Japanese companies across the world with ever more resources, while their nations were growing weaker. Governments were less able to confront or regulate the multinationals as they themselves became more insecure and inward-looking, trying to hold their own coalitions together. 'In the closing years of the twentieth century,' wrote Richard Barnet twenty years after his *Global Reach*, 'the "deglobalisation" of world politics is occurring even as the globalisation of economic activities proceeds.' The labour unions in rich countries could no longer protect wages as the companies built factories abroad to employ cheaper labour. The American worker could no longer assume that 'What's good for General Motors is good for America.'

The clash with the multinationals never came. In fact most nations – and regions within nations – were competing desperately to attract them, as a precious source of investment, jobs and technology. The more the global market opened out, the more the multinational men could play governments and regions against each other, choosing whichever offered the cheapest labour, the greatest freedom, or most generous tax concessions. Developing countries, which had led the attack on multinationals in the sixties and had nationalised many of their assets, were now most anxious to attract them. They were learning the painful lesson 'If there's one thing worse than being exploited by a multinational, it's not being exploited.' The reviled world managers of one decade had become the guests-of-honour of the next.

But Western multinationals were themselves becoming less monolithic as they faced more competition with each other. The old military command structure based on a massive headquarters was outdated; and the model of ITT, with its dread controls, proved unworkable. By the end of the eighties, as we will see in Chapter 14, many of the bigger companies were becoming more like federations of small companies. Multinationals no longer had to be giants. As communications quickened and opened up, quite small companies could provide services across the globe, based on special skills or technology.

In 1970, according to the UN Center on Transnationals, there were 7,000 multinationals, of which over half were based in the US and Britain; by the 1990s there were 35,000, including hundreds based in developing countries. And the new multinationals included networks of individual operators – whether bankers, lawyers, accountants or salesmen – who had the experience to comprehend the global market-place.

It was not so much multinational corporations which were now undermining societies and governments as the flow of capital, which provided constant scope for speculation against currencies or bonds. The chief beneficiaries of world trade were not the company men but the dealers, like the 'Masters of the Universe' described by Tom Wolfe in his *Bonfire of the Vanities* (1988), spending their day yelling and swearing as they moved billions in bonds across the globe. 'Everyone woke up to it when the Arabs suddenly jacked up oil prices in the early 1970s,' as Wolfe put it. 'In no time, markets of all sorts became heaving crap-shoots: gold, silver, copper, currencies, bank certificates, corporate notes – even bonds.' By the late eighties $400 billion was crossing the frontiers every day, providing opportunities for investors and speculators who could use savings in one continent to buy and sell assets between the hemispheres. Local communities found themselves at the mercy of dealers at the other side of the world whose gambles could shut down a whole plant – or a town.

The most successful money-makers were individual speculators, like George Soros, the Hungarian-American who in 1993 made a personal profit of over a billion dollars – putting him among the top multinationals. Soros had no interest in fixed investments – he joked that 'an investor is just a failed speculator' – and made his fortune from the instability of currencies and capital. But he was also passionately concerned to build up stable democratic institutions in Eastern Europe, to which he devoted most of his time and money; and he became disillusioned, as he explained in London in June 1994, with Western governments which had not followed his lead. But governments were becoming subject to the same short-term pressures as corporations; and like speculators they were reluctant to make long-term commitments to distant countries.

*   *   *

As the pace quickened, multinational men became more cut off from the earthbound masses, as they moved between international conferences, conventions and grand hotels. For them the word community no longer meant a neighbourhood or district but a group of specialists, like the legal or medical community, whose bounds were set by skills rather than frontiers. They had more interests in common with their foreign counterparts than with most of their own people, who were being left behind by the world market-place. 'As the top becomes ever more tightly linked to the global economy,' wrote Robert Reich in 1991, before he became Secretary of Labor in Washington, 'it has less of a stake in the performance and potential of its less fortunate compatriots.'

The 'world managers' were in some respects reverting to the world before 1914, before it was broken up by the First World War: when European bankers were more concerned with their loans and investments across the oceans than with less promising prospects at home; when Edwardian capitalists knew more about Johannesburg or Buenos Aires than about Glasgow or Leeds. But since then the industries in the developing world had multiplied while European industries had relatively shrunk. And the biggest supplier of international investment was no longer either Britain or America, but a country which was only just emerging in 1914: Japan.

CHAPTER ELEVEN

Wind from the East

The American and European multinational men who were competing in the seventies were remarkably slow to notice the intruders from a third continent who were to provide a much more serious challenge to them in the eighties.

The American oversight was the more surprising, after they had done so much to revive and reform Japanese business in their own image after the Second World War. Like the British in Germany, they had been determined to democratise the Japanese political system, to break up the pre-war cartels, to purge business of warlike leaders and to forbid any military industry. They did not realise that the combination was to provide the ideal seedbed for a spectacular industrial revival. The disasters of war had already provided the conditions for the kind of 'creative defeat' which challenged the Japanese – like the earthquake of 1923, which had been followed by a massive boom. The Americans also ensured that the corporations would be run by modernised and highly-motivated company men.

The old Japanese owner-families were compelled to sell their shares in the trading groups or *zaibatsu* like Mitsui, Mitsubishi or Sumitomo, which dated back to the nineteenth century or earlier. But the old connections still lurked below the surface, and the combines soon publicly re-emerged in a more dynamic form, run by younger managers from the universities with no capital, who made their own contacts with the shareholders, arranged exchanges of shares, and virtually hijacked the companies. 'The business world in Japan,' wrote Professor Morishima, 'was transformed from a club of rich men to a circle of university graduate businessmen.' And as the occupation forces retreated, the new groups, called the *keiretsu*, re-established close links to the government, who through MITI, the ministry of industry, helped to guide them towards successful exports to strengthen the economy. The *keiretsu*, according to one American investigation, came to be 'the most dynamic and efficient system of industrial finance yet devised'.

These new company men were a genuine meritocracy, much more classless than the old families, selected through highly competitive examinations from their companies' favourite universities. Mitsubishi had always favoured Tokyo University; Sumitomo had regional links with Kyoto; Mitsui was linked with Keio. The universities were much more practical than Oxford or Cambridge: they had left behind Confucian ideas that technical and commercial questions were unfit for gentlemen, and had embraced engineering as well as science. They were as meritocratic as the French *grandes écoles*, and as Ronald Dore puts it, 'They were built for a country which took industrialisation, and especially manufacturing, seriously.' They were not hotbeds or forcing-houses: they kept their distance from the world of profit, and allowed Japanese undergraduates to be remarkably idle. But they provided the motivation which enabled companies to train sophisticated engineers and managers with a network of like-minded friends. University friendships took the place of family connections, and reinforced the information system within each group: the ablest executives were far better informed about the world than their British or French equivalents. Company men from rival groups could work together closely when necessary, through the chairmen's connections over breakfasts or dinners, and when they faced a national crisis – like the oil-shock of 1973 – they could quickly work out an emergency plan.

The lack of a defence industry proved Japan's biggest advantage, for it deprived companies of the feather-bed of safe government orders at home and compelled them to compete fiercely abroad. Akio Morita, the son of a rich industrialist who had lost most of his money, started up a small electronics company which later became Sony, and realised that his only hope lay in export markets. 'In a defence industry if we achieve a target we don't have to pay too much attention to the cost,' he told me in 1988. 'But in a consumer industry we have to create new products at a reasonable cost. So we need more creativity than the defence industry.' Sony forged ahead with brilliant innovations and global marketing which made it a world leader, competing with the giant Matsushita (Panasonic) for electronic wizardry. While engineering giants in America and Britain were easily satisfied with profitable defence orders, Japanese companies were challenged to develop peaceful new technologies; ex-military engineers were given civilian tasks with spectacular results, like the bullet trains which pioneered high-speed railways. The name 'bullet train' – which the Japanese adopted – seemed to symbolise the conversion of warlike ambitions into peaceful projects. The pride in the regiment or the battleship was transferred to the company, and management schools channelled aggression into salesmanship. Military man was converted into company man.

The attitude to business as a kind of war was reminiscent of the nineteenth-century American era of business, when Rockefeller or Carnegie behaved like privateers or pirates; but the Japanese approach also had deep Asian roots. Sun Tzu, the classic authority on the art of war 2500 years ago, became the guide for many Japanese company chairmen, providing much advice which was relevant to contemporary business:

> All warfare is based on deception.
> If you know the enemy and know yourself, you need not fear the result of a thousand battles.
> Energy may be likened to the bending of a crossbow; decision, to the releasing of a trigger.
> The clever combatant looks to the effect of a combined energy, and does not require too much from individuals.
> Regard your soldiers as your children, and they will follow you into the deepest valleys.
> Keep your army continually on the move, and devise unfathomable plans.
> Be subtle! Be subtle! And use your spies for every kind of business.

Many Westerners regarded these aggressive strategies as part of a secret Japanese conspiracy to replace military conquest with commercial domination. But the motivation emerged naturally from people living in a crowded group of islands without their own resources who had to export to survive. The overriding need for exports compelled Japanese company men to become sensitive to the precise requirements of consumers all round the world. They instigated elaborate market research and intelligence systems which alerted them to every change in fashion and taste. They studied foreign customers as keenly as their own, as they designed typewriters, computers and calculators for the alien Western alphabet. It was the opposite priority to American manufacturers, who were conditioned to a profitable home market and ventured abroad as an afterthought.

The Japanese companies which emerged from the ruins of war were always more highly motivated than their Western equivalents. Two American consultants in Japan, James Abegglen and George Stalk, observed four main characteristics of these companies: they were determined to keep growing; they were preoccupied with their competitors; they ruthlessly pressed home their competitive advantage; and they were able to borrow heavily to finance their growth.

They were also more firmly committed to providing lifetime employment than most Western companies – which encouraged them to keep growing, to provide jobs. In return their employees were expected to be much more flexible than Westerners, and to shift when necessary into new industries. The more secure they were, the more they could adapt. This life commitment had only begun in big companies after the Second World War, partly in response to socialist trades unions, partly as a convenience when labour became scarce; and it was confined to about a third of the workforce. But in the bigger companies it massively reinforced the earlier Japanese tradition of familial companies and paternalist bosses: workers and managers knew their company would look after them like fathers. And like the IBM people at Endicott, they willingly joined in the demonstrations and company songs:

> For the building of a new Japan,
> Let's put our strength and mind together,
> Doing our best to promote production . . .
> Grow, industry, grow, grow, grow!
> Harmony and sincerity!
> Matshushita Electric!

The Japanese company men appeared to Westerners to be comically formal and conformist, deferring to strict hierarchies. At the bottom young men were underpaid and subservient to their elders; at the top old men were surrounded by underlings. Seniority appeared to depend on age: in the 1960s most presidents and chairmen of big companies were aged between sixty-two and sixty-six, ten years older than their American counterparts; presidents stayed in their job for an average of 13.4 years, compared to 5.7 years in the US. In the middle were the 'salarymen', all in dark suits, bowing to each other, exchanging business cards, striding out together in eager groups. There were reckoned to be twenty-five million Japanese salarymen by the late sixties. As for the factory workers, they seemed thoroughly military and obedient as they paraded and ran to work in their company uniforms.

This picture corroborated the traditional Western assumption: that the Japanese were a people with a collective brain but no real individuality or originality, like ants – a comparison lovingly repeated by the French prime minister Edith Cresson in 1991 – who were imitating Western ideas without understanding them. But the appearance was misleading. The basic culture of the Japanese company was derived not from Western models, but from the old structure of family enterprises before Japan was opened up, in which artisans were included within the family enclave. The family feeling in Japanese companies contributed more than paternalism and loyalty: it allowed easier communication between its members, and an ability to balance the stability of the older generation with the vigour of the young. While the Japanese companies looked gerontocratic, there were only a few old men at the top. The senior managers gave many opportunities to young men in new technologies, and allowed ideas and suggestions to flow up as much as down, with the middle-managers absorbing from both: what has been called 'middle-up-down management'. 'It is middle-management which is charged with integrating the two viewpoints emanating from top and bottom,' explained Tadashi Kume of Honda. 'There can be no progress without such integration.'

The Japanese, in spite of their fascination with machines, had a more organic and less mechanistic attitude to companies than the Americans or even the Europeans. They liked to use metaphors from the family or from nature, particularly from the forest, and to depict corporations like trees with branches and roots. To quote the authors of *The Seven Cultures of Capitalism*: 'The company resembles an organism that grows and develops, even more, it is a family with deep and affectionate bonds.'

Japanese companies, like Sun Tzu's armies, were much more flexible and fast-moving than they looked; and prepared to take bold decisions and act on them swiftly. They seemed to follow what some Westerners called the '80–20 rule': they spent 80 per cent of their time reaching decisions, and 20 per cent in implementing them – compared to the opposite in the West. They had no formal organisation charts, narrow specialisations or job descriptions: they were largely run by generalists who moved up through different departments, working closely with small teams through a mysterious but crucial process of consensus. How did they really reach decisions? Westerners inside Japanese companies were baffled. As one described it to me: 'You can't tell their seniority or hierarchies from their desks or offices – they keep on moving around. But they're very sensitive to what others are thinking. And they're amazingly candid in their small groups which meet every morning. They don't seem to have egos, yet they can be stubborn. They really do seem to have communal minds: they're scared of taking decisions alone.'

By the sixties the Japanese were already devastating their Western rivals across a whole range of industries, from radios and televisions to motorcycles and outboard motors. Their success seemed at first to depend on cheap labour and economies of scale. But they were learning how to achieve consistent quality and reliability, with the help of the American expert W. Edwards Deming, who had been largely ignored in his own country. They had embraced Deming's teaching that the flaws in mass-produced products were the fault of managers who failed to provide motivation, and they gave workers more responsibility and involvement. By the seventies Japanese companies were increasingly improving their quality.

They were confident that others could not replicate their own system of management. As Konosuke Matsushita told visiting Westerners in May 1979:

We are going to win and the industrial West is going to lose; there is nothing much you can do about it because the reasons for your failure are within yourselves ... For you, the essence of management is getting ideas out of the heads of bosses into the hands of labour . . . For us, the core of management is the art of mobilising and putting together the intellectual resources of all employees in the firm. Because we have measured better than you the scope of the new technological and economic challenges, we know that the intelligence of a handful of technocrats, however brilliant and smart they may be, is no longer enough for a real chance of success.

TOYOTA MAN

By the seventies the Japanese could challenge the United States in making the most American of products, the car, with a success which would eventually change the world's ideas about how to run a company. The story can be told through the development of a single company, Toyota. The Toyoda family – they changed the company's name because their own meant 'abundant rice field' – had begun to make cars before the Second World War, with meagre results. They were determined to succeed after the war, and in 1950 Eiji Toyoda, the nephew of the founder, visited Ford's plant in Detroit, like so many Western industrialists in search of the secrets of mass-production. After three months studying Ford he decided that he could improve on this rigid system, and back in Japan he asked his brilliant engineer, Taiichi Ohno, to devise something better suited to the different needs of both the Japanese consumers – who required a wider and more reliable range of cars – and Japanese workers, who were still influenced by craft traditions and reluctant to undertake repetitive tasks.

Ohno proposed a quite new kind of assembly line which could turn out a variety of cars by giving individual responsibility to the workers. He devised a far quicker way of changing dies – the hard metal moulds which shape the sheet-steel to make parts of the car – which allowed for rapid changes without holding up the line. He gave much greater scope to the workers by putting them in teams responsible for total quality at each stage in the assembly, with the right to stop the assembly line when any fault was discovered. It was not easy to persuade the union, as Ohno recalled: 'Although there was no increase in the amount of work or working time, the skilled workers at the time were fellows with the strong temperament of craftsmen, and they strongly resisted change. They did not change easily from the system of one man, one machine, to the system of one man, many machines in a sequence of different processes.'

Ohno gained the co-operation of the workers, who soon provided their own solutions, and welcomed closer involvement. To avoid the build-up of huge stocks from suppliers he devised a revolutionary system which would order parts only when they were about to be used, simply by sending back the empty container for the supplier to fill up. It was this *kanban* system, which Westerners called 'just-in-time', which was the most spectacular feature of the new 'Toyota Production System'; it eliminated the huge inventories and waste which cluttered up car factories. It was a ruthless discipline, squeezing the suppliers for ever cheaper and faster parts production; and Toyota was attacked as 'the factory of despair' in reports of the 'gloomy darkness of the auto kingdom'. But the real secret of Toyota was greater attention to the individual: both to the customer, who could order his special car without extra cost, and to the worker, who was much more involved in maintaining quality, much more 'industrially literate', and also better educated generally. He was part of a human team, rather than of a machine. The conveyor belt was turning out not only a different car, but a different company man.

The contrast with the old-style Western plants can be seen immediately at Toyota City, the huge complex of car-factories outside Nagoya, two hundred miles west of Tokyo, which has now become a place of pilgrimage for Western car-makers as Detroit was in the twenties. It is one of the world's great company towns, containing 300,000 people, of whom 73,000 work for Toyota. It was originally called Koromo city, after its silk industry, but in 1959 it was renamed after Toyota, which already dominated the town; in the same year the company built the Motomachi plant which has turned out Crown cars in successive models ever since, with one car emerging every four minutes. (The Japanese have continued to give their cars English names, including the quaint Gloria and Cedric – which deceived some foreigners into thinking that they copied their whole industry from the West.)

The Toyota system is laid bare at the Motomachi assembly plant.

Outside, trucks from suppliers unload containers full of parts at their separate stalls, and take back empty containers to be redelivered 'just in time'. Inside, the vast shed looks more like an exhibition hall or a theme park, with banners hung across the roof bearing the slogan 'Good Product', and a long walkway from which visitors can look down on the bright components gradually converging on the finished car. The empty car-bodies, painted different colours – mostly white, the Japanese favourite – trundle slowly across the floor, while their doors move above them, hanging from another line, waiting to be joined on. The car-frames pass through a succession of assembly areas – which look like artisans' shops with their collection of parts, screws and spanners – while the workers clamber over them, fitting the seats, dashboards or petrol tanks, and eventually lowering the engines into the frames. Each car's separate needs are indicated by a sheet of symbols, including a snowman indicating icy-weather conditions, a rectangle for American fittings, a P for power windows. At the far end of the shed the finished cars emerge from twenty hours of assembly to be tested, put into blizzard boxes to ensure that they're watertight, and driven round a track. Then they wait to be driven off – and to come to a standstill in the traffic-jams of Nagoya.

Every two hours loudspeakers play the tune of the Toyota company song ('Our company is young and energetic'), and the workers relax for ten minutes with their team, sitting round a small table, smoking and drinking tea. Some wear jerseys with 'Toyota' on the back, but most wear casual clothes. They all look at home, as if they owned the place, without a sense of dependence on management. 'We regard blue and white collar as the same,' I was told. 'In the US the blue collars can't move up to management, while the MBAs can become managers straight away: it's a mismatch.'

Why was Toyota so open, so prepared to show foreigners its secrets? I asked my guide Isao Inoue: 'We're more open because we're more confident,' he replied. 'We know it will take five years for others to copy us. If we lose confidence we'll become closed. We need to have continuous improvement: if we think there can be no improvement, the Toyota Production System will perish.'

How much further can the plant move away from human manufacture? I asked the director of Toyota in charge of the plant, Mikio Kitano, an exuberant man with a square-clipped beard and alarmingly wide grin: 'They regard me as an orang-utang, so I have to prove I'm a human being.' He was sceptical about further cuts in people. 'You can't drastically increase the rate of automation,' he replied. 'Assembly is for human beings, and machines won't replace people. The system isn't mathematical or systematised, it's a question of atmosphere – it's a quite different atmosphere from mass-production. The Toyota man shouldn't be a special person, but a natural human being.' My guide Inoue took the same view: 'General Motors had a fiasco when they used robots in the Lordstown, because they hadn't trained humans to control them. The final perfection of the car depends on the human being.'

INVADING AMERICA

During the seventies Japanese cars rapidly followed electronics into America and Europe; by 1979 Toyota had exported ten million cars. By the eighties the Japanese were increasingly building their own plants abroad, to move closer to their markets and to avoid being shut out by protection, and after 1985 the combination of the high yen and low interest rates encouraged Japanese companies to both build and buy abroad. During the eighties they had invested $280 billion overseas – equivalent to buying the whole economy of Australia. Cars accounted for half of this foreign investment. In the decade from 1982 the Japanese built in the mid-west of America a car industry bigger than that of Britain, Italy or Spain. In the words of the team from MIT which investigated their achievement, 'Nothing like it has ever occurred in industrial history.' Honda, which set up a factory in Marysville, Ohio in 1982, had the most spectacular success when in 1989 its Accord model became the biggest-selling car in the US. But Toyota remained the largest Japanese company.

Complete Japanese factories rose up from green fields in America, Britain and elsewhere, bringing Japanese methods into the old heartlands of Western industry; and with them came cohorts of Japanese company men, who dramatically increased the productivity of local workers. The enigmatic people who were hardly heard of two decades earlier were now crucial to Western economies: by the early nineties the number of Japanese managers abroad (according to Bill Emmott of *The Economist*) was around 300,000: most brought their families with them, and stayed between three and five years. They kept a low profile and remained discreetly detached from the local populations, staying in favourite hotels, using Japanese restaurants or food shops, living near the factories. But the broader Japanese success was apparent from the wave of purchases of highly visible properties, particularly in America, culminating in two famous Hollywood studios: Columbia Pictures bought by Sony, and MCA (with Universal Studios) by Matshusita. Japanese multinationals emerged as bogeys to Americans in the eighties, as American multinationals had emerged to Europeans in the sixties.

The Japanese company men were confident that they brought a better working life to the West. Their mass-production system still depended on an assembly line; but it provided a much greater human element which dispelled the nightmare visions of Chaplin's *Modern Times* or Fritz Lang's *Metropolis* or Aldous Huxley's *Brave New World*. It marked in fact the end of Fordism, and of Henry Ford's terrible assumption that 'A great business is really too big to be human.' It was more like a return to the earlier vision of industrial harmony outlined by Frederick Taylor before it was corrupted and brutalised by the tyranny of Detroit. The irony was striking: while the Japanese were being depicted by Westerners as a collective ant-heap with no real individuality, they had pioneered a system of mass-production which gave much more scope than Western factories for individuals, both workers and customers. And it was so successful that the American car companies could only survive by negotiating a quota for Japanese imports, to give themselves a breathing-space to catch up.

JAPANESE IN EUROPE

The Japanese impact on European companies was less drastic and less traumatic, for Europeans had long ago lost their economic domination. Britain was by far the biggest receiver of Japanese investment in the European Community, with 37.6 per cent in 1990, compared to Holland's 24 per cent and Germany's 8.2 per cent. And the British, in spite of lingering wartime memories, were quite hospitable to the Japanese who were prepared to build factories in decaying industrial areas. Akio Morita of Sony was encouraged to build a factory in Wales by the Prince of Wales, who opened it in 1974: 'Nobody could be more surprised than myself,' Prince Charles said after describing his first meeting with Morita, 'when two years later the smile on the face of the inscrutable Japanese chairman turned into an actual factory in South Wales.'

Sony and other Japanese electronic companies multiplied their British investment; but by the late eighties cars were making the most impact, as in America. Nissan opened a factory near Sunderland in the north-east, which had a history of hopeless labour relations; Honda opened a plant in Swindon which soon doubled in size; and Toyota opened in Derby. Japanese economic power was also becoming more visible in London, including Bush House and the old general post office in the City which became the plush headquarters of Nomura. Japanese restaurants and shops, led by Mitsukoshi, proliferated across London.

The Japanese interest was less flattering than it looked: they chose Britain partly because its workers were cheaper than most Europeans, and more prepared to do boring work. But the Japanese managers revealed how much they could improve on British managers. They attracted more company loyalty. They negotiated with a single union instead of the rivals that had caused so many disputes. They rapidly increased productivity, without strikes. Soon some factories could compete with their equivalents in Japan. And by the eighties the Japanese influences were beginning to change the relationship between British managers and workers in many industries. To quote Sir Christopher Hogg, the chairman of Courtaulds:

Thanks to Japan, we know we need the involvement of our workers: the Japanese have changed the whole way the British managers think about their workforces: they're much more conscious about motivation and commitment. When I was at the Harvard Business School thirty years ago they were talking about the maximum specialisation for workers to increase their productivity: it was the extreme of Taylorism, very exploitative.

Now everyone is aware of how the Japanese have motivated their workers.

The British-owned car factories had already been devastated in the seventies, and had only been revived by reaching agreements with Japanese. But the big European companies like Fiat, Volkswagen and Renault were at first less pressed to respond to Japanese methods. By the sixties they had only belatedly caught up with the full implications of the Detroit mass-production of fifty years earlier, and had hardly noticed that the Japanese were using new methods and teamwork to improve quality and efficiency. The Europeans, who had been rightly proud of their craft production of cars, were now trapped in the American system they had so despised. By the time they eventually faced the full blast of world competition in the early nineties they had to impose successive layoffs, with devastating political and social consequences (see Chapter 17).

The success of Japanese company men caused inevitable tensions with their European and American counterparts. They had quickly managed to convert the workers to their methods, but they were reluctant to promote Western managers to their higher ranks. The corporate citadel of Toyota in Nagoya seemed much more remote than the headquarters of Ford in Detroit or Shell in London, and the Japanese lifestyle and language remained a high barrier.

By the eighties Japanese multinationals were beginning to loom as villains in Western fiction and movies like *Black Rain*, as American multinationals had loomed in *Network* a decade before. The worst new American fears were reflected in *Rising Sun*, the novel by Michael Crichton published in 1991 and made into a successful movie. It portrayed a mysterious murder inside the skyscraper-headquarters of the Nakamoto Corporation in Los Angeles, filled with surveillance technology and ruthless executives who were bribing American politicians, paying off police and journalists. In his novel Crichton explains the sinister skills of Japanese company men, with their close-knit relationships, their inscrutable façades, their constant improvement in technology and their resistance to foreigners who can only succeed in their companies if they know their place. Americans must control their own destiny, or be overwhelmed. 'Japan is not a Western industrial state; it is organised quite differently,' he explains in his final chapter. 'And the Japanese have invented a new kind of trade – adversarial trade, trade like war, trade intended to wipe out the competition – which America has failed to understand for several decades.' But there was nothing new about adversarial trade: where Americans had failed was in catching up with the global pace of it.

Japan was now providing Western science-fiction writers and cartoonists with their nightmare visions of the future; human beings programmed by super-computers, transformed by bio-tech into mutants and whirled round the globe above desolate cities. William Gibson in *Burning Chrome* conveys a world dominated by Oriental multinationals who compete for brainpower with industrial espionage and corporate crime, while the hero sleeps in a plastic capsule in a coffin-rack hotel outside Tokyo airport. But Japan was exporting its own nightmares to the West, with its violent comic-strips and animated videos about Tank Girls and super-killers and its weird confusions between men and machines, as in the film *Tetsui, the Iron Man*, where flesh turns into metal.

Japan was influenced by the West more than the West was influenced by Japan. The changes on the surface of the big cities were breathtaking. When I first visited Tokyo in 1975 it still showed a forbidding face to a foreigner, with bewildering rows of jumbled low buildings covered by Kanji symbols and hoardings, and very few European letters or English-speaking people to show the way. Two decades later the skyline was barely recognisable, with clusters of skyscrapers and shiny new buildings: every crossroads had English-language as well as Japanese street names, subway maps and shop signs, while hoardings proclaimed Dunkin' Donuts and Kentucky Fried Chicken, French restaurants and Italian shops, and the streets were full of European fashions favoured by returning tourists. Some of the city-vistas could be mistaken for Manhattan avenues, concealing narrow lanes between the skyscrapers which still contained sushi-bars and cafés which made no concessions to foreigners.

The changes in Japanese attitudes were even more significant. Many company men who had spent years abroad maintained contacts with foreigners in this cosmopolitan world, and felt detached from their own traditional way of life. Living abroad they had become accustomed to a more relaxed lifestyle, while their wives enjoyed more freedom from the home, and their children enjoyed less discipline at school. They faced a shock as 'returnees' to more constricted surroundings, back to strict Japanese schools and social segregation between genders. In Toyota City there were seven hundred returnees, many of whom faced psychological problems. 'It takes about two years to be reabsorbed into the Japanese culture,' explained one Toyota man. 'It's hardest for the children between five and ten.' But the returnees with more cosmopolitan tastes and attitudes were also making themselves felt, particularly in Tokyo. For they held the keys to the next stage in Japan's development, as the exporter of capital and technology round the world.

CHAPTER TWELVE

The Raiders

The heroic role of the captain of industry is that of
a deliverer from an excess of business management.
It is a casting out of businessmen by the chief of
businessmen.

THORSTEIN VEBLEN, *The Theory of
Business Enterprise*, 1904

In the eighties American and British company men were finding their
security threatened not only by Asian competitors, but by a radical
change in the political mood, which questioned the basis of corporate
bureaucracies. They had come under heavy fire from the Left in
the sixties and seventies, for manipulating society, denying personal
freedom and collaborating with the military. But now they came under
more devastating attacks from the Right for being bureaucratic and
complacent in the face of global competition. The entrepreneur was
the ally of the neo-conservatives, and company man their enemy.

The words capitalism and capitalist made a triumphant comeback.
In the post-war decades the champions of free enterprise were
defensive, very conscious that socialism, communism and other ideal-
isms were far more stirring and confident forces in much of the
world. 'The prevailing theory of capitalism suffers from one central
and disabling flaw,' the neo-conservative economist George Gilder
wrote in 1984: 'a profound distrust and incomprehension of capitalists.' Peter Berger the political scientist complained in 1986 that:
'Capitalism, as an institutional arrangement, has been singularly
devoid of plausible myths. By contrast, socialism, its major alternative
under modern conditions, has been singularly blessed with myth-
generating potency.' Only a few adventurers extolled unreconstructed
capitalism, like Malcolm Forbes, the exhibitionist owner of *Forbes*
magazine, which he proclaimed (as early as 1965) 'the capitalist's

tool' – a slogan which he blazoned across giveaway shopping-bags as he toured the world on his yacht.

By the mid-seventies the neo-conservatives were heralding the return of the unrestrained capitalist; and the election of Ronald Reagan in 1980 – preceded by Margaret Thatcher in 1979 – was the cue for a major rehabilitation. The capitalist was reinterpreted as a heroic life-force, a bringer of growth, innovation and riches to others as well as himself, associated with giving and generosity rather than meanness and avarice. As Gilder explained: 'Capitalism transforms the gift impulse into a disciplined process of creative investment based on a continuing analysis of the needs of others.'

The central hero of this new drama was the raider, the champion of oppressed shareholders demanding higher share values and dividends, attacking the strongholds of big business. And company men became suddenly vulnerable, both to raiders and to politicians: Richard Darman, the Deputy Secretary of the Treasury under Reagan, blamed the sluggishness of the American economy on the 'corpocracy' who were preoccupied with their own comfort and their companies' interests. The men who were acclaimed a decade earlier as captains of all-powerful industry were now mocked as corpocrats and blamed alongside the government bureaucrats for the nation's decline.

The champions of the new entrepreneurs reverted to the older mythology of the late nineteenth century, which was influenced by Herbert Spencer, Social Darwinism and 'the survival of the fittest'. Capitalists once again adopted the metaphors of the jungle and ocean – lions, eagles or sharks pursuing and devouring their prey. When the British entrepreneur Sir Owen Green retired from the chairmanship of the conglomerate BTR in 1986 he was presented with a stone sculpture of an elephant, which he still keeps by his fireside, with the inscription 'King of the Industrial Jungle'. 'It *is* an industrial jungle,' he explains, 'but it needs a framework of law.'

Much of the glorification of the entrepreneur was due to economic upheavals, including the failure of Western companies to compete in world markets, the surge of deregulation and the growth of new opportunities in electronics and computers. But it was also part of a profound change in the social atmosphere which was turning against all the assumptions of collective responsibility which lay behind company men. And the dramatic imagery and personalised battles made business epics much more exciting.

The political shift coincided with a shift in thinking among zoologists, who were developing Darwin's theories of natural selection with special reference to genes. This was popularised by Richard Dawkins' book *The Selfish Gene*, first published in 1976, and admired by entrepreneurs, particularly in Silicon Valley. Dawkins debunked the theories of group-selection promulgated by books like Robert Ardrey's *The Social Contract*, which were popular, he suggested, because they were 'thoroughly in tune with the moral and political ideals that most of us share'. Instead, he argued that

We, and all other animals, are machines created by our genes. Like successful Chicago gangsters, our genes have survived, in some cases for millions of years, in a highly competitive world. This entitles us to expect certain qualities in our genes. I shall argue that a predominant quality to be expected in a successful gene is ruthless selfishness. This gene selfishness will usually give rise to selfishness in human behaviour.

The neo-Darwinian theories were also taken up by sociologists. 'Anyone who thinks life isn't a jungle isn't around,' the gangster Jimmy Hoffa had allegedly boasted: and the leading British sociologist Lord Runciman took this as his text in a lecture on competition in 1993. 'In all human societies, even the almost egalitarian foraging bands,' he explained, 'there is competition for control of the means of production, persuasion and coercion.' But Runciman found no evidence that competition was working towards any end-state. The new entrepreneurs of the late twentieth century liked to present themselves as part of a grand social purpose like their predecessors a century earlier; but Runciman sees human competition as a random process like that in the rest of the animal kingdom. We have to accept that 'nature is red in tooth and claw, that the human species is no less haphazard an outcome of evolution than the dinosaurs were'.

RAIDERS' WARS

The basic opportunity for the raiders lay in the low valuation of the shares of big corporations after the high inflation of the seventies; while new means of borrowing and raising capital, including 'junk bonds', gave them access to unprecedented sums of money with which to bid for the shares.

The most tempting prey were the oil companies, including some of the 'Seven Sisters' – three of them descended from the grandfather of all corporations, Standard Oil. Faced with the world oil shortage of the 1970s they had poured billions into new exploration which was always expensive and often fruitless, while their existing oil reserves had spectacularly increased in value, which was not reflected in their share price. Shareholders had an obvious grievance, which the boards were too complacent to face up to.

The first to exploit this was a maverick Texan, T. Boone Pickens, who had begun his career with Phillips Petroleum and left in disgust to build up his own company, Mesa Petroleum. After wasting millions drilling for oil in the Gulf of Mexico he realised in 1983 that it was cheaper, as he put it, 'to buy oil on Wall Street than to go out and look for it yourself'; and he embarked on a succession of raids on companies which, even when they failed, left him with huge profits after he had pushed up their share price. Pickens cast himself as a folk-hero, the champion of shareholders against the 'good ol' boys' in the big companies who were preoccupied with their 'four Ps' – pay, perks, power and prestige – and engrossed in their company planes, yachts and hunting lodges. 'It's the empire syndrome,' he explained. 'The managers look to their survival and the increasing size of their company.'

After Pickens failed to capture his old company Phillips he bid for Gulf, the venerable Sister which the Mellon family had established at the beginning of the century, run from its ornate thirties skyscraper in Pittsburgh. Gulf was now the weakest of the Seven Sisters, after it lost its half-monopoly of oil in Kuwait. Again Pickens failed to gain control, but his company made a quick profit of $500 million from the increase in Gulf's share price. He was outbid by rivals including

Chevron, a more prosperous Sister based in San Francisco and enriched by Saudi oil, which swallowed up Gulf. Gulf was lost to Pittsburgh, and the skyscraper was bought by New York investors.

Another Sister faced greater humiliation. Texaco, which like others was afflicted with dwindling reserves and unsuccessful exploration, made a bid to buy Getty Oil, which had been torn apart by rifts in the Getty family. Texaco outbid the Texan company Pennzoil which had just concluded an 'agreement in principle', but Pennzoil argued that their agreement had to be honoured, and sued Texaco: they were awarded record damages – later reduced to $3 billion. Texaco remained a separate company, but after a period of bankruptcy they sold off key assets, and emerged as a relatively small player. Only five Sisters now remained intact; and they were rapidly re-organising themselves into much leaner and more rational organisms (see Chapter 14).

The raids on the old oil companies were the precursors of much wider upheavals. By the mid-eighties raiders were beginning to unsettle all company men, both in America and Britain, as they challenged the security of corporations. A new breed of financier was mastering complex deals, underwritten by the banks who were looking for profitable loans, and by the invention of high-interest 'junk bonds' by Michael Milken, the 'grand sorcerer' who conjured up billions to finance American raids and earned half a billion dollars a year before he went to jail. The financiers were supported not by companies but by aggressive law firms and investment bankers who saw immense profits in 'mergers and acquisitions' and who could perceive opportunities more clearly than company executives. The lawyers masterminded teams of accountants, public relations experts and private detectives to encircle the target companies, with a single-minded ruthlessness which was often compared to war. They relished the language of combat as they filled their war-chests, launched their dawn raids from war-rooms, sprayed their enemies with bullets and took no prisoners.

Old-style attorneys and investment bankers watched the warriors with distaste. The lawyer-novelist Louis Auchinloss in *Honorable Men* (1985) described a ferocious raid in which a law firm hires private investigators to examine the personal lives of company officers: the hero Chip reads aloud a report about an executive who has indecently assaulted an office-boy in the washroom. His friend Lars exclaims: 'I haven't seen you so aroused since the war.' 'But it *is* war!' says Chip. 'And these people are as bad as any we fought in the last one.' In Auchinloss's next novel, *Diary of a Yuppy*, an immoral lawyer enjoys a raid which includes examination of 'abandoned property' – a euphemism for searching trash-baskets for incriminating documents. He discovers that the rival president has been protecting his alcoholic brother who has embezzled company cash; he is determined to exploit this information, to the distress of his idealistic wife. As lawyers became the buccaneers of company warfare they were acquiring a much less respectable popular image, projected in John Grisham's novel *The Firm*.

There had been four earlier waves of mergers and raids. The first had created the giants of the late nineteenth century, including Standard Oil. The second had created the new giants of the twenties, including General Motors and ICI. The third had produced the conglomerates of the late sixties, led by aggressive outsiders including Harold Geneen of ITT. But the fourth wave were less interested in conglomerating and empire-building. They had to restructure their acquisitions and cut down the company men to pay for the huge loans they had raised. They were financiers first, industrialists second.

One of the most enduring was Carl Icahn, a Wall Street trader with little presence or charisma who turned to buying companies and became one of the bidders for Texaco. He was even more critical of the corpocrats than Pickens: 'Texaco is the quintessence of what is wrong with corporate America,' he told a group of analysts. 'We have a corporate welfare state in this country, which is why we can't compete.' He failed to buy Texaco, but he did buy TWA, which had been one of the world's great airlines twenty years earlier but was now struggling against bankruptcy. He drastically reorganised it, reached an agreement with the unions, and managed to keep it flying. To his rivals' surprise he began deploring the 'casino mentality' of American business, and the decline of basic services: 'The infrastructure is crumbling, nothing new is built and nothing old is maintained.' But TWA itself was still flying on the edge of bankruptcy, too preoccupied with its short-term survival to make long-term plans.

GOLDSMITH

The most daring of the raiders were much more theatrical than Icahn, more interested in publicity and Hollywood-style glamour: for they needed fame to attract shareholders and raise loans. Anyone observing their raids (said the French economist Michel Albert) 'may be forgiven for thinking that he or she had accidentally strayed onto a film set'.

The most filmic, the Anglo-French financier Sir James Goldsmith, became the spokesman for all the raiders. He brought with him a European historical perspective, as the descendant of a German-Jewish family which had helped to finance the first Industrial Revolution; and he now presented himself as an activist in a new revolution, based on communications and information, which was destined to transform old structures. He made a plausible case for raids or takeovers as the means to liberate companies from complacent managers for the benefit of shareholders, and to force them to concentrate on profits. He firmly criticised the conglomerations after the earlier wave of mergers in the sixties: they 'had underperformed in growth, profitability, worthwhile capital investment, creation of employment and innovation'. He saw his own opportunities in breaking them up, and making their components more profitable. The role of takeovers, he said, was 'to improve unsatisfactory companies and to allow healthy companies to grow strategically by acquisitions'.

Goldsmith despised all bureaucrats, but especially the industrial corpocrats. 'I don't believe there's any difference under the microscope,' he told me in 1989, 'between the bureaucracy of General Motors, the Pentagon, the Kremlin, the Vatican or any of these major bureaucracies.' He relished the role of predator in the world's jungle and loved to depict companies in zoological terms, constantly needing challenges to revive them. 'One of the basic rules of nature,' he says, 'is that every organism including the human organism does the minimum needed to survive. People operate very differently when the pressure's on.'

Goldsmith was an actor on the stage he had created, with a tall frame and powerful eyes. He could fascinate both businessmen and women – he openly kept separate households for successive wives and mistresses. He seemed to have stepped out of a romantic novel with his combination of magnetism and confidence, like Scott Fitz-gerald's Last Tycoon: 'Like many brilliant men, he had grown up dead cold. Beginning at about twelve, probably, with the total rejec-tion common to those of extraordinary mental powers, the "See here: this is all wrong – a mess – all a lie – and a sham –", he swept it all away, everything, as men of his type do.'

Goldsmith moved his base to America in the early eighties, despair-ing of the constraints in Europe, particularly in Britain. He gambled heavily on Wall Street, buying up undervalued companies in the expectation of economic recovery. He specialised in timber companies with forests which would become much more valuable in a house-building boom. He bought the Diamond Corporation, which had first introduced the safety-match to America in 1882 and had suffered from diversifying, and sold off its assets to give him a profit of $500 million. He tried to buy another timber company, St Regis, but had to back down, taking a profit of $50 million. He then bought half the shares of Crown Zellerbach, became its chairman, and made a paper profit of about $400 million in a few months. His timber deals seemed like modern versions of old European myths about invaders cutting down forests: he was exploiting natural resources rather than bringing innovations or improving manufacture. Paradoxically he was to re-emerge in the nineties as a crusading environmentalist, persuaded by his brother Teddy to help protect the world's resources.

The most dramatic of Goldsmith's raids, against Goodyear, was turned into a kind of fairy-tale, of a foreign bogey threatening happy company men. The old tyre company had been established for a century in the rubber town of Akron, Ohio, and had grown rich through the car-plants in Detroit. Goodyear was now the only major American-owned tyre company, employing 133,000 people in twenty-eight countries: in Akron the sons and grandsons of Goodyear workers enjoyed a paternalism and local pride symbolised by its great rubber airship, the Blimp. The chairman Robert Mercer, who had spent thirty-three years with Goodyear, was the archetypal company man. Then in 1986 Goldsmith bought 12 per cent of Goodyear's shares. Mercer depicted Goldsmith as a predatory villain threatening the company town: 'You can't shoot down a Blimp and expect to get away.' He mobilised the local community into a righteous crusade with the help of the local Congressman, the grandson of Goodyear's founder, who compared the shock of Goldsmith's assault to Pearl Harbor. Goodyear took the case to the Ohio state legislature, whipping up political feeling against the foreign invader.

Goodyear also took it to Washington, where Congressmen were already holding hearings about raiders. Goldsmith himself popped up with panache, claiming that Goodyear had shamefully neglected its core business and wasted money on disastrous projects including a lunatic oil pipeline. He presented himself as the saviour who was restoring 'the life-giving link of ownership and management' and who had rescued many companies from tired conglomerates: 'Up and down the country, hundreds of erstwhile stagnant divisions of large bureaucratic corporations have been freed.' When he was accused of only being interested in his own profit he retorted: 'I can think of no other reason for doing business . . . I strongly recommend that the United States, which was built on that idea, remain on that idea.' Mercer complained that Goldsmith had forced Goodyear to abandon its long-term plans for the sake of instant gratification: he could not compete with Goldsmith's heroic style.

But Goldsmith saw the political mood turning against him, after opposition in Ohio and Washington and the arrest of the crooked financier Ivan Boesky. He decided to settle, and sold back his shares to Goodyear at a profit of $90 million. Goodyear organised a victory rally, and Mercer lamented that the company had sold its aerospace and oil interests and contracted heavy debts to fend off the raid. But in reality Goodyear still had a surplus bureaucracy, and when Mercer's deputy Tom Barrett succeeded him as chairman he soon complained that 'There were still too many layers of executives. We've got to break down the matrix system that's been building at Goodyear over the years.'

The melodrama of Goldsmith versus Goodyear – the lone raider riding into the company town – expressed two extremes of attitude towards business: the protective, paternal company challenged by the aggressive, short-term global dealer. Neither extreme made sense by itself. The company men could not adjust fast enough to the pace of world trade, while Goldsmith was always a dealer, never a builder.

And there remained a basic contradiction between Goldsmith the raider, surfing on the waves of mobile money, and Goldsmith the conservationist who respected the equipoise of settled environments. 'No matter how brilliant the technological revolutions, no matter how useful the economic and political initiatives,' he said in October 1989, 'there can only be hope if man can cast away his anthropocentric delusions and seek to find his place in nature, a place from which he can live in harmony with his universe.'

MOTHER OF BATTLES

By the late eighties the raiders had lost much of their political support and economic justification, but they retained their glamour, and could still make fortunes. Ivan Boesky, at the peak of his glory, had told graduates at Berkeley that 'You can be greedy and still feel good about yourself.' After his fall he became the model for the central character of the film *Wall Street* in 1987, appropriately the year of the Crash, in which Gordon Gekko, played by Michael Douglas, assures shareholders that 'Greed is good.' Gekko, like Boesky, is caught cheating through inside information and goes to jail; but he still appears a much more creative force than the complacent company men. By the late eighties corporate managers and directors were counterattacking the raiders through the state courts, and defending themselves with legal deterrents called 'shark repellents' or 'poison pills'. But the sharks were still more exciting than the repellents, and the concept of corporate loyalty was now at a discount.

The stock-market crash of 1987 induced a new sobriety and anxiety, but the raids still continued, more hectic and less rational. Between 1987 and 1989 mergers reached a new intensity: in the US 2730 firms were acquired, with an aggregate market value of $860 billion. And in 1988 the extraordinary battle for RJR-Nabisco, the tobacco-and-biscuit giant, provided a climactic extravaganza in which finance merged with showbiz.

The tobacco company R.J. Reynolds had its roots in the last century, firmly based on Winston-Salem in North Carolina. In 1913 it introduced its Camel cigarette and reaped huge profits from its cigarettes ever afterwards, dominating the company town from its twenty-two-storey skyscraper. But by the 1970s the anti-smoking movement was taking its toll: like other cigarette companies, Reynolds looked for a healthier partner, and in 1985 it acquired the huge biscuit company Nabisco which had originated from the 'biscuit trust' monopoly set up in 1898. Nabisco's conservative style had already been disturbed by a new chief executive, Ross Johnson, a relaxed and fun-loving Canadian accountant with a flashy young Californian wife, who was depicted as a new kind of 'non-company man': he was bored by biscuits, and relished the corporate perks, the luxury apartments, the fleet of planes and golfing holidays. He was a brilliant boardroom intriguer, and after the biscuits were merged with the cigarettes he took over as chief executive of both.

Johnson was impatient of the stuffy old cigarette town: he sold off some old tobacco lines, moved the headquarters to Atlanta, and spent much of his time in New York with cronies and celebrities. He wanted more financial activity, and in 1987 the banker Henry Kravis proposed a leveraged buy-out which, by borrowing huge sums of money, would give Johnson and six co-directors not only control but personal gains of up to $2 billion. It would be a triumph for individual ambition over collective responsibility.

There followed the mother of corporate battles, featuring many of the showmen-financiers of the eighties. Johnson made his first bid through Peter Cohen, the young chairman of Shearson Lehman, which was in turn controlled by James Robinson III of American Express; then John Guttfreund of Salomons joined the contest; then Henry Kravis, enraged at being left out, came back fighting. Johnson and Cohen raised their bid; but at the last moment Kravis made an offer which the directors accepted. Ross Johnson bailed out of the company with his golden parachute, worth $53 million.

Kravis had to raise $19 billion in cash to take over the giant company. He set about selling off components to reduce the vast debt, and hired Louis Gerstner from American Express to become new chief executive. Gerstner brought in McKinsey's, the consultants from his old firm, moved the headquarters to New York, and fired armies of managers. The surviving company men scarcely recognised the place: 'I don't feel I work for a company any more,' as one manager put it. 'I feel I work for an investment.'

The battle for RJR-Nabisco marked the climax of the raiding

frenzy: soon afterwards Michael Milken went to jail, Congress moved against tax loopholes, the banks clamped down on their loans, and mergers and acquisitions almost stopped. Five years later nearly all the chief participants had collapsed from their pedestals. Shearson's came close to bankruptcy, Peter Cohen was fired by his boss Robinson, who in turn was ejected from American Express. Henry Kravis was devastated by the death of his son, retreated from the public world, and separated from his dress-designer wife. John Guttfreund was deposed from Salomons after a scandal over fixing auctions for Treasury bonds. Only Ross Johnson appeared undamaged, enjoying his $53 million, travelling, playing golf and deal-making, quite unashamed of the attacks on his greed. 'I love the notoriety,' he said five years later to Bryan Burrough, co-author of the best-seller *Barbarians at the Gate* which had depicted him in scathing terms: 'Everybody knows me now. I still sign autographs.'

As for the company, it sold off several lines, fired thousands of employees, verged on bankruptcy and survived in a leaner form. But many investors now doubted the sense of combining biscuits and tobacco; and they talked of splitting RJR-Nabisco up into the original core businesses which had been set up in the nineteenth century.

THE BRITISH HEROES

The change in British attitudes in the eighties was more spectacular. Thirty years earlier a small group of raiders including Charles Clore, Isaac Wolfson and Maxwell Joseph had been reviled for undermining respectable family firms, exploiting workers and reverting to the laws of the jungle. Lord Attlee, the former Labour Prime Minister, called it 'Jungle red in tooth and claw, and particularly Clore.' But the arrival of Mrs Thatcher in 1979, and the subsequent privatising of nationalised industries, changed the whole mood. The raiders of the eighties were depicted by the media as national heroes, liberating companies from their overmanned bureaucracies. Even the most reckless gamblers were made to appear brilliant financiers, including Asil Nadir, the Turkish Cypriot who later fled back to Cyprus; the Australian billionaire Alan Bond, who went bankrupt; and the crooked newspaper-owner Robert Maxwell, who later disappeared from his yacht.

But a handful of serious entrepreneurs built up more enduring conglomerates with more dynamic and less complacent company men. The most influential was Sir Owen Green, an ex-accountant from Stockton-on-Tees who expanded his rubber company BTR into a group of niche companies with connected interests which he knew something about: what he called 'contiguity'. He despised the earlier financial conglomerates like ITT ('It was just milking cash cows, buying companies to prevent the benefit going to shareholders'), and he put much emphasis on leadership and motivation. As he explained to me: 'The secret of management is commitment to growth: it must never be static. I aimed to reproduce the most exciting time of people's lives, up to the age of twenty-five, when you think you can do anything. You can capture that era in a company, bringing out the feeling of growth, so that you can go higher and higher. Managers' morale depends on their sense of identity, the feeling that they're needed: they respond to being noticed.'

The most publicised of the British raiders was James Hanson, who had been knighted by Harold Wilson and in 1983 was ennobled by Mrs Thatcher. Like Goldsmith he developed a theatrical presence and striking entrances: he had once been engaged to Audrey Hepburn. He came from a Yorkshire family who, starting out with pack-horses, had built up a road-haulage business until it was nationalised in 1948; but in the privatised eighties he could reassert his entrepreneurial blood. In a succession of bold raids he captured old British companies including Ever Ready, Imperial Tobacco and Gold Fields, cut away their managers and overheads, sold off properties and enhanced their profits. Behind his stage-craft he was always watching the numbers: when he took over a company, as he explained to me, 'We'd do nothing for six months, while we put the ferrets in.' His ferrets, the accountants Ernst & Young, told him how to maximise profits: at Imperial Tobacco he halved the number of employees by rationalising the competing brands of cigarettes.

Hanson extended across the Atlantic, with his colleague Gordon White, another showman who duly became Lord White, and bought a succession of American companies. Hanson was not dominating the company men, he explained, but liberating them. As his vice-chairman Martin Taylor told me: 'It's not the bosses who judge the managers, it's the market.' Hanson's headquarters in London has only a hundred people, with another 150 in New Jersey, and he insists that his conglomerate gives much more opportunity for effective managers than the separate companies ever did. 'If people ask where they'll be in ten years' time, I can't tell them in which industry; when one is up, another is down: "What goes around, comes around".'

British company men felt vulnerable to the raiders who had benefited shareholders and shown up wastefulness and incompetence. The argument was dramatised in March 1989 in a private debate at the Bank of England (which I infiltrated) on the motion that 'Contested bids tend to be bad for industry', in front of an audience including both financiers and industrialists. The motion was proposed by Sir John Harvey-Jones, the former chairman of ICI, and Paul Nicholson of the Vaux Group, and opposed by Sir James Goldsmith and Martin Taylor from Hanson. Harvey-Jones pointed to Japanese and German companies which were efficient without the help of raiders, and protested that industry was not a casino: it needed long-term stability for research, which should be Britain's strong point. Goldsmith described how whole industries in Britain had rotted away under complacent bureaucracies; while raiders cleared the way for renovation and prosperity – a view endorsed by Martin Taylor of Hanson's. The audience soon sided with the raiders, encouraged by sharp interventions. Sir Owen Green attacked the hubris of company men and claimed that takeovers shook them up more thoroughly than competition. Robert Horton of BP thought the appeal to public interest was the last refuge of the scoundrel. Even Sir John Banham, then Director of the CBI, conceded that management needed to be 'under the gun' of potential raiders – though raiders, too, needed some discipline. The eventual show of hands showed massive support for the raiders – to Goldsmith's surprise. But it was a vote not so much for the raiders as against the captains of industry. 'They were in defensive mood,' said Sir Owen Green afterwards. 'They showed their non-leadership. The big companies are still far too bureaucratic: they can predict their careers for years ahead.' It was the bureaucrats who were the villains of the time, whether in private or public service. As Goldsmith told me afterwards: 'All organisations have an inbuilt tendency to degenerate. That is true of governments, political parties, international organisations, charities, trade unions, and also business enterprises. The almost universal symptom of decay, when it occurs in such organisations, is the swelling of central bureaucracy.'

But the drastic raiding, merging and firing brought dangers in Britain as well as America. They gave much more incentive to buying and selling rather than building up companies. 'A system which favours dealing in existing assets rather than generating new assets, physical and intangible, cannot in the long run be dynamic,' wrote Stanley Wright, an ex-banker from Lazards. And they inevitably devalued the specialists in products in favour of accountants who were inclined to see all products in the same terms. Consumer industries were taken over by managers who had little interest in the product – managers of drinks which they did not drink, tobacco managers who did not smoke, publishing managers who did not read. Whisky experts were swept aside by marketers trained to sell toothpaste or chocolate. The raiders indignantly denied that quality suffered: Hanson explained that his American coal company was run by a leading authority on coal. But people who took pride in their product were easily demoralised by the ferrets. Many proud British traditions suffered from the domination of accountants – even British beer was overwhelmed by a flood of better-marketed rivals from Australia, Belgium and even Mexico. And in manufacturing industries the neglect of the product was specially dangerous: for it played into the hands of the Japanese, who were obsessed with the quality of their products.

But the raids and rationalisations brought a greater danger to companies in flux: of more concentration of power at the top. However much managers were liberated and decentralised, the financial power was more tightly held by the single entrepreneur at the centre. The personality cult, the elimination of senior managers and the importing of outside consultants, all tended to strengthen the man at the top. The committees of the fifties and sixties, with all their weaknesses of indecision and self-indulgence, were often being replaced by the opposite extreme, by dominant leaders surrounded by yes-men and place-men. Republics were being succeeded by monarchies.

COMPANIES AND COMMUNITIES

By 1990 the main wave of mergers in America and Britain – the largest and longest in history – had ended. The American public's fears about raiders were dramatised in Norman Jewison's film *Other People's Money* in 1991, in which Danny De Vito played the boss of OPM holdings, which makes a bid for an antiquated cable company. The chairman, played by Gregory Peck, appeals to his shareholders to support him and accuses the raider of 'playing God with other people's money', while creating nothing. The raider replies: 'I don't make anything. I make money,' and persuades the shareholders to sell out to him. The community is eventually saved by the Japanese, who buy up the factory to make airbags.

The raids had been part of a deeper groundswell of economic forces which was continuing to transform the balance of power in big corporations. The high interest rates of the mid-eighties had massively increased the cost of capital, making cash-flow far more precious. Companies were pressed by the markets to pay out more money to shareholders. The raiders had greatly increased the burden of debt, which compelled managers to improve their performance to prevent the bankers taking over control. And the biggest shareholders, the insurance companies and pension funds, were becoming much more conscious of how they could exercise power, with very different interests from others concerned with corporations – management, customers and communities.

The pressure for short-term profits undermined the whole concept of the socially responsible corporation. The paternal companies of the sixties, like Goodyear in Akron or Imperial Tobacco in Bristol, had seen their future bound up with the communities in which they worked, and supported them with donations, artistic patronage or support to universities. Now that whole relationship was being undermined by the pressure to please shareholders and the threat of the raider. The confrontation between Goldsmith and Goodyear was part of a much wider conflict between more demanding capitalists and protective communities which could not be reconciled. 'The improved returns to shareholders,' as the American economist

Margaret M. Blair wrote in her study *The Deal Decade*, 'had to be achieved at the expense of other social goals of the corporations.' There was a clear contradiction between the two perceptions. 'However much we want our companies to be lean,' wrote the American Lloyd Cutler, 'we do not want them to be mean.'

It was not the same everywhere. The frenzy of raids, mergers and buy-outs had been largely confined to America and Britain. The Japanese and Continental Europeans looked on with growing amazement, seeing raiders encouraging the short-term greed of the shareholders, as they believed, against the long-term interests of both communities and corporations.

German companies, protected by the big banks which had large stockholdings and were strongly represented on their boards, had always been much less vulnerable than their British and American counterparts to shareholders; while most European companies were closer to the German than the American model. But the upheavals of American companies in the eighties had sharpened the contrast between different versions of capitalism which had quite separate historical roots and social assumptions. It was only the common enemy of communism that had forced them into the same category, and without communism they looked more distinct as they competed with each other. The European differences were described in 1991 by Michel Albert, the French economist and company president, in his book *Capitalism Against Capitalism*. Albert distinguished between the neo-American model of capitalism under President Reagan – which also heavily influenced Britain – and the 'Rhine model', embracing Germany, Switzerland and the Netherlands, which saw the company as a social institution and an enduring community, which earned the loyalty and affection of its members in return for its care and protection.

Albert observed the American raids and financial manipulations with alarm, against a broader background of American industrial decline, lawlessness, drugs and a widening gap between rich and poor: he took Tom Wolfe's *Bonfire of the Vanities* as his text. He saw the influence of showbiz as producing a caricature of capitalism which was undermining the discipline of industry and corrupting entrepreneurs: 'They have become personalities in a drama, and they must live up to the script or disappoint an audience of millions.' He believed the French were being torn between the two models, and urged them to choose the Rhine. But he feared that the glamour of the transatlantic financier was already corrupting the austere restraint of the Rhine company man or 'the discreet charms of a Zurich banker'. The Rhine model, he lamented, 'has no more status than some unmarried cousin from the provinces in dowdy attire, laden down with old-fashioned moral scruples and "afflicted" with the laughable virtues of prudence, patience and compassion'.

Albert's picture of the Rhine capitalist was too flattering; prudence and patience could mask a great deal of complacency and rigidity, which became more evident in the nineties as German companies failed to face up to the challenge from Japan. And Albert largely ignored the Japanese model of capitalism, which had been able to combine responsibility to the community with more flexibility and sensitivity than the German model. But he provided an important reminder that corporations were always part of the societies in which they operated. He saw how the raiders helped to transform the concept of the corporation which had first evolved in the Renaissance:

Things have come a long way since the word 'company' meant, as its etymology suggests, a community of interest, a mutually beneficial partnership of employers, employees and investors. Gone is the *esprit de corps* implicit in incorporation; companies are now merely cash-flow machines, subject to the whims of finance and exposed to the cruellest elements of stock-market speculation.

CHAPTER THIRTEEN

Computers: Command or Escape?

The easiest way to predict the future is to invent it.
Slogan of Xerox Palo Alto Research Center, 1970

While raiders and Asian newcomers were battering company men from the outside, a more insidious force was slowly undermining their strongholds from within. The computer was not only competing with them for their jobs; it was providing the means to create new kinds of company, run by irreverent youngsters with no respect for structures or loyalties, who thrived on apparent anarchy and near-chaos. Before trying to assess the transformation of companies in the eighties it is important to look at the accelerating influence of the instruments which became crucial to that change.

The computer bogey at first appeared as an extension of the long-running drama of machines versus men. After the Second World War many experts warned about its likely social consequences. In 1950 Norbert Wiener, the brilliant mathematician who invented and named the new science of cybernetics – the theory of the control of communications – wrote *The Human Use of Human Beings*, in which he warned that the power of computers to make decisions could overtake human priorities and decisions, and that American worship of know-how could prevail against know-what. 'Whether we entrust our decisions to machines of metal, or to those machines of flesh and blood which are bureaux and vast laboratories and armies and corporations, we shall never receive the right answers unless we ask the right questions.'

Over the next two decades computers appeared to give an advantage to big organisations over small – since they needed a large scale to justify their cost – and to autocracy at the top. They helped to dehumanise crucial decisions – a trend that reached a climax with the computerised bombing of Vietnam. And the big computer companies themselves tended to be conformist and hierarchical. IBM effectively maintained a semi-monopoly, all the more after its massive investment on its new 360 computers: the industry was sometimes called 'IBM and the Seven Dwarves'. Throughout the seventies the trustbusters had sought to challenge this monopoly, which IBM resisted with a huge team of lawyers who eventually won out in 1980.

The new industry at first required obedient company men. The future Presidential candidate Ross Perot joined IBM from the navy as a salesman, but left when his commissions were restricted, after reading in *Reader's Digest* a quotation from Thoreau: 'The mass of men lead lives of quiet desperation.' 'If I had stayed,' he said later, 'I would have become a grey, middle-management problem.' He set up his own company, Electronic Data Systems in 1962, selling IBM computers and systems; but he was determined to avoid the image of nerds and dropouts in jeans, thongs and beads. He recruited many naval and military officers, insisting that all men (like IBM-ers) wore dark suits and white shirts, and that all women wore skirts. His autocracy paid off: he made his fortune – ironically enough, given his later political views – by supplying computers for the burgeoning welfare system in the sixties, and by the age of thirty-eight he was a billionaire.

But the mid-sixties also saw the emergence of mini-computers, which were smaller and more flexible than IBM machines, after the invention of transistors and silicon chips. They gave scope to more rebellious young programmers and entrepreneurs, many of whom were rebels against the Vietnam war. The pioneer Digital Equipment Corporation (DEC) was soon rivalled by Data General, set up by defectors from DEC in 1968 – at a time of financial boom, Vietnam offensives and student revolt.

The eccentric style of the managers and programmers at Data General was vividly described by Tracy Kidder in his book *The Soul of a New Machine* (1982). They had discovered the secret computer language as schoolchildren, and still lived in a world of lonely childhood fantasies and science fiction: when they built two prototypes they called one 'Coke' and the other 'Gollum' – after a creature in Tolkien's *Lord of the Rings*. They called their boss 'Darth Vader', the villain of *Star Wars*. They were more challenged by machines than by people: one of them compared his excitement at work to Steven Spielberg's early movie *Duel* (1971), in which a car driver is relentlessly chased by a huge truck whose driver he never sees. Their view of life was clearly influenced by the computers' binary system, which accepted only two choices – right and wrong. 'It's a binary world; the computer might be a paradigm,' wrote Kidder. 'And many engineers seem to aspire to be binary people within it.'

The leader of Data General, Tom West, had left Amherst for a year to play the guitar in coffee-houses, and had become a computer engineer partly to escape the draft to Vietnam, partly to gain some control over complexity. 'I wanted to see how complicated things happen,' he said. 'There's some notion of control, it seems to me, that you can derive in a world full of confusion if you at least understand how things get pulled together.' He showed all the symptoms of the obsessive control-freak: at home he worked in a basement full of machines and ordered gadgetry, with a notice for his wife: 'What's a Place Like this Doing to a Nice Girl Like You?'

Kidder concluded that computers were not really revolutionary in their impact: they basically supported the status quo. But he endorsed Wiener's view thirty years earlier that they 'offered unbounded possibilities for good and evil'. And he prophetically warned that 'they might be used extensively to increase the reach of top managers crazed for efficiency and thus would serve as tools to destroy the last vestiges of pleasant, interesting work'.

SILICON VALLEY

It was not till the seventies that a new explosion of innovation in computers gave scores of young inventors the chance to bypass all existing corporate structures. They were concentrated in an area south of San Francisco known as Silicon Valley, which became the world centre of a new kind of company man. His spirit is expressed in the 'Tech Museum of Innovation', an exhibition building in San José still waiting for a grander home. It is a magnet for young computer freaks, who cluster outside the entrance gazing at an 'audio-kinetic sculpture' designed by George Rhoads, in which balls roll down from the top of an intricate structure and are sorted and distributed, sounding a bell as they pass. Inside the exhibition a bevy of children – nearly all boys, many with Asian faces – gaze at and play with gadgetry: a robot which can be told to dust a telephone; holograms with dogs and flowers in three dimensions, as a first step to Virtual Reality; tiny chips being wired up to provide the core to computers. The boys are engrossed in their private world of discovery and control, on the threshold of their magic kingdom.

There was already a climate of innovation in Silicon Valley in the fifties, as there had been around Newcastle where George Stephenson had built the 'travelling engine' in 1814, or in Detroit where Henry Ford had made his 'quadricycle' in 1896. In these climates ideas and news travelled quickly, inspiring young inventors like Ford, who saw a copy of the magazine *The American Machinist* which explained how to build a gasoline engine, and exclaimed: 'a barrel of money was to be made in it'. Several young computer inventors dreamt of huge fortunes; but the real prizes came to those who adapted others' inventions to the market-place, with a wary eye on copyrights and eventual profits.

The resources of Silicon Valley were not iron ore, coal, or any raw material: only education and brains. But its success was not as individualistic or anarchic as it could appear to visitors, for it had been underlaid by larger organisations backed by capital and inspired leadership. They were centred on Stanford University in California, which had enabled clever young engineers to set up new companies alongside the campus itself in part of the old ranch which its founder had endowed to the university. Near the campus at No 267 Addison Avenue, a leafy street of high-gabled houses, is a garage beside which is a bronze plaque, put up in May 1989, which commemorates its historic role:

This garage is the birthplace of the world's first high technology region, Silicon Valley. The idea for such a region originated with Dr Frederick Terman, a Stanford University professor who encouraged his students to start up their own electronics companies in the area instead of joining established firms in the East. The first two students to follow his advice were William

R. Hewlett and David Packard who in 1938 began developing their first product, an audio-oscillator, in this garage.

Hewlett-Packard grew into a giant corporation which became the grandfather of many small computer companies, encouraging many others who sought to benefit from young engineers emerging from Stanford and elsewhere. But the greatest benefactor of the new computer revolution was the Xerox company, which had made its fortune from a near-monopoly of copying machines: in 1970 it set up the Palo Alto Research Center (PARC), which it hoped would put the company in the forefront of the office revolution. They hired a brilliant Texan psychologist, Bob Taylor, who had worked for NASA and the Pentagon until he had been disillusioned by organising computer systems in Saigon; and he hired young graduates whom he supervised very informally, creating one of the first 'flat' organisations without middle-managers. Xerox PARC invented the laser printer and Ethernet, the first device to connect computers to printers: most important, in 1972 it produced the Alto, the first personal computer. But Xerox could not work out how to apply it, and the chief beneficiaries of PARC were researchers who set up their own small computer companies. PARC lost out, though it would show signs of recovering its vigour in the nineties, as it looked for entrepreneurial partners while protecting its own intellectual property.

The other historic seedbed was Fairchild Semiconductor, the company set up in 1957 by a group of young friends including Bob Noyce, the son of an Iowa preacher, who had been working with William Shockley, the inventor of the transistor. Noyce invented the integrated circuit, with tiny components on a piece of silicon which provided the crucial 'chip' for the personal computer. He also produced a thoroughly informal new kind of company without hierarchy: when his Eastern shareholders refused to let him give his employees stock options he left to found a new company, Intel, which remains today the leader in producing microprocessors. Other defectors from Fairchild were responsible for breakthroughs, but Fairchild itself languished: eventually in 1979 it was bought by the Schlumberger company, and was finally 'merged out of existence' by National Semiconductor in 1987.

Under Noyce, Intel developed the silicon chip into a 'microprocessor' which was itself a tiny computer, with immense potential but no immediate use. But Ed Roberts, a former air force engineer in Albuquerque, set up a company, MITS, which used the microprocessor to make a small computer which he called Altair. He sold it to a few experimenters, and in January 1975 an undergraduate at Harvard, Bill Gates, read about the Altair and realised that he could make a fortune by devising a standard programme for a massproduced version. It was the moment of truth for popular software. In six weeks Gates, with his friend Paul Allen, put together a programme called Basic which translated English words into computer commands. Gates realised, as his professor Tom Cheetam noticed, that the computer was about to cause a revolution. He dropped out of Harvard and moved to New Mexico with Allen to establish a new company, Microsoft, with a mission to produce 'a computer on every desk and in every home'.

The Altair computer, which had no keyboard, soon fizzled out, and its creator Roberts became a doctor in Georgia. The real breakthrough for the personal computer, as opposed to the software, came from a much more anarchic background – from the Homebrew Computer Club south of San Francisco, where Steve Wozniak, a young engineer from Hewlett-Packard, invented a small computer which he called 'Apple'. He improved it to the Apple II with the help of his still younger friend Steve Jobs, who realised that the machine could be sold to a mass-market. 'Woz' was the genius who devised the programme, the disk controller and the video display; but it was Jobs who saw the full possibilities. Jobs was a creative genius in the tradition of the inventor-pioneers a century earlier: like Gates, he compared himself to Henry Ford. He presided over his young engineers or 'artists' in jeans and trainers with the casual style of a professor at an alternative university, relishing fierce argument like a rap session. He wanted his kind of company town to be a model of a liberated corporation. He saw himself as a rebel leader – 'It's more fun to be a pirate than to join the Navy' – and compared Apple to Ellis Island, a colony of misfits. He was the champion of the individual: 'We build a device that gives people the same power over information that large corporations and government have had over people.'

Apple II found an exciting new application when Dan Bricklin, a young programmer at Harvard Business School, devised a software device called Visicalc which enabled businessmen to make complex calculations on the screen, on a 'spreadsheet'. Apple was sceptical at first, but enterprising managers found Visicalc a thrilling way to work out accounts without needing a big company computer. This came just at the time when business schools were turning out thousands of MBAs, trained in analysing balance sheets, cash-flows and business plans. Visicalc made Apple indispensable to them, and the tiny company in a garage infiltrated the heart of big business.

IBM's company men were slow to understand the significance of these new machines from an alien world which threatened both their central product and their style of management. But by 1980 their chairman, John Opel, took a bold step – to set up a separate division, detached from IBM's rigid hierarchies. He told its dynamic boss, Bill Lowe, to produce a personal computer within a year. IBM also needed an operating system or language; and for that they turned to Bill Gates, who had now established Microsoft in his home town of Seattle. Gates at twenty-five was both a master of programming and a shrewd negotiator (his father was a corporate lawyer): for $50,000 he bought an existing operating system from another Seattle company called QDOS (Quick and Dirty Operating System) and agreed with IBM to provide a modified system, to be called PC-DOS. It was a double whammy, for Gates retained the right to sell the programme to anyone else; and he was soon establishing his own monopoly, while IBM was losing theirs.

The IBM personal computer appeared a brilliant success: anyone (like myself) who was then confusedly trying to choose between untried machines found its name reassuring and safe; it soon outsold the Apple and gained a new boost from an accounting programme, Lotus 1–2–3, which rapidly overtook Apple's Visicalc. IBM established the personal computer as an essential work-horse for business, with a standard operating system, like a standard gauge for railroads. For a short time the powerful giant seemed even more powerful.

But the IBM PC was made of standardised parts that anyone could copy; and by 1984 it was competing with clones made by smaller companies which could respond to each new innovation more quickly. In Texas the Compaq company, set up in 1981, was soon making cheaper and more ingenious versions; not long afterwards Michael Dell, who had begun selling IBMs cheap as an eighteen-year-old undergraduate in Texas, began making his own clones, which became a major competitor. IBM, held back by its commitment to mainframes, could not keep pace. The contrast between the individual PC and the corporate mainframe became a metaphor for opposite kinds of company. But the more extreme contrast was between the makers of hardware and software, who had mind-sets worlds apart. It was not until 1985 that an IBM chief executive, John Akers, visited Silicon Valley. While IBM was heavily committed to its huge manufacture, Microsoft needed only brainpower and shrewd business sense. And the new software giants were now connecting up with new communications across the world.

The software innovators who made fortunes in the eighties came from a wide range of backgrounds. Mitch Kapor, who invented Lotus 1–2–3, came from Brooklyn and taught transcendental meditation. Charles Simonyi, who worked with Gates at Microsoft, was a teenage computer hacker in Hungary, the son of an engineering professor. Bruce Bastian, a Mormon, was studying computer science at Brigham Young University in Utah when he began writing a programme with his professor which developed into WordPerfect, one of the most successful of all systems. John Warner, who invented Adobe, which initiated desktop publishing, was a graduate student at the University of Utah.

These pioneers were not politically rebellious, and most came from middle-class homes. But they were cut off from ordinary human beings not just by their profession but by their boyish lifestyles and hobbies, including new-age religions and video games about dungeons, monsters or lonely battles. They were held together by their common obsession and language, a secret from others. They came from outside conventional business, and many were psychologically resistant to any kind of organisation. 'It doesn't matter whether you're ugly or graceless or even half crazy,' as Tracy Kidder described their attitude. 'If you produce the right results in this world, your colleagues must accept you.'

They revealed their isolation in the vocabulary of their software programmes, which seemed designed to bewilder ordinary customers while claiming to be 'user friendly'. They liked to give existing words quite different meanings; like 'default' to mean standard, or 'dedicated' to mean restricted, or 'icon' to mean symbol. Manuals which

were supposed to instruct secretaries were full of scary phrases like
'fatal error', 'abort', 'phantom rubout' or 'attempted write-protect
violation'. There were occasional grim jokes: an early Wordstar begin-
ners' manual showed a photograph of two policemen arresting a
young woman with the caption: 'Operator pushes wrong key.' When
it explained that 'J' stood for Help it said: 'This is a joke; there is no
J in "help".' The cryptic humour was a symptom of the insulation
of the 'nerds' from the rest of society.

APPLE

The isolated individuals had to come to terms with some organisation,
but all the tensions emerged in the stormy history of Apple, the
pioneer of personal computers. As it expanded Steve Jobs realised
that it needed rational administration and marketing, and found a
new chief executive in John Sculley, a master-salesman at Pepsi-Cola,
a company with legendary conformity and marketing skills. Sculley
was 'the guy from corporate America': he described how the Pepsi
men would gather in blue pinstripes, white shirts and 'sincere' red
ties, to analyse sales figures. He was the most eager of all: 'I was just
going through people, chewing them up.'

Jobs lured Sculley away with a question which became famous:
'Do you want to spend the rest of your life selling sugared water, or do
you want a chance to change the world?' At Apple Sculley redesigned
himself as a showman-salesman wearing an Apple T-shirt: he and
Jobs had a glorious honeymoon, culminating in launching the Macintosh computer with a $1.6 million TV commercial proclaiming it as
the champion of the individual against the Big Brother of George
Orwell's *1984* – the year of the launch. But the honeymoon soon
faded, and the arch-individual was on his way out. Sculley rashly
promoted Jobs to run the Macintosh group and soon decided he had
'created a monster'. 'When I look into your eyes,' Sculley's wife told
Jobs, 'I see a bottomless pit, an empty hole, a dead zone.' When
sales collapsed Sculley, pressed by his board, sacked Jobs from the
company he had created.

Apple recovered with the help of drastic cutbacks, new models, programmes and desktop publishing, and celebrated its tenth anniversary in 1987 with triumph. But Sculley was now caught up in his own hype. He depicted himself as a hero of the third wave, 'caught between the industrial and new-age times', a prophet of creative management like the conductor Rudolf Bing, or Harold Ross, the first editor of the *New Yorker.* 'The clues and inspiration for business systems in the future,' he wrote in his book *Odyssey* (1987), 'are to come from new disciplines and new paradigms. From biological cell theory, from Tao, from architecture, and from art.'

Behind all this verbiage Apple was falling apart, undercut by cheaper foreign models, overstaffed and with no real new breakthroughs. In June 1993 Sculley was replaced as chief executive by his lieutenant Michael Spindler, a much steadier influence, a German electrical engineer who had begun with Siemens and had made his name as a patient cost-cutter. Soon afterwards Sculley left to lead a rash new venture which came unstuck.

When I lunched at the Apple headquarters in Cupertino early in 1994 the company already seemed middle-aged, though the average age of its employees was still only thirty-five. The symbol of the munched apple was displayed everywhere, as a reminder of its early casualness; and there were exhibits of its daring new inventions, the Powerbook laptop and the Newton message-pad. But the atmosphere was now staid and unexciting, with grim regulations on the wall, including: 'Apple prohibits slurs or jokes based on any protected class.' Apple had not expanded for five years, and did not intend to expand further. Spindler had explained that Apple was making the transition 'from college campus to real business': he had set up a 'technology council' to weed out the many unprofitable projects which Sculley had endorsed. Apple was concentrating on its 'core competitivity', which rested on its ability to relate to the home; and Sculley was now a non-person, erased from Apple's memory. 'We still maintain a sense of insecurity by creating new enemies,' I was told. 'Bill Gates is now our iconic demon.'

But Apple was still very different from any conventional corporation. Their 'corporate mouthpiece' Frank O'Mahoney, who had recently moved from London, described how he found Apple's culture:

We're still very fluid. It's hard to have a career-structure: you can't impress the boss if you're working alone in a quiet room: you may be noticed but not necessarily recognised: you have to do some bullshitting. But your peers know much more than your boss.

After a new product has been launched 30 per cent of the team are looking for a job outside, for the next eight weeks. There's still constant movement in Silicon Valley: cultures carried from one group to another, creating all kinds of hybrids with the help of venture capital. Companies are always changing shape like amoebas. And it's full of individuals working from home: they only need a good brain and an understanding spouse.

There's not much institutional memory at Apple. When we celebrated the tenth anniversary of the Macintosh it was hard to find people who remembered it. We wanted to have an Apple museum but not enough early products had been kept. The consultants seem to know more about the history of Apple than we do.

In the shifting sands of Silicon Valley Hewlett-Packard withstood the winds and tides, retaining its special character. The two founders, 'Bill and Dave', were both billionaires in their eighties, but still came into the office. The company prided itself on a family feeling, an informality and sense of equality, expressed by open doors and first names: the chief executive, like many of the staff, arrived in a Ford Taurus. 'The HP way', said co-founder Bill Hewlett, was based on 'the belief that men and women want to do a good job, a creative job, and that if they are provided the proper environment they will do so'. HP liked to 'grow their own people', including many researchers from Stanford across the road, and found new ways of motivating and directing them: through widespread profit-sharing, through flexible time (imported from Germany) and through developing 'management by objective' (MBO) to give junior managers and supervisors more responsibility. By the seventies the personnel chief John Doyle was talking about 'management by wandering around' or 'staying in touch with the territory' – which might seem obvious techniques, but which other companies later welcomed as crucial discoveries.

Hewlett-Packard had kept ahead of most American companies in facing up to world competition: they moved into Germany in the fifties, and allied with Yokogawa in Japan in the sixties, which gave them a head start in strategic planning and quality techniques: 'We got religion,' as they put it. They rode high on the electronic and computer boom of the early eighties, with clever new products including cheap laser printers. By the end of the decade they looked more sluggish, held back by an overweight bureaucracy, but they began downsizing and decentralising: 'Almost no decisions are made here,' I was told in 1994 at their headquarters, a ribbed concrete block still next-door to Stanford University. Their new chief executive, Lewis Platt, was giving a new push towards digital communications, and the company appeared to have the right formula for the nineties: a big player which could retain its profitable core business, while making constant alliances with smaller companies. 'The HP way is still very strong, though people are always criticising it,' their 'communicator' Mary-Ann Easelee assured me. 'We still don't recruit from other companies: a lot of people leave, but they take the HP culture with them. We've become less paternalist: we offer employment security but not job security. We call it institutional paranoia.' Other big companies admired HP for its balance between organisation and freedom, big and small, and looked for its secret. But much of the secret came from the rare continuity of the two men who set it up over half a century ago.

Beyond Hewlett-Packard, Silicon Valley became legendary for its lack of loyalty. The turnover of staff went up to 50 per cent a year, and many top computer engineers knew they could easily find jobs elsewhere: 'If I want to change jobs,' said one, 'I just turn my car into a different driveway.' The cluster of venture capitalists in San Francisco encouraged young engineers with no money to break away and start their own businesses. Companies seemed more like temporary teams: like a Broadway production (as one Intel executive put it) whose producer brings together a cast of actors for a play, after which they disperse and look for a new play. They were reverting to the original meaning of a company in the sixteenth century, as a ship's company or company of investors, before the joint-stock system and the railways created impersonal giants.

This discontinuity caused many worries. In 1990 two well-

197

informed critics, Richard Florida and Martin Kenney, in their book *The Breakthrough Illusion*, complained that the 'hypermobility' was wasteful and destructive, as research programmes were disrupted, companies lost their institutional memory, and employees burnt themselves out, often ending their careers after ten or fifteen years. Venture capitalism, they warned, could become 'vulture capitalism' as it confined its victims to short-term perspectives, while the Japanese investors took a much longer view.

Yet it had its advantages. In the early eighties Silicon Valley faced an economic crisis as the Japanese invaded the market for semiconductors, and the Californian inventiveness appeared to be fading. But by the late eighties a new crop of companies had mushroomed, including Sun, Conner and Cypress, producing a new wave of innovations; while older companies including Hewlett-Packard and Intel fought back with more dynamic managers. The rival computer region along Route 128 in Massachusetts remained relatively stagnant: Digital Equipment (DEC), the pioneer of mini-computers in the sixties, was losing out to Hewlett-Packard in the nineties; Apollo, which had first developed engineering work-stations, fell behind Sun in California and was eventually bought by Hewlett-Packard.

A comparison of the two regions by AnnaLee Saxenian in 1994 suggested that the Californians' main advantage lay in their much more fluid business culture and environment. Massachusetts had relatively fewer companies, with centralised structures and information flowing vertically, which encouraged corporate self-sufficiency and loyalty. Silicon Valley bred a more individual culture with more porous boundaries between companies, but with a common infrastructure of education, finance and ideas which provided its own continuity, or 'controlled chaos'. 'When industrial networks are embedded in such a supportive local environment,' wrote Saxenian, 'they promote a decentralised process of collective learning and foster the continual innovation that is essential in the current competitive environment.'

Talking to computer experts in California, I found some agreement. John Markoff, the computer correspondent for the *New York Times*, explained: 'Silicon Valley has been innovative for thirty years. The innovation is linked to instability, with engineers wanting to become millionaires, and it does seem to thrive on chaos: it hasn't become stagnant like Route 128. It's survived the decline of defence spending and the shift of manufacturing to the third world.'

Or Paul Saffo of the Institute of the Future: 'Darwinism still prevails in Silicon Valley, with a wild contrast between success and failure. It's still a simmering cauldron of innovation, and insecurity makes for innovation: perhaps it's helped by being on the San Andreas Fault. But it's a very different place from Hewlett-Packard's garage: now it's a seedbed where things are born and transplanted elsewhere.

The veteran management expert Peter Drucker, though he lives in California, was much more sceptical, as he explained in his still strong Austrian accent:

> Silicon Valley is in bad shape: it confuses technical virtuosity with innovation. They used to get money by talking hi-tech but now they don't deliver: they suffer from a total refusal to be disciplined. Very few hi-tech projects work out in the marketplace. The successes are high-engineering companies, usually making one quite mundane project. It's been the same for every new technology over a hundred and fifty years. You know how many auto companies there were in 1920? Eleven thousand.
>
> They're anti-bourgeois people who still want to be billionaires, and greed ruins them: I've no sympathy. They don't want to run a business, it's too like hard drudgery: I've seen them kill the most promising markets by always trying to improve the product. They can't keep their fingers off. Companies in Route 128 are far more disciplined: they don't promise to make everyone rich. They bring in a few key people, with financial, personnel and marketing experience who know how to run companies.

Certainly Silicon Valley provided a unique business environment and fluidity, as different in its atmosphere from other regions as a rain forest from a copse, which enabled its inhabitants to break through into personal computers. It was both more individualistic and more communal: the innovators were motivated by direct personal gain more than by any corporate loyalty, but they shared a common outlook, and could pick up ideas and pass them rapidly to each other. Foreign businessmen flocked to California in the seventies to discover the secret; and soon no country felt complete without its own Silicon

Valley, Glen or Delta. But none created the same inventiveness, which depended on the mix of ambitious individuals, universities, finance and prevailing optimism. The profit-motive which elsewhere had been disconnected from industrial ambition was connected in Silicon Valley to genuine innovation and a vision of the future; and it provided the spur to a succession of breakthroughs.

The balance between organisation and chaos became more difficult as the first personal computer boom subsided and young companies had to adjust to middle age. The era of pure inventions has been succeeded by the more difficult stage of applying them to popular needs and tasks, which involves a long time-lag, as with steam engines or electricity. And it requires alliances with other companies who hold the keys to wider markets. By the 1990s the big computer companies were concentrating their energy on trying to infiltrate homes as well as offices. They were spurred on by the prospect of the 'information superhighway', which would link entertainment, information and communication over the telephone lines – all using the digital technology which computers had originated. This heady prospect brought computer bosses together with entrepreneurs from quite different cultures and experiences, like John Malone from the cable company TeleCommunications, or Barry Diller, chairman of QVC which pioneered home-shopping on TV. Each company was hoping to exploit the other: they were, as Malone called them, 'seven octopuses each with their hands in each other's pockets'.

But the battle for the home market would not be easy. Even Bill Gates, who invented the slogan 'A computer in every home,' had decided that offices, not homes, were the first target for the new technology: 'Once business is using multimedia,' he said in March 1994, 'then we can move to the home environment.' The term 'information superhighway' was anyway misleading. William Gibson, the science-fiction prophet who had first coined the word cyberspace, said the highway was more like a shopping mall, trying to sell people things they did not want. And the new networks along the telephone lines would be more like railways than roads, vulnerable to powerful cartels and to eventual regulation: there was a real risk (warned John Browning of *Wired* magazine) 'that instead of information highways, America will get information railroads run by information robber barons'. Who will be the robber barons of the future? The barons of the telephone lines, like AT&T or British Telecom? The barons of news and entertainment, like Rupert Murdoch or Ted Turner? Or the barons of software, like Microsoft or Novell?

The infiltration of the home requires skills which are very alien to most programmers and computer managers – the least domesticated of animals. The average family remains as fearful of computer technology at home as they were of 'the electricity' at the beginning of the century, which took years to be trusted. Computers, the marketing experts say, are only accepted by ordinary people when they are invisible, and most homes are already full of them, concealed in dishwashers, video-cassette players and telephones. The next stage of acceptance will be harder, when computer chiefs will require a much wider understanding to connect up their specialised technology to the broader needs of the home.

COMPUTERS AND CUTBACKS

The office remained the main territory of the computer, which had taken a long time to exert its full influence. Back in 1950 Norbert Wiener had warned that the automatic machine, when applied to factories, would produce a wave of unemployment which would make the Depression of the thirties look like a joke. But the next three decades showed no serious signs of automation or computers leading to mass-unemployment, while they achieved a huge expansion in mass services like telephones or airlines, and made possible the expansion of multinationals across the world. The vast roomful of typists or clerks commemorated in the film *The Apartment* was obsolete by the seventies, partly replaced by whirring mainframe computers; but new industries were growing up which still required the human touch. And in the eighties the arrival of personal computers brought about no corresponding departure of office-workers.

Computers were constantly being installed by businesses, ostensibly to save money; yet they showed no real evidence of increasing office productivity. In the decade to 1992 service companies in the US were reckoned to have spent $860 billion on information technology, while the service sector (which employed three-quarters of

American workers) was only increasing its productivity by 0.5 per cent a year – compared to 3.8 per cent in manufacture. A survey by *Fortune* magazine in 1991 found office productivity lagging far behind the factories; and the most productive companies tended to spend less per employee on management information systems than did companies with average productivity.

Managers who were fascinated by computers could easily be led to extravagant wrong solutions, without analysing the root of their problem. Big American companies, faced with huge inventories in warehouses, devised elegant computerised systems for storing and retrieving components, while the Japanese were discovering they could abolish inventories altogether through the 'just-in-time' system. As an MIT investigation concluded in 1989: 'We have spent over a decade and millions of dollars developing elegant Materials Requirements Planning Systems, while the Japanese were spending their time simplifying their factories to the point where the materials can be managed manually with a handful of Kanban (just-in-time) cards.'

The arrival of personal computers tempted office-workers to play games with them. (When I first installed WordPerfect for Windows I was surprised that it kept offering me a game of solitaire – until I was told that it was the favourite game of bored secretaries.) Computer buffs loved to smuggle their own games on to their hard drives, to play with each other in office hours, which was hardly surprising since they saw themselves as liberating computers from the bureaucrats. Office managers counterattacked by installing their own surveillance programmes to track down the culprits: Electronic Data Systems, the company founded by Ross Perot, installed 'data security co-ordinators' to inspect employees' computers to ensure that they were not having fun with them – or using them to run their own businesses. But dedicated computer-freaks could easily outwit corporate controls.

Computers were also creating their own bureaucrats, and the new industry of information technology (IT) was itself becoming a huge employer. Management consultants and accountants' firms were making fortunes by installing and managing expensive systems, which often needed more people to run them than the old one, and were soon outdated by yet newer systems.

In Britain some computer salesmen were practising the same kind of fraudulent tactics as horse-dealers in the nineteenth century; and by the nineties large-scale disasters were coming to light. The London Stock Exchange spent over £250 million on a much-hyped 'paperless' computer system called Taurus which had to be scrapped; while the British government, which was spending £2 billion a year on information technology, was involved in successive fiascos. Andersen Consulting, an offshoot of the accounting partnership, successfully lobbied for a computerised system for Wessex Health Authority in the mid-eighties which proved a disaster and cost taxpayers £63 million, with no effective redress. 'The civil servant doesn't really understand what he is being sold,' explained Robert Sheldon, the chairman of the Public Accounts Committee in 1993.

By the late eighties and early nineties, computers were beginning to show their power to take away jobs. In America recession at last compelled companies to take more advantage of computers to replace office employees, leading to gains in productivity. Alan Greenspan, the chairman of the Federal Reserve, explained in Washington in 1993: 'A new synergy of hardware and software may finally be showing through in a significant increase in labour productivity.' The banks and insurance companies were becoming more ruthless – or realistic – in firing employees. 'There has been a tremendous reversal of complacency,' said Stephen Roach, an economist at Morgan Stanley who had frequently criticised computer spending: 'Managers are finally getting the long-overdue payback from computing.' Roach found that the annual growth in the number of white-collar jobs in America had gone down from 3–4 per cent in the eighties to zero in 1991, since when productivity was growing equally in services and manufacture. Many experts saw this as only the beginning of a much deeper, longer trend towards cutbacks in offices. John Skeritt, managing partner of Andersen Consulting in the US, reckoned that 'Technologies like image processing, voice recognition, telephone banking, expert systems for doing loan evaluations, will continue to cause massive layoffs.'

As personal computers became more integrated into office organisation, they lost much of their idealistic appeal of the previous decade, as the liberators of young people from bureaucracies and officialdom. They were still thrilling instruments for loners, including writers, dealers and designers. But inside companies they were becoming part of the power-structures, associated with centralisation rather than liberation. They were linked up to central networks and databanks which could provide bosses with mechanical all-seeing eyes, showing them how to make cuts, enabling them to check on salesmen's performances, to bypass middle-managers and to replace them. Decisions taken through computers, as Norbert Wiener had warned forty years earlier, were overtaking human decisions: know-how was prevailing over know-what. And the spread of computers was speeding up the most ruthless purge of company men since the Depression of the thirties.

CHAPTER FOURTEEN

Corporate Crisis

Computer programmers, Japanese managers and global raiders had all challenged the assumptions of Western company men, and had thrown doubt on their solid pyramids of 'scientific management'. The computer, the strictest enforcer of logic, proved the most devastating enemy of the bureaucracies which had once appeared so logical. By the eighties nearly every big company faced a crisis of identity as it faced a more hostile and fast-changing world.

In 1980 two management experts, Robert H. Hayes and William J. Abernathy, published a devastating article in the *Harvard Business Review* entitled 'Managing Our Way to Economic Decline', which put the blame firmly on company men. They found evidence of 'a broad managerial failure – a failure of both vision and leadership'. And they blamed management principles which encouraged analytic detachment rather than hands-on experience, and preferred short-term cost reduction to long-term technological competitiveness. Strict financial controls were creating an environment in which no one dared risk a failure or 'even a momentary dip in the bottom line'. And too many top executives were 'pseudo-professionals', specialists in finance or law who moved between companies and ran them with no special expertise or interest in the product.

The keys to long-term success – even survival – in business are what they have always been: to invest, to innovate, to lead, to create value where none existed before. Such determination, such striving to excel, requires leaders – not just controllers, market analysts and portfolio managers. In our preoccupation with the braking systems and exterior trim, we may have neglected the drive trains of our corporations.

Leadership soon became the new rallying cry of the eighties, acclaimed as it had not been since Hitler had given it a bad name in the Second World War. In the post-war decades the complex committee-structures of companies like General Motors and Shell had been deliberately designed to limit the powers of leaders, while their scientific management was meant to be impersonal. Britain in the late seventies, said Sir John Banham, a future Director-General of the CBI, 'was a world in which people were seen as machines; leadership was best left to the discredited military'. But now chief executives, like raiders, were encouraged to see themselves more as predators in a jungle, or as leading guerrilla armies, 'slashing and burning', 'searching and destroying'.

The cry for leadership was taken up in 1982 by two management consultants, Thomas J. Peters and Robert H. Waterman, in their influential book *In Search of Excellence*. They urged managers to return to first principles: to attend to their customers, to be concerned with people, to experiment with trial and error. And they debunked the supposedly rational beliefs of the seventies: the assumption that big is better, that low-cost producers always win, that everything can be analysed. They warned against the kind of 'abstract, heartless philosophy' typified by Robert McNamara in the Vietnam war. And they urged more personal and risk-taking leadership which would concentrate on pathfinding and implementing decisions rather than just making them. 'If America is to regain its competitive position in the world,' they concluded, 'or even hold what it has, we have to stop overdoing things on the rational side.'

The whole system of scientific management established by Frederick Taylor, they insisted, had ceased to be a useful discipline. They called the change of thinking a 'paradigm shift'; but in fact they had not shifted their own paradigm far enough, for their ideals of excellence were based on several giant companies, including General Motors and IBM, which were soon to be models of what *not* to do. In his next book ten years later Peters confessed to an 'enormous error' when he was under the influence of earlier academics like Galbraith and Chandler who saw big corporations as 'almost perfect instruments'.

The American crisis was later summed up by the Massachusetts Institute of Technology which had set up its own commission to report on the decline of American industry, which they published in their book *Made in America* (1989). 'The international business environment has changed irrevocably,' they concluded, 'and the United States must adapt to this new world.' They criticised American companies for not 'sticking to their knitting': for failing to develop their own inventions, and preferring to buy up other industries for short-term profits, thus losing out to Japanese technology. And they gave their own devastating judgment on American company men:

> In the immediate post-war years they were complacent; they held stubbornly to an outmoded mass-production model; they set inappropriate financial goals; they relegated product realisation and production engineering to second-class status; and they failed to make the investments in plant, equipment, and skills necessary for timely product development and efficient manufacturing.

American individualism had been at the expense of teamwork. The American system of mass-production was no longer appropriate; it had destroyed the old craft tradition, and neglected the customer, without organising alternative systems of choice. And it had failed to provide human motivations and involvement.

The Commission's recommendations had an unmistakably Japanese flavour:

> Under the new economic citizenship that we envision, workers, managers, and engineers will be continually and broadly trained, masters of their technology, in control of their work environment, and involved in shaping their firm's objectives. No longer will an employee be treated like a cog in a big and impersonal machine.

The American turnabout was part of a broader rejection of business lifestyles and values which was forcibly expressed by Charles Handy, the British management 'guru' (the word itself implied that consultants were now acquiring a more philosophical dimension). In his influential book *The Age of Unreason* Handy argued that the world was entering a phase of rapid change and discontinuity which called for 'upside-down thinking', questioning such assumed needs as big companies, fixed working hours and even the need for managers at all. 'Management ceases to be a definition of status, of a class within an organisation, but an *activity*, an activity which can be defined, and its skills taught, learned and developed.'

The eighties saw a spate of books, articles and speeches which proclaimed the end of the once-admired 'scientific management' and the discrediting of conventional company men. The management consultants reclaimed their kingdom, with all the zeal of revivalist preachers, lecturing dramatically with flip-charts, diagrams, slogans and lists of imperatives. The missionary style was partly a throwback to earlier salesmen like Patterson and Watson, but now embraced also an Oriental element, reminiscent not so much of Japan as of Mao's Cultural Revolution, with magic numbers and rules: the three Cs, the five Fs or the seven Ss of McKinsey's. The rules helped to reassure demoralised bosses who did not know what had hit them, and who wanted consultants to take responsibility for cutbacks which they could not face by themselves; but consultants were also moving closer into the heart of business. There was an old joke that 'A consultant is someone who borrows your watch to tell you the time.' Now, they said, he was keeping the watch.

The battering from Asia put a premium on the more international consultants, of whom the most successful were McKinsey's, who had acquired a special authority and mystique. Their 3,000 consultants had the austere, puritanical style of a priesthood, wearing dark suits and white shirts, talking with cool analytical detachment, drawing neat diagrams and prescribing precise cures. 'The firm' had been established in 1926 by James O. McKinsey (who later ran the Chicago department store Marshall Field), and had expanded into Europe in the 1950s, and later to Japan, where their exuberant Japanese partner Kenichi Ohmae promoted the concepts of the Triad trading-blocs and a borderless world. McKinsey's lost their way in the seventies, after the oil shocks which they had failed to predict, and they were slow to diagnose the bureaucratic diseases of big corporations – they advised General Motors on a disastrous restructuring in the mid-eighties. But they benefited from their global range, multiplying the number of their consultants fourfold in fourteen years, and in 1994 they chose their first non-Western managing director, Rajat Gupta, who was born in Calcutta. They had extended their role from producing one-off reports to becoming semi-permanent advisors in a 'transformational relationship', and many McKinsey men took over as chief executives of big companies – including Harvey Golub at American Express, Michael Jordan at Westinghouse, Robert Haas at Levi-Strauss and Louis Gerstner at IBM (see next chapter).

The success of the consultants marked the failure of the company men throughout America and Europe who had lost sight of the market-place, which outsiders could see more clearly, or confidently. But the consultants had their own limitations. As global operators they were inevitably detached from any grass roots: 'A citizen of the world,' said Robert Reich, 'the management consultant may feel no particular bond to any society.' And they instinctively assumed that they could apply the same financial yardsticks anywhere, to any product. The conflict between the engineer devoted to his product and the financial expert devoted to numbers had recurred since the beginning of industry; but it reached a new bitterness as consultants told the experts how to cut back their lines – which seemed at odds with 'sticking to the knitting'.

Consultants usually strengthened the hands of the chief executives who hired them. Their proposals often turned out to concentrate more power at the top, by cutting out rival executives and simplifying the lines of command, with separate departments reporting direct to the boss. A dominating chief could employ consultants on short contracts to bypass and undermine the senior managers who might contradict him and get in his way. Ernest Saunders, the boss of Guinness who was later jailed for manipulating the company's share price, fortified his power through a young group of 'Bainees' – consultants from Bain & Company – who depended on his patronage. Any autocrat is likely to prefer mercenaries to an organised army, and consultants played their part in the shift of many corporations away from republics towards monarchies.

But the demand for consultants stemmed basically from the severe sense of shock which had hit most Western chiefs in the eighties, making them realise they must shake up their companies if they were to survive. Their danger was summed up in the much-quoted fable of the boiled frog. A frog sitting in water which is gradually boiled will die; but if he is thrown straight into the boiling water he will jump out again. The Westerners could learn much from the Japanese companies which had responded to past shocks with still greater energy and innovation, and which could trace their dynamic back to their greatest shock – the 'creative defeat' after the Second World War. The Western corporations had to face up to their defeat in order to fight back; and their case-histories showed that they would only do so at the last moment.

But the shock-treatments brought their own dangers; for in their desperate short-term need to cut back and turn round into profit, the corporations could easily forget the longer-term need to develop the products which were the reason for their existence.

GENERAL MOTORS' DELUSION

It was the American car companies which faced the most humiliating shocks. Japanese success called in question their mass-production and mass-marketing which had led the world since the 1920s, and the scientific management which Alfred Sloan had adapted from Taylor. The great pyramids of delegation, with all their specialists, middle-managers and lines of command, turned out to have lost contact with the ground – with the quality of their product and the needs of their customers. Managers had indulged in the hierarchies and the extravagant welfare system, while the pride of the old craft traditions, which still survived in Japan, had been obliterated.

The Detroit companies had based all their plans on producing a few basic models of the big family car, designed for driving long distances, using cheap gasoline. Their first warning came from the invasion of small European cars in the fifties, led by the Volkswagen. But the Japanese in the seventies produced a far deeper shock, as they provided cars which were cheaper, more reliable and closer to American tastes, while their production system was far more flexible in shifting from one model to another.

Ford was the first to feel the shock, and the first to recover. In the late seventies, when it began losing market-share to the Japanese in America, it responded by buying 24 per cent of the Japanese car company Mazda, which opened up its secrets. But by 1982 Ford was like the frog in the boiling water, with massive losses which threatened its survival, and it jumped. In the words of the MIT study *The Machine that Changed the World*: 'Suddenly, employees at all levels of the company were ready to stop thinking about how to advance their careers or the interests of their department and to start thinking about how to save the company.' Ford adopted Mazda's techniques in its American and European factories, and eventually exported Mazda cars under the Ford name to South-East Asia. It exchanged managers between three continents, and became the most genuinely global car company. Its executives harangued managers on the need for team pride, streamlining, customer-driven ethic, benchmarking and group dynamics. The underlying message was clear: they must become more like the Japanese.

General Motors took much longer to react realistically to its crisis, and its decline provided the most alarming warning of the immobility of huge bureaucracies. By the late seventies it too was losing out to Japanese and European imports, and in 1980 it made a loss for the first time since 1921 – of $763 million. The company, with low productivity and growing safety defects, clearly needed shock-treatment, but it jumped the wrong way. In 1981 it chose a new chairman, Roger Smith, short and squeaky-voiced, who was determined to be bold. He closed plants, cut down the staff and preached the importance of the three Rs – risk, responsibility, reward. Like his predecessors he was a lifetime company man: he had even helped Sloan write his book *My Years with General Motors*. But he had climbed up as a 'numbers man', detached from the plant and the product, and with a 'brilliance unimpeded by humanity'. He presented himself as a visionary of the 'factory of the future' who could turn GM into a high-tech conglomerate and beat the Asians at their own game. He built highly automated plants in Delaware and New Jersey, with robots costing $350 million per plant. But the new plants produced only two body-styles, with only average productivity. Smith's financial mind was removed from the practical concerns of the bureaucracy and the work-face, and he could never apply himself to the central problems – the people and the product.

Peter Drucker, revisiting General Motors forty years after he had written his first report, found it acting on the oldest delusion of managements: 'If you can't run your own business, buy one of which you know nothing.' Roger Smith was fascinated by other businesses. He bought Hughes Aircraft, the biggest producer of military satellites, and then in 1984 made a rash deal with Ross Perot, the autocratic boss of Electronic Data Systems, to connect up with computerised systems. Perot collected $2.5 billion for his half-interest and joined the board of GM, but he soon despaired of its slow-moving organisation and the pomposity of its fourteenth floor. 'I could never understand why it takes six years to build a car,' he said, 'when it only took us four years to win World War II.' He was ejected two years after he had joined.

Smith was more successful in dealing with the Japanese. After GM had lost a billion dollars in 1982 he negotiated a joint venture with Toyota, and his executives began their pilgrimages to Toyota City, where they belatedly discovered its secrets. 'It was the first time we really had a clear understanding of how they ran,' admitted Jack Smith, later GM's chairman: 'The data was just unbelievable.' GM soon collaborated with Toyota managers in a joint company, NUMMI (New United Motor Manufacturing Inc.), which in 1984 rebuilt an old plant in Fremont, California, strictly according to the Toyota Production System. The Toyota managers moved to California to supervise the team system, while the United Auto Workers union abandoned their elaborate job categories in favour of only two, workers and technicians. By 1986 the NUMMI plant was turning out cars with the same quality and almost the same productivity as Toyota City. It was clear proof that GM's past faults were not with the workers but with the managers. Mikio Kitano, the 'orang-utang' from Toyota City who planned the NUMMI project, described to me how it was done:

> It was a question of atmosphere, of people working in teams to help each other. Some Japanese said Americans couldn't learn it. At first the Americans didn't want to help each other, but then it became natural. You have to feel it not just in the brain, but in the body. I always argued that it could be done because we're all basically human beings. Now I'm more confident.

But Roger Smith did not extend the NUMMI revolution to other existing plants, which would involve massive layoffs and job-changes;

and the Japanese were much more interested in NUMMI than were the Americans. GM still did not feel sufficiently threatened to respond to the challenge. It was not till the early nineties that it faced its real moment of truth, when it closed six assembly plants and offloaded 74,000 employees.

The bitterest commentary on GM's decline was the film *Roger and Me* in 1989, which depicted the decay of Flint, the town where GM's founder Willy Durant set up his workshop, and which became one of the most prosperous communities in the world. Now GM was virtually closing it down, laying off 30,000 workers while opening up new plants in Mexico. Flint's decline was so great that it was voted the worst city in the United States. Michael Moore, the movie's director, had been born and brought up in Flint, where all his family worked for GM, and he filmed the symptoms of collapse: the main street boarded up, the houses disintegrating, the sheriff's deputy evicting twenty-four families a day. When he tried to interview Roger Smith – in the Grosse Point Yacht Club, in the plush suburbs or in GM's Detroit headquarters – he could never get through. Eventually he caught him on camera at GM's Christmas party, giving seasonal greetings while yet another family was being evicted. GM's public relations man Tom Kay explained: 'Cradle to grave security can't be accomplished under the free enterprise system.'

The film gave a poignant epitaph to Flint. But the real tragedy of General Motors lay not so much in the firings and evictions as in its past failures to understand its own success, which did not only depend on its mechanical systems and structures, but on the human motivation and involvement which alone could guarantee quality.

DISAPPEARING GIANTS

Nearly all the old-established corporations were devastated by the economic storms of the eighties: whether by Asian competition, by deregulation, by raiders or by more demanding shareholders. Some were shocked into recovery, some into death.

Among the 'Seven Sisters' of oil Gulf had vanished, and Texaco was much diminished after its lawsuit with Pennzoil. The oldest and biggest, Exxon – as Standard Oil of New Jersey was now called – had embarked on acquisitions and projects in the seventies which proved disastrous: they lost a billion dollars in Colorado shale oil. In 1983 Exxon changed course, offloaded 40 per cent of its employees, and began buying back its own shares to enrich its shareholders while protecting itself from raiders. All the Sisters now had a less confident identity. Chevron, which had gobbled up Gulf, was restructured as a looser group of companies. 'Whither the Chevron Way?' it asked in the final issue of its old house magazine, in which the chairman Ken Durr explained how decentralisation and cutbacks had put all Chevron's values and behaviours in flux.

The idea of 'the company way' was in retreat everywhere. Until recently nearly all companies had liked to emphasise their own corporate culture as the 'best way': what Marvin Bower of McKinsey's had described as 'the way we do things around here'. In 1982 a McKinsey book on corporate cultures had explained that 'A strong culture has almost always been the driving force behind continuing success in American business.' But the 'company way' turned into a bad joke as the bosses fired more and more managers: 'That's the way we do things around here.'

The Company Way had been specially visible in the airlines, which became the worst casualties of deregulation. Pan American, the most famous of all, had once seemed immortal. It had been the first international airline when it first flew in 1928 between Florida and Cuba, and over four decades it was the pioneer of global travel: first to fly across the Pacific, first to fly 707s, first to fly 747s. It was the 'chosen instrument' of the State Department, and its representatives were courted like ambassadors. Its omnipresence was proclaimed by its fat tower above New York's Grand Central Station, by its circular Worldport at Kennedy Airport, and by its chain of Intercontinental Hotels. But Pan Am had no domestic air routes to give it a firm base, and it overreached itself with the Jumbo, which burdened it with huge debts, followed by the oil crisis which took it to the edge of bankruptcy. The shock was still not sharp enough to save Pan Am in time. It sold off its hotels and routes and moved out of its skyscraper, but it was still top-heavy with layers of expensive managers – who deterred potential buyers like Sir James Goldsmith. Eventually in 1991 Pan Am disappeared without trace. Its collapse was rightly blamed on years of complacency, but fierce competition was undermining loyalty to all airlines and their 'company way', while their staffs now appeared interchangeable.

One giant company had the benefit of a compulsory shock. AT&T had virtually monopolised American telephones since its creation in 1899, and in the 1970s it reasserted its confidence from an overbearing new tower on Madison Avenue. In keeping with Parkinson's laws this marked its Nemesis, for in January 1984 AT&T was broken up by anti-trust action which divided its domestic telephones into seven 'Baby Bells' competing across America. But the break-up, like Standard Oil's in 1911, proved a blessing in disguise, for it released new energies among the components, who raced ahead while the rump company AT&T, under its chairman Robert Allen, expanded its long-distance network to forge links with computers and cellular systems. It was ironic that IBM, which had ruthlessly defied anti-trust action, was now withering while AT&T had been revived by the shock. As for the grandiose skyscraper, it was taken over by Sony – which was showing its own symptoms of over-reach.

Some of the old corporations still survived virtually intact after a century; notably those that 'stuck to their knitting', making the same product in the same place. King C. Gillette, a bottle-cap salesman, had invented the replaceable razor blade in 1895 in Boston, where the company is still based. John Pemberton had invented Coca-Cola in Atlanta in 1886, whence it still competes with its rival Pepsi, invented ten years later. William Wrigley began making chewing gum in Chicago in 1891; H.J. Heinz sold bottled sauces in the 1890s in Pittsburgh; W.K. Kellogg discovered corn flakes in 1894 at Battle Creek, Michigan. They still all make similar products in the same cities.

But many veteran companies were confused about their products as they finally emerged from 'the lengthened shadow of one man' into a world of fierce competition. Eastman Kodak had dominated the company town of Rochester, New York since George Eastman invented his camera in 1888. For most of the next century it had retained its lead, based on the same basic technology producing pictures on silver-halide film, and adding new inventions like the Brownie (1900), Kodachrome (1935) and the Instamatic camera (1963). But Kodak was slow to compete with Polaroid's instant camera, or Xerox's copying machine, and its markets were invaded by Fuji from Japan and Agfa from Germany, until by the eighties its profits were seriously slipping. It suffered from acute indecision and the familiar conflicts between product-people and finance-people. In 1983 a new chairman, Colby Chandler, cut it down, separated its components, and bought other companies. In 1990 Kay Whitmore, a company engineer, reversed the cuts, sold off the newly-bought companies and concentrated on research in electronic photography until he too had to cut back. In 1993 the board chose George Fisher, the ex-chairman of Motorola, who returned to electronic photography, proclaimed Kodak at the centre of the information revolution and sold off irrelevant companies. But he still faced a huge task to wrench Kodak away from its safe past into the unknowable future.

GENERAL ELECTRIC

Of the top twelve American companies in 1900 only one, General Electric, kept its place ninety years later. By the 1990s it had become the most admired American model for corporate recovery. But it was scarcely recognisable from its original character.

It was founded in 1878 by Thomas Edison, who invented the light bulb, and had expanded for almost a century without a serious upheaval, into everything from pop-up toasters to aero-engines and nuclear power. It maintained cosy agreements with its American rivals, only occasionally disturbed by anti-trust complaints. After two world wars it became one of the corporate 'generals', a key part of the military-industrial complex, with its own quasi-military structure which looked more permanent than an army's. Strong chief executives deployed divisions of conformist company men: plays devised by the company (as Kurt Vonnegut described them) 'made clear the nature of good deportment within the system, and the shape of firm resolve for the challenging years ahead'. General Electric developed strict financial controls, like its separate British namesake, and in the seventies it was ruled sternly by Reg Jones, a British-born master-accountant who reorganised its huge workforce of 400,000, with a team of 'sector' executives to assess future research and development.

But General Electric too felt the gales of world competition, with low productivity and dwindling profits; while its nuclear programme was set back by the accident at Three Mile Island, which revealed its true dangers. In 1981 the board chose a new boss: Jack Welch, the son of a train-conductor, a chemical engineer who had already asserted himself in the plastics division. Welch soon faced still fiercer competition led by the Japanese Matsushita and the Dutch Philips, who in 1983 bought part of GE's old American rival Westinghouse. At first Welch appeared modest and unassuming. 'I don't want to be part of a book,' he told Ralph Nader in 1984. 'I'm just a grungy, lousy manager.' And he showed a lively interest in allowing freedom of expression: 'It's really the heart of the issue. Can we take the punitive aspects out of having people tell us the truth?' But he had a driving zeal to reinvigorate the old corporation. He believed in passionate leadership, looking back to Churchill and Roosevelt as models. He had studied the Prussian military strategist von Moltke, who preached the necessity of flexibility. And he had learnt much about Japan. He realised long before most other corporate chiefs the full impact of unrestricted global trade, and vowed to make GE 'the most competitive enterprise on this earth'.

He developed a simple rule: every GE product must be either first or second in its own market, or be got rid of. He offloaded whole industries, including computers and the household appliances which had been GE's greatest pride. He reinvented General Electric with a clarity of mind which avoided the disasters of GM and IBM. But he also bought huge disparate businesses about which he knew little, including Employer's Insurance, the TV network NBC, and the investment bank Kidder Peabody. NBC soon sank from first to third place in the networks, and by 1994 Kidder Peabody was giving Welch appalling problems, with insider dealing and bogus profits which revealed a serious loss of control. Was Welch suffering from the same delusion as Harold Geneen or Roger Smith: 'If you can't run your own business, buy one of which you know nothing'?

Welch laid into the giant bureaucracy, rejecting the old obligations of lifetime employment, which he complained produced 'a paternal, feudal, fuzzy kind of loyalty', and offering instead jobs which were 'the best in the world for people who are willing to compete'. He fired people with a ruthlessness which earned him the nickname

'Neutron Jack': like the neutron bomb, he eliminated people while leaving buildings intact.

He was much influenced by the East, by China as well as Japan. He developed slogans and principles and devised educational sessions called Work-Outs which (said one of his consultants) was 'one of the biggest planned efforts to alter people's behaviour since Mao's Cultural Revolution'. There was indeed a Maoist tinge to Welch's 'Corporate Message', which proclaimed permanent revolution, and to his lists of five principles and three objectives. He could argue that nothing short of a crusade could change the mind-sets and habits of an entrenched bureaucracy, but was this a real liberation?

Welch certainly saw himself as a liberator, inspiring others to realise their responsibility and talents: his key slogan was 'Control your destiny or someone else will'. But everyone knew who was really in control. He had chosen his own men to push through his reforms and weed out 'resistors'. He replaced the old wedding-cake corporate structure with a 'cartwheel', with the thirteen spokes of the business units all radiating from his own office. There was now much less scope for opposition and balancing forces: he had replaced a republic with a monarchy.

Welch's methods influenced hundreds of companies including BP in Britain and Boeing in America, which sent executives to study his Work-Outs and systems of assessment. His consultant Noel Tichy, who had produced his own book, *The Transformational Leader*, promoted team-building courses which modernised the psychological systems of the sixties, to bring managers together for intensive courses to play games and learn how to communicate more candidly and solve common problems. But without the corporate security of the sixties some participants were worried about the real object of the courses: were they really for self-development, or for brainwashing?

DANCING GIANTS

By the nineties the shocks of global trade were forcing most American corporations to become much more flexible and agile, more like small companies. Rosabeth Moss Kanter, a Harvard professor who advised several, told them to 'learn how to dance'. But there was a huge gap between the bold precepts of management experts and the long, patient process of persuading lifetime company men to change their attitudes. To fire hundreds of employees was relatively easy: it was far harder to remotivate the rest to take a long view, in a much less secure atmosphere. And while American companies had taken much from the Japanese, they were now rejecting the principle of loyalty and security which was still central to nearly all Japanese corporations.

Entrepreneurs and raiders might know how to shake up, cut down or break up a corporation, but few knew how to build one up again for a continuous future. The eighties, with their huge rewards for financial operators, had diminished the status of the most effective company men who could plan steadily and inspire others to work harder. The business wars had thrown up two extreme types – the corpocrats and the cowboys, as Kanter called them – but neither by themselves could revive a company, while the combination was much harder to find. And the resolution was all the more difficult because the basic character of a corporation was in doubt. In the words of Kanter:

The corporation is an artificial construct; nothing about its definition says that it must endure or that it must be the central instrument for ensuring social welfare. But the corporation is also much more than a bundle of transactions; it is infused with meaning and value by all who devote their life to it and who, therefore, find that it is indeed the primary determinant of their families' welfare. We have counted on corporations to take care of people, and to take care of them for the long term. Today, however, even those corporations with strong values and concern for their people must make more gut-wrenching changes more rapidly.

CHAPTER FIFTEEN

Daddy's Run Away

Could Western corporations still take care of their people and remain 'the primary determinants of their families' welfare'? If not, who could take their place? Of all the downfalls of the eighties and early nineties, the most spectacular was that of IBM, which for most of the century had been a paragon of paternalism and security, apparently invulnerable to the vicissitudes which afflicted others.

Thomas Watson Jr had retired early from the chairmanship in 1970 after a heart attack; but his successors Vinson Learson, Frank Cary and John Opel had maintained the Watson tradition of lifetime employment and care for their employees, as profits and jobs continued to rise. In 1984 IBM's earnings doubled to $6.6 billion, a record for any company anywhere, while *Fortune* magazine reckoned it was the most admired company in America.

But John Akers, who became chief executive the following year, soon faced a succession of shocks which left him bewildered, with mounting competition from mainframe computers abroad and personal computers at home (see Chapter 13). The shrewder senior managers realised that IBM was suffering from bureaucratic paralysis – 'The management seemed to have totally lost contact with the product,' said one of them – and many able British executives left IBM at that time for top jobs in government, British Telecom or industry. But while IBM's profits were slipping their employees found it almost impossible to be fired, and there were still nearly 400,000 of them in 1989. It was not until 1992 that the full disaster became clear, as IBM made the greatest loss of any company in history, and was compelled to cut back its vast payroll through voluntary retirements.

The next year the board fired Akers, and after a desperate search they chose as his successor Louis Gerstner, who was reorganising

RJR-Nabisco. Gerstner was another ex-consultant from McKinsey's, who came from outside the computer culture, and had little reverence for IBM's paternal traditions. In March 1993 he made the break by announcing that for the first time IBM would lay off tens of thousands of employees.

To look at the social effects of this decision, six months later I made a tour of the IBM communities in New York State, where the company had grown up and built its biggest concentrations. I began at Endicott, the town on the Susquehanna River, north-west of Manhattan, where IBM was born. It still looked like a caricature of a company town, with the IBM clock-tower looming above Watson Boulevard, lined by a succession of IBM plants which provided a history of civilised industrial architecture. Outside the town the IBM Country Club looked out onto the IBM golf course. At the Homestead, the mansion on the hill, IBM people still came for training courses under the benign gaze of Watson's portrait.

It all looked fatherly, but there was now no father. During 1993, IBM Endicott had shed a thousand of its seven thousand jobs, and everyone was waiting for the next stage. The site manager, Thomas Ruane, assured me that there had been no layoffs, only voluntary retirement through the 'Endicott Transition Opportunity Program' (ETOP). He was himself about to retire at fifty-three, he said, on terms so generous that he could hardly afford not to: he could not wait to spend his time on the golf course. Ruane's successor Michael Flanagan, with an outgoing style and a wide grin, said that he had only two retirees who hated it. He had found no real psychological disturbance. I asked about a notice I had just seen at the entrance warning retirees not to enter without a permit: wasn't that an abrupt shock? Ruane and Flanagan looked at each other in wonder, and explained it was only a question of office security.

The IBM workers gave a rather different story. Lee Conrad, who was making cheque-sorting machines at Endicott, represented 'IBM Workers United' and was publishing a monthly newsletter called *Resistor*. It claimed that employees have been harassed and humiliated to make them retire through ETOP, which really meant 'Eliminate the Older People'. 'The stress level has increased remarkably,' Conrad told me.

The loss of capital had affected the local economy almost as much as the loss of jobs. All round Endicott there were enclaves of rich families who had inherited IBM shares: now the share price had toppled, and the dividend had been cut twice during 1993. But the workers remained much more vulnerable and dependent than the senior managers, who could always move on, while the workers were more static. 'There was always a very strong sense of community,' said one banker. 'The managers would joke about "IBM – I've Been Moved," but the workers were deeply rooted, with strong church traditions. They were personally loyal like lemmings.'

Local citizens confirmed the growing strains on society. 'IBM affects everyone, including other businesses and kids at school,' said the Mayor of Endicott, David Archer. 'It has a ghost-town effect. We have to re-invent our society.' 'There's a lot of stress,' said Irving Rothe, a thoughtful and respected doctor, the son of an IBM-er with many IBM patients. 'They didn't think it would happen. You can see it in the hospitals.' 'The layoffs have affected the whole psychology of the community,' said Dan Coughlin, the commissioner for mental health in Broome County which includes Endicott. 'We thought IBM was the Rock of Gibraltar. The demand for mental services has gone up by 33 per cent over eighteen months. There's a greater likelihood of fathers whacking their children. People think that as IBM goes, so goes the community.'

From Endicott I drove down to Dutchess County, alongside the Hudson River seventy miles north of Manhattan, which was really IBM County. The three IBM centres along the Hudson – Pough-keepsie, Kingston and East Fishkill – were employing 21,000 people at the end of 1992: six months later there were only 14,000. IBM never used the word layoff, but it was now an understatement. Stephen Cole, their manager of community relations at Kingston, said: 'It's a metamorphosis.'

Dutchess County has a look of rural prosperity, with fine farm-houses, wooded hills and pretty small towns; but it has always had a history of poverty and dependence – ever since the Duke of York, the future King James II, established it in 1683 and named it after his 'Dutchess', Maria Beatrice d'Este. In the eighteenth century the ports along the Hudson became centres of industry and trade, but the opening-up of the mid-west made the big estates uneconomic and the ports out-of-date. Many workers depended on families like the Roosevelts at Hyde Park, and during the Depression they came to rely on public institutions including prisons and psychiatric agencies which were provided (with FDR's help) by New York State.

Then in 1942 IBM had come to Dutchess: the company acquired a former pickle factory at Poughkeepsie and converted it into a massive plant, followed by others making mainframe computers, microprocessors and office machinery. IBM was soon the county's biggest employer, supporting a discreetly prosperous lifestyle. The plants along the Hudson were clean and landscaped, and IBM managers restored the old farmhouses surrounded by woodlands, from which they could drive to work in twenty minutes. Behind the rural façades IBM money was lurking everywhere – in the schools, roads, churches and colleges like Vassar or Marist.

But the county became dangerously dependent. As Hamilton Meserve, who owns five local newspapers, described it: 'IBM drained the responsibility from the county politicians: because IBM was there, they felt they could be against everything. IBM sucked up everything, creating a labour shortage. The county felt no need for economic development.' The vast IBM plants became the economic hub of Dutchess County, while the IBM Country Club became the social hub – an idealised retreat with trim lawns and manicured gardens where IBM children could play all day, and retirees could play continuous golf and compete for the Thomas J. Watson trophies.

This was in poignant contrast to downtown Poughkeepsie, the official county capital. The Main Mall looked like a faded film-set for a period drama, with dingy merchants' buildings from the 1870s, a low art-deco building and an old-fashioned department store called 'Up to Date'. It displayed notices saying 'I have a stake in Poughkeepsie'. But the only big stake was IBM's.

When IBM announced its first massive layoffs the county officials took some time to realise that no other employer could fill the gap. The empty buildings were full of expensive installations ideally equipped for data-processing, but not for much else. The county chief executive, William Steinhaus, watched the shock from painfully close quarters: he had been brought up as an IBM child, his father had been a corporate buyer for IBM, and he had watched the factories grow up from green fields. 'When we had health or family problems, my dad always said "IBM will take care of it,"' he told me in his spacious office overlooking the Hudson. 'I can't tell you how many social situations I've been in when the only thing an IBM-er could talk about was IBM. Their family, kids, travels, were all bound up with the corporation.' Now Steinhaus was having to face all the dislocations. 'We've realised that the community is very fragile: there's much more stress, domestic violence and need for mental services – directly linked to the layoffs. Even inside IBM, the environment has changed radically: they have great unease, without their security.'

The local churches felt the impact most keenly. I talked to Father James Heron, a tall, bearded ex-teacher who presided over the beautiful colonial church at East Fishkill, and half of whose congregation was dependent on IBM. 'We're ground zero,' Heron explained. 'This is real IBM country, and I was caught up in it as much as anyone. I've never experienced mass grief like this. It's as if Daddy has run off and abandoned them.'

He thought that IBM was too benign towards incompetent managers: 'It was like trying to get rid of a rector: it wasn't healthy.' But he blamed employees as much as the company. 'Paternalism is always two-way. IBM didn't impose their values: they gave people what they valued, and they ran with it. They were like parents who gave their kids too much.' He did not lament the collapse. 'People will come out from it with a better set of values. The IBM community was always a myth: they provided services but no real community or personality. I'm seeing an increase in the congregation, as in wartime. But the church doesn't provide a father-figure like IBM: it makes people accountable to each other. We're going to be a much healthier and more realistic place. God is teaching us a lesson in humility.'

Another local pastor, David Way, was himself in IBM before he saw the writing on the wall, and left to run a small church in Pleasant Valley, with IBM-ers in his congregation. 'They feel bitter and betrayed,' he told me. 'We were made to feel as if we were the cause of their failure, while the big guys were making millions.'

Could any other community take the place of IBM? Both pastors were doubtful. 'In the sprawl we live in here there are no clear emotional frontiers,' said Jim Heron. 'I'd like to respond that the church will,' said David Way, 'but it's not true.'

The retirees themselves took some time to realise what had hit them. To be an IBM-er or 'Beemer' was more like a nationality than a job: to lose that identity was almost like becoming stateless. When I sought out a sample of retirees, I found nearly all of them at home, and longing to talk about themselves. 'I don't think people understand the sacrifice and stress we've been through,' said Brian Moore, who had been a facility engineer at East Fishkill for twelve years. 'It was a family-oriented company, giving family parties and Christmas shows for the children. Now I can't even go to the country club. That hurts.'

'In January I was told my job was the safest in the nation,' said Mary-Francis Mitchell, who was in IBM's marketing services before she was 'surplused'. 'In February we were told half the jobs would be gone. People can't handle this stress: a lot of them have given up.' She decided to run her own counselling service with her husband.

'IBM was always very family-minded,' said one IBM parent. 'They gave a Christmas present to every young child, they had their quarter-century club, they sent flowers if someone passed away. Of course people became dependent, but who caused it? Now it's all changed: I went back to find an empty parking lot. Wow! It was like a movie about devastation in the year 2006.'

So who was to blame? Most of the ex-IBM-ers criticised the middle-managers, about 25,000 of them. What had they all been doing sitting by their open office doors in their dark suits and white shirts, looking at their notices saying 'THINK'? Programmers and workers called them 'zipperheads' (with heads full of facts waiting to be unzipped) or the 'Big Gray Cloud'. 'There were all kinds of people doing not very much,' said one IBM supplier who often visited their offices. 'One engineer left us for IBM and came back six months later, complaining that he could do his day's work in two hours.' 'There were definitely too many managers,' said Joe Davis, who had been IBM's international counsel before leaving in 1990. 'Every time they had a problem they wanted to be sure it would never go wrong again, so they set up another department.'

The middle-managers were blamed for IBM's inability to communicate with itself, in a corporation whose business was communicating. Michael Maccoby, the psychologist who wrote *The Gamesman* in 1970, was a former consultant for IBM, and continued to watch them closely. 'They had a highly-structured hierarchical system,' he told me, 'just when other companies were going the other way. The hardware of mainframes helped to create an inflexible psychostructure.

Their greatest strength became their greatest weakness.' Certainly the rigid mind-set appeared to make it harder for ex-IBM-ers to find work. Gene Moser had worked on the huge 360 mainframe computers until he was laid off in 1993. He saw the contrast between corporate mainframes and personal computers as representing the transition from corporate to individual enterprise – for which IBM had failed to prepare him. 'Half the IBM débâcle,' said Moser, 'was due to the mismatch between small machines and their management methods.'

IBM had anticipated that their laid-off managers would be in shock, and they hired the firm of Drake Beam Morin who specialise in the new arts of 'employee transition', 'outplacement', 'downsizing' and 'revitalisation'. As corporations got smaller, DBM got bigger: by 1993 they had sixty-five offices in the US, and another sixty-two abroad. The chairman, William Morin, saw the process of downsizing as part of a fundamental weakening of corporate loyalties. 'Companies are still shying away from saying people are responsible for their own careers.' For six months after the first layoffs, a team from DBM led by Charles F. Albrecht were installed in an IBM building in Poughkeepsie. Albrecht had the benign style of a family doctor. 'The more paternal the firm,' he told me, 'the harder it is for people to understand what has happened to them. But once they understand, they're marketable.'

The hardest ordeal was 'The Conversation', in which an IBM manager first breaks the bad news to his employee: he has to prepare it carefully, to ensure that the employee both understands the message and retains his dignity. The experience, Albrecht assured me, could affect the manager almost as deeply as the employee. The employee's first problem was usually: What do I say to my spouse? The advice was not to phone immediately, but wait to tell him or her face-to-face, to get the emotion under control and allay the spouse's first worry, which is usually about losing the house. Afterwards someone from DBM tries to identify the most brittle ex-employees, and revive their confidence. As Albrecht described it:

They've got to appreciate their value apart from the corporation. Many IBM people are naive about the worth of their skill-bank: they're much like the military in being team-oriented, and don't want to take credit. They haven't needed to sell themselves. The first need in the job-search is networking. In IBM they were in a family situation, with an imploded network. But outside it's different. Once they understand what an outside network is like, they're up and running.

But wasn't their whole identity threatened, I asked, after always being identified as an IBM-er? Some of them even wore their name-tags when they went shopping, to make sure they were recognised. 'It's a weaning process,' said Albrecht: 'When they're asked to give up the card which admits them to the building, they feel they're losing the last vestige of corporate identity. So we provide limited access, for a time.'

Surely it's more fundamental than that, I suggested, recalling conferences where everyone else wore a name-tag with their 'affiliation'. How do they survive without that? That's all changing, Albrecht assured me. 'In five years' time people won't be saying they're in IBM or in GM: they'll define themselves by their skill-bank. My own sons identify themselves as an accountant and a lawyer.'

But most outsiders in Dutchess County reckoned that IBM-ers have special difficulties in adjusting to the modest identity of self-employment, or a small company. 'We had two IBM-ers who came to us,' said Ham Meserve the newspaper-owner, 'but they only stayed two weeks. They live in an unreal world. Now when I advertise for jobs I'm tempted to say "IBM-ers need not apply".'

George Zornetsy, who ran a networking group in Poughkeepsie called JobNet, found ex-IBM-ers hardest to re-employ: 'They're used to a gilded cage. They've never had to write a resumé or to interview. They've had narrow and specialised skills, defined by their job. For some, being laid off is a social catastrophe. At first there's denial, then deep shock and fury. When they walk down the corridor their ex-colleagues pretend they're not there. Even kids ask them: "What do you do?"'

Dr Peter Leonard, who was teaching urban studies at Vassar, worked with the Dutchess Alliance for Human Needs which tried to ease the ordeal of the layoffs: 'The IBM people have pale confusion in their faces. We've tried to remove the social stigma, but we couldn't. They took the blame on themselves, felt the corporation had rejected them. They've always looked down on the problem of welfare: now they can't recognise that they're part of it.' He put much of the blame on the lack of community spirit: 'People always looked to the corporation, not to the county, and now they're paying a big price. The American ideology of individualism still maintains itself, even though it prevents our working together.'

How did it all look from the top? I revisited IBM's headquarters at Armonk, which I had first seen soon after it was built a quarter of a century ago: a chaste white palace in the middle of parkland, built round a symbolic Japanese garden to encourage reflection – now enhanced by a glass entrance-pavilion designed by I.M. Pei. Inside, the top floor still looked much the same, with spacious galleries with orange carpets and romantic portraits of the Watson family. Senior executives still kept their doors open; though they now had no notices saying 'THINK', and some even wore coloured shirts.

But the corporate line had totally changed. The new chairman, Lou Gerstner, had admitted many of IBM's past mistakes, its arrogance and introversion. In the September 1993 issue of *THINK* – still the house magazine – he complained that the bureaucracy had run amok, were too slow to market, and had lost control of the cost structure. But it was unfair 'to keep slicing quarter after quarter, laying off people. I mean, it is awful!'

To take charge of 'human resources' Gerstner had appointed an ex-banker and accountant, Gerald Czarnecki, an athletic man who enjoyed an argument. Czarnecki did not play down the problem. 'IBM *did* deliberately foster paternalism, with a social contract between employer and employee,' he told me. 'But economic realities forced us to rethink the relationship. Now we're no longer asking people for total commitment to us. They're eager to stay, but prepared to leave.' He put the collapse of paternalism in a long perspective:

A hundred years ago capitalism was pretty ugly, and unforgiving for those who failed. Later the big corporations created a kind of balancing act with governments, who supported big business even if they said it was bad, as a kind of quid-pro-quo for looking after their employees' welfare. But the market system didn't really work properly. Lots of corporations were semi-monopolies which dominated their markets; so they could do things which were not really economic.

Now there's a readjustment which needs a new balancing act. Every experiment in paternalism like this one has fallen. Local government is having to pick up burdens they can't deal with, and individuals get hurt in the dislocation. There's a real challenge to society: it's even worse in defence installations. But young people have got their heads screwed on: they are recognising the changing relationship with the company, and they're not discouraged. I never thought it was good for a corporation to take over the role of the family unit, which is more dependable for society. Now the pendulum will swing back, to give a larger role to the family. But there's still a role for all three – family, business and government – in parenting.

After my tour of the IBM company towns I could not feel it would be as easy as that. For IBM had deliberately embraced its employees in its corporate hug, while both families and governments had weaker pulls. The Poughkeepsie Country Club – now renamed the Convention Centre – remained a symbol of benign care, but it was closed to the layoffs. And the county, the churches and the communities could provide no easy substitute. 'IBM people have been locked into such innumerable benefits that they couldn't be ready for anything else,' said Walter Goldstein, a professor at the State University of New York who once worked for IBM: 'It's like being demobilised from the Red Army.'

But the IBM cutbacks were only an extreme case of the insecurity which was spreading across the West. Everywhere managers were suddenly finding themselves outside the 'comfort zone' and the 'security blanket' of the big corporations. And in Europe the break with traditional paternalism was made more abrupt by the underlying political swing.

CHAPTER SIXTEEN

The European Alternative

The American purges were part of a fundamental change in attitude to big companies across all Western countries. As the corporate lawyer Martin Lipton described it to me in New York in 1993:

> There's been a basic change in business philosophy. At the beginning of the century the purpose of corporations was to grow big, which led on to the creation of cartels worldwide. Then there was a shift of power to professional managers. Now there's disaggregation across the world, from AT&T to ICI.
>
> The basic reason is that big business has failed. The corporations haven't provided a steady increase in the standard of living, and corporate managers have fallen flat on their faces. In the seventies many of them lost their capacity for self-analysis and self-correction. Basically they've faced the same problem as the communist regimes in the East: the failure to perform.

The Europeans were in some ways coming closer to the American pattern, as they revolted against high taxes and bureaucracies and privatised nationalised industries, while their big companies were compelled to jettison managers to keep pace with the world competition. But they were traditionally less mobile, more community-conscious, and more reluctant to make extreme turnabouts than the Americans. They still preferred to see their companies in organic rather than mechanical terms, using metaphors from the landscape or from gardening (a favourite hobby of British chairmen). They talked about growing their own timber, cutting out the dead wood to make room for new growth, preserving the roots and extending the branches, transplanting and grafting, seedbeds and nurseries. They preferred personnel to human resources. The organic approach had its own dangers, for it could often justify vegetating and decay; but serious gardeners could be as ruthless as the most ardent corporate radical, 'slashing and burning'.

Europeans were more sceptical about the language of American management in the eighties, words which, observed the *Financial Times*, were 'creeping stealthily out of the software like a tarantula out of a banana crate, arousing a mixture of terror and curiosity'. The American management experts stressed the importance of human relations, but their vocabulary was still mechanical, about downsizing or right-sizing, re-engineering, delayering or re-architecting with interfaces or cross-functional interactions; while phrases like 'reducing the head-count' were euphemisms for firing people.

The accountants and Masters of Business Administration who spread out from the business schools developed their impersonal systems of business units, profit centres, internal markets and bottom lines. Many were essential disciplines which brought financial realism to amateur managers. But they often crudely ignored the human equations which were becoming still more important in creative enterprises. 'Who ever heard of anyone being loyal to a business unit or a cost centre?' asked John Tusa, the former managing director of the BBC World Service.

The British were more inclined to embrace the aggressive American model of management than other Europeans – or than the Japanese. 'It's bizarre that British managers look to it,' said Cary Cooper, the American Professor of Industrial Relations at Manchester, 'when the real success stories are Japan, Korea and Germany.' And the British managers' position was weaker, compared to directors and shareholders, than on the Continent. 'Employees in Britain, unlike those in virtually every other European country, just do not have the mechanisms to bring their influence to bear,' said Neil Millward, an ex-civil servant now with the Policy Studies Institute. 'We keep looking to America.'

Many British companies adopted American methods of 'team-building' like those of Noel Tichy, the professor of business who had helped Jack Welch to revolutionise General Electric. Some managers had to play 'touchy-feely' games, confess their mistakes, and discuss each others' faults; others had to wear masks, build houses with Lego, or work with handicapped people in the local community. But the

American imports appeared naive and conformist to most Europeans, with their greater scepticism and sense of irony. As Tichy observed in his study of General Electric: 'These touchy-feely, egalitarian methods may strike people from other countries as peculiarly, perhaps even laughably American. Without question they are rooted in American culture.'

END OF EMPIRES

The British had experienced many earlier layoffs in the course of their industrial retreat. The oil shock and recession of the mid-seventies had forced many companies to cut back their employees, most of all the stricken car company British Leyland. It had been nationalised in 1975 by the Labour government after it effectively went bankrupt, and to revive it the board in 1977 brought in a complete outsider, Michael Edwardes, a tiny South African without hang-ups about class who did not mind making enemies. He closed down factories, fired hundreds of managers and laid into the cosy privileges of the car-towns. He still could not revive Leyland as an international competitor, and after he left in 1982 it faced a new series of crises. But he had made history as striking an early blow for realism.

A more resilient casualty was Courtaulds, the old textile company which had been battered by Asian invaders. In 1979 they chose a forty-three-year-old chairman, Christopher Hogg, who showed his puritanical spirit by bicycling to work and writing his letters in long-hand. He had already been disillusioned about bigness when he worked in the Labour government's Industrial Reorganisation Corporation, which encouraged several giant mergers, including the General Electric Company run by Lord Weinstock. 'I came to think big mergers were daft,' Hogg told me later. 'The problems weren't structural; they were lack of professional management. Big companies may sometimes be necessary, but there are all sorts of negatives. All organisations are drags.'

At Courtaulds Hogg faced ferocious new foreign competition as the pound soared: he shut down almost-new factories, stopped making nylon, and reduced the workforce by 35 per cent in two years, down to 65,000. 'It was bloody awful but there was no alternative. The factory managers knew it; they took it so well, they almost fell on their swords – which made it still worse for me.' But when the world economy recovered, Courtaulds was again profitable and became a model for the leaner and fitter company of the future. Hogg later became still more sceptical of big companies and in the eighties he began planning to de-merge Courtaulds – with much internal opposition. 'Management always likes bigger companies: to get smaller seemed wimpish. But I knew from the start that it would release new energies.' So in 1990 Hogg finally split up Courtaulds into two smaller companies, with two chief executives, while he remained chairman of both. Hogg remains today an austere example (at least in his office) of the rational manager, working from his modest London headquarters in between serving as chairman of Reuters and adviser to the Ford Foundation. And he has provided his own mini-history of British industry over thirty years: reacting against bigness, cutting a company to the bone, then splitting it up.

There was one merger from the sixties which had remained intact and enlarged by further acquisitions: Weinstock's GEC (see Chapter 8). Weinstock remained a legendary financial controller, overseeing his plants from his dingy and dimly-lit offices in Mayfair, with sharp phone calls and alarming statistical questions. But he (like Geneen at ITT) showed all the limitations of purely financial disciplines, as GEC became more like a bank than a technological leader; and he dreaded risk-taking or delegating responsibility to engineers. 'To get Arnold to leave his desk,' said one of them, 'that's an event!'

The eighties had brought about a much more extreme change of mood, coinciding with the fall of the Labour government and the arrival of Mrs Thatcher. The public sector was most obviously affected as services were cut and successive nationalised industries were sold off. But private corporations were soon hit harder, as they were exposed to world competition and deregulation, without protection from governments. In the late seventies chairmen were still boasting about how many people they employed; by the early eighties some were boasting about how many they had fired. By the mid-eighties neither government nor companies felt any responsibility for maintaining employment, which had been a priority of post-war politicians. Both managers and workers found themselves facing a hostile world for which they had little preparation, and they rapidly lost the sense of security which they had seen as their birthright.

British company men faced different kinds of shock to the Americans. Older hands had seen themselves more as public servants than had American executives, enjoying a similar dignity and security to their counterparts in Whitehall. Many of the biggest companies, including Shell, BP and ICI, had after all grown up as ancillaries to the British Empire; and part of their downsizing reflected the tail-end of imperial attitudes, the final acceptance that they were multi-nationals in a global market-place, dependent on trading and dealing.

BP: DOWN FROM THE TOWER

The most spectacular cutbacks took place in BP, the oil company which had grown up from 1914 as a commercial arm of the British government, but which by the eighties was exposed to all the hazards of the global oil market. It had been run by a succession of autocrats, like imperial proconsuls, who had dominated both the company and Iran, whose oil they controlled, until Mossadeq nationalised it in 1951. BP retained its imperial style, with privileges and overmanning which were the envy of others. Its City skyscraper, appropriately called Britannic House, had fleets of company cars at the bottom, layers of managers all the way up, and the chairman's suite at the top.

But by the early eighties BP was becoming more like its multi-national rivals, while its managers were being squeezed by lower margins which forced them to cut back. The more they sold off superfluous businesses and sites, the more they realised the extent of their fat. In 1990 the board chose a new chairman, Robert Horton, an abrasive ex-engineer who had already swung an axe through BP's American subsidiary Sohio, and was much influenced by American ideas like those of Jack Welch at General Electric. Horton put forward a vision statement and a mission statement, devised a bold 'Project 1990', then a 'Project 2000' which abolished the company's elaborate hierarchy and committees, and trained managers to work in teams. 'There's only one sacred cow,' he pronounced: 'the existence of the corporation.' But there was another sacred cow, the managers observed, who never became part of a team: Robert Horton. He moved BP out of its skyscraper and into its earlier Edwardian head-quarters designed by Lutyens. It was smaller but more like a palace – with only one monarch.

The British managers accepted the team-building exercises more reluctantly than the Americans; but the promised new era never came. As BP's troubles continued, Horton cut still deeper, and the remaining managers coined the word BOHICA – 'Bend over, here it comes again'. In a decade the two thousand headquarters staff were cut to 350. Horton alarmed his own board as much as his juniors by his domineering style and by maintaining dividends which cut into the reserves. The outside directors, who were unusually independent, were persuaded to revolt by Patrick Sheehy of the conglomerate BAT and Lord Ashburton from Baring's Bank. In 1993, in an unparalleled coup, Horton was ousted and replaced as chief executive by his deputy, David Simon, with Ashburton as chairman. Simon has an almost opposite style to Horton: a small, unassuming man working in shirtsleeves, he seems a world away from the old proconsuls whose portraits stare down at him. He sees the empty BP tower as the symbol of an outdated command system which passed orders down from the top, while the Edwardian palace, redesigned with maximum internal visibility, encourages a democratic openness. He insists that the global hazards call for much faster flows of information: 'It's like a grocer's shop – you have to know where the margins are.' He sees differences with America: 'My hardest learning curve was realising the difference in Sohio,' he told me. 'They were much more Germanic, more regimented, paternalist than the Brits. In America they needed words like empowerment because they were really breaking the mould. In this country it's happening more naturally.' But Simon still pressed on with the cutbacks, and welcomed the end of the traditional BP company man. As he told me:

> The jobs-for-life syndrome is over. Young recruits don't expect to progress up the tower: they have no implicit promise of life-time employment, and don't expect it. Instead they ask: 'What can you offer me, to develop my skills? Am I growing, becoming more marketable?' We've discovered from surveys that most think they are responsible for managing their own career.

There's still a massive corporate loyalty among those who remain; but it's a change from dependence to partnership, and it's based on much more information. The more they know, the more their loyalty: and they feel proud that they're all competing. It's like a difference in families, between dependence and emancipation. I'm amazed by the difference in five years. We have to escape from the tower.

ICI DISMEMBERED

It was ICI which took the most drastic step. It had been through an earlier crisis in the seventies, when it too was hit by the oil shocks: its new chairman in 1978, Sir Maurice Hodgson, cut his employees from 90,000 to 73,000 in two years. But its performance was still lagging behind its three powerful German rivals, and it faced growing problems in the early eighties.

For once in 1982 the board made a bold decision, to appoint a chairman who they knew would rock their boat. John Harvey-Jones looked like a maverick, with his long hair and loud ties – his puzzled German rivals called him *der Zigeuner*, the Gypsy – and his giggling extrovert style was disarming. But he was both thoroughly rational and prepared to take risks. 'Big companies don't value risk-taking,' he told me afterwards. 'There's no way I would have been chosen if they hadn't been in deep shit.'

In five years as chairman Harvey-Jones provided a colourful new kind of British leadership: accessible, noisy and provocative. The boss, he insisted, must take responsibility for the company, and blame for mistakes. He criticised ICI's paternal, quasi-military hierarchies, its hoarding of scientific brains and its heavy bureaucracy, which he compared to the elephants' ballet in Walt Disney's *Fantasia*. He leased off most of ICI's palace on the Thames, cut the board down to eight and the support staff from 1200 to 400. He played up to his big shareholders, the pension funds, pushing up the share price. He became a model for industrial leadership in the Thatcher era, but he supported the Social Democrats and publicly criticised Thatcher for favouring the City over industry. His showmanship antagonised Tory industrialists: 'He's just a box o'tricks,' said Sir Owen Green, the former head of BTR. But he was the much-needed champion of British industry. 'I find it very difficult to convey to young people at universities the excitement and sheer honour of the job,' he told me; but he did convey it, first by his leadership of ICI, then as a TV hero in the series *Troubleshooter*. He believed passionately in individual commitment: 'You have to love the people, and the products,' he told me. 'Man isn't an economic animal, thank Christ.'

But ICI was still an unmanageable giant, and Harvey-Jones was less radical than he sounded; it was left to his successor to take the ultimate step of breaking the company up. Denys Henderson was an Aberdonian lawyer, less inspiring and outgoing than Harvey-Jones. He called himself 'an ICI man through and through'. By October 1990, facing lower profits, he set up task forces which concluded that ICI was trying to run too many different industries at once, just when Britain was entering a deep recession. In particular, the pharmaceuticals were as different from heavy chemicals as apples from pears, racing ahead while chemicals lagged behind. In May 1991 Henderson was already discussing restructuring ICI when he heard that the raider Lord Hanson had bought twenty million of the company's shares. He rejected a honey-hug from Hanson, who promised that he had no hostile intentions, but soon talked about his own plans to break up ICI. Both sides prepared for the mother of all British industrial battles – the biggest raider attacking the biggest manufacturer – and spread the usual smears about each other's extravagance and incompetence. By the end of the year Hanson had retreated, with a profit of £42 million for his shareholders.

Henderson was now more worried about ICI's bulk. The rigours of global competition, and the troubles of other giants like GM and IBM, were already making bigness look less attractive. Henderson borrowed a banker from Warburgs, John Mayo, to advise him, who three months later proposed breaking ICI up. Henderson was still cautious, but he consulted Sir Christopher Hogg, who told him that splitting Courtaulds into two had released new energies among the managers in both components. Henderson began talking publicly about how size didn't necessarily mean success, and in July 1992 he broke the news to the divisional heads: ICI would be broken in two.

It was a huge upheaval, involving a massive reorganisation and issue of shares, but it went ahead smoothly. A new pharmaceutical company, called Zeneca, was established with its own board and shareholders, and prepared to move out of the ICI building. 'I'm either a visionary or an iconoclast,' Henderson told me soon afterwards. 'I won't know for some time.' He quoted Sophocles: 'It will be evening before we know how splendid the day has been.' What was more certain was the clean break with the past. The United Kingdom's biggest manufacturing company had voluntarily broken itself in half, and turned away from the pursuit of bigness for its own sake.

SHELL, THE SURVIVOR

Shell remained the shrewdest and most flexible of the giants, the model for the multinational man. By 1990 it had overtaken Exxon to become the world's biggest oil company by turnover, and the most consistently profitable. It had avoided the buying-binges of the eighties which had weakened the American companies, and after massive losses in nuclear energy it concentrated on what it understood: 'sticking to the knitting'. 'I think diversification has to come from below, where the ideas and entrepreneurs are,' its British chairman Sir Peter Baxendell told me in 1982. 'Managers often don't realise themselves how much they fly by the seat of their pants.' Baxendell gave subsidiaries much more autonomy, while providing expertise and maintaining financial control as a 'friendly merchant bank'. By 1990 there were 260 separate units, largely autonomous.

Shell always took a long view, by looking at alternative scenarios developed by experts. They were less surprised than their rivals by the oil-price increase in 1973 after their chief forecaster, Pierre Wack, had warned them of a potential shortage. In the eighties, while American companies were buying up high-priced oil reserves, Shell was considering a scenario which saw OPEC weakening and the oil price collapsing. When that happened in 1986 they were better placed to buy their oil more cheaply, and to develop more as a trader than an explorer or producer. By 1993 they were looking at new rival scenarios ranging from 'Barricades' to 'Wider Frontiers', including the implications of electric cars. And Shell were shrewd in maintaining their relations with awkward countries: when their British chairman Sir Peter Holmes was faced with an anti-apartheid boycott against Shell's South African operations, he helped to finance training programmes for young ANC supporters.

The basis of Shell's success was its decentralisation, and the continuity of its company men. It had pioneered graduate recruitment, as we have seen; and despite its over-cautious attitudes in the late sixties and seventies it still had one of the most intelligent of all management teams, still 'growing its own timber' as its Dutch chairman Lo van Wachem explained in 1991. It still attracted exceptional loyalty: it recruited about 400 graduates each year from Britain and Holland, and had kept three-quarters of them five years later, while the average company only kept a half. It still moved them for regular stints across the world, like diplomats, planning their future fifteen years ahead. If they did leave Shell they usually prospered elsewhere (like Bob Reid, who became chairman of British Rail; or Charles Handy the guru).

But in the nineties Shell, too, was feeling the gales of competition, and having to rethink its attitudes to loyalty. Young recruits were less prepared to be packed off to Nigeria or Syria, while veterans complained that the tradition of service had died. The managers tried to find a middle way, between human and mechanical solutions. In the words of Mourik Broekman, their 'Co-ordinator for Human Resources', in 1993:

> We have to choose between the control model of the past, and the organic model of the future. If you rely on control you won't get as much out of managers as before; but the organic model can be dangerous – unless you believe that people are naturally virtuous. The old steep pyramid gave more control: now the pyramid is much flatter, which makes control harder. There's a danger of trying to clone people, but we don't go out of our way to break the Shell mould.
>
> Managers now spend more time managing people, and providing leadership – not necessarily leading into battle, but sharing with others what you want to achieve. Sharing information

becomes more crucial, and it's only secondary to people. People want to know the purpose of what they're doing, even if it's a menial task.

But it can take six months to make people understand a change of direction, and people are unbelievably clever in justifying their jobs. Shell has a gradualist culture, but can we afford the luxury of gradualism?

THE EUROPEAN CRISIS

Like the Americans, most of the biggest European companies were facing some crisis of identity: realising that centralised control prevented the flexibility and creativity that were essential to keep up with change. Some prophets foresaw the collapse of all the giants, like dinosaurs, or a succession of break-ups like ICI's. Yet large resources and concentrated skills were still essential in most heavy industries engaged in world competition. And the most successful companies, like Shell, still maintained a core of senior company men who could combine institutional experience with innovation, who could maintain a corporate network across the world with political agility.

Unilever, the other Anglo-Dutch giant, was constantly changing the balance between the centre and the provinces as it fought back its global rivals including Procter & Gamble, Nestlé and Colgate. It cut its headquarters and managers with the help of computers: in the decade to 1994 the number of employees had stayed at 300,000 while it doubled its turnover. It had developed subtler centralised controls, while still sending young managers into the developing world, where it found more scope for expansion, particularly in Asia. Its British co-chairman Sir Michael Perry insisted to me that there were only four layers of managers between him and the ground; and there was no question of Unilever breaking itself up.

Every big company faced the same problem of balancing the big and the small, the central control with the liberated provinces; but the Europeans were more inclined towards organic solutions, based on trust between individuals as much as financial disciplines. Charles Handy, the most intellectual of management gurus, saw corporations developing a federalism which was not unlike political federations – or the notion of 'subsidiarity' adopted by Jacques Delors for the European Union. Many of the European giants, including Shell, Unilever and the Swiss Ciba-Geigy, had already adopted federal systems which were more like mini-societies than impersonal systems. As Handy put it in 1992:

> The concept of federalism is particularly appropriate since it offers a well-recognised way to deal with paradoxes of power and control: the need to make things big by keeping them small; to encourage autonomy but within bounds; to combine variety with shared purpose, individuality and partnership, local and global, tribal region and nation state, or nation state and regional bloc. Change a few of these terms and these political issues can be found on the agendas of senior managers in most of the world's large companies.

Companies on the Continent, with their long traditions of family control, paternal attitudes and close links with communities, faced greater difficulties in building up decentralised structures which combined the advantages of bigness and smallness. But many family companies were being forced into larger units by the pressures of world markets; and one new giant became a model, both in Europe and America, for a new kind of federalism.

ABB: THE BARNEVIK MODEL

In the mid-eighties two venerable engineering companies, Asea in Sweden and Brown Boveri in Switzerland, both founded in the nine-teenth century, were facing crises; and in 1987 they secretly agreed on the biggest cross-border merger in history – to become Asea Brown Boveri, or ABB, based in Zurich. It was a sensational move which offended national pride in both countries, and it was made more sensational by the arrival in Zurich of the young Swedish chief executive, Percy Barnevik: a tall, gaunt figure with big dark eyes and a trim beard who had a clear vision of how to rationalise the merger.

He was determined to break down national rivalries and duplications, from a compact headquarters of a hundred people, speaking English as its official language. He wanted his company to be 'as lean as humanly possible': 'I believe you can go into any traditionally centralised corporation and cut its headquarters staff by 90 per cent in one year.' He moved rapidly into Eastern Europe, and began buying up American companies, including part of Westinghouse. Within a few years he had decisively turned the company round.

Barnevik's ideas arose out of his experience. He had learnt the importance of small companies when he began in the family printshop, working a linotype machine. He studied business and computers, first at Gothenburg then at Stanford in California, and gained practical experience of a multinational when he joined the Swedish tool company Sandvik and took over its subsidiary in America. He developed his own concept of federalism, which was more human and imaginative than his global competitors, including GEC in Britain and GE in America. He had learnt about mergers and statistical controls from Weinstock in London; but he rejected the purely financial yardsticks. He had competed with Jack Welch in America, and had lured away some of his staff; but he avoided buying companies – like television stations or banks – which distracted from the central business of engineering and gave no opportunities for synergy. He saw no sense in becoming a financial conglomerate, like Harold Geneen at ITT. He wanted to create a new kind of multinational, with a 'multi-domestic' structure like Unilever or Shell, which combined national benefits with global planning; but also to co-ordinate the specialised engineers, making the most of their strengths. Above all, he saw his giant company as a group of small ones – with five thousand separate profit centres, each with its own sense of achievement and responsibility.

Barnevik was the most thoughtful and intellectual of the company reformers I talked to on my travels. In a long talk in Zurich he gave his own answers to questions and themes that have emerged so far in this book: about multinationals, computers, autocrats, and above all the new company man.

Doesn't the rapid downsizing, I asked him, make everyone too insecure to be efficient?

Whether you call it downsizing or firing people, it's a serious human problem. This 'jobless upturn' is part of a major trend, not just a business-cycle matter, like the loss of jobs in agriculture a century ago, when they went down from 50 per cent to 5 per cent of the working population.

But reduced employment in the industrial sector shouldn't be a threat. We have to handle the transformation in our own way. I think people behave worse, not better, when they're insecure. I detest the macho view of some Americans who rank managers by their toughness. It can be a bloodbath. To downsize effectively you have to have empathy with the people who are losing their jobs. You have to pay money, take time, handle them with honesty and respect. What you say to them has a lot to do with the attitude of the survivors: whether they see the company as a money-machine or keep their respect and trust for it.

Isn't there a limit to how much change people can take?

No doubt about it. I've been reading recently about how long human genes and mutations take to develop. We can't suddenly adapt to machines: they have to adapt to us.

I have to remind myself that there's a limit to the speed. We discovered that our companies which performed worst were those where the managers didn't give people enough time to commit themselves to the changes – to 'make them their own thing'. If you spend time persuading people face to face instead of giving orders, you save time in the end.

Engineers can find it very difficult to change. At first I couldn't understand how they could be so in love with the systems they develop: how machines were part of their human lives or even national pride. It's extremely painful to have to choose between two factories in Spain and Germany for making transformers. As a Swede I realise it will always be difficult to promote anything Swedish without a very good reason.

The pace of change is the biggest problem in Continental Europe, which is used to stability. After a factory has cut costs and increased production, I still want more. Germans ask me:

haven't you done enough? Isn't it your own mental problem, that you're never happy? But if you stand still you're on a down-ward-moving escalator. You have to present change as a positive life, which is more *fun*.

Don't the drastic changes inevitably concentrate too much power at the top?

Analysts keep asking me that, because they reckon the share price would go down substantially if I disappeared. After the merger, a lot depended on me, because someone had to decide. But now the idea of continuous change is taking hold. There's a top executive committee of eight, who all know what is happening.

We have a strong supervisory board, who are not just fee-collectors and are not afraid to disagree. It is an advantage to have a non-executive chairman who is different from the chief executive. Politically Switzerland has avoided strong leaders ever since Napoleon, which is why they have a different president every year.

But in business, today the person at the top is seen as an integral part of the company's image, which is encouraged by the mass media. Much of my work is communicating internally and externally, which comes back to me. But now the executive committee members and the national leaders in ABB are becom-ing much better known. We're deliberately trying to project a multi-faced picture.

Could you achieve these changes without computers?

Without the modern information technology, ABB couldn't exist. Computers have transformed our company as much as any of the IT companies like ATT or IBM. They've transformed not just our management but the engineering process itself.

I was lucky because I wrote my first programme when I was eighteen and then studied computer science at Stanford; but many managers have difficulty in understanding computers. I divide them into BC and AC: before or after computers – which usually means under thirty-five. Only about half our managers are AC – and fewer among the senior ones – so we have to try to convert BC to AC.

But we must at all costs avoid becoming mechanical in our attitudes. The most serious errors I make are not financial: they're about judging human beings. Computers can be a tool for decentralisation and empowerment: by giving PCs to workers you can reinforce the human factor. But computers can easily be used for the opposite, for centralisation, as they spit out their paper from central terminals.

Can you really reverse the historical tendency towards bureaucracy?

Centralisation is always lurking round the corner. And it takes time to break up a centralised system. When we bought part of Westinghouse in Pittsburgh, which had a headquarters of several thousand people at that time, I got an insight into the power of American bureaucracy. Decentralisation has to be a kind of religious belief, like democracy.

But I think what we're doing is irreversible: we've let the cat out of the bag. I couldn't reverse it if I tried: like the old men in China if they tried to reverse free enterprise which is booming there.

So Europe is really going through a fundamental historical change?

Yes: it's a tremendous sorting out between winners and losers. They're very exciting times. Much has gone better than I thought. We're really succeeding in developing from the bottom up. But I know there are still very great problems.

Are you producing a new kind of company man?

We have two separate breeds of manager. Most of them are working in small units, as if they were in small family companies, proud of their own country. They need to have a charter, so they know what they're doing: they need their own self-interest, as Adam Smith said. You can't tell a Scotsman to abstain from making something so that Germans can make it.

But we have about five hundred people who have to see the whole picture. They must be able to talk to people in the factories, but also provide a global umbrella, and they must have the integrity not to favour their own countries. They're rare, and they're worth their weight in gold.

CHAPTER SEVENTEEN

Disorganisation Men

Fleeing the short-haired mad executives,
The subtle useless faces round my home ...
W.H. AUDEN, 'The Climbers', 1933

In the summer of 1994 several coachloads of company men and their
wives arrived at the grey Georgian mansion of Castlemartin outside
Dublin, on the banks of the Liffey. They were shown into a hall
filled with modern Irish paintings round a handsome double staircase,
where a butler offered them drinks and showed them into a marquee
almost as big as the house, framing one side of the house like an
opera set. At the centre of the marquee a tall, commanding Irishman
welcomed each of them with a joke and an intimate smile before they
mingled and sat down at dining tables round the dance floor.

It could have been a scene from Scott Fitzgerald. In fact it was
the annual outing for senior Heinz executives, who had flown in
from Pittsburgh and elsewhere. The host was Dr Tony O'Reilly, the
chairman and chief executive who was also Ireland's leading entrepreneur, with his own interests round the world. Next week he would
fly to South Africa with an entourage including his family, editors,
accountants, advisers and a separate plane for luggage, to reorganise
his newspapers there and talk to his friend President Nelson Mandela
(it's because I was involved in South Africa that O'Reilly invited me
to this jamboree). But in this marquee he was the Prince of Heinz,
the monarch of tomato ketchup and baked beans, transforming an
office party into a private ball. And he seemed totally committed to
Heinz – with good reason: the *Irish Independent* newspaper (which
O'Reilly controls) had just reported that the value of his personal
shares in the company had increased by $30 million in the last week,
after he had briefed investment analysts.

O'Reilly had become the most legendary of the new master-tribe of industrial entrepreneurs: in America he had been billed as the highest-paid executive, earning $105 million in 1991 and 1992, apart from his own free-booting deals which made him the richest man in Ireland. Henry Kissinger had called him 'the modern Renaissance man', and he had been invited to be a cabinet minister both in Dublin and in Washington. Like all tycoons O'Reilly created his own aura. It went back to his youth as an international rugby star, and it suited the tradition of Heinz, which had begun as an entrepreneurial, paternalist company when the first H.J. Heinz founded it in 1876, and built model factories in Romanesque style in Pittsburgh. Now the entrepreneur was back in fashion, and when Jack Heinz had appointed O'Reilly as President he compared him to his grandfather, with the same energy, vitality and genius. O'Reilly seemed to have come down from the sky – where he still spends much of his time in his private airliner. Like Monroe Stahr, Scott Fitzgerald's Last Tycoon in Hollywood:

He had flown up very high to see, on strong wings, when he was young. And while he was up there he had looked on all the kingdoms, with the kind of eyes that can stare straight into the sun.

Down at his dinner table in the marquee he was making everyone feel taller while dominating their talk. My neighbour, a minister in the Dublin government, was telling a joke about an Irishman discussing styles of management with an American and a Japanese: 'We follow the mushroom principle,' says the Irishman. 'Keep 'em in the dark and cover 'em with muck.' O'Reilly asked him what we were talking about. He replied, 'Management,' and O'Reilly told him: 'Talk to him about South Africa.' My other neighbour was from the Morgan Stanley bank – which had just advised clients to hold on to their Heinz shares – and he was relishing the news that a rival bank, Kidder Peabody, had visibly lost control over its employees – to the discomfiture of their boss, Jack Welch of General Electric, whose systems were supposedly foolproof.

The marquee embraced two almost opposite cultures: the Protestant ethic of the Pittsburgh company men, dedicated to their

specialised tasks, and the Catholic ethic of the Irish, putting everything in the wide context of family, the big heart and universal values.
But the puritanism was rapidly dissolving in a sea of jokes and alcohol
as O'Reilly and his wife Chryss – herself a Greek heiress – were
transforming the business outing into a family party. And the Irish,
whatever their past business shortcomings, were showing all the
talents which management gurus were now stressing: communicating
casually, escaping from hierarchies, inspiring enthusiasm, relating
work to the family. As the band struck up with 'Hello, Dolly' the
company wives come into their own, and inhibitions disappeared on
the dance floor. The party ended at 3.30 a.m., with O'Reilly showing
no signs of sagging, when the coaches drove the Heinz people back
to their Dublin hotels.

The next morning they emerged, bleary-eyed, to exchange remi-
niscences about previous celebrations. 'You're lucky ever to get to
bed before 3 a.m.,' explained one Pittsburgh man who had often
stayed at Castlemartin. He'd learnt to sleep in the afternoon, so that
he could outlast the others into the small hours. O'Reilly always
noticed who left early, said another, and recorded that they lacked
stamina. Another recalled how O'Reilly once stayed up till 4 a.m.
and started a conference four hours later, continuing for eight
hours with no sign of missing a trick. Every Heinz man seemed
to see himself in the context of the boss: watching him, specu-
lating about him and regarding him as the personification of the
company.

Yet they could not feel very secure. Since he became chief executive in 1979 O'Reilly had been more impatient than the Heinzes from
whom he took over. With his own style of genial directness he had
closed down old plants which the family had clung to. In the nineties
Heinz was downsizing, delayering and restructuring as enthusiastically as the rest. Many company men in the marquee were worried
about the future of their famous products, which had survived so well
over the last century: from Heinz tomato ketchup and baked beans
to Star-Kist tuna, Great American Soups and 9-Lives cat food. Even
the British, who had made Heinz part of the language and consume
1¼ million tins of baked beans every day, could no longer be taken
for granted. In the early nineties Heinz's total profits had slipped,
and there were rumours of a takeover by an even bigger company

like Unilever. O'Reilly had eloquently reassured the investment analysts, but he still faced many problems.

Heinz had reinsured themselves by acquiring Weightwatchers, which sells both diet programmes and low-calorie food, in order to profit from dieting as well as overeating. At dinner the head of Weightwatchers, Al Lippert, appropriately lean and energetic, talked to me passionately about the need for constant self-denial, encouraged by his wife Felice, whose wide, smiling face seems out of place with her thin body. But another Weightwatcher said that America was experiencing an epidemic of overeating and a decline in dieting which was a serious setback for Weightwatchers. All the Heinz products were vulnerable to the price wars in the supermarkets, which suggested that customers might be losing their loyalty to brand names, and looking to less famous and cheaper products. As the products were less secure, so were the managers: no Heinz man – not even the boss – could feel really sure of his future.

That Heinz jamboree seemed to sum up the paradoxes of company men in the nineties. The more multinational their business, the more they looked for somewhere to belong. The more insecure their jobs, the more they wanted to feel part of a paternal family. The more impersonal and mechanical their systems, the more they needed to relate to a single leader. The more unsure they were of their future, the more they looked to a risk-taking entrepreneur – who was more likely to get rid of their jobs.

THE PURGES

What had happened to the loyal old company men, the managerial class? In the sixties they were the admired professionals, who had wrested power away from the owners of industry and built up the elaborate 'technostructure', the great pyramids on which Western civilisation depended. Yet by the late eighties they were facing purges in nearly all the big Western corporations, while the old pyramids were mocked not just by the raiders, but by management experts and by the bosses themselves, who were looking for 'flat organisations' which had no room for managers in the middle.

The computer was the most obvious enemy, which, with the help of telecommunications, had replaced the middle-managers as the source of information. In the old days they had been the essential intermediaries through which information flowed up and decisions flowed down. Now information technology had undermined their monopolies, making facts and figures far more widely available. But the computer was also the internal spy which revealed what became evident anyway: that the top-heavy armies were full of unnecessary troops who were not equipped to face serious industrial warfare, and who had become detached from the customer who should be their overwhelming concern. 'To suit the customer you needed to know about four things,' said Rhiannon Chapman at the Industrial Society in 1993: 'The product, marketing, technology and personal service. And all the traditional functions of management got in the way.'

Already by the mid-eighties American company men were in full retreat, and a third of all Americans were switching jobs each year. 'We are witnessing the beginnings of a tremendous whittling away of middle-management, a flattening out of the hierarchies that were the norm in industrial America,' John Naisbitt wrote in 1985. Many big companies were beginning to hire managers on short-term contracts: sometimes the same ones they had recently laid off. Citibank in New York offloaded hundreds of bankers and took back 'temps' for specific tasks and negotiations. The word 'temps' no longer meant secretaries: they could be senior managers – with no security, no health benefits, no payment for days off work.

By the late eighties the flow had turned into a flood, as overweight companies like Kodak and Honeywell followed one purge with another – without completing their cure. 'Companies have been labouring to become "lean and mean" for nearly a decade,' noted Ronald Henkoff in *Fortune* in 1990. 'Shouldn't they be honed, toned, and sinewy, ready to face the world by now? The Fortune 500 industrial companies sweated off 3.2 million jobs in the eighties. Isn't that enough?' But it wasn't. The purges continued, with no end in sight, as new methods and theories made even more managers look redundant.

As they retreated, the managers revealed their lack of political clout. Back in 1983 Peter Drucker had noticed that the emerging employee class of 'knowledge workers' was a group who had 'no political home as yet', and who had not developed 'any leadership types of its own' – which might, he suggested, explain the emergence of 'political adventurers' like Jimmy Carter or Margaret Thatcher. But by the nineties the lack of a political home was much more evident, as the unemployed 'knowledge workers' kept their distance from the rest of the workless masses. The much proclaimed 'new class' now seemed more politically homeless and helpless than the apparatchiks of Eastern Europe and Russia who were to find some support from revived communist parties. But the redundant managers in the West might yet look to an authoritarian leader in the future, to a 'man on horseback', to recover their self-respect and sense of purpose.

The organisation man now looked sadly disorganised. William Whyte, who had first analysed him in 1956, insisted that he was still very much alive in the late eighties, despite the revived cult of the individual entrepreneur. And the corporate bosses did not look very different: when *Business Week* surveyed the top thousand companies in 1988 they found that the average chief executive had worked for his company for a quarter of a century, was aged fifty-six, was 'middling rich, and resolutely middle class in his tastes and avocations'. All but four of the thousand were men.

But the ordinary company men were much less sure of their commitment and future in the corporation. Michael Maccoby, who had written *The Gamesman* in 1976, conducted exhaustive interviews again in the eighties which showed managers to have become less loyal than either the organisation men or the gamesmen. They were now 'self-developers' who looked for continual personal development and jobs which sharpened their skills and marketability, and trusted no company to take care of them. They were strongly influenced by women moving into companies and by dual-career families – the most dramatic change in corporate life since the fifties. They wanted enough flexibility to balance family and career, while in return they offered 'entrepreneurial initiative, real teamwork, and honest information: less careerism, more commitment to the productive project'. Maccoby looked forward to more tolerant corporate cultures which could be reconciled to these self-developers, though bosses looking for short-term profits would be impatient with them. 'In the afterglow of the eighties, one might be nostalgic for the helpful, co-operative organisation man as contrasted to the rugged Wall Street individualists who in fact set the temper of the times.'

In 1991 two writers, Paul Leinberger and Bruce Tucker, decided to trace the 'organisation children' – the offspring of the company men Whyte had interviewed in Park Forest outside Chicago – who were now reaching positions of power. These 'baby boomers' were less prosperous than their elders, indeed they were likely to be 'the first generation in American history that will not do better economically than its parents'. They had come of age in the sixties and seventies, and began by resisting the pressures of organisations and cultivating their private selves. They looked towards self-expression, self-fulfilment or self-assertion: many had artistic aspirations, to be musicians, film-makers, actors, poets, novelists, dancers or visual artists. But their aspirations retreated as they were battered by recession and competition. They emerged seeing themselves as artists manqués, or artisans rather than artists. They became businessmen who were prepared to take risks, change jobs and abandon orthodox careers. They accepted the need for collective effort, but were uncommitted to particular institutions, and unwilling to 'seek niches in immortal hierarchies'. And like Henry Adams at the turn of the century, they longed for a sense of wholeness: 'For what the successor generation is doing, without consciously realising it, is seeking to recreate a way of working that dates back to the pre-industrial age, when there was less separation between art and craft, creativity and creations, personal identity and public identity.'

THE BRITISH EXODUS

The American organisation men were already losing their total commitment to their companies in the eighties; but by the nineties the purges were changing the whole relationship both in America and Europe. The consultants Drake Beam Morin – who specialised in 'outplacing' fired employees like IBM's – foresaw all Europe following the pattern of American layoffs, as the single market intensified competition and privatised companies cut back their employees.

In Britain the purge of managers was specially abrupt. Many commercial hierarchies had survived the earlier crises of the seventies surprisingly unscathed: particularly insurance companies and banks. 'I hadn't seen so many layers of bureaucracy since I read Milton's *Paradise Lost*,' said one senior manager at the National Westminster Bank in London: 'Archangels, angels, seraphim, cherubim everywhere!' But by the later eighties the layers had lost their associations with eternity. As one disappeared without visible damage, the next appeared more vulnerable, and managers turned on each other. 'When people talk about soggy management,' one Shell veteran explained, 'they usually mean the layer just above them.'

Middle-managers were demoralised by the late eighties. 'Most writers portray the middle-manager as a frustrated, disillusioned individual caught in the middle of a hierarchy, impotent and with no real hope of career progression,' wrote Sue Dopson and Rosemary Stewart in a study of them in 1989. 'The work is dreary, the careers are frustrating, and information technology – some writers argue – will make the role yet more routine, uninteresting and unimportant.'

The nineties brought a succession of purges which undermined them further, although they took some time to realise their danger. When the British Institute of Management surveyed a thousand middle-managers in 1992 they found that 80 per cent had experienced at least one restructuring in the previous five years. Yet they still felt that delayering posed no threat to their current job. 75 per cent expected to be managers for the rest of their careers. The Institute could only warn them: 'Stop assuming that it won't happen to you.'

The cutbacks continued. 'Organisation after organisation has taken the axe to its unwieldy layers of management,' warned Roger Young, the director of the Institute, in 1993, 'chopping them out with a remorselessness which has left thousands shell-shocked and out on the streets.' 'There's no sign of it easing off: chief executives are still obsessed by the head-count,' Howard Davis, the director of the CBI, told me in July 1994. 'Bosses who have been through two recessions don't want to be caught with too many people in a third one.'

The talk of axes and shell-shock suggested a war-footing and a ruthlessness which could ignore human casualties, in Europe as well as America. Bosses could apply the same theories to managers as to inventories and components which could be 'outsourced', bought in or supplied 'just in time'. And they could use the crisis atmosphere as a pretext for avoiding human encounters altogether. But behind all the apparent impersonality the purges were often an excuse, like the civil war in Yugoslavia, for paying off old tribal scores or feuds between rival cultures – American v European, Scots v English, patricians v working class. They made it easier for impatient bosses to fire people because they didn't like their face or voice. As one headhunter said, 'It's what we call the why-don't-you-piss-off syndrome.' Some companies became so carried away by the excitement of downsizing that they soon had to re-engage managers – even the same managers – at higher cost in a new role as consultants; the salaries for information-technology consultants went through the roof. Even *The Economist* showed some worry about the dangers of 'corporate anorexia': 'Far from being redundant parasites, some middle-managers were often important allies in the fight against anarchy and corruption.'

Middle-managers who survived felt less secure, and less confident of promotion: successive studies by the British Institute of Management suggested that as the number of layers was reduced the gap between them became wider, and the jump harder. Managers complained that while there was more information, there was less communication and less caring. They had less scope to reach higher grades as the bosses streamlined decision-making. And they were exasperated by short-term restructurings, which sometimes took longer to implement than the shelf-life of the changes they were meant to achieve, and could hasten the collapse of the company. Above all, there was more concentration of power at the top: 'Delayering has meant that decisions have gone upwards and taken even more control away.'

The reactions of the survivors were often ambiguous. Most of them worked under greater pressure, sometimes doing the jobs of two or three people; and many indicated a sense of helplessness and lack of redress against the bosses. 'Two-thirds of our members report they're under stress, and half show actual physical symptoms,' Roger Young told me. 'But there's an apparent contradiction, for most members also say they're enjoying the change: it gives more job satisfaction.' There was a clear difference between the generations;

many younger executives had perceived before their elders that their future was insecure, and that the old-style company was incompetent. They were adjusting their expectations, and often enjoying the challenge.

CORPORATE DISLOYALTY

No corporation could now promise lifetime employment, and no manager could expect it. 'There's no such thing as a job for life,' said Paul Charlesworth of Coutts' Career Consultants in June 1988. He estimated that 300,000 professional and managerial people in Britain were out of work. Five years later the consultants were still more confident. 'Corporate loyalty is dead,' Stephen Rowlinson of Merton Associates assured me with relish.

The headhunters, or 'executive search consultants', were the new princes of industry. Their scope increased as loyalty dwindled, for it was they who separated the swans from the geese. While no one wanted most middle-managers, everyone wanted the high-flying managers and directors who were qualified for the more competitive world. The headhunters made the most out of them, earning commissions of a third of their first year's salary. They had confident military styles and plush offices in Mayfair, and they knew the private fears of the chairmen and the secrets of the market-place. They realised that big corporations could no longer 'grow their own timber' – even ICI, which had exported so many chairmen, had to find its own new chairman in 1994 from Unilever – so they became timber-merchants. Some chairmen blamed the headhunters for bidding up the salaries of finance directors and marketing experts to dizzy levels; but the chairmen had only themselves to blame.

The big companies had ceased to expect total loyalty. Sir John Harvey-Jones remembered how when he joined ICI he had to go wherever they sent him; but by the late eighties recruits no longer felt obliged to surrender their rights: 'In the future it will be the company that conforms to the individual that attracts and motivates the best people.' 'Security from the womb to the tomb is no longer possible,' his successor Sir Denys Henderson told me. 'But the lack of loyalty is going too far the other way. It comes from the City, where they're always thinking of money. When I was younger I never debated about money: I just expected annual increments. Now they're always arguing about money; and if they don't get what they want, they won't stay.'

Shell, with its long tradition of lifetime employment, faced a more traumatic adjustment than most. As Mourik Broekman said: 'There's a growing individualism all through Europe: people don't want to be tied down. Young graduates are less interested in loyalty, or in pensions: they want to get the training and information which can improve their own market position, and give them qualifications they can use anywhere.'

In theory the loyalty had been relaxed from both sides, as part of a more grown-up relationship of 'adult-to-adult contracts'. Young recruits realised, often better than the personnel managers, that they could not be secure, and demanded more information and experience in return. 'The old contract was basically: I worked for a person and I did the person's bidding,' said William Morin of DBM. 'Often I did not tell the person what I did know or did not know about the given situation.' Now you must 'tell everybody everything you know about what's going on'.

But many companies tried to have it both ways, demanding intense loyalty in the short term, which they could not reciprocate in the long term. Robbie Gilbert, the director of employees' affairs at the CBI, warned them in 1994: 'The dilemma of employers is that whilst they want loyalty, certainly from their core employees, they are often seen to be less than loyal to those that work for them. Employers want to be able to face those that work for them with new challenges; but sometimes to close the door, with them on the outside.'

The loss of loyalty was, of course, part of a much wider insecurity which had spread through professions and nations in the late eighties. The assumption of a lifetime job had long been the pattern of professional and public-service careers, at the heart of the middle class. The unemployment of the thirties had made security still more valued in the post-war decades, while the war had encouraged quasi-military attitudes and loyalties, making public and private service seem more alike. 'It wasn't the corporations that demanded loyalty,' argued Nigel Humphreys of Tyzack Accord. 'They were part of a social pattern, with the church, the army and the professions, in which lifetime jobs were expected. In the eighties there was an attitudinal change: people felt freer, and wanted to be in control of their own destiny.' But by the nineties many people had little choice about their destinies as global competition stepped up, boom was followed by recession, and the state felt little responsibility for employment. Even accountants and lawyers were no longer confident of their jobs, and academics and vicars were losing their time-honoured 'tenure'. By 1994 a poll by Mori was showing that 35 per cent of the British middle-class respondents were worried about losing their jobs over the next year. Middle-class parents looked in vain for occupations where their children could be safe: only vets and undertakers appeared relatively sure of steady demand.

The company men were the most vulnerable of the middle classes, both economically and psychologically. For they had never enjoyed the same social identity and acceptance as the older professions. Their qualifications were less defined, while their status and self-respect had always depended heavily on corporate politics and prospects. In the wider society 'the manager' never carried the same resonance as 'the doctor' or even 'the major'; he was simply 'something in industry'. Once forced into early retirement, away from his social supports, he could find himself in an environment for which he was unfitted and unprepared. Behind all the language of downsizing and reducing headcounts were individual human tragedies which received little publicity or sympathy. Dignified figures in the office suddenly found themselves no longer noticed or valued as they were ousted by highly-paid young upstarts; they could be asked to clear their desk in a morning, and be shut out from the building which had been their village for half their lifetime.

The very phrase 'company man' was now suspect. When John Harvey-Jones was introduced on *Desert Island Discs* as 'an industrialist, a company man', he was indignant. 'It is his individuality that is needed, his individual contribution, rather than the conformity to some sort of ideal "company man."' Some ageing employees who looked back on their lifetime of loyalty wondered what had been the point of it all. 'I've often thought how we spent all our lives,' one Shell veteran recalled, 'dedicated to doing down the opposition, just for the sake of the company.'

THE LIBERATION?

What kind of manager was flourishing after the purges? Among the crumbling pyramids, the most qualified and self-reliant had more opportunities than before. In America there was a burst of hopeful theorising, particularly by the most popular guru Tom Peters, author of *Liberation Management* and *Crazy Times Call for Crazy Organizations*. The rejection of scientific management had provided scope for all kinds of theories of unscientific management and a resurgence of interest in spiritual development, new-age training, intuitive and creative thinking: IBM had even tried teaching its employees the Chinese rituals of I Ching. Californian-born ideas like 'organisational development' and 'personal growth' which had grown up in the sixties came back reinforced by new psychological evidence. Psychologists saw companies as 'living laboratories in which to try out their ideas', and launched new kinds of 'touchy-feely' exercises to bring managers together. But the old suspicions remained: were they meant to develop the teams, or to fortify the boss?

A few high-flown chief executives revelled in far-out new theories, particularly in Silicon Valley, like the philosophising of John Sculley before he departed from Apple Computers (see p. 195) about new disciplines and new paradigms, and comparisons with biological cell theory. Corporations, he said, should see their future in terms of genetic change: 'As cells grow and divide, genetic code is always present.' Oriental ideas were at a premium after the Japanese success, and American individualists tried to connect up with Asian collectivism, linking the inner harmony of the individual with the larger harmony of the firm – while rejecting the corporate loyalty which still lay at the heart of the Japanese idea of harmony.

Many younger company men, too, were looking for more creative scope, more rounded lifestyles and more connection with the home – as Michael Maccoby had perceived in the eighties. Some were again dreaming of rediscovering a lost unity, and reconnecting family life with the company, like earlier farmers or artisans; and the vague notion of 'holism'- the 'whole-making tendency' which General Smuts first defined in 1926 – became fashionable again.

There were exciting visions of a new era. In Britain Charles Handy expanded his optimistic, Christian view of future company men in *The Age of Unreason* in 1994. He looked forward to a 'post-heroic manager' whose job was to develop other people's capacity, like a good teacher, and saw the word 'manager' itself disappearing, as society became less stratified. 'The young don't want to be managed, and the word sounds low-class, like canteen manager or office manager.' Handy saw company jobs developing in the wider context of people's life-pattern, leisure and fulfilment; and he anticipated people only engaging in formal office work for twenty years, from the ages of twenty-five to forty-five, before embarking on more individual challenges.

Undoubtedly the most ambitious and well-qualified executives had more scope in the nineties to liberate themselves from the bureaucratic constraints. The lone manager, the 'hired gun' or the 'mercenary' became the new role model, flexible and mobile, joining and leaving short-term assignments and teams, or forming and reforming small companies like the entrepreneurs of Silicon Valley. Creative young people could thrive in fast-changing industries where managers were too old at fifty; including computers, software and all kinds of media, all the way from the TV network CNN in Atlanta to the publishers Dorling Kindersley in London. With ideas at a premium, the intellectual was no longer necessarily at odds with the manager: there might even be a return to the pattern of the East India Company men 150 years earlier, who wrote poetry and philosophy between planning sea-routes and supplies.

But most established corporations still reveal a huge discrepancy between the outward theories of liberation and opportunity, and the realities within. Despite all the talk about personal development and inner harmony, internal competition and insecurity have pressed employees towards greater commitment to immediate commercial goals; while computerised controls impose their unseen discipline. The market-place is a more demanding master than any single boss, while customers are constantly unreasonable, demanding instant availability and flexibility. The managers who serve them are always fearful of losing business to harder-working rivals, inside or outside their company, and worried about taking any holidays. And the pressure for instant responses is stepped up by the new gadgetry of faxes, e-mail and mobile phones which tolerate no hiding places.

Young American executives are expected to be still more thoroughly committed to their business, leaving still less time for hobbies or philosophical thoughts; while leisure-time is associated with failure or opting-out. 'At school I was told there would soon be a three-day week,' said one financial manager in his thirties. 'Now it's seven days a week and I only dare take one week's holiday a year.' But while the company demands this commitment from the young, it can quickly lose interest in the middle-aged; and the pressure towards workaholic zeal can soon be followed by suggestions of early retirement – which is all the more unwelcome without hobbies or counter-interests.

How many managers were really controlling their own destiny? Many of the most successful retail companies, like McDonald's hamburgers, which became a model for others, had learnt how to monitor and control their scattered empires more strictly than ever, with total conformity to their rules. The delayering and restructuring of companies could concentrate more power at the top, with more direct lines of command. And even companies which genuinely tried to empower their employees faced difficulties, for the old habits of giving and taking orders died hard. 'For people brought up in an authoritarian atmosphere,' says the management writer Robert Heller, 'it's a natural reaction to ask what to do. It needs a colossal effort on both sides, not to order, and not to obey.' Or as John Harvey-Jones put it to me: 'The whole process, all the way from the shop floor, encourages decision-making to flow upwards. It's against human nature to stop it. The only solution is to have no upwards. But delegating from the top takes a lot of balls: when people ask you to advise, you simply have to refuse.'

And many bosses were not altogether honest when they called for drastic changes, which if taken too literally could threaten their own security, near the end of their careers. Some chief executives who most insist on downsizing, team-building and flexibility are themselves inflexible and reluctant to work in a team, or to downsize their own directors' suites. It is an old complaint: as Henry Ford wrote in 1923: 'Sometimes it is the men "higher up" who most need revamping – and they themselves are always the last to recognise it.' But at a time of much faster change, the resistance is all the greater;

and the small band of 'change-makers' who are called in to rescue companies are often eased out by the board before their task is completed.

While managers became more mobile and insecure, they saw a widening gap between themselves and the top, which became more visible when directors paid each other huge fees in the midst of the layoffs (see Chapter 21). The 'flat organisation' was really more like a plateau, with a high peak in the middle which was partly in the clouds. For despite the talk of free access to information, corporate chiefs could still make their own plans and arrangements with little fear that their underlings would find out, protest or blow the whistle. In Britain Robert Maxwell could embezzle company funds and cheat his pensioners without any whistle-blowing from senior executives who noticed suspicious signs; while British Airways embarked on a rash and dishonest campaign of 'dirty tricks' to dissuade passengers from flying on the rival Virgin, without any apparent protest from employees. In America autocratic chiefs can maintain much more secrecy – still more when their influence extends through company towns. In Cincinnati Procter & Gamble still dominates both its employees – 'the Proctoids' – and the city, a bastion of conservative conformism. In 1990 their macho new chief Ed Artzt was obsessed with company secrecy. When a persistent reporter from the *Wall Street Journal*, Alecia Swasy, published some inside information he persuaded the county prosecutor to obtain a subpoena to track all local phone calls, and mobilised the chief investigator in the Fraud Squad, who was a part-time security officer with Procter's. After the *Journal* reported these strong-arm tactics Artzt had to admit an 'error in judgement', while the reporter went on to write a book about Procter's which raked up the maximum muck.

In such autocratic companies the talk of liberation management rang very hollow. The more managers were fired, the more the survivors felt themselves dependent on the vagaries of successive bosses, each with his own likes and dislikes, his plans for 'corporate cleansing'. As the layers of managers were removed, they left a barer structure, with fewer continuous elements to provide reinforcement and reassurance.

The headquarters building itself was changing its whole character. It was no longer a secure home-from-home, a benign support system, let alone a playground where you might 'succeed in business without really trying'. It was more like a battleground for internal fights which gave thrilling challenges to ambitious newcomers, but constant dangers to old-style company men. And the whole idea of the office, as we will see, was now in flux.

CHAPTER EIGHTEEN

Office versus Home

The richness of life, which we accept as private
selves and when we turn to novels and poetry, seems
abandoned at the front door of the business or public
agency establishment.

TOM PETERS, *Liberation Management*, 1992

Company man had grown up inside the office block, which reflected
and reinforced the structures and layers of the organisation and symbolised his own security. The purges of middle-managers in the
nineties inevitably undermined this settled existence and the depend-
ants who had accumulated around it. Yet many younger managers saw
the business revolution bringing a much more flexible and liberated
lifestyle, without the strict duality between the home and the office,
and allowing a return to the human scale of activity before those giant
buildings had first emerged at the beginning of the century. How far
could they really achieve that?

Corporate life had, after all, interacted with the rest of society. By
the sixties and seventies the office had come a long way from the
'dingy little back office' of Dickens, the 'airless cage' of Henry Miller
or the 'enormous file' of Wright Mills. In Britain the office had
acquired a special cosiness. For millions of executives, secretaries,
messengers and receptionists it had become the central arena of their
daily lives, where they would always be recognised and acknowledged,
replacing the church, the village or the regiment. If they were ill their
office colleagues would visit and reassure them; and their recovery
was marked by their return to the building. Many companies extended
their long arms to clubs and sportsgrounds and into suburbs where
people from the same company converged: like Shell employees in
London who clustered round Southern Region stations which were

served by Waterloo, next-door to the Shell Centre. Big offices had established their own social calendar which reached a climax before Christmas, when office windows and filing cabinets were festooned with decorations, Christmas cards and letters addressed to 'Dear Office'. The celebrations culminated in the office party where drunkenness was obligatory, bosses flirted with secretaries and equality prevailed for a few hours in the year. The extended-family feeling still seemed like a hangover from the old country-house life – or at least the nostalgic version of it expressed in TV series or films like *The Remains of the Day*. And like the country house, the office block encouraged a dangerous illusion of solid permanence and continuity.

It was a more sustaining and realistic community than many of the villages lovingly depicted by contemporary novelists. Intellectuals mocked office-life, and many young graduates found it absurd until they were broken in. 'I decided that, in the office system, society had created an aberration which it could not control,' wrote Jonathan Gathorne-Hardy in the introduction to his novel *The Office* in 1970: 'It was monstrous that I should submit to it.' But the daily encounters and social opportunities of easy-going offices could become thoroughly reassuring and habit-forming to their denizens. It was left to strip-cartoonists to convey the daily comedy and pathos of the office employee, like Dagwood in the American strip 'Blondie', or Bristow, Frank Dickens's office hero of the Chester Perry organisation in the London *Evening Standard*.

The hero of Keith Waterhouse's 1978 novel *Office Life* finds the daily rituals 'as pleasant a way of passing the days as any he could think of'. He works in an office-tower engrossed in sociable tasks, exchanging dockets, chits and vouchers, chatting in the lavatory and beside the copying machine, organising raffles, football pools and an office sweet-stall. But the company turns out to produce nothing at all. The boss explains that the 'company man is among the most valuable assets that a healthy business concern can possess'. When some inquisitive employees question him further he admits that the office is secretly financed by the government to provide jobs which are totally unproductive, to reduce unemployment.

Office-life had become a central but segregated part of the social history of the twentieth century. The self-containment of offices, and their separation from other lives, had been enhanced by the architects who established their characters as vertical villages within their own towers. By the mid-1920s the innovations of skyscraper-offices in America, which had lasted forty years, had come to an end, and the developers and realtors had taken over, imposing their own standardisation. 'During most of this period, from 1920 to 1970, office organisations, office technology and the expectations of office workers remained more or less constant,' wrote Francis Duffy, the leading British architect of office-buildings. 'The office manuals of the early 1920s and those of the 1960s differ little in content and not at all in their underlying assumptions about the mission and conduct of office work.'

The architects set the pattern of the corridor offices with rows of cells, each with their own window; later followed by the open-plan – which began in America and Germany and spread to Britain in the sixties – in which hundreds of employees could be supervised. Both extremes became rigid, limited by the structure of the main building, while the realtors encouraged symmetrical, repetitive designs into which company-clients had to fit. In Continental Europe many companies were able to commission and design their own headquarters, with some spectacular results like the Pirelli tower in Milan or the Thyssen tower in Düsseldorf. By the late 1950s some German companies were favouring a third kind of office design, the *Bürolandschaft* or office-landscape, with huge open floors split up by screens, foliage and desks scattered apparently at random, which deliberately discouraged hierarchies and encouraged informal communication and participation. But British companies preferred a structured style, and developers preferred to build the more conventional towers which maximised the rent per square foot. The architects conspired in the conformity of company man.

In the eighties office-buildings showed a new surge of exuberant confidence. Across the world big banks were moving into monumental new palaces which increased the sense of permanence and security, while adopting an international style with no feeling of place. In Manhattan the World Financial Center set a new scale with its giant conservatory, high ceilings and Egyptian columns, which its developers Olympia & York soon repeated in Canary Wharf in London's Docklands. In Hong Kong the Bank of China and the Hongkong and Shanghai Bank competed with dazzling skyscrapers by I.M. Pei and Norman Foster. They were (said Francis Duffy) 'the first genera-tion of buildings anywhere which fully reflect the placeless, global corporatism of a financial services industry freed by, and yet utterly dependent on, information technology'.

In London developers built exotic prestige or 'signature' towers to attract industrial headquarters, within range of Heathrow airport: a turreted façade like a Sultan's palace, an overgrown Swiss chalet with its steep roof almost down to the ground; a mock Tudor barn with a belfry; a 'London Ark' with comical bulges and bubbles looming above the Hammersmith flyover like a grounded balloon, which has remained empty since its completion.

For all their architects' fantasies, most of these buildings were still designed to command and dominate, with assumptions almost opposite to the domestic buildings around them. In the words of Jeremy Myerson, the author of *The Work Aesthetic*:

> Our cities are still defined by monuments to work. Urban sky-lines are punctuated by tall office buildings which signify not just real estate prices on the ground but an overt desire for mastery of all the corporation or developer beholds. And our psyches are conditioned by the banal pseudo-functional imagery of the office – all potted plants and blinds, metal filing cabinets and modern systems furniture. The British don't put up with that kind of hard-edged stuff in their homes but they are willing to tolerate it at work in the name of productivity.

But there was a dangerous time-lag in the eighties: big buildings took more than a decade between conception and occupation, and could be outdated before they were completed. Most architects had been slow to realise the full impact on office design of the computer, which was requiring a complete rethinking of the working environment. And there was not only a deep recession, but a swing against large, flamboyant headquarters which went against the new thinking of management experts about downsizing, outplacement, delayering and customising. The aspirations of managers and their architects were constantly at odds with sensitivity to the customer.

Many British companies were already, as we have seen, cutting back their central staffs to minimal headquarters. When ICI wanted to move out of their Millbank palace they could find no other company to move in. Courtaulds had slimmed down to a modest courtyard in the rag-trade district; BP had moved back to its Edwardian building; Unilever had halved its headquarters staff, still based in its renovated old palace at Blackfriars. The peak of grandiose office-building, in keeping with Parkinson's Laws, coincided with the mass exodus of managers. The office society that had grown up around them diminished like camp-followers left behind when a regiment had marched on. The dear office with its odd jumble of people, its reassurers, its carers, its marriage-brokers and office parties, was dwindling with the downsizing. It now looked like an outdated luxury, a distraction from the competitive business, which could not survive global competition and clamour for profits. But in the meantime it had drained away much of the social energy and initiative from the real villages and neighbourhoods. The new job-hopping managers, temps and consultants who could uproot themselves every few years had to make their own social arrangements in a much more insecure world.

All the assumptions about offices were called into question, as managers and architects rethought their attitudes to space, time and work. 'One hundred years after the great explosion of invention in Chicago which created the office building,' wrote Duffy in 1981, 'offices are certainly not dead but are perhaps the ultimate design problem of the twentieth century.' A report on British cities published by English and Overseas Properties in November 1994 predicted that office blocks would be the social and economic dinosaurs of the next century.

Many bosses now wanted their head offices to appear more related to their business, to reflect (as Christopher Lorenz put it) 'the individual character of the organisations within them, rather than some glossy theatrical norm'. Architects were devising unpretentious, flexible structures like warehouses or souks. In Europe, the Swedes were again in the forefront of innovation. Electrolux provided an austere, minimal headquarters by converting a warehouse in Stockholm. The Scandinavian airline SAS moved into a daring new headquarters designed by Niels Torp to provide creative inspiration and meeting-places, including an internal street with café tables and restaurants, which was acclaimed as 'the most important office-building of the 1980s'.

In July 1994 *Business Week* held a conference on 'the virtual office' at its Manhattan headquarters, where experts described the new flexibility of work with 'the 3 Ws' – whenever, wherever, whatever you choose – and predicted the disappearance of office blocks. The old cathedrals of commerce, said real-estate consultant Sandy Agpar, were now 'sterile hulks that wall in their occupants, break down communication and turn people inward'. He foresaw office-hotels where executives could book in for a few hours, bringing their 'emotional kitbag' of personalised stationery or family pictures.

Many bosses now debated whether office space was necessary at all as they totted up its cost, second only to the cost of the employees themselves. All the old accoutrements now began to look dispensable in the new world of mobility and fast communications, of empowerment and customisation. Companies, they argued, could liberate their employees from the office, to control their own destinies.

Do they even need a desk? Since the eighteenth century it had been the basic symbol of organised work, all the way from Charles Lamb's high desk, to the great roll-top desk of J.D. Rockefeller, to the high-tech console bristling with computers and gadgetry. But the desk was now seen as the symbol of bureaucracy and territorial disputes – while the mobile telephone and the laptop computer provided the means to escape. Already some companies are depriving their employees of their desks altogether, or making them share with others through 'hot-desking' (like the 'hot-bunking' of wartime sailors sharing bunks in submarines). The avant-garde advertising agency Chiat/Day has commissioned a weird new building in Los Angeles with cellular phones and a computer network instead of fixed desks and filing cabinets: 'The phone has become a symbol of non-communication,' said the chairman Jay Chiat, 'because people are never in their offices.' IBM, which was always associated with grand offices and desk-bound grandees, is now pioneering deskless work; and its British subsidiary gives some managers a choice between a desk and a job. In New Jersey IBM have closed down six branch offices, fired half their employees, and moved the survivors to a warehouse which they converted into an office-building for 800 employees, but with only 350 desks, in minimal cubicles with only a telephone and a computer jack – so that the workers had to keep moving around, and were encouraged to leave the building. Their office manager explained: 'No walls, no boundaries, no hierarchies, no epaulettes.'

Yet at the top of the company the desk remained both the symbol and the instrument of power. A few restless entrepreneurs, it is true, had no fixed abode and kept all their facts in a briefcase and a laptop; but the control over any complex business still centred on a desk, as it had for several centuries. Today's merchant bankers, the guardians of capital, still favour the atmosphere of the old partners' room: Robert Fleming's directors sit facing each other from behind antique desks, with green lampshades on one side and computer-screens on the other – the symbols of continuity and modernity.

Do employees need a telephone receptionist? The telephone, which a century ago enabled managers to distance themselves from the factory, now appeared to be dismantling the office itself as answering machines were linked together to provide 'voice-mail'; by 1993 three-quarters of America's biggest corporations were using it. Recorded messages could remove the geographical sense of an office altogether, so that a caller booking an airline ticket in New York could be answered in Nebraska (where the booking staff can be paid less).

But outside callers were exasperated, as they were passed from one voice-machine to another, in a closed circle of recordings with no real voice to rescue them, or maddening jingles and bursts of music, never knowing whether their contact was away, out of the office, or simply not wanting to talk to them. The exasperation caused the voice-mail producers in July 1992 to form an Educational Committee which published a guide to voice-mail etiquette. It advised clients to update the 'greeting' every week, to avoid shunting callers into a second voice mailbox, to always answer calls when they were at their desks, and to tell callers how to find a 'live' person. But even the most sophisticated companies trapped themselves in their own voice-mail. In Seattle I tried repeatedly to make contact with a senior manager at Microsoft, until I was told after two days: 'I've left several messages on her voice-mail with no reply: I'm afraid I'll have to walk over to her office.' Voice-mail really works against modern management principles of tactful consultation and empowerment. 'It only gives me time to give abrupt instructions,' said one Seattle manager:

'I must sound very autocratic. I never see the expression at the other end.'

Do employees even need a telephone? The most revolutionary intruder was electronic mail, or e-mail, which allows people to communicate directly on personal computers linked by telephone lines. It was naturally favoured by computer companies like Microsoft, whose employees used it to create their own social networks and communities. But e-mail inevitably reduced communications to more mechanised formulae, with their own artificiality. John Seabrook, who prepared a magazine profile of Microsoft's chairman Bill Gates through e-mail, decided: 'We were intimate in a curious way, in the sense of being wired into each other's minds, but our contact was elaborately stylised, like ballroom dancing.' Gates himself spends two hours a day writing and reading his e-mail, and sees it as a breakthrough which gives employees easy access to their boss, without formalities. But it also cuts out any casual contact. 'If someone isn't saying something of interest,' Gates explained, 'it's easier not to respond to their mail than it is not to answer the phone.'

Finally, do employees need to come to the office at all?

As daily commuting became longer and slower, many executives began to use their car as an alternative office, with the help of telephones, laptops and faxes. In Tokyo, where traffic frequently comes to a standstill and where living-rooms may be smaller than cars, the mobile office is a natural solution. Many cars, I noticed, now have two telephones – one mobile, and one for the chauffeur who can reschedule appointments delayed by the traffic jams. But the more obvious solution in Europe and America was not to come into the office at all, and to work from home. Already in the 1970s the idea of 'teleworking' or 'telecommuting' was encouraged by congestion and high rents in cities. Teleworkers remained a small minority: by 1993 only about 7.6 million Americans – 6 per cent of the workforce – were reckoned to be telecommunicating, and only 1.2 million British, or 4 per cent of the workforce. But in the future the video-telephone promises more intimate links between office and home, while commuting becomes more nightmarish. In Los Angeles the earthquake of 1993 immobilised crucial freeways for months and the Pacific Bell telephone company recorded a surge of interest in telecommuting; while in the eastern and mid-western United States the freeze-up in February 1994 brought much commuting to a halt.

In more informal businesses which can benefit from flexible hours the office at home can provide a solution which is both more efficient and more enjoyable, while some offices are becoming more like homes. 'The duality between the home and the office is no longer necessary,' said Rhiannon Chapman, the former director of the Industrial Society in London. 'The man is becoming less like a hunter, more like a farmer, involved in his family. Some fathers are even bringing their children to the office.' Will there be a reversal of the long trend in industrial society since the early nineteenth century, when the workplace was increasingly separated from the home?

But home-working does not necessarily imply more humane or independent conditions of work. In Victorian times many of the most menial activities, like bleaching, dyeing or dressmaking, continued to be performed in the workers' houses, for minimal wages; and some home-workers in late-twentieth-century Europe are perpetuating an earlier kind of dependence, sometimes in the same regions, where there has been a continuous tradition of cottage-workers doing piece-work for low wages. Women with young families often choose tele-working as an alternative to a long daily commute: like keyboard operators working for printers who farm out jobs below union rates. But there is little sense of liberation in this kind of home-working. A study of home teleworkers by two academics at the University of Sussex in 1994 found them facing repeated strains between the demands of their families and their business tasks.

There is much more liberation at a higher level. Many entrepreneurial loners and consultants can work profitably and effectively from home, electronically linked with their offices. Highly-motivated salesmen can revel in the gadgetry which keeps them constantly in touch and instantly available as they drive between their clients. And home is the natural fixed base for the new-style roving manager envisaged by Charles Handy, who sees him having a career like an actor's: engaged with the rest of the cast for a single run, frequently resting between parts at home, constantly looking for new shows. Creative new businesses involved with communications are throwing up thousands of this kind of mobile managers, who need (as Handy suggests) not so much offices as clubs to provide casual meeting places for camaraderie, teamwork and face-to-face contact.

But the average executive who makes the transition to home-working can face a deep psychological shock. When I interviewed laid-off IBM managers in Chapter 15 any talk of liberation from the office sounded hollow. For the company had encouraged their employees to see themselves as part of their larger unit, a 'family', a 'community', a 'group', with the office at the centre of their lives, while keeping their actual family at a distance and maintaining the duality between office and home. Paternalist companies had taken over the role not only of the real father, as the breadwinner and provider of security, but also of the real mother as the caring parent, arranging children's parties and Christmas festivities, country clubs and sports grounds. And the traditional nuclear home had dwindled as wives went to work and left their children at crèches and day-nurseries, or with home helps. A parent staying in the house all day felt isolated and excluded from the centres of activity; and the corporation appeared still more impregnable behind its defences.

Whom do you represent? Who are you with? What is your affiliation? Which company? The telephone interrogation emphasises the barriers between the home-worker and the office-building, as all freelancers like myself are constantly reminded. Outside callers must often explain their reason for calling before even being put through to a secretary, to whom they must repeat it. The individual remains suspect, despite all the rhetoric of empowerment and customerisation. In the biggest bureaucracies, like government offices, the very fact of an external call is seen as a threat: 'Are you calling from *outside* the building?' Conferences and conventions still demand corporate identities. Every list of delegates has a column headed 'representing'; and everyone has a name-tag – which looms bigger and bigger – including their company's name, which provides the context to explain why they are there and what they can talk about. Mere individuals represent no one but themselves.

Much of the talk of liberation from the office conceals the simple fact that bosses want to cut overheads and avoid responsibility for housing their employees. Voice-mail, e-mail, hot-desking and home-working all put a greater distance between employer and employee, and reduce the social obligations that have revolved around the office. But inside the corporate castles the managers need more than ever to be close to the boss, to inhabit the suites, the dining rooms or the jets, to watch the winks, nods and silent gestures which have always been the stuff of power-struggles: 'Nothing propinqs like propinquity,' as George Ball said of the White House. No video-phone or conference call can be a substitute for that closeness, and the traditional symbols of status – the secretary with the intimate voice, the big desk and the thick carpet – are as important as ever. Managers who are shifted to outlying offices or to their own homes can prosper so long as they prove their market value, but in office politics or palace intrigue they are out of sight, out of mind. Despite all the emphasis on measurement and numbers, the centre still depends on human relationships; and the leaner the system, the more it depends on personal cohesion and trust.

Conformity still prevails, I realised after my tour of office-life, including conformity in dress. Much is made of the new informality. In America Tom Peters, who began with McKinsey's, appears on the cover of his book in pink boxer shorts, while software companies on the West Coast have established their own code of jeans, T-shirts and trainers. In Britain Sir John Harvey-Jones flaunted his long hair and outrageous kipper ties while chairman of ICI. By the nineties bankers' offices in New York and Chicago were encouraging staff to wear country clothes on 'casual Fridays' to show they could relax, while even IBM was allowing coloured shirts. But most consultants themselves, including McKinsey's, still favour dark suits and white shirts, and most managers remain cautious in their dress. The more insecure and changeable the job market, the more they need to impress, not with daring or creativity, but with reliability and neatness: a barber in California assured me that he was busier than ever during the recession as customers needed haircuts before their interviews. Only the most successful entrepreneurs can wear pony-tails and garish open-necked shirts without arousing distrust, because everyone knows they are successful – like the eighteenth-century duke who was asked why he dressed so badly: 'Why bother? In the country everyone knows who I am. In the city, no one knows.'

If homes do not become offices, will offices become more like homes? Certainly contemporary work-places are far more congenial and less austere than the old barrack-like spaces with their military style. They are often more welcoming and varied than the employees' homes; a visitor to New York, practising 'office tourism', can see how, inside the same outwardly uniform skyscraper, different floors can be turned into an art-nouveau fantasy, a Renaissance gallery, an avant-garde art show or a baroque boudoir.

But grandiose new buildings are becoming still more cut off from everyday life and casual visitors, as they become obsessed by security. In Los Angeles new urban developments provide office complexes protected by electronic surveillance, private police forces and razor-walls. Part of the downtown business area has been converted into a self-contained fortress which can be quickly insulated from any disaster outside. Mike Davis, the radical professor at the Southern California Institute of Architecture, described how 'Fortress Down-town' responded to the LA riots of 1992: 'By flicking a few switches on their command consoles, the security staffs of the great bank towers were able to cut off all access to their expensive real estate. Bullet-proof steel doors rolled down over street-level entrances, escalators instantly stopped and electronic locks sealed off pedestrian passageways.'

American corporate headquarters are increasingly detached from the old city-centres. In New York they have moved steadily out of Manhattan to the ex-urbs where land is cheap, cars can park, and company people can live close to their work. Though AT&T com-missioned a Manhattan tower its real heart was in New Jersey, between routes 278 and 78, where it moved into the Pagoda, its world headquarters: by the late eighties it was employing 51,000 people in New Jersey – despite the breakaway of its Baby Bells – and occupying as much office space as the whole of downtown Seattle. AT&T's Manhattan tower was taken over by Sony as a showplace for their communications, while IBM were evacuating their tower next door. Skyscrapers were becoming part of global showbiz, while the real business was run from the ex-urbs. Many companies were building headquarters far from any city, looking more like campuses or farms. Nike, the sportswear company, developed an estate like a university round a man-made lake ten miles outside Portland, Oregon; Apple computers planned a campus in Cupertino, modelled on Stanford University; Chrysler projected its extravagant 'Technology Centre' at Auburn Hills, Michigan. Microsoft, as we saw in Chapter 1, com-missioned a new campus outside Seattle in the style of a monastery.

Many corporations preferred a no-man's-land, beyond the

suburbs and close to freeway intersections: at Tysons Corner outside Washington, at the Galleria outside Houston or at Irvine outside Los Angeles. Office blocks appeared suddenly, like slabs descended from the sky, their backs turned to their natural surroundings, surrounded by car-parks and highways like islands in fast-flowing estuaries. Developers see these 'Edge Cities' as the natural consequences of the free market, as they rise up from the crossroads of trade: as decisively as Venice in the fourteenth century, or Hong Kong in the twentieth. But they may also satisfy a specifically American kind of self-assertion. 'Maybe it worked like this,' wrote Joel Garreau in *Edge City*, a perceptive book about the phenomenon. 'The force that drove the creation of Edge City was our search deep inside ourselves for a new balance of individualism and freedom. We wanted to build a world in which we could live in one place, work in another, and play in a third, in unlimited combination, as a way to nurture our human potential.'

But the dominant side of the triangle is the work-place, which determines where employees live and play, and provides their main identity. The enveloping high-tech office blocks become still more self-enclosed, wired up and plugged into global systems detached from any territory. Magic cards open their doors to a privileged world, with its own rules and assumptions. It is much more exciting than life inside the Standard Oil building a century earlier, wearing the 'Standard Oil collar'. But it is still more detached from the world outside it. The gap between the home and the office, with their different values and priorities, is wider than ever. And life becomes more difficult for the people who have to bridge it, particularly the company women.

CHAPTER NINETEEN

Company Women

In the late twentieth century, women were more than ever torn between conflicting values. They had become much more confident of their abilities in key areas of business, particularly small business. But big corporations were still a man's world; and as they became leaner, more computerised and competitive they became more demanding. Many women were having doubts about the human costs of success: was it really worth it?

Ambitious women had always been caught between two attitudes since they had first come into men's offices with the typewriters and telephones, like Sinclair Lewis's Una Golden (see Chapter 4): they wanted to succeed in a man's world, while defending their human values and family priorities. Corporations had always been closely associated with masculine virtues and virility, and competing in male games. They appeared thoroughly rational. Max Weber saw bureaucracy governed by impersonal rules, and Frederick Taylor's scientific management appeared neutral and objective. But it was always male-based: corporations and offices very soon established their own 'emotional economy' based on men's needs, as Michael Roper described it in his useful book *Masculinity and the British Organisation Man Since 1945*. 'Managerial work offered organisation men a wide range of expressive modes, from typically masculine postures of cold-hearted calculation, to being "mothered" by a secretary, or "mothering" young managers by developing them in career terms.' (Men liked to think of their secretaries as office wives, but the secretaries themselves felt more like mothers.)

The corporate images of success, from the family patriarch to the committee-man, always reflected male models. Champions of rugged male virtues mocked corporations for producing 'the sanitised, hairless, shallow man' (as Robert Bly called him in *Iron John*), and critics of Western industry blamed its decline on feminine cosseting and the nanny state. But these macho criticisms were confused, as Roper points out, for big companies were cultivating just the kind of intimate relations between men that the critics wanted to revive. The feminist management guru Rosabeth Moss Kanter saw corporations being governed by close male relationships which she called 'homosociality'.

Until the sixties British company men were inclined to regard women colleagues as dependent people who had failed to get married or who needed the money. Intellectuals who looked down on business were patronising about businesswomen. As John Betjeman described the 'poor unbelov'd ones':

> From the geyser ventilators
> Autumn winds are blowing down
> On a thousand business women
> Having baths in Camden Town.

Feminist academics largely ignored the study of organisations until the eighties, when a series of sociological studies provided evidence of how bureaucracies had been constructed on the basis of maintaining women in junior positions. In Britain the growth of big organisations at the turn of the century had coincided with the 'white blouse' or 'pink collar' revolution which brought women into clerical work. 'The modern organisation came into being depending on cheap female labour,' wrote Anne Witz and Mike Savage in 1992, 'and in turn helped define women as subordinate workers to men within white collar labour markets.' Lloyds Bank, for instance, hired large numbers of women in the twenties who were not eligible for promotion, thus giving men more scope for elevation from junior grades; while many organisations compelled women to retire when they married. The inflow of young women fortified the security of company men.

The ownership of big companies did not diminish the bureaucratic bias. America was full of rich women shareholders who might have exerted pressure on management to appoint women to key jobs in companies; but they did not. There were a few phenomenal businesswomen in specifically feminine products – particularly in cosmetics which produced such dragon-ladies as Helena Rubinstein,

Elizabeth Arden and Estée Lauder. A few women took over control of big companies from their parents or husbands and turned out to be formidable bosses. The most influential was Katharine Graham, who became chairman of *Newsweek* and the *Washington Post* – which her father Eugene Mayer had built up – after the suicide of her husband Phil Graham. She took over as a shy and self-effacing new-comer, bewildered by the very male editors and managers, but within a few years she became one of the toughest of all newspaper owners. She outstared the printers' union to install new technology, supported her editor Ben Bradlee when he exposed Watergate, and boldly fired top executives. She said 'Power is neither male nor female', but she plays down her own achievement. 'It was an accident of family and a lot of luck,' she told me. 'I began in a small and private company and had time to learn before it went public, with the help of Warren Buffet who taught me what a public company was. But I'm not sure that I ever broke into the male mafia.' She did not noticeably shift the balance of management towards women, and she was succeeded not by her journalist daughter Lally, but by her more conventional son Donald.

Until the seventies company women usually meant wives, who were expected to be loyal and supportive of their husbands without showing too much interest in office politics. In big cities most company wives led social lives which were not much affected by corporate hier-archies; but company towns or suburbs were much more influenced by company values. The predicament of the lively wife subjected to corporate conformity became a favourite theme for fiction, summed up in the haunting film *The Stepford Wives* (1974), based on a novel by Ira Levin, in which the obedient, long-suffering women turn out to be produced by a mechanical process. Several novelists depicted idealistic wives who tried to identify with their husbands' business ambitions, only to be disillusioned as they realised their ruthless compromises. 'When you married me you wanted Lancelot,' the businessman tells his wife in Louis Auchinloss's novel *Honorable Men* (1985). 'And now you'll settle for George Babbitt. I suppose that's the story of the American wife.'

In overseas expatriate communities, where businessmen were watched like diplomats, the wives were expected to be specially loyal. Shell wives belonged to a para-diplomatic tradition in which entertainment was important for promotion – a world which Thomas Hinde (an ex-Shell man) captured in his novel *For the Good of the Company* in 1961. The demands of loyalty could be heavy: Shell operated in many unstable third-world countries, and some wives could face harrowing ordeals. Nien Cheng, author of *Life and Death in Shanghai* (1984), was the widow of the general manager of Shell in that city. She took over the role of the company's special adviser and was persecuted under the Cultural Revolution, accused of being the imperialists' running dog and imprisoned in solitary confinement for seven years. *Shell Wives in Limbo* was the title of a sociological study by Soraya Tremayne in 1984. She found that the overseas wives were expected to identify strongly with the company, to display 'loyalty, resilience and sociability', and to conform to Shell standards: to fill up their car with another company's petrol would raise eyebrows, and bosses could learn about their employees' faults through the wives' careless remarks. Senior managers could flirt with the wives of juniors, but never the other way round. They would refer to 'a lousy manager: if he could not even control his wife'. When Shell wives returned to their home country they faced a further culture shock, leaving the limelight of community life for 'a dimlight of private lives with no incentives for displaying hard-won qualities'. But more cosmopolitan young wives were already resisting the identification with the company as a threat to their own identity.

The evolution of the real company women, as opposed to the company wives, was very slow until the sixties and seventies. There were a few exceptions. Women were most obviously needed in companies which were selling to other women, particularly in advertising agencies, which were always trying to get inside the mind of the housewife. Already in the thirties agencies were employing clever women both to write copy and to deal with clients, including novelists like Dorothy L. Sayers and J.P. Marquand (see Chapter 8). But few of them promoted women to key positions. Procter & Gamble in Cincinnati spent huge sums advertising to women, but until the sixties their women employees had to wear skirts and to eat in a separate canteen, and not until the seventies could they be promoted from 'brand assistants' to sales training. Women employees complained about Procter's male-based images of housewives obsessed with cleanliness and preoccupied with pleasing their menfolk, like the jingle for Prell shampoo in 1949 which caused an uproar (and a lawsuit from Tallulah Bankhead):

> I'm Tallulah the tube of Prell,
> And I've got a little something to tell.
> Your hair can be radiant, oh so easy,
> All you've got to do is to take me home and squeeze me.

The complaints within Procter's about discrimination and sexist advertising intensified in the mid-seventies, when a group of women employees in Cincinnati protested against the portrayal of women as 'dopey housewives, sex objects and half-wits', and brought a shareholders' resolution to the annual meeting in 1975, supported by a church group and the National Organisation for Women. But Procter's board successfully defeated the resolution.

Unilever, Procter's main European rival in soap and detergents, was also reluctant to promote women, in spite of a serious shortage of male managers. In January 1964 their magazine *Progress* reported that 'the limits to Unilever's expansion will largely be set by its managerial resources ... we are still having to search for the right man in the right place'. A later study of women in business commented:

> Perhaps companies like Unilever ... could find that they are overlooking talent in the shape of the highly qualified young women they have within their organisations. Companies of this size and stature spend vast sums of money on management development, and still succeed in having discontented and under-employed young women on their staff, who have not been given the opportunities to test whether or not they have management potential.

Other service industries were employing new armies of women in the post-war decades, without conceding promotion at the top. The most visible were air hostesses, or flight attendants, who were trained to project a sense of caring and security for passengers, and presented in airline advertising with images of beautiful submission – specially effective among Asian airlines like Singapore and Cathay Pacific. In *The Managed Heart*, Arlie Hochschild in 1983 described the

281

manipulation of women into a male image and analysed the 'emotional labour' carried out by flight attendants who were required to smile as part of the service: 'The emotional style of offering the service is part of the service itself, in a way that loving or hating wallpaper is not a part of producing wallpaper.' The companies developed 'corporate feeling rules' which dictate emotional behaviour: 'Years of training and experience, mixed with a daily carrot-and-stick discipline, conspire to push corporate feeling rules further away from self-awareness.'

While businesses remained firmly controlled by men, the growing presence of women as receptionists, secretaries and assistants was giving offices a much more feminine atmosphere, particularly in America. 'While management was being defined as a "masculine" pursuit,' wrote Rosabeth Kanter, 'more routine jobs were being "feminised".' As *Fortune* described the office of the early fifties:

> The male is the name on the door, the hat on the coat rack, and the smoke in the corner of the room. But the male is not the office. The office is the competent woman at the other end of the buzzer, the two young ladies chanting his name monotonously into the mouthpieces of a kind of gutta-percha halter, the four girls in the glass coop pecking out his initials with pink fingernails.

But the female images were often suffused with male sexual expectations, as was reflected in fiction and films. The hero of Joseph Heller's novel *Something Happened* (1974) combines timid ambition with an obsession with laying office girls among the filing cabinets: 'The company is in favor of getting laid if it is done with a dash of élan, humor, vulgarity, and skill, without emotion.'

The late sixties, with Women's Liberation and the surge of interest in sexual freedom, self-fulfilment and far-out fashion, brought new opportunities to enterprising businesswomen including designers, retailers and agents who could cater for creativity in the younger generation. In Britain the successful woman entrepreneur was publicised by names like Mary Quant, Barbara Hulinicki of Biba, Laura Ashley, and Marjorie Hurst of the Brook Street Bureau. Women were most clearly advancing in the media which depended on easy and fast communications, including advertising, television, journalism and publishing. In these activities even the old barriers between secretaries and executives were beginning to break down. Bright typists could find out how offices really worked and reveal their talents to their bosses, and young men took up secretarial courses with the same ambition. By 1993 60 per cent of publishing assistants and secretaries in America were men.

Sometimes the familiar stereotypes of office-life were turned inside out, as timid men were dominated by bossy women or 'killer bimbos'. A few women could show themselves as ruthless as men in office politics, and women's networking began to rival the traditional old boys' nets. The changing relationships between women and offices were caricatured in successive movies. In *Nine to Five* (1980) the male chauvinist boss of an insurance company bullies and harasses his secretary (Dolly Parton) and tyrannises two other women (Jane Fonda, Lily Tomlin). He tells the 'girls' to 'spare the women's lib crap' and talks like a baseball coach, urging his staff to 'cut the balls off the competition'. The three women have a theme song – 'You're just a step in the boss-man's ladder . . . they never give you credit' – until they plot to kidnap the boss and chain him up in his house. They take over the office and introduce flexible hours, a day-care centre and bright furniture, which rapidly boost productivity; when the boss returns to the office the chairman sends him off to Brazil.

Working Girl (1988) shows a dominating woman boss (Sigourney Weaver) in an office making mergers and acquisitions, who employs an ambitious secretary (Melanie Griffiths), promising her 'a two-way street' but stealing her ideas without credit. While the boss is away the secretary impersonates her, revealing a shrewd head for business which attracts the admiration of a master-financier. The boss returns in fury to discover the deception, but the secretary wins out, explaining: 'You can't get there without breaking the rules.' *The Temp* (1993) tells a still less probable story of a sexy and super-efficient temp secretary who takes over from a wimpish male who leaves in a panic when his wife is having a baby. She brilliantly reorganises her boss's life and tax returns, but is haunted by the refrain 'It's only temporary,' and eventually murders her boss.

But other films of the mid-eighties were reflecting women's rejection of business in favour of babies, including *Baby Boom* (1987),

where a successful woman in advertising (Diane Keaton) is suddenly
landed with a baby who takes over her life, until she leaves her
boyfriend, the boss, in favour of a vet.

By the eighties even the banks appeared to be giving way to women:
the female stockbroker or analyst with a tailored business suit, Filofax
and mobile phone became a new role-model. In the City of London
the fall-out from the Big Bang brought women dealers into highly-
paid jobs for the first time, competing with men in fast thinking, hard
drinking and bad language. Caryl Churchill's play *Serious Money*,
performed in 1987, the year of the Crash, depicted international
money-women – a British stockbroker, a Texan arbitrageur and a
Peruvian businesswomen – converging on London for ruthless
double-dealing, too absorbed by money to find time for love or sex.
As the heroine Scilla Todd says:

> Zac, you're so charming. I'm almost as fond
> Of you as I am of a Eurobond.

The British high-street banks brought in a cohort of women, including many with degrees and specialised qualifications, committing
themselves to equal opportunities and showing evidence of widespread promotion. In 1985 8 per cent of the Midland Bank's
managers were female; in 1991, apparently 20 per cent. But there
were suspicions that this merely reflected new titles – like a secretary
renamed 'office manager' – rather than a real breakthrough. The big
banks were all re-forming themselves into structures that separated
skills from authority, which still kept women out of the top grades:
in 1991 none of the top forty-two managers of the Midland was
female. Women in banks, concluded the sociologist Mike Savage,
'have not moved into the sorts of sectors where managerial discretion
is important, or where they are likely to be in charge of a specific
unit'. The really big financial deals, including raids and mergers,
remained an aggressively male preserve. The competitiveness of the
eighties, as we have noticed, thrived on images of virility and war –
cutting off the balls, searching and destroying – which had little
place for women. Many of the most publicised entrepreneurs, like
Sir James Goldsmith, Lord White and Sir Ralph Halpern, acquired

reputations for sexual as well as business triumphs, in the macho mould of the traditional master-financier, like Theodore Dreiser's *Titan*.

In the wider field of industry women also appeared to be advancing. By the eighties a new generation was challenging male strongholds across a much wider battleground of careers, including science and engineering, in both developed and developing countries. 'It is almost as though a magic wand has been waved over millions of sleeping beauties,' wrote John Harvey-Jones in 1988, 'for in countries as diverse as India and Japan, the USA and Latin America, we are seeing the emergence of a new, and very welcome, field of female talent. Highly trained, highly motivated and very involved in their work.' On the face of it, American women were making strides towards the top. In 1977 only forty-six women were on the boards of America's top companies; by 1993 five hundred women had one or more directorships among the thousand biggest industrial and service companies. But they were still only 6 per cent of the total number of directors in those companies. Almost half of America's top companies – including Disney, Lockheed, Safeway, Apple, Black & Decker and Digital Equipment – had no women on their boards. And most female directors were 'name-brand' women who came from outside business, from education or government. Of 4,012 listed as the highest-paid officers and directors of their companies, nineteen were women – less than half of one per cent.

In Britain, too, women were becoming more ambitious for business careers. By the early nineties they made up 45 per cent of students in business and management; and the Henley Centre for Forecasting predicted that women would get more jobs than men over the next decade. Over the twenty years from 1974, according to the Institute of Management, the proportion of women directors had gone up from 0.6 per cent to 2.8 per cent, and of department heads from 2.1 per cent to 8.7 per cent.

But by 1994 the trend appeared to be reversing, both in Britain and North America, where the downturn in women managers caused some puzzlement. 'It has come about because of two filtering biases,' wrote Professor Michael McCarrey of Ottawa University: 'sex-biased stereotypes and performance management or appraisal.' In Britain the Institute of Management reckoned that the proportion of women managers and directors in the largest organisations had fallen for the first time, from 10.2 per cent in 1993 to 9.5 per cent in 1994; and Trudy Coe of the Institute found confirmation inside the big companies: Marks & Spencer had seen a huge attrition of women in their mid-thirties, most of them being replaced by men.

The reversal was not altogether surprising, for many women had become managers just when big organisations were laying off middle-management in their thousands. 'Now that hierarchy is fast disappearing before their eyes,' wrote Tom Peters in 1992, 'along with the toehold so painstakingly gained.' The layoffs could be more demoralising for women, who lose the security of a fixed base, than for men. 'It's observably true that women are more loyal than men, and readier for a job for life,' said the headhunter Stephen Rowlinson in London. 'They put more value on the job, its status and importance: perhaps because it's harder to achieve, perhaps because of their nesting instinct.' Yet women also appeared resistant to big companies. 'Some women could be reacting against the non family-friendly policies of large companies,' said Roger Young, the director of the Institute of Management, 'and are opting to leave behind the stresses of corporation life for the buzz of being in control of their own companies.'

In Britain the assumptions of conventional companies remain emphatically masculine. When in 1992 the Institute of Directors polled its women directors (8 per cent of their members) a third claimed direct experience of discrimination, and three-quarters believed that the work-place discriminated against women. A study by Arthur Andersen showed that boards had been little changed by the supposed social upheavals: the typical director was a fifty-two-year-old chartered accountant, probably a golfer, from a grammar school; his most likely club was the RAC or the MCC. Out of 20,000 directors and senior executives, only 426 were women. The women in business who had gained most financially were chief executives' secretaries, whose average pay in central London went up from £11,200 to £18,600 in the five years to 1992. But this had more to do with the enhanced grandeur of chief executives than with women's promotion; and senior secretaries found it hard to transfer into management jobs with comparable pay.

Women who reached the top were still very conscious of discrimination. Rhiannon Chapman, the director of the Industrial Society in 1993, gave me her own explanation:

> The glass ceiling still operates. I know, because I've been turned down for a senior post because I was a woman: the chairman just couldn't bring himself to work with a woman. It's not really a question of gender, but of being different. The chaps always like to be with the same kind of people – you can see from the surveys of the boards – with wives who come from the same kind of backgrounds. I understand that: they're living in an uncertain world, and they only feel comfortable with people like themselves. They really think that the world is male.

Women appear to find better prospects in 'flat' organisations without formal hierarchies, or in small and flexible companies which require skills in human relationships and communications. Mary Baker, the president of Women in Management in Britain, maintains that: 'In these more open corporate structures, where partnership and discussion allow space for new ideas and new styles of management and, above all, where the performance of an individual is measured on objective not subjective grounds, the sort of business culture is created where women stay and prosper.'

The rejection of 'scientific management' and of mechanical systems should in theory give more opportunity for women's intuition and human values. In America Sally Helgesen in *The Female Advantage* has portrayed women as providing the kind of breakthrough that American companies need. Judy B. Rosener, a professor of management in California, maintained that women succeed by 'behaving like women' – sharing information and power, working interactively, inspiring enthusiasm and individual confidence – while men were too preoccupied by power-structures, rationality and commands.

Domestic experience suggests that women cope better than men with complicated day-to-day resources – which is the basis of management. Charles Handy insists that small dynamic companies need:

> People who can juggle with several tasks and assignments at one time, who are more interested in making things happen than in what title or office they hold, more concerned with power

and influence than status. They want people who value instinct and intuition as well as analysis and rationality, who can be tough but also tender, focused but friendly, people who can cope with these necessary contradictions. They want, therefore, as many women as they can get.

But most company women still have to resolve the same basic conflict that they faced when they first entered office life at the beginning of the century: between pursuing a business career and raising children. In some respects the combination is now easier. British companies must by law grant six months' maternity leave, and many allow more flexible hours to their brightest women executives: mothers are not noticeably less successful in business than unmarried or childless women. But the insecurity and competitiveness of the nineties has widened the gap between the two activities: the young mother in the office faces tensions between opposite demands, rhythms and paces – the computer versus the cradle, the telephone versus the tantrums. And many mothers who reach the top remain worried about neglecting their family life. As Phyllis Swersky, executive vice-president of the aluminium company Alcorp in America, explained: 'I don't cook, I don't take my children to malls and museums. And I don't have any close friends.' British business women may be less driven than Americans, but they face greater pressure as they reach the top. 'The ambition on the part of many women to have it all – career, management and family –' said a survey by the headhunters Spencer Stuart in 1992, 'has been proved to be possible but costly and fraught with compromise.' In November 1994 one of the highest-paid women in the country, Penny Hughes, President of Coca-Cola in Britain, announced that she was going to give up her job in order to have a baby.

Was a demanding job worth it? By the nineties surveys and interviews were suggesting growing disillusion among career women, particularly in bigger companies. Kate Figes, the author of *Because of Her Sex* in 1994, found that 'Nearly all the women I spoke to felt that work was essential, both financially and to keep them sane,' but was shocked to discover that 'because of the pressures of work and families, women aren't having any fun'. 'Women have been succeeding in the male-dominated corporate culture as a challenge,' said

Dr Judi Marshall, psychologist author of *Women Managers*, 'but when they have done it they quite often become disappointed and disillusioned about what they have found and become.'

The more fiercely big companies competed in the nineties, the less welcoming they became to senior women with different values. Directors might have been expected to look for more diversity at the top, to reflect the diversity of their customers and markets. But they were more inclined to close their ranks. 'Customers are not cloned like directors,' as one woman director put it sharply. 'But as the boards are more threatened by competition outside they don't want to feel threatened by women inside.'

JAPANESE WOMEN

The fear of women was magnified in the big Japanese companies, which were facing their own crisis of the genders. Until the eighties most Japanese company men assumed that their success depended on women playing a submissive or supportive role, whether in the office or in the home, to give the men both the time and the confidence for their successful careers. Japanese women appeared content to be 'office ladies', receptionists or tea-pourers looking after all their men's needs: most were in their early twenties, waiting to get married, sometimes with growing anxiety: after twenty-five they were known as 'Christmas cake after Christmas'. A marriage within the same office, *shokuba kekkon*, had an aura of romance, but women could not remain in the same firm as their husbands, thus stressing the separation between the firm and the home. A few women protested against their subservient role: in the early sixties the tea-pourers at the Kyoto City Office rebelled, only to fail without the support of their union. The Japanese government passed an Equal Employment Opportunity Law in 1986, but many Japanese women criticised it, including a career woman, Michiko Hasegawa, who wrote a popular article which complained that it introduced an alien concept, and demoralised the status of housewives.

The eighties brought some signs of change, particularly in smaller companies. In the early nineties a Japanese researcher, Takie

Sugiyama Lebra, interviewed twelve women company presidents who had broken through the gender barrier. Most were involved in communications, using their skills in foreign languages: 'No man can do anything about women's language ability,' said one of them. Most kept a low profile, adopting a humble, self-denigrating style which was effective in handling men: 'If a woman tries to do business on an equal footing with men,' said another, 'pretty soon she will be crushed under a hail of kicks and blows.' The twelve were not typical: only half were mothers, and the younger ones had husbands who actually helped with home chores. But they showed that women's skills in communications and language were becoming more valuable with the globalisation of business. The author concluded that 'Women entrepreneurs will in future come to play an increasingly greater role in Japan's internationalisation.'

Well-educated Japanese women were also widening their horizons, marrying later – at an average age of twenty-six – travelling abroad and seeing other societies. Some of them were staying abroad, marrying Western husbands who gave them more freedom. Yuriko Koike, a cosmopolitan TV presenter who in 1993 became a minister in the Hosokawa government, was a role-model for more questioning women: 'The high yen has helped to change attitudes,' she told me in Tokyo in December 1993. 'In the last few years millions of Japanese went abroad and saw how well other people lived: they asked themselves why they should work so hard, when they couldn't buy those gorgeous houses. They began to think about the whole of life: what is it?'

When skilled labour was scarce in the eighties Japanese companies were compelled to hire more women, and to give them more opportunity and choice: they could even refuse to work overtime. They were still, like Western women, more successful as specialists than as generalists, but they were competing seriously with men: far from slowing down the men's ambition – as some Westerners had hoped they would – they appeared to be intensifying it. They could excel at financial services, which became more valuable as Japanese interests stretched abroad, and they often had a shrewder understanding of people than men. 'You could say women are humanising the workplace,' said Mariko Fujiwara, research director of the Hakuhodo Institute of Life and Living in 1993, though they still had not 'figured out the right strategies to work within a large corporation'.

But it was a false dawn: in the recession of the nineties many companies offloaded women employees in their hundreds, while retaining their men: Mitsubishi, the giant trading company, stopped recruiting women altogether in 1994. In May 1994 the Minister for Industry, Eijiro Hata, admitted that women had been the last to be hired and the first to be fired, and appealed to employers to comply with the Equal Employment Opportunity Law; but he received little response. At the top of big companies the male dominance had hardly diminished.

Japanese company women, in fact, provided a more extreme example of the predicament of Western women. They were showing a mastery of skills which had once been the monopoly of males, and adding their own skills in communicating and human understanding. Yet the corporate citadels of finance and manufacture were becoming more aggressively masculine and less prepared for diversity, as they faced harsher competition, which was becoming less like a game and more like a war.

CHAPTER TWENTY

Global Battleground

> The twenty-first century capitalism will be domi-
> nated by a spectrum of capitalisms, some successful,
> some not. The crucial question for Americans, and
> perhaps for the world as a whole, is where our own
> nation will be located along the spectrum.
>
> ROBERT HEILBRONER,
> *Twenty-First Century Capitalism*, 1993

By the early nineties the global battles were making all company
people less secure and less confident, as they looked anxiously at
their rivals overseas. The industrial confrontation across the Pacific
was taking a new turn as the Americans saw themselves achieving an
industrial renaissance, while the Japanese faced yet another state of
shock. Japanese companies were suffering their worst crises for forty
years, made worse by past overborrowing and financial corruption.
The recession revealed all the faults in the system which had been
concealed during the boom, like beach rubbish in an ebb tide, and
threatened the whole tradition of corporate loyalty and paternalism.

Returning to Tokyo after two years away in December 1993, I
found the business atmosphere overcast. The diminished confidence
and lifestyle of the company men was evident everywhere: many of
the 3,000 bars and clubs in the Ginza were closing down for lack of
expense-account customers. On my last visit I had taken part in the
triumphal fortieth anniversary of Japan Air Lines, a showpiece for
the whole economy which had boomed with each new surge of trade
and tourism: it had just bought the Essex House hotel in New York,
and was preparing a twenty-five-storey headquarters on the Tokyo
waterfront. JAL had celebrated with an imaginative conference on
the New Global Age, with speeches from astronauts, poets and philo-
sophers about the nature of space and the future of air travel. But

soon afterwards it faced a global retreat, after a slump in tourists and business travellers and fiercer competition from Asian rivals with lower costs and a cheaper workforce. In the year ending March 1993 JAL lost 55 billion yen and paid no dividend. The visions of the future had evaporated into gloomy cost-cutting and doubts. As one JAL director said: 'We used to take the Americans' ideas. Then they took ours. Now there are no new ideas.'

Investors and bankers in Tokyo were drastically reducing their expectations of the big companies, and looking to America for solutions. In the words of Nobumitsu Kagami, Executive Vice-President of Nomura Investment Management:

The days of big business are really over. It's the end of the era which began with the Meiji restoration, when we first started to catch up with the West. The big companies won't be able to dominate anymore. The recession has eroded the authority of business leadership: it showed that the father wasn't infallible. It's also changing the lifestyle of the employees, allowing them to go home to their families. The problem is that they like it. At Nomura, people don't want to work late any more.

We need more small businesses for service industries, with better people, like the Americans: but it will cost us some social stability. The American recovery started with their changing corporate structure: we need to make our adjustments, with deregulation and training, to give more help to small companies.

Radical critics were welcoming the decline of the giants. 'Our society has been constructed on dependencies,' said Masataka Itoh of the newspaper *Asahi Shimbun*. 'Now we are liberated: we're finding ourselves.' And criticism of big companies was encouraged in 1993 by the coalition government led by the new party of Morihiro Hosokawa, which owed little to corporate donations and much more to small service companies in the large cities which had been hurt by big business. 'The fear of risk is linked to corporate habits,' said Yuriko Koike, the Vice-Minister for the Management Agency. 'We're trying to help small companies, which can reduce unemployment and encourage risk. We're a party of ventures; we must get back to them

– like Honda, Toyota or Sony in the early days. But it will take time to restart the adventurous spirit.'

The big companies themselves were much less confident, all the less after the death or retirement of their founders. In 1989 the pioneer Konosuke Matsushita died, the man who had set up his electrical company in 1918 and made it a model of paternalism and phenomenal exports, selling Panasonic electronics round the world. After his death the company faced scandals, defective products and collapsing profits. In 1993 Akio Morita had a stroke which removed him from the Sony corporation which he had founded in 1946. Morita had maintained his originality into his seventies: he had first out-spokenly criticised American management and then attacked Japanese companies, urging them to be more concerned with workers and shareholders and less with market share. His successor at Sony, Norio Ohga, was also an original – a former opera singer who commissioned a Sony building in Berlin because he had learnt to sing there. But he could not compete with Morita's inventiveness and salesmanship. Morita's departure spelt out the end of the heroic age of entrepre-neurs after the Second World War. Now Japanese companies were becoming more like Western bureaucracies, in which risk-takers were much harder to find.

Japanese company men were becoming more influenced by the Americans as they ventured abroad. Professor Naohiro Yashiro, of the Institute of International Relations in Tokyo, saw working customs in Japan beginning to converge with those in America and Europe, with more fairness and more opportunities for women. 'In some cases, Japanese management is applied in a more refined manner abroad, blending the Japanese efficiency with the fairness,' he said in December 1993. But Japan's managers were less sure of the lifetime employment which had given them such past stability. Young salarymen who had tolerated low pay in return for steady promotion now saw their ladders collapsing, and university graduates were experiencing unemployment for the first time. Both employers and employees were modifying their views of loyalty, though less than their counterparts in the West. 'I want to pick young men who are more confident and resilient, because we can't promise the same kind of security,' said Masahiro Oga, president of the Shogakukan publishing group. 'But the loss of loyalty is one-way: employees want their company to be loyal to them, without feeling loyal to it.'

Most big Japanese companies had accumulated far too many office-workers: Sony's white collar staff had gone up by 139 per cent in the eight years to 1992, its blue collars by only 6 per cent; Matsushita's white collars went up by 47 per cent while its blue collars had gone down by 24 per cent. By 1994 both companies were drastically reorganising: Sony divided itself up into eight almost autonomous companies; Matsushita reduced forty-eight divisions to ten. Honda was trying to purge its middle-aged managers with the new formula that if they were not promoted within twelve years they would cease to be managers. But all these companies remained overmanned in comparison with America.

Could the big companies keep their promise of lifetime employment? It was less expensive than the past commitment of Western companies like IBM: the Japanese had a lower retiring age (fifty-five), and they could shift ageing managers into their subsidiary companies, or into dignified non-jobs known as *madogiwa-zoku* ('sitting by the window'). By the early nineties the window was a euphemism, as the old employees were moved into basements without daylight or told to work at home. Many company men were pressed to take early retirement, which was given the new name *kata-tataki* ('tap on the shoulder').

But most Japanese corporations still saw mutual loyalty and commitment as the key to the harmony and long perspective which distinguished them from the Americans: for the more secure their employees, the more flexible and enterprising they could be.

The problems seemed to bear down on Toyota City when I visited it in December 1993, in the depths of the recession. The high yen – which had appreciated 2.5 times against the dollar over seven years – had made Japanese cars far more expensive abroad, and Toyota was ruthlessly cutting back its costs. It had already reduced the range of choice that it had extended to customers in the 'variety wars' of the eighties. 'We gave people more options than they really wanted in those bubble years,' said my guide Isao Inoue. 'We had too many different steering wheels or radios – some with six speakers. Now we're reducing the choice, without customers objecting.'

The cost-cutting was causing much resentment; the suppliers were beginning to protest against the relentless pressure of 'just in time' on their profits (in the plastics industry, suppliers had effectively revolted against the system). Even the Toyota workforce was less loyal in the recession. 'In the first thirty years workers took pride in the growth of the company itself,' said one manager. 'Now we have to give our workers job satisfaction, too. We need to make people understand all the systems.' Toyota was even looking critically at its headquarters staff: 'Every big organisation has the bureaucratic disease. You have to recognise the symptoms and try to cure it, but there's no panacea. We can't reduce management any faster without causing big social problems.' Some younger Toyota managers were calling for a much more radical restructuring. A ginger-group of 3,000 set up what they called the Revolutionary Group; though when their jobs were threatened they changed the name to the Restructuring Group.

The Toyoda family, who still own 3 per cent of the company, were losing their hold. Eiji Toyoda, the founder's nephew – the man who had visited Detroit in 1950 and perceived its limitations – was now eighty, and honorary chairman of the company. The founder's two sons, Shoichiro and Tatsuro Toyoda, were chairman and president. Younger Toyodas were climbing up the management, but there were no obvious successors. And the company, with all its paternalism, was beginning to loosen its commitment. As the plant manager Mikio Kitano described it:

> We're trying to maintain lifetime employment, but it's much harder. Toyota started as a very local company where people worked together like a family; and we've tried to keep a feeling of equality between young people and managers. But Toyota became too like IBM in its paternalism, and we see the danger: paternalism is ending in Japan too, and the next generation, like the politicians, have a more independent attitude.

American observers were now predicting that Toyota would have to reinvent itself, laying off tens of thousands of employees, which would undermine company loyalty. But they underestimated its resilience: by March 1994 Toyota had not fired a single employee. And it still had immense strengths. Its cash holdings – 'the bank of Toyota' – were worth $14 billion, and it survived the recession much more strongly than its rivals Honda, Nissan and Mazda. It was selling computer software, digital telecommunications, car phones, even pre-fabricated houses. And its plants abroad, unaffected by the rising yen, were stepping up their production, while the British factories were building a precious beach-head in the European market.

Above all Toyota still maintained flexibility, through the process of *kaizen*, or continual improvement. 'Why do you so openly reveal your methods to foreigners?' I asked when I was shown round the assembly plant. 'Because we still think we can keep five years ahead of the West.'

'I'm concerned that Toyota people may be too arrogant. That's the real danger: like the Americans in the fifties,' said the plant director Mikio Kitano. 'We have to have continual improvement. But the Japanese have the advantage of a continual inferiority complex: they're never sure of themselves.'

AMERICA FIGHTS BACK

Across the Pacific, there could be no doubt that the Americans were both catching up and becoming more like the Japanese. By the early nineties nearly all big American companies were talking in Japanese terms – suitably disguised – about teamwork, participation and contin-ual improvement, encouraged by the hundreds of books, lectures, manuals, and courses on Japanese methods, filled with evangelical zeal. As they said at Hewlett-Packard: 'We've got religion.'

The Americans were finally succeeding in translating theory into practice. In Detroit the car-makers had been temporarily saved by the Japanese trade agreements which restricted the imports of cars, giving them a few years to reorganise; and they were at last learning the merits of the 'lean production' which Japanese companies were practising in factories next-door. Only the galloping losses which threatened the American car-makers with collapse made them face up to the drastic changes needed.

Ford, as we saw in Chapter 14, were the first to go through the 'creative crisis', which forced them to transform their manage-ment methods and become the leanest of the Big Three. In the late seventies they employed over 200,000 people: by 1974 they were down to 100,000. They made no bones about the Japanese challenge; at their world conference in 1992 managers appeared in sweaters and open-necked shirts, vowing to match Toyota by 1997 and committing themselves to the new policy of 'collective intelligence' – a thoroughly Japanese concept.

But Ford's real secret was a new dedication to their basic purpose, the quality of the car. As Lindsay Halstead, the former chairman of Ford in Europe, put it: 'Most of us are in the company because we love the product.' In 1993 they chose a chairman who typified the new global dedication. Alex Trotman was a working-class Scotsman, the son of an Edinburgh carpet-layer who spent time with the RAF and joined Ford in Dagenham without going to university. He made his name working on the Cortina, became chief product analyst, and transferred to Detroit to escape British taxes and get close to the centre of power. He rose quickly to the top, where he wielded his axe on the committees, the perks and executive dining rooms, and never lost sight of the Japanese competition. 'They're not going to change in the foreseeable future,' he said in June 1994, 'except to get tougher and more efficient.' Trotman remained an expert on his product. When Michael Moore, the director of *Roger and Me*, made a television series for the BBC he stood outside successive company headquarters with a megaphone and challenged the bosses to come out and show their knowledge of their product with specific tasks: only Trotman agreed, efficiently changing the oil in a Ford truck.

General Motors had remained the most intractable. When Roger Smith left as chairman in 1990 he was replaced by Robert Stempel, the first engineer to reach the top in three decades. Like his predecessor he talked much about the company in the twenty-first century, but he could not cope with the immediate crises, and the losses which recurred every quarter. In December 1991 he dropped a bombshell by announcing the closure of twenty-one plants, which would cost 74,000 jobs. But he had no correspondingly positive plans, and shareholders and politicians were appalled: what was bad for GM was bad for the US.

By April 1992 the General Motors board, which included powerful outsiders, had had enough. In a historic coup they put in their own man as president, Jack Smith, who six months later replaced Stempel as chief executive. Smith was an unassuming company man from a modest Irish family, but he had been through a gruelling shock-treatment. He had been converted to Japanese methods when he negotiated the NUMMI joint venture with Toyota (see Chapter 11), and when he visited Toyota City he knew it held the key to his company's future. When he was put in charge of GM in Europe he swiftly applied Japanese principles, pressing the suppliers to cut costs and deliver just in time with the help of a fanatical Basque manager, Jose Ignacio Lopez, and his team of 'warriors'. He co-ordinated GM's scattered plants, from Opel in Germany to Vauxhall in Britain, and moved the headquarters to Zurich, in a modest building near the airport adjoining the Novotel, which could not hold more than two hundred people. He turned GM Europe into a big profit-maker which offset the losses in America: a triumph which put him in line for the succession.

Smith did not conceal his Asian influences, from ancient China as well as modern Japan: in his chief executive's office he displayed a stone inscribed with a motto from Lao-tze which begins: 'A leader is best when people barely know he exists.' In America he repeated his European strategy, beating down suppliers with the help of Lopez and causing much bitterness until Lopez defected amid huge contro-versy to Volkswagen a year later. Smith left the notorious fourteenth floor of the corporate headquarters, cut the bureaucracy from 13,000 to 2,000 and moved to GM's new technical centre fifteen miles away in the suburbs. 'The problem was never the people,' he explained. 'It was the screwed-up structure we had . . . We had a history I'd like not to repeat.'

By 1994 the Big Three car companies were again making hand-some profits; and they had all become much more like the Japanese. Their chief executives were much less complacent, after all the humiliations and trips to Tokyo. They were all recruiting better-educated workers, including some graduates, instead of the old 'cattle-call'. They were all squeezing their suppliers and testing their quality, like the Japanese. And they had begun talking to each other, and to the government in Washington, almost as if they were Japanese companies talking to their Ministry of Industry, MITI. 'The three of us have had more direct contact with the Administration in the past nine months than existed for the past twelve years,' said Bob Eaton of Chrysler in December 1993.

Other American company men were also more optimistic about their competitiveness with Japan, boosted by adopting Japanese systems, by massive layoffs and by the fall in the dollar. Corporations like General Electric and Boeing had shown they could respond to shock-treatment, and fight back with new energy, while the Japanese were still recovering from their own past self-indulgence and worried about their loss of leadership. 'Japan has completely lost out to the United States in the industrial race in leading sectors like electronics,' said Ryuzaburo Kaku, chairman of Canon, in 1994. In one area Americans were specially confident – computer software, which held the keys to the information highways of the future, which the Japanese could not replicate. The Japanese made pilgrimages to Silicon Valley and the Microsoft Campus in Seattle, and many Japanese-Americans graduated from Stanford to become computer-freaks. But they could not transplant the culture back to Japan. The government planners in Tokyo saw this as their most intransigent problem: it struck at the heart of the educational and cultural background which provided their strength in other industries – and even at their language, with its thousands of ideograms. 'Silicon Valley depends on half-crazy people who thrive on chaos and can think the unthinkable,' as one Japanese technocrat told me: 'But our schools can't train people for that.'

The success of American software brought out all the Japanese concerns about their lack of basic inventiveness in scientific areas, which was implied in their shortage of Nobel prizewinners and went back to the fundamental conflict between the individual and the collective mind which acquired a new significance in the new information age. 'In this new world,' wrote Professor Peter Berger in 1994, 'Americans may again discover that their economic culture, shaped by individualism and irreverence towards institutions, including the ones that employ them, is a source of cultural advantage.'

But the success of extreme individualism in California was not necessarily applicable to more organised businesses elsewhere. And the Japanese economic culture, with its emphasis on corporate loyalty, still had considerable advantages. It was still true, as Matsushita had warned Westerners in the seventies (see Chapter 11): 'For you, the essence of management is getting ideas out of the heads of bosses into the hands of labour . . . For us, the core of management is the art of mobilising and putting together the intellectual resources of all employees in the firm.'

The Japanese still had much easier communications between top and bottom, more sense of common purpose, better education and more industrial literacy. They could still combine individual initiative with passionate teamwork. And the companies' long-term commitment and loyalty still gave them more scope to plan far ahead into a fast-changing market-place.

Behind the apparent convergence of Japanese and American methods, the Japanese company men still believed in a quite different kind of capitalism, with responsibilities to employees and communities rather than to shareholders; and behind that was a much more organic, less mechanistic view of the company, with a sense of its roots and its need to be slowly nurtured and trained like a garden or a tree.

EUROPE DETACHED

European company men were watching the Japanese–American duel with some detachment, feeling more cushioned against the shock-treatment. German and Italian managers had already been through their own 'creative defeat' after the war, and had responded with their own miracles, throwing up self-made entrepreneurs and dynamic export industries. But they lacked the continuing insecurity complex of the Japanese, and they had become more complacent in the seventies, protected by their monopolies, by controlling families or banks, even though many industries were falling behind America and Asia. Many of the biggest companies which operated across Europe, including GM, Ford and ITT, were American-owned, while much of the British car and computer industries, including ICL, was Japanese-owned.

The car industry, which the Europeans had invented, was now especially vulnerable, caught between American and Japanese rivals, and left behind by both. The founders, like Renault, Agnelli and Morris, were protected by tariffs from American competition and had never fully transplanted the original mass-production system of Detroit. It was not till the fifties and sixties that they seriously adopted American systems – just when the Japanese were beginning to improve on them. By the late sixties their workers were fiercely revolting against their inhuman conditions.

Within Europe the car manufacturers could compete with the American-owned Fords and General Motors, but they were protected against Japanese intruders. When Volkswagen and Renault acquired factories on the American mainland in the seventies they both suffered deadly losses; they retreated back to Europe and a few developing countries. Paradoxically, both Ford and General Motors owed part of their revival to the experience in Europe, and to their use of Continental engineers, while the Europeans were less able to mobilise their skills across the frontiers.

The remaining European-owned car companies each had their own strong national culture, sustained by families or banks which could help them through crises and provide a long view. In Germany Mercedes was supported by the Deutsche Bank, and BMW by the Quandt family: both exported desirable quality cars, which could even penetrate the domestic Japanese market. Fiat remained a unique private fiefdom, of which the Agnelli family still owned over 30 per cent, still ruled by Gianni Agnelli after twenty-eight years. It still had a flair for engineering and design which could produce an elegant popular car like the Uno. And it wielded heavy political clout which protected it from Japanese competition.

But by the nineties BMW and Mercedes were facing Japanese cars which were cheaper and of equal quality, led by the Toyota Lexus. And Fiat was much more vulnerable, politically as well as financially. In 1993 its chief executive Cesare Romiti and other senior managers were charged with corruption, its losses were escalating, and it would face a Japanese invasion when it lost its protection in 1999. Agnelli was giving way to his brother Umberto and his nephew Giovanni, who were more likely to merge with another company and turn Fiat into a European combine which they could not control.

The British in the meantime had virtually abdicated from their own mass-car production, which had never been competitive abroad, and put their hopes in the Japanese-owned factories of Toyota, Nissan and Honda.

The original British Leyland, stripped down and renamed Rover, had been revived with the help of a quarter-share owned by Honda, and bought by British Aerospace. But it was still torn between the continents, and when BMW needed a British base Rover was sold to them, which made a quick gain for shareholders but antagonised the Japanese. The resulting row revealed all the contrast between Japanese and British attitudes to capitalism, short-term versus long-term: as Sir Peter Parker put it, it was 'the same bed, different dreams'.

Most European-owned car companies now looked weaker compared to the Japanese and Americans. The Europeans had never quite come to terms with the assembly-lines of the twentieth century, whether Fordism or Japanese lean production; and now they were again slow to catch up with the new challenges. Newer European industries, too, including electronics and computers, lacked the resources and commitment to compete with the other continents.

Significantly it was the makers of luxury goods, based on the tastes of the nineteenth-century bourgeoisie, who achieved the most striking European successes, with their brand names glittering from international airports and hotel boutiques in the Far East. Louis Vuitton's hand-made luggage was turned into a global status symbol in the 1970s by Henri Racamier, who had married a Vuitton descendant. Cartier, who had been the French court jewellers, had extended into leather goods, pens, spectacles and watches: 'We're not selling watches to tell the time,' their president Dominique Perrin explained in 1987. 'We're selling them to people who belong to a certain social class ... who want to show off.' Many of Britain's most dynamic exports were based on the masculine appeal of an earlier country-house lifestyle – including Dunhill, Burberry and Barbour, with the later addition of the Range-Rover, all of which conjured up the grouse moors. The European managers themselves were experts on leisure, accustomed to a month's holiday compared to the single weeks of many Americans and Japanese; and the most admired companies were the purveyors of leisure and status, which could project images of châteaux and salons before mass-production existed. They provided very marketable exports, particularly in Asia, but they were no substitute for successful mass-industry; while the Europeans were looking to Japan for their electronics, and to America for their software and entertainment. Even the old European myths and folk-tales were left to Disney to popularise, mass-produce and sell back to Europe.

GLOBAL MIX

The European company men were still immersed in their separate national cultures and styles, formed by their educational systems which each had their own specialities and limitations. French industry was still dominated by mandarins from the *grandes écoles*, who had moved more enthusiastically into business in the 1980s, with impress-ive qualifications but still resistant to the global market-place. German managers were the most confident, entering companies after a long education at about twenty-seven, with a strong technological tradition and support from the banks; but they were increasingly complacent and resistant to change, attacked as 'fools in pinstripes' (*Nieten in Nadelstreifen*, the title of a German best-seller attacking managers).

The British managers had become much more professional since the class divisions of the fifties which divided them into gentlemen and players. But companies were controlled by accountants rather than engineers (Britain had 120,000 accountants, while Germany had only 4,000, Japan only 6,000). And British managers remained less well-educated than most Continentals: a report by Charles Handy for the Manpower Services Commission in 1987 found that only 21 per cent of managers appeared to have any professional qualifications. 'Companies have asked too little from their would-be managers,' Handy commented, 'and given them too little in terms of education, training and development.' He pointed out that 'For no other role in life, other than parenting, is there no proficiency test, no preparatory education or early apprenticeship.'

The Continental versions of capitalism remained very distinct from the Anglo-American. The cross-holdings of German banks and the influence of supervisory boards gave German companies greater security and immunity to raiders, while the French government retained far more leverage over private as well as nationalised com-panies. The boards of most Continental companies preserved a more collegiate structure than British or American boards, which limited the powers of the chief executive and the tendency towards autocracy, while slowing down the decisions. The two huge Anglo-Dutch combines Shell and Unilever had both long ago developed their own versions of the Continental college; but the full contrast between the systems emerged after the Dutch publishing company Elsevier had merged in 1992 with the British Reed Group, under two co-chairmen. Peter Davis, the British chairman who had been a prime mover in the deal, wanted to dominate the board as he had dominated Reed, but came up against resentful Dutch colleagues led by their chairman Pierre Vinken. 'Moving from a classic Anglo-Saxon chairmanship to the Continental executive committee style is requiring a change of gears,' Davis later explained. 'I think a company needs a clear focus and clear leadership.' The Dutch insisted on their collegiate control, and the board refused to endorse Davis as sole chairman when Vinken retired, preferring an executive committee with two members from each country. Davis resigned in protest in June 1994 – 'I didn't want to keep living like this' – and picked up a £2 million golden handshake.

But many Continental companies were becoming more influenced by Anglo-Saxon pressures, as they acquired foreign shareholders who demanded more information and immediate results. When Daimler-Benz began selling shares in New York they came under American rules which compelled them to become much less secretive. Percy Barnevik at ABB in Zurich accepted the need to compromise between the systems: 'British analysts are beginning to realise we must look five years ahead,' he told me in 1994. 'Continentals complain that I'm being too American, while Americans tend to say: he's running it with his heart, not his brain.'

The national loyalties of companies were becoming altogether more blurred, as they bought up foreign businesses and more managers worked outside their own country. The Frenchman Daniel Goudevert joined the board of Volkswagen, the American Bob Beckman chaired the Anglo-American SmithKline Beecham, the Scot Alex Trotman took over Ford. Within the United States the contest between the hemispheres was confused further by the success of immigrants from Asia, both managers and workers, whose intelligence, hard work and flexibility were helping to make many companies more competitive with the other side of the Pacific. The Asians in America were competing with the Asians in Asia. Even products are less nationalistic than they look. All the major car companies are now interlocked with shareholdings and are buying key components from each other: it is hard to know where Mazda begins and Ford ends. Airliners or computers, too, include parts from two or three continents. American multinationals are becoming less like national industrial champions, more like global assembly-points. 'The core corporation is no longer even American,' wrote Robert Reich in 1991, before becoming Secretary of Labor in Washington: 'It is, increasingly, a façade, behind which teems an array of decentralised groups and subgroups continuously contracting with similarly diffuse working units all over the world.' And he summed up: 'There is coming to be no such thing as an American corporation or an American industry. The American economy is but a region of the global economy.'

But it is not true that 'ownership is unimportant' – as Michael Heseltine claimed when the German BMW bought the British Rover company. The rhetoric of multinationals still conceals much humbug. Only a very few multinational companies like Unilever, ABB and Shell have become genuinely detached from a single national interest. Several attempted mergers, from Dunlop-Pirelli to Volvo-Renault, have come apart through national rivalries, and most so-called transnational companies are firmly based on a single nation. While they may be able to run subsidiaries abroad peacefully so long as they have complementary skills (as Christopher Lorenz points out), they face political rows as soon as they shut down factories to suit their domestic interests.

Most skilled activities remain deeply rooted in their own country, or region or town, with a pride and motivation which cannot readily be transplanted; while much of the appeal of luxury products, including food and fashion, is associated with their home country. While companies need global managers to co-ordinate them and link them to the market-place, their excellence stems from their local roots, and their relationship with the surrounding society. And the greatest danger in the wave of mergers, layoffs and restructuring of company men is the destruction of the continuity on which that quality depends.

CHAPTER TWENTY ONE

Corporate Kings

'O brave new world,' said Robyn, 'where only the
managing directors have jobs.'
DAVID LODGE, *Nice Work*, 1988

The traditional company man with his confidence in annual
increments and a growing pension is as extinct as an eighteenth-
century clergyman. His decline has taken nearly everyone by surprise,
particularly politicians who preferred not to face up to it; yet it is
causing one of the biggest social upheavals of the twentieth century,
and its repercussions are still spreading.

In the mid-seventies the big corporations seemed as permanent as
nations: many of them were confidently preparing for their centen-
aries. The great signs of Ford, IBM or Fiat which shone above the
city skylines appeared to bind together the world's consumers and
producers in their confident embrace. Now once-great names like
Pan Am and Gulf have disappeared altogether; the loyalties to old
brand names are diminishing; and some of the healthiest survivors,
like General Electric in the US and Courtaulds in Britain, have been
transformed into quite different creatures. Most of them no longer
feel paternal towards their employees and communities; and they
are quick to replace lifetime employees with short-term specialists,
consultants and temp managers with no commitment.

The promise of corporate loyalty began to look like an absurd
indulgence which preserved incompetents and built up extravagant
bureaucracies. What *were* they all doing through the fifties and sixties
– those co-ordinators, liaison officers, in-house specialists, advisers
and lawyers – if they could eventually be dispensed with so easily?
But at the time the emperor's clothes were real enough. The hierarchy
symbolised by the skyscraper and the elevator was taken for granted.

Company men assumed that they must spend a lifetime climbing up it. The opaque structure with its hundreds of managers and specialists looked indispensable. The most profitable companies, which were monopolies or oligopolies, equated their success with the size of their bureaucracies.

The corporation everywhere was consciously or unconsciously part of a political system and a society to which it had to justify itself. Over the post-war decades it responded to the challenges of socialism, communism and labour unions by developing its own kind of private welfare state. In America the big companies made unwritten bargains with governments, which supported them in return for their looking after their company people: a political balancing act, as Gerald Czarnecki of IBM described it in Chapter 15. In Britain the company men in Unilever or ICI were hard to distinguish from managers in nationalised industries or the civil service. In Japan the post-war corporations promised lifetime employment partly in response to their fears of communist unions. Everywhere big business felt vulnerable to attacks from the Left, and responded with its own security.

But that bargain was broken in the eighties, as corporations exposed to the gales of world competition could no longer feel any responsibility for maintaining employment. Throughout the West the political mood turned fiercely against bureaucracies, whether public or private. The raiders mocked the complacent corpocrats for betraying their shareholders, while fund managers complained about their quarterly earnings and pressed them to cut back their overheads. Within a decade chairmen had stopped talking about social responsibilities and communities, and started boasting about reducing the headcount. The company men who had been clambering up the corporate ladders were now back on the pavement, with the doors shut against them.

The ex-company men were of course part of a much wider disruption. They like others were facing a reversion to an earlier kind of capitalism before it was countered by powerful unions and softened by corporate welfare, when it more clearly resembled 'nature, red in tooth and claw' and seemed to threaten all stable human relationships. As Karl Marx described it in 1848: 'It has pitilessly torn asunder the motley feudal ties that bound man to his "natural superiors" and has left remaining no other nexus between man and man than naked

self-interest and callous cash payment.' The capacity of capitalism
to destroy as well as create was a familiar concept, summed up in
Schumpeter's theory of 'creative destruction'. But its ferocity was
restrained over the post-war decades by unions, state regulation and
corporate monopolies. It was not till the mid-eighties that it showed
its force again, with growing momentum, so that even in the recession
of the early nineties it was gathering speed. As Edward Luttwak
described it in 1994, echoing Marx, 'The engine turns, grinding lives
and grinding down established human relationships, even when the
car is stopped.' The central problem of our days, he said, is 'the
completely unprecedented personal economic insecurity of working
people, from industrial workers and white collar clerks to medium-
high managers'. Luttwak saw this insecurity leading to a new wave
of fascism.

There were growing doubts as to whether the West could keep
up with the pace of change without a major political upheaval. Some
European politicians now believe that global free trade and competition from cheap Asian labour will become so destructive of settled
communities that they will have to abandon not only a closer European union but also the global trade agreement. In 1994 Sir James
Goldsmith, who had made his fortune in the global market-place,
was elected a member of the European Parliament on his protectionist
policy, encouraged by his ecological brother Teddy. But the long-
term costs of protectionism are alarming, as it cuts Europe off from
the challenges of competition and innovation. And the global engine
is still gaining a momentum which appears unstoppable.

The most devastated class in the West were the unskilled workers,
who found themselves competing both with further automation and
with cheaper and more flexible labour in Asia and Latin America.
They were faced once again by the insecurities of their nineteenth-
century forebears, but with less prospect of protection by unions.
The old servant class had been replaced by a migrant army of hotel
and restaurant workers catering for a mobile clientele who never even
learnt their names.

But the more politically significant impact was on the middle
classes, who were more seriously hit than in Marx's day. Robert
Reich divides the American population into a 15 per cent underclass,
another 15 per cent 'over-class', and a large majority between them

whom he calls 'the anxious class', who will be increasingly tempted to support protectionism: 'The coming political battle will be for the souls of the anxious class.' The middle classes, it is true, have often squealed before, whether about high taxes, education or earlier waves of unemployment; but today their fears are more justified. All middle-class institutions across the West are now vulnerable to the growing insecurity and competition. Governments are themselves cutting their bureaucracies and welfare; even the old professions, including the law and medicine, can no longer guarantee jobs for life, and universities demand performance-related pay. 'No one can feel altogether secure, even if we do see years and years of steady growth with low inflation,' warned Andrew Britten, the director of the National Institute of Economic and Social Research, in 1994. Conservative politicians are caught between two ideologies: as neo-liberals they praise competitiveness and deregulation, while as traditional conservatives they deplore the decline in stable family values which is blamed for crime, drugs and social disintegration. But these are two sides of the same coin: the industrial dynamism has been achieved at the cost of social stability. We are back again to the nineteenth century; but with much less support from the churches or extended families which provided some kind of social safety-net in Victorian times. And the stronghold of the twentieth-century middle class, the corporation, is now its most vulnerable sector.

The company men who seemed most secure are now the most vulnerable. In Britain they were quite unprepared for the speed of the change, and remained weak in political organisation. They could find little support from their former conservative allies. As the political scientist John Gray wrote in *The Undoing of Conservatism*:

> The social and cultural effects of market liberalism are, virtually without exception, inimical to the values that traditional conservatives hold dear. Communities are scattered to the winds by the gale of creative destruction. Endless 'downsizing' and 'flattening' of enterprises fosters ubiquitous insecurity and makes loyalty to the company a cruel joke.

In this fast-changing scene the company employees are much more vulnerable to the controllers of capital. The more aggressive fund managers are determined to maximise their clients' profits, monitoring quarterly earnings and pressing chief executives to wield the axe further, even in companies which are very profitable. The more office workers are laid off, the more the shareholders benefit; and the gap between the generations is widened. Already by the seventies few young middle-class people could aspire to their parents' standard of living: by the eighties employees were much less secure, while shareholders were richer. The older generation, largely retired, benefit from the layoffs, while the younger generation are the victims. The profits for the old are at the expense of the security of the young.

NEW MONARCHIES

Inside the companies the balance has changed even more dramatically, with a shift of both power and money towards the top. This is most obvious to the ordinary workers: the unions which grew up a century ago as their champions have been undermined by the competition from cheaper labour abroad, and by rising unemployment at home. Many workers, it is true, enjoy more responsibility and involvement than before: the need for effective teamwork and quality, influenced by the Japanese, has compelled the best managers to take much more note of their workers' motivation. But empowerment becomes meaningless when it leads to the sack. Some chairmen are themselves worried about the lack of counterweights. 'Managers are really too strong,' said Sir John Harvey-Jones, the ex-chairman of ICI. 'Management has never been so powerful, or so unaccountable,' said Christopher Haskins of Northern Foods. Even some Republican businessmen in America are concerned about the weakness of the unions. 'The employees need to have proper representation,' said George Shultz, the former Secretary of the Treasury. 'It's all the more unfortunate that the unions are so badly run.'

The middle-managers too are much more dependent on a few men at the top. Contemporary theories of business present a picture of power being disseminated, as headquarters palaces are evacuated and their inhabitants dispersed into small offices and even homes. Chief executives in Britain as well as America talk about empowering managers, about 'taking ownership' or 'controlling your destiny'. 'It's not the bosses who choose the managers,' says Martin Taylor of Hanson's, 'it's the market.' But the men at the top can interpret the market-place in a very personal way, as they make judgements about hiring and firing; and they can inspire much more fear in an age of high unemployment.

The appearance of delegation can be misleading, for computerised financial systems can effectively conceal where the real power lies. The manager of a supermarket or a small factory may be told that he controls his destiny, but his real controllers are the constant printouts, assessments and financial checks from his headquarters. The computer tells him much more about the cash flow and demand in his own branch, but the key decisions about strategy and investment, which may close down his whole operation, are held close at the centre. Even the leanest headquarters offices can maintain very strict controls, like Percy Barnevik's ABB offices in Zurich. 'ABB is not as decentralised as it may appear,' said one of its engineers, Bertil Nordqvist of the Federation of Graduate Engineers in Sweden: 'Responsibility has been decentralised – but not power.'

The biggest and consistently best-managed companies like Shell and AT&T have maintained a tradition in which the chairman is part of a committee, with limited powers; but companies undergoing drastic reforms and cutbacks inevitably give more power to a single boss. As they become leaner, cutting back their layers of fat, they tend to look less like republics, more like monarchies. Investors, managers and the media all look for a charismatic, flamboyant boss with a distinctive image, who can personify the company, while the revived emphasis on leadership encourages a more personal and regal style. A leader can surround himself with a miniature court of favourites and flatterers. When he is ousted or retired, his successor can bring in his own courtiers whom he can trust, and embark on 'corporate cleansing' to remove suspect influences and establish his own culture. The most radical reformers inevitably favour more centralised systems, like Jack Welch of General Electric, who was the model for many others. He replaced the company's 'wedding cake' structure with the 'cartwheel', whose spokes all converged on him, while he eased out the 'resistors' who stood in his way (see Chapter 14). Dissidents can be portrayed as traitors, and autocratic chiefs can replace their senior managers – who might become rivals – with consultants who are paid to agree with them. Some of the chiefs begin to look more like the corporate grandees of the thirties, like Teagle, McGowan or Deterding (see Chapter 5), who could dominate their boards with their own company's money. The new monarchs may be less secure than the old, for they are subject to fiercer competition and more inspection; but they are all the more tempted to fortify themselves at the expense of their rivals. 'Business isn't naturally democratic: the early owner-managers were all autocrats,' as Christopher Haskins puts it. 'But leadership is a dangerous concept: we need accountability. Capitalism has really failed to achieve it.' Boards produce their own political correctness, to conceal their dominance: high fees become 'compensation', 'rewards' or 'remuneration'; firing becomes 'letting people go', 'restructuring', 'downsizing' or 'rightsizing'; centralising becomes 'decentralising'. Directors, like most other human beings, protect their own interests and fortify their power.

Headhunters argue that employees prefer their chairman to be surrounded with appropriate splendour. 'Tribesmen like their chieftain to be beautifully attired,' said Nigel Humphreys of Tyzack Accord. 'Privates in the army like a general to appear grand. Factory workers in the Midlands like to see the chairman in a Roller. The boss must be chromatic, not monochrome.' But while the chieftains regale and protect themselves, they can no longer deliver what the tribe most wants: protection from the insecurity outside.

The biggest companies in America, Europe and Asia all have problems with controlling autocrats, within their widely varied versions of capitalism. The Japanese claim to organise retirements and successions better than the West through their system of consensus, but they also find it harder to dislodge dominating bosses. Many of the post-war industrial pioneers in Japan were both inventive and democratically-minded, but their successors are more inclined to relish the trappings of power: the bowing acolytes, the elaborate feasts, the grand corporate headquarters (no British bank can compete in grandeur with the London headquarters of Nomura). 'The corporate bureaucracy and power structure have no real checks,' said Kiichi Mochizuku of the Pacific Institute in 1994. 'They are absolute corporate kings.'

The German chairmen are becoming harder to dislodge, in spite of their supervisory boards and the industrial failures of the nineties. 'The chairmen always begin to think they own the company,' said one Anglo-German sociologist. 'They're acting like seventeenth-century princes, or like business in the 1880s before the unions became stronger. Companies are less well organised than politicians to get rid of their bosses and choose a successor.'

Even the French are becoming more worried about their tradition-ally over-centralised power. 'The French caste system, based on a mandarinate, gives huge power to presidents: it's really based on monarchic principles,' said Octave Gelinier, ex-president of Cegos, the Commission for Scientific Organisation. 'Decentralisation allows more centralisation of major decisions,' said Jean-Pierre Tirouflet, the joint director-general of Rhône-Poulenc. 'Leadership becomes more important than diplomas.'

But British and American companies face the greatest difficulties in controlling their autocrats. They are more conditioned to individual leadership at the top, as we saw in Chapter 20, against the more collegiate tradition in Continental Europe: this was dramatised in the Anglo-Dutch merger of Reed-Elsevier. They have had a more fragmented ownership, with fewer dominant shareholders. They lack the restraints of the supervisory boards, or a broader commitment to stakeholders. And their lack of accountability was spotlighted by the rush of high salaries in the nineties.

THE SCORE

It is with their salaries that the chiefs show their ultimate power over the company men. While middle-managers have been helpless to protect themselves from layoffs, rewards at the top have increased to levels which have exasperated employees, shareholders and politicians on both sides of the Atlantic.

In America huge rewards were part of a more risk-taking entrepre-neurial tradition and respect for money-values. When Sir Owen Green of BTR asked one of his American directors why he demanded such a high salary he replied: 'It's the score.' As Green put it to me:

'America is still a kind of frontier society which respects the richest man in town.' But even American investors were becoming worried about who really decided the score, and they were protesting against some of the biggest payments, like that to Michael Eisner, the chief executive of Disney, whose salary has been reckoned as close to the entire gross national product of Grenada – or to the pay of all 4,000 gardeners in Disneyworld in Florida. The disconnection between the rising salaries of chief executives and the mediocre performance of their corporations – for instance Rand Araskog at ITT – was infuriating American fund managers.

In Britain, where people live closer together, businessmen in the post-war decades had seen themselves as more accountable than Americans to their surrounding society, which helped to restrain their demands; so their change of attitude in the eighties was all the more spectacular, just when managers and workers were facing mass lay-offs. At first higher salaries were explained as essential to offset high taxes, or to compensate for dwindling company perks; but as taxes went down and perks remained, the salaries went up. They were most spectacular in the City of London, where a few went above a million pounds a year; and the City soon influenced the demands elsewhere in industry – to the dismay of industrial chairmen like Sir Denys Henderson of ICI, who sat on banks' boards. The competition for salaries acquired its own momentum, speeded up by the headhunters who could play companies against each other and create new markets in directorships, breaking down corporate loyalties and encouraging mobility. By the early nineties the escalation of fees and payoffs appeared to some observers to be out of control. And as the American pay expert Professor Graef Crystal warned the British in 1994, comparing their salaries to the Americans': 'You ain't seen nothin' yet.'

A few of the British high earners were genuine entrepreneurs on the American pattern who had been brought in to turn round a somnolent company, with a salary, bonus and share options linked to the performance. But many were very conventional company men, often in ex-nationalised industries, who could benefit from the new mood to double or triple their salaries and exact huge payoffs when they retired or were fired. They were loudly criticised by shareholders, the media and even Conservative ministers: 'I wish more of our business leaders showed a decent level of restraint,' complained Kenneth Clarke, the Chancellor of the Exchequer in 1994. But wishes were not enough: in November 1994 there was a new outcry when the chief executive of British Gas, Cedric Brown, was awarded a 75 per cent pay increase just as domestic gas prices were going up. The bosses appeared immune to criticisms and social sanctions: 'In this business you must have a thick skin,' one of them explained. They were determined to separate themselves from the rest of the company men, and from the society around them, to become part of a new elite of owners of capital. They seemed to be re-establishing a class system, as they installed themselves as a new aristocracy in country houses and estates. The rise of this new class coincided neatly with the retreat of old landowners who had lost their fortunes in Lloyds insurance market, and whose estates could be taken over. They began to look more like the caricatured fat cats of the 1920s and 1930s, or the 'hard-faced men who looked as if they had done very well out of the war'. But they were now operating in a much more transparent atmosphere, with much greater pressure for accountability: and they were doing serious political damage to the Conservative Party which had first unleashed their ambitions.

THE OWNERS

Who could control them? The abuses of power have revived the uncertainty about the basic legitimacy of the corporation. There had always been doubts about the safeguards of the limited liability company or *société anonyme* which took shape in the mid-nineteenth century and expanded with the railways, run by entrepreneurs who were remote from their thousands of shareholders. After the original owners or families distanced themselves from the control of production, the idea of 'managerial capitalism' was welcomed, with salaried professionals who appeared dedicated to the long-term good of the company, and often achieved spectacular growth and stability. But confidence waned as their performance diminished, while the more ambitious managers could exploit their companies to suit themselves. In America a few unscrupulous bosses could enrich themselves without any effective control: Ross Johnson could treat the giant company RJR-Nabisco as his personal domain, using its private airline and luxury hotel suites to entertain his friends and conspire for their own enrichment.

The major shareholders, the pension funds, were slow to assert themselves against the chairmen and directors, but they became more impatient in the eighties. They took the side of raiders who promised to increase profits by dislodging the corpocrats in sleepy companies, and they became more restless as the giant corporations failed to face up to the global challenge. By the early nineties the biggest American funds were collaborating in a succession of dramatic boardroom coups: against IBM, Westinghouse, GM and Kodak.

In Britain the pension funds were more reluctant to move, but the scandals in the late eighties, including Guinness and Polly Peck, forced them to intervene more vigorously. The monstrous dominion of Robert Maxwell, who bullied directors, auditors and pension funds into submission and treated his managers as courtiers, showed up all the lack of safeguards for both shareholders and employees. And the huge increases in bosses' salaries and payoffs in quite ordinary companies in the nineties exposed the general lack of accountability. The British funds began to intervene more visibly, led by the Postel funds who handle Post Office and Telecom pensions. Their chief executive Alastair Ross Goobey, supported by his chairman Sir Martin Jacomb, publicly opposed the 'rolling contracts' which allowed directors three years' pay if they were fired. 'Frankly, some payoffs have been astonishing, quite obscene,' he complained. 'They cause resentment in the workforce, are not good for morale and don't give capitalism a good image.' But the funds were still wary of having to choose chief executives, or to become involved in management. 'The funds can't manage – we couldn't even run a candy store,' Ross Goobey told me in 1993. 'We can only set a framework for management. We want structures which give us confidence that companies aren't being managed for managers' sake.' And the scope for fund managers to ban rolling contracts was severely limited by their own directors, many of whom had similar contracts.

Faced with over-powerful bosses, the major investors in Britain and America became more seriously worried about what they discreetly called 'corporate governance'. In the United States General

Motors published guidelines for corporate governance in 1994 which influenced many other corporations: they gave much more independent power to outside directors, to meet separately under their own leader, to review the chief executive's performance each year and to make plans for the succession. In Britain a committee headed by Sir Adrian Cadbury recommended more effective accountability, including separating chief executives from chairmen, and giving more power and information to non-executive directors; but the proposals remained voluntary. Outside directors remained very reluctant to challenge their chairmen when that would risk forgoing their own fees, and those who fixed chairmen's and chief executives' salaries were often familiar 'remunerators' who had their own interest in higher fees.

The reformers underestimated the power of a monarchic boss to intimidate his board and silence his opposition. The problem was personified by Lord Weinstock, who for thirty years had dominated GEC, Britain's biggest engineering company, as managing director, choosing his own chairmen and directors who dared not contradict him – including his son Simon, whom he favoured as his successor – while the company's engineering languished. At the age of seventy Weinstock's position was renewed for another two years, against opposition from Postel, but with the reluctant assent of other funds.

Uncertainties about succession remained the greatest danger for monarchic companies, as they were for earlier European kingdoms – or for Dombey and Son. Most brilliant autocrats, like Weinstock and Hanson, have some kind of Napoleonic wish to establish a dynasty, thus creating their own succession problem, consciously or unconsciously weakening any rivals. It is an unsettling atmosphere for the dedicated engineers or executives on whom the actual products depend.

In the nineties loyal company men watched their departing bosses making their fortunes out of failure; and saw personal profit becoming increasingly divorced from production, added value and teamwork. The sense of corporate loyalty was often too solid in the past; but it was now dissolving so fast that it threatened to undermine any continuity. And the problem was more serious in the face of global competition with Asian corporations which maintained a continuous commitment, more closely related to the rest of their society.

Corporations are back with the problem of unaccountability with which they began. The directors who were managing other people's money, as Adam Smith warned, could never be expected to be as vigilant as the earlier partners looking after their own. The loss of accountability was a recurring problem as corporations got bigger, and directors more remote; but it reached a new crisis in the 1980s, with the weakening of corporate loyalty and the burst of individual ambition, spreading from America to Europe, which further separated the top from the bottom.

This was inevitably becoming a political problem, as it affects the competitiveness of nations and the health of their societies, while threatening to widen the rift between employers and employees. The excesses are unlikely to be effectively restrained by existing plans for corporate governance. The only effective counterforce must come from the broader representation of both employees and shareholders, with elements of the Continental system, but with greater transparency and more frequent meetings – which can only be achieved through sustained political pressure: but Social Democrat politicians remain reluctant to make any moves that might be attacked as anti-capitalist.

The most effective pressure must come from the company people themselves. It is the managers, for all their past mistakes and weaknesses, who remain the keys to production and prosperity; and they, more than anyone, suffer from the disruption and disintegration of corporate loyalty. They are beginning to realise, as they watch the abuses of power at the top, that the accountability of their companies is essential to their own continuity and achievement, and to the health of the capitalist system. And accountability will become a more explosive issue in the twenty-first century.

Source Notes

INTRODUCTION

ix 'Read more novels': quoted in Charles
    Handy, *The Empty Raincoat*, p. 126,
    Hutchinson, London, 1994

CHAPTER ONE

3   'We feel the machine slipping':
    Robert Lowell, 'Since 1939', 1977
3   'The enemy of the market': J.K.
    Galbraith, *The New Industrial State*,
    p. 33, Hamish Hamilton, London,
    1967
3   'The very scum of the earth': *Seattle*,
    edited by John Wilcock, PTERAPA
    Publications, Hong Kong
    (distributed by Houghton Mifflin,
    Boston), 1993
9   'Mike Hallman had defected':
    Stephen Manes and Paul Andrews,
    Gates, pp. 394, 434, Touchstone
    (Simon & Schuster), New York,
    1994
12 'Well, someday': ibid., p. 456
14 'It is the Age of Machinery': Thomas
    Carlyle, *Signs of the Times: Critical and
    Miscellaneous Essays*, 1838
14 'the mechanical control of man':
    Norbert Wiener, *The Human Use of
    Human Beings*, pp. 209–10, Eyre &
    Spottiswoode, London, 1950
15 'from ordered individuality': Thomas
    Pynchon, *Slow Learner*, p. 86
    (paperback edition), Picador,
    London, 1985

CHAPTER TWO

16 'The first stock-exchanges': Fernand
    Braudel, *The Wheels of Commerce*,
    pp. 100, 101, Collins, London,
    1992

17 'Corporations have neither bodies':
    see John Poynder, *Literary Extracts*,
    Vol. 1, p. 268, 1844
17 'Corporate bodies are more corrupt':
    William Hazlitt, *Table Talk*, Essay
    XXVII: 'On Corporate Bodies'
18 'Royal Charter': Holden Furber,
    John Company at Work, p. 268,
    Harvard University Press,
    Cambridge Mass., 1948
18 'Most profitable part': John Keay,
    The Honourable Company, pp. 454–5,
    HarperCollins, London, 1991
19 'The business, though laborious':
    Bruce Mazlish, *James and John
    Stuart Mill*, p. 141, Hutchinson,
    London, 1975
19 'he wrote much': ibid., p. 199
19 'found office duties': John Stuart
    Mill, *Autobiography* (unaltered
    edition), Chapter 3, Columbia
    University Press, New York, 1924
20 'From ten to eleven': Carl Van
    Doren, *Thomas Love Peacock*, p. 222,
    J.M. Dent, London, 1911
20 'model man of business': ibid.,
    pp. 211–22
20 'Ushered to his office': ibid., p. 223
20 'Quill-driving gentlemen': E.V.
    Lucas, *Life of Charles Lamb*,
    pp. 309–11, Methuen, London,
    1921
21 'Reproved for arriving late': William
    Foster, *The East India House*, p. 178,
    John Lane The Bodley Head,
    London, 1924
21 'Confusion blast all': E.V. Lucas,
    op. cit., p. 434
21 'Thirty years have I served': ibid.,
    p. 600

21 'Like passing out of': Charles Lamb, *Essays of Elia 1818*: 'The Superannuated Man'

21 'That dry drudgery': ibid., 'Work'

21 'a soul had been put into': Mrs Craik, *John Halifax, Gentleman*, Chapter 27, 1857

22 'possessed to the full': ibid., Chapter 8

22 'Cash nexus': Mrs Gaskell, *North and South*, Chapter 26, 1855. 'Cash nexus' was the phrase of Carlyle

24 'When the house is finished': Thomas Mann, *Buddenbrooks*, p. 332, Penguin, London, 1952

24 'the villian escapes': Mrs Gaskell, *North and South*, Chapter 9

24 'more disciplined world': Frank McKenna, quoted in Nicholas Faith, *The World the Railways Made*, p. 214, Carroll & Graf, New York, 1990

25 'One can sit with': Keith Robbins, *Sir Edward Grey*, p. 103, Cassell, London, 1971

26 'In a joint-stock company': Henry Fawcett, *Political Economy*, pp. 1,6,77, 1863

26 'This new corporation': Peter Drucker, *Frontiers of Management*, p. 170, Dutton, New York, 1986

26 'This little world': Emile Zola (trans. Leonard Tancock), *La Bête Humaine*, p. 151, Penguin Books, London, 1977

26 'three-quarters of a million': J.H. Clapham, *The Economic Development of France and Germany* (4th edition), p. 349, Cambridge University Press, 1961

26 'In Prussia railway employees': Faith, op. cit., p. 223

27 'A peculiarly American type': Daniel Boorstin, *National Experience*, pp. 115–16, Weidenfeld & Nicolson, London, 1966

27 'The corporation came to be regarded': Joseph C Furnas, *The Americans*, Putnams, New York, 1969 (Longman's, London, 1970)

28 'created a class of': Charles Francis Adams, *A Chapter of Erie*, New York, 1870

29 'There was growing up': Theodore Dreiser, *The Titan*, p. 395, Constable, London, 1928

29 'A wonderful look of power': Trollope, *The Way We Live Now*, Chapter 4, London, 1875. See also introduction by John Sutherland to World's Classics edition, OUP, 1982

29 'Finance is an art': Theodore Dreiser, *The Financier*, p. 120, Meridian Classics, New York, 1986

29 'It was a powerful mind': ibid., p. 396

29 'What would you say': ibid., p. 447

30 'careful, internal organisational structure': Alfred D. Chandler Jr, *The Visible Hand*, p. 97, Harvard University Press, Cambridge Mass., 1977

30 'managerial capitalism': ibid., p. 491

31 'All New York was demanding': Henry Adams, *The Education of Henry Adams*, p. 499, Houghton Mifflin, New York, 1961

31 'In Tokyo live': Hugh Cortazzi and George Webb (editors), *Kipling's Japan*, p. 215, Athlone Press, London, 1988

32 'The world's first': Michio Morishima, *Democracy and Economic Growth: The Japanese Experience*, London School of Economics

32 'To build modern enterprises': Johannes Hirschmeier, in *The State and Economic Enterprise in Japan*, edited by William L. Lockwood, pp. 232–43, Princeton University Press, New York, 1965

32 'Unspeakable business': Thomas Adams and N. Kobayashi, *The World of Japanese Business*, p. 37, Ward Lock, London, 1970

32 'The role of samurai families': Yasuzo Horie, 'Entrepreneurship in Meiji Japan', in *The State and*

Economic Enterprise in Japan, op. cit., p. 195

33 'Although this enterprise': ibid., p. 233

33 Rodney Clark, *The Japanese Company*, p. 37, Yale University Press, 1979

33 'The business world was already': Michio Morishima, *Banking and Industry in Japan*, London School of Economics Financial Markets Group, Special Paper No. 51, January 1993

34 'city of light': Edwin Seidensticker, *Low City, High City*, pp. 81, 109, Tuttle, Tokyo, 1984

34 'While Japan continues to think': Lafcadio Hearn, *Japan: An Attempt at Interpretation*, p. 496, Macmillan, New York, 1904

CHAPTER THREE

35 'Capitalist societies': Robert Heilbroner, *Twenty-First Century Capitalism*, p. 104, W.W. Norton, New York, 1993

35 'The huge jagged city': Henry James, *The American Scene*, New York, 1907. Reprinted by Granville Publishing, Angel Bookshop London, 1987, p. 10

35 'each of these huge': ibid., p. 59

35 'his descendants were never': Fred Kaplan, *Henry James*, p. 7, Hodder & Stoughton, London, 1992

36 'a line of research': James, op. cit., p. 82

36 'I aimed at the public's heart': *The Autobiography of Upton Sinclair*, pp. 125–6, W.H. Allen, London, 1963

36 'snuffy little man': Theresa Whistler, *Imagination of the Heart*, p. 44, Duckworth, London, 1993

36 'could not recall': ibid., p. 104

37 'The bank was no place for us': P.G. Wodehouse, *Psmith in the City*, A. & C. Black, London, 1910

37 'We are in the presence': Woodrow Wilson, *The New Freedom*, Doubleday, New York, 1913

38 'the old pictures': H.H. Gerth and C. Wright Mills, *From Max Weber*, p. 15, Routledge, London, 1948

38 'Among these masses': ibid.

38 'happy returning natives': H.G. Wells, *The Future in America*, p. 53, Chapman & Hall, London, 1906

38 'The individuals': ibid., p. 55

38 'That steady trend': ibid., p. 110

38 'an amazing cliff': Joseph C. Furnas, *The Americans*, p. 768, Putnams, New York, 1969 (Longman's, London, 1970)

39 'this amazing city': Theodore Dreiser, *A Book About Myself*, p. 417, Constable, London, 1929

39 'Gilbert who finally': Mark Sullivan, *Our Times: 1900–1925*, Vol. VI, p. 112 (new edition), Scribners, New York, 1972

39 'as though the life': Dreiser, op. cit., p. 417

39 'a great believer': Theodore Dreiser, *Sister Carrie*, Chapters 29 and 36, Heinemann, London, 1901

39 'hierarchies of engineers': Chandler, *The Visible Hand*, op. cit., pp. 399, 414–16. See also Thomas C. Cochran, *Social Change in Industrial Society: Twentieth Century America*, Allen & Unwin, London, 1972

40 'an institution is the lengthened shadow': Ralph Waldo Emerson, *Essays: First Series 1841*: 'Self Reliance'

40 'the most famous': Allan Nevins, *John D. Rockefeller*, Vol. 2, p. 100, Scribners, New York, 1940

40 'Solid as a prison': Thomas Lawson, *Frenzied Finance*, p. 181, Heinemann, London, 1906

40 'When the secretary': ibid., p. 181

41 'sanctum sanctorum': ibid., p. 14

41 'I never came into': Nevins, op. cit., Vol. 1, p. 624

41 'this movement was': ibid., p. 622

41 'he would make up': Austin L. Moore, *John D Archbold*, Macmillan, 1930

41 'Every Standard Oil man': Lawson, op. cit., p. 8

42 'the very genius': Daniel Yergin, *The Prize*, p. 109, Simon & Schuster, New York, 1991

42 'the young fellows': Nevins, op. cit., Vol. 2, p. 605

42 'have absolutely retired': Gibb and Knowlton, *The Resurgent Years*, p. 38, Harper, New York

42 'The day of combination': Nevins, op. cit., Vol. 1, p. 622

42 'the nightnurse heard': John Dos Passos, *The Big Money*, p. 48, Signet Classics (paperback edition), New York, 1969

43 'workers and bosses': Frederick W. Taylor, *The Principles of Scientific Management*, pp. 10, 26, 128, Harper, New York, 1913

43 'had as much impact': Peter F. Drucker, *Toward the Next Economics*, p. 104, Harper & Row, New York, 1981 (Heinemann, London, 1981)

43 'On their claims': Rosabeth Moss Kanter, *Men and Women of the Corporation*, pp. 20-21, New York, 1977

44 'Power and machinery': Henry Ford (with Samuel Crowther), *My Life and Work*, p. 2, Heinemann, London, 1923

44 'When his son Edsel': Robert Lacey, *Ford: The Men and the Machine*, pp. 270, 264, Heinemann, London, 1986

44 'There is no bent of mind': Ford, op. cit., p. 91

45 'It is not necessary': ibid., p. 92

45 'Marx made theory': Lacey, op. cit., p. 320

45 'Year of our Ford': Aldous Huxley, *Brave New World*, 1932

46 'The destruction of crafts': Paul Krause, *The Battle for Homestead, 1880-1892: Politics, Culture and Steel*, University of Pittsburg Press, 1992

46 'The real and effectual': Adam Smith, *The Wealth of Nations*, Chapter 10, Part 2, 1776

46 'the triumph of this system': MIT Commission on Industrial Productivity, *Made in America*, p. 47, MIT Press, 1989

47 'When the global marketplace': For the story, see the MIT study *The Machine that Changed the World*, pp. 48-69, Random House, New York, 1990

47 'drummers or greeters': C. Wright Mills, *White Collar*, p. 162, Oxford University Press, New York, 1953

47 'His suit was of a striped': Theodore Dreiser, *Sister Carrie*, op. cit., Chapter 1

49 'Standard Oil of New Jersey': Hill and Knowlton, op. cit., p. 244

50 'The American businessman of 1840': Chandler, *The Visible Hand*, op. cit., p. 455

50 'instead of investing': Thorstein Veblen, *The Theory of Business Enterprise*, p. 23, Scribners, New York, 1904

50 'Modern business enterprise': Chandler, op. cit., p. 339

CHAPTER FOUR

52 'the dingy little back office': Charles Dickens, *Sketches by Boz*, 1837

52 'a pallid forlorn young scrivener': Herman Melville, *Bartleby*. Originally published in *Putnam's Monthly*, 1853, reprinted in *The Piazza Tales*, 1856

53 'raised above the level': Charles Wilson, *The History of Unilever*, Vol. 1, p. 48, Cassell, London, 1954

53 'The office was beginning': David Landes, *The Unbound Prometheus*, p. 322, Cambridge University Press, 1969

53 'a new kind of': Francis Duffy, *The Changing Workplace*, p. 132, Phaidon, London, 1992

53 Shan F. Bullock, *Mr Ruby Jumps the*

Traces, Chapman & Hall, London, 1917

54 'He was always bending over': Sinclair Lewis, *Our Mr Wrenn*, Harper, New York, 1914

54 'the Clifton aims': Henry B. Fuller, *The Cliff-Dwellers*, Introduction, Harper & Brothers, New York, 1893

54 'the Larkin building': Duffy, op. cit. p. 136

55 'and soon it will be': George Gissing, *In the Year of Jubilee*, Laurence & Bullen, London, 1894

55 'I advise fools': ibid.

55 'The casual wanderer': Dreiser, *Sister Carrie*, op. cit., Chapter 2

56 'the machine and the maiden': ibid., Chapter 5

56 'beat them altogether': *St James's Gazette*, 22 December 1884. Quoted in *New English Dictionary*

56 'wondering at the amazing': Theodore Dreiser, *The Titan*, Chapter 16, uniform edition, Constable, London, 1928

56 'a brisk little woman': George Bernard Shaw, *Candida*, Act 1, *Plays Pleasant and Unpleasant*, Constable, London, 1898

57 'the marriage of the type-writer': *How to Get Married*, 1895. Quoted in *New English Dictionary*

57 'the air of unmerited wrong': William Dean Howells, *Silas Lapham*, David Douglas, Edinburgh, 1885

57 'He gives her letters': Henry Fuller, *The Cliff-Dwellers*, op. cit., p. 187

57 'Evangeline Côté': Lacey, op. cit., pp. 184–91

57 'Head office, in a smart quarter': Peter Young, *Person to Person: The International Impact of the Telephone*, p. 18, Granta Editions, Cambridge, 1991

58 'the telephone has been': Hugh Thomas, *Unfinished History*, p. 393, paperback edition, Pan Books, London, 1981

58 'E.H. Harriman was reported': Peter Young, ibid., p. 69, quoting Herbert

Casson's *History of the Telephone*, 1910

58 'With the new instrument': *The Times*, quoted by Peter Young, ibid.

58 'of such stentorian efficiency': Michael Holroyd, *Bernard Shaw*, Vol. 1, p. 79, Chatto & Windus, 1988

58 'exploited his experience': George Bernard Shaw, *The Irrational Knot*, Constable, London, 1905

58 'Strindberg first introduced it': Peter Young, op. cit., p. 48

59 'Even in Tokyo': ibid., pp. 27–31.

59 'A man who has no office': George Bernard Shaw, *The Irrational Knot*, op. cit., Chapter 18

59 'Between 1861 and 1911': Alan Delgado, *The Enormous File: A Social History of the Office*, p. 38, John Murray, London, 1979

59 'In the morning, at nightfall': M. Mostyn Bird, *Women at Work*, p. 130, Chapman & Hall, London, 1911

59 'She is at the service': ibid., p. 126

60 'women secretaries are': ibid., pp. 134–50

60 '*Ladies' Home Journal*': Rosabeth Moss Kanter, *Men and Women of the Corporation*, op. cit., p. 26

60 'an efficient, intolerant': Sinclair Lewis, *Our Mr Wrenn*, op. cit.

61 'in this fumbling school': Sinclair Lewis, *The Job*, p. 31, 1916

61 'A world is this': ibid., p. 47

62 'He could not run his machine': Adams, op. cit., p. 445.

63 'The workshop and the office': Walther Rathenau (trans. Eden and Cedar Paul), *In Days to Come*, p. 153, Allen & Unwin, London, 1921

63 'I'm not complaining': Franz Kafka, letter to Hedwig. Quoted in Ronald Hayman, *K: A Biography of Kafka*, p. 63, Weidenfeld & Nicolson, London, 1981

64 'each time it passed': ibid., p. 145

64 'the only true hell': ibid., pp. 160–1

64 'Kafka came and went': ibid., p. 278

CHAPTER FIVE

65 'This world, which has': Landes, *The Unbound Prometheus*, op. cit., p. 554

65 'No longer does': Sinclair Lewis, *The Job*, op. cit., p. 31

65 'Business itself was': Frederick Lewis Allen, *Only Yesterday*, p. 177, Harper & Brothers, New York and London, 1931

66 'greatest Human-nature Expert': ibid., p. 179

66 'Moses was one of the greatest': ibid., p. 180

66 'picked up twelve men': Arthur M. Schlesinger Jr, *The Age of Roosevelt*, Vol. 1, p. 75, Heinemann, London, 1957

66 G.K. Chesteron, *What I Saw in America*, p. 109, Hodder & Stoughton, London, 1922

67 Thorstein Veblen, *The Engineers and the Price System*, 1921 (reprinted by A.M. Kelley, New York, 1965)

67 'turned upon its masters': see Schlesinger, op. cit., pp. 477–80

68 'No executive has fulfilled': Larson et al, *New Horizons*, Harper & Row, New York, 1971

68 For details of Teagle's career, see Bennett H. Wall and George S. Gibb, *Teagle of Jersey Standard*, Tulane University, New Orleans, 1974

69 'I wanted one': Alfred P. Sloan, *My Years with General Motors*, p. 22, Doubleday Anchor Books edition, 1972

69 'any rigidity': ibid., p. 514

70 'an ideally bullish address': Allen, *Only Yesterday*, op. cit., pp. 302–3

70 'not the appropriate': Sloan, op.cit, p. 510

70 'Decentralisation or not': ibid., p. 59

71 'He created in the': Peter Drucker, *The Frontiers of Management*, op. cit, p. 284

71 'The street might as well': Robert Manning, *The Swamp Root Chronicle*,

p. 16, W.W. Norton, New York, 1992

72 'Loyalty saves the wear and tear': William Rodgers, *Think*, p. 100, Weidenfeld & Nicolson, London, 1970

72 'We're here to cheer': ibid., p. 114

72 'Magazine cartoonists': Thomas J. Watson Jr and Peter Petre, *Father, Son & Co*, p. 69, Bantam Press, New York, 1990

72 'I want my IBM salemen': Drucker, op. cit., p. 282

74 'Now what has produced': Charles Wilson, *The History of Unilever*, op. cit., Vol. 1, p. 292

74 'you had to cable London': W.J. Reader, *Fifty Years of Unilever*, pp. 24, 32, Heinemann, London, 1980

75 'the Empire would be': W.J. Reader, *Imperial Chemical Industries, A History. Vol. 1: The Forerunners, 1870–1926*, pp. 463–4

75 'competition was essential': W.J. Reader in *Dictionary of National Biography 1961–70*, p. 695, Oxford University Press, 1981

75 'it is quite impossible': H. Withers in *Dictionary of National Biography 1922–1930*, p. 603, Oxford University Press, 1937

75 'artistically Billingham is': Aldous Huxley, 'Sight-seeing in Alien England', *Nash's Pall Mall Magazine*, lxxxvii, June 1931. Reprinted in *The Hidden Huxley*, p. 69, Faber & Faber, London, 1994

76 'They can't do without me': W.J. Reader, *Imperial Chemical Industries, A History, Vol 2: The First Quarter-Century, 1926–1952*, pp. 239–47, Oxford University Press, 1975

76 'inspired by the Raj': Robert Henriques, *Sir Robert Waley Cohen*, pp. 61, 167, 170, 258, Secker & Warburg, London, 1966

76 'spend their lives': ibid., pp. 332–3

77 'Sir Henri's word': Yergin, *The Prize*, op. cit., pp. 369–70. See also Adrian Hamilton, *Oil, The Price of Power*, p. 50, Michael Joseph, London, 1986

77 'Always be determined': Letter 31 March 1856. See Werner Sombart (trans. M. Epstein), *The Quintessence of Capitalism*, p. 186, T. Fisher Unwin, London, 1915

78 'You pass no judgement': ibid., p. 189

78 'Three hundred men': Count Henry Kessler, *Walther Rathenau: His Life and Work*, pp. 121, 108, Gerald Howe, London, 1929

78 'The de-individualisation': Rathenau, *In Days to Come*, op. cit., p. 121

79 'The immediate guardians': Hans Speier, *German White-Collar Workers and the Rise of Hitler* (written but unpublished in 1933), p. 105, Yale University Press, 1986. Translation by the author.

80 'banality of evil': Hannah Arendt, *Eichmann in Jerusalem*, Chapter 15, 1963

80 'The greatest evil': C.S. Lewis, *The Screwtape Letters*, Preface, p. 9, (new edition) Geoffrey Bles, London, 1961

CHAPTER SIX

82 'Authors and actors': Dorothy Parker, *Bohemia: The Collected Dorothy Parker*, p. 223, Duckworth, London, 1974

82 'self-contained blocks': C. Wright Mills, *White Collar*, op. cit., p. 192

82 'the new American profession': ibid., p. 193

83 'sounds more like': Sinclair Lewis, *Babbitt*, Chapter 1, 1922

83 'austere towers of steel and cement': ibid.

83 'he beheld the tower': ibid.

83 'The little unknown people': ibid., Chapter 3

83 'huge, circular, frameless lenses': ibid., Chapter 1

83 'his car is poetry': ibid., Chapter 3

83 'It's here in Zenith': ibid., Chapter 14.

84 'the Company must make the boy': Robert Ferguson, *Henry Miller: A Life*, p. 65, Hutchinson, London, 1991

84 'was in an airless cage': ibid., p. 90

84 'my own master absolute': ibid., p. 99

84 'I want to prevent': Henry Miller, *Tropic of Capricorn*, p. 279, John Calder, London, 1964

85 'He would disclaim': John O'Hara, *Butterfield 8*, Chapter 3, New York, 1935

85 'he came home that evening': Andrew Turnbull, *Scott Fitzgerald*, Bodley Head, London, 1962

85 'Grandpapa Pulham made hooks and eyes': J.P. Marquand, *H.M. Pulham, Esq.*, Robert Hale, London, finished 1940

85 'Advertising, what a thing': ibid.

86 'I have lived': ibid.

86 'I think this is': Dorothy L. Sayers, *Murder Must Advertise*, Gollancz, London, 1933

86 'He had never realised': ibid.

86 'as far as I can make out': ibid.

86 'an actual rest': John Stuart Mill, *Autobiography*, op. cit., Chapter 3

87 'Oh forget it': Peter Brazeau, *Parts of a World: Wallace Stevens Remembered*, Random House, New York, 1983

87 'Wallace was such a giant': ibid., pp. 24, 48, 21, 39

87 'he needed the discipline': Peter Ackroyd, *T.S. Eliot*, pp. 78–9, 100, Hamish Hamilton, London, 1984

88 'as dreary and as permanent': Booth Tarkington, *Alice Adams*, Doubleday, New York, 1921

88 'pretty girls turned into': ibid.

88 'In your day': John Dos Passos, *The Forty-Second Parallel*, Constable, London, 1930

89 'ammunitioned with paper': Arnold

Bennett, *Lilian*, Cassell, London, 1922

89 'lose the typewriting girl': ibid.

89 'she was the most romantic': ibid.

89 'Well, I got the job': George Orwell, *Coming Up for Air*, Secker & Warburg, London, 1939

89 'shedding a part of themselves': J.B. Priestley, *Angel Pavement*, Heinemann, London, 1930

89 'his days at the office': ibid.

90 'some huge, some overwhelming grievance': ibid.

90 'they're half dead': ibid.

90 'I love Sir Phoebus': Stevie Smith, *Novel on Yellow Paper*, pp. 16, 204, Jonathan Cape, London, 1936

90 'As skyscrapers replace': C. Wright Mills, *White Collar*, op. cit., p. 189

CHAPTER SEVEN

92 'If America ever destroyed': See William H. Whyte, *Organisation Man*, p. 396, Jonathan Cape, London, 1956

92 'Less than ten years': Peter Drucker, *The Concept of the Corporation*, pp. 5, 9, 142, Transaction Publishers, New Brunswick and London, 1993

93 'The management cadre': C. Wright Mills, *White Collar*, op. cit., p. 86

93 'The prime contractors': Chandler, *The Visible Hand*, op. cit., p. 483

94 'A policy of nonaction': Adolf Berle, *Power without Property*, p. 50, Sidgwick & Jackson, London, 1960

94 'from the type of society': James Burnham, *The Managerial Revolution*, p. 17, Indiana University Press, Bloomington, 1960

95 'We had then, in effect': T.K. Quinn, *Giant Business*, p. 145, Exposition Press, New York, 1953

96 'any loss of imagination': Mabel Newcomer, op. cit.

96 'a vast system of passing the buck': Edmund Wilson, quoted in Wright Mills, op. cit., p. 107

96 'All managers are "middle managers"': ibid., p. 106

96 'the capitalist spirit': ibid., p. 107.

96 'What became of the independent spirit': Clark Kerr, *Fortune*, July 1953

96 'if one is successful': David Riesman, *The Lonely Crowd*, pp. 127–30, revised edition, Yale University Press, 1961

97 'I want to eat': Sloan Wilson, *The Man in the Gray Flannel Suit*, 1954

97 'I really don't know': ibid.

97 'The conflict between individual and society': Whyte, op. cit., pp. 400, 404

98 'been neglected by': Crawford Greenewalt, *The Uncommon Man*, p. 12, McGraw-Hill, New York, 1959

98 'Teams of labourers': ibid.

98 Vance Packard, *The Status Seekers*, Chapters 1, 20, 22, New York, 1959

98 Vance Packard, *The Pyramid Climbers*, McGraw-Hill, New York, 1962

99 'All but shattered': Henrietta Larson et al, *New Horizons 1927–50*, p. 585, Harper & Row, New York, 1971

99 'Millions of people': ibid., p. 639

99 'the social order of things': ibid., p. 650

99 'developing reserves of key personnel': Holman, ibid., p. 595

100 Drucker, *The Concept of the Corporation*, op. cit., pp. 291–303

101 'The committees are the company': Joseph Kraft, *The Downsizing Decision*, p. 140, *New Yorker*, 5 May 1980

101 Watson: 'You can make wild ducks tame': see also Thomas J. Peters and Robert H. Waterman, *In Search of Excellence*, p. 222, HarperCollins, London, 1982

102 'If I'm ever confronted': Peter de Vries, 'A Hard Day at the Office', from *Without a Stitch in Time*, 1974

102 'reaches forward': J.K. Galbraith, *The New Industrial State*, p. 168, Hamish Hamilton, London, 1967

104 *How to Succeed in Business Without Really Trying*, film version directed and produced by David Swift, 1967. Loosely based on the book of the same title by Shepherd Mead.

104 'Nobody is sure anymore': Joseph Heller, *Something Happened*, p. 19, Corgi Books, London, 1975

105 'orgy of morale building': Kurt Vonnegut, *Player Piano*, p. 34, Dell, New York, 1988

105 'short story about': Kurt Vonnegut, 'Deer in the Works', from *Welcome to the Monkey House*, Jonathan Cape, London, 1969

105 Alan Harrington, *Life in the Crystal Palace*, pp. 19, 215, Jonathan Cape, London, 1960

CHAPTER EIGHT

106 'In a culture of being': Alistair Mant, *The Rise and Fall of the British Manager*, p. 117, Macmillan, London, 1971

107 'The basic fact is': Anthony Crosland, *The Future of Socialism*, p. 480, Jonathan Cape, London, 1956

107 'Jelly-fish where their predecessors': Anthony Crosland, *The Conservative Enemy*, p. 55, Jonathan Cape, London, 1962

107 'when the house is finished': see Chapter 2

108 'But you couldn't do that': Nigel Balchin, *Sundry Creditors*, William Collins, London, 1953

108 'I am a young executive': John Betjeman, 'Executive', from *A Nip in the Air*, John Murray, London, 1974

108 'faced the plod': Roy Fuller, *Spanner and Pen*, p. 63, Sinclair-Stevenson, London, 1991

109 'Here was an organisation': Roy Fuller, *Image of a Society*, Andre Deutsch, London, 1956

109 'they sidelined their most': see Felicia Traun, *You Keep Moving . . .! A Biography of FAC Guepin*, Jaques & Sitwell, London, 1988

111 'it is quite impossible': see Chapter 5

112 'The oldest of all': see *Financial Times*, 16 February 1993

113 'Tercentenarians Club': Letter from Henry G. Button, Hon. Secretary of the Tercentenarians Club, Christ's College, Cambridge

113 'in 1968 fifteen families': See Anthony Sampson, *The New Europeans*, p. 109, Hodder & Stoughton, London, 1968

114 'more continuous commitment': see W.D. Rubinstein, *Capitalism, Culture and Decline in Britain, 1750–1990*, Routledge, London, 1993

114 'You are the only one': Arrigo Levi, *Interview on Modern Capitalism*, Chapter 1, Laterza, Italy, 1983

114 'I am what the Italians call': ibid.

114 'I would never make a decision': ibid., Chapter 11

114 'I have never compared myself': ibid., Chapter 3

115 'So marked was the middle-class origin': M.M. Postan, *An Economic History of Western Europe*, p. 291, University Paperbacks, London, 1967

115 'At the top of German enterprises': Ralf Dahrendorf, *Society and Democracy in Germany*, p. 259, Doubleday, New York, 1967

116 'that Continental nuisance': Thomas Carlyle, *Latter-day pamphlets*, IV, 1872

116 'the best symbols': Michel Crozier (trans. David Landau), *The World of the Office Worker*, p. viii, University of Chicago Press, 1971

116 'Young people will have to discover': ibid., pp. xii–xiii

117 'The US is a country': Levi, op. cit., Chapter 11

117 'had often wondered why people': Vikram Seth, *A Suitable Boy*, p. 1009, Phoenix, London, 1994

117 'The endless rows': ibid., p. 993

118 'today's economic conditions': interview with Thomas Bata in *McKinsey Quarterly*, No. 2, 1994

118 'I worked at a factory': Edward Crankshaw, *Khrushchev*, p. 19, William Collins, London, 1966

119 'the industrial manager is kingpin': David Granick, *The Red Executive*, p. 8, Macmillan, London, 1960

119 'the Russians are still fighting': ibid., p. 166 (see also Milovan Djilas, *The New Class*, 1957)

119 'don't buck the system': Hedrick Smith, *The Russians*, p. 305, Ballantine, New York, 1977

120 'the only sector': ibid., p. 312.

120 'The lone wolf': Vladimir Dudintsev (trans. Edith Bone), *Not by Bread Alone*, Hutchinson, London, 1957

120 'Like an enormous ship': ibid., p. 243

120 'Now at last I see': ibid., p. 430

120 'We speak boldly': ibid., p. 243

CHAPTER NINE

122 Thomas Whiteside, *The Investigation of Ralph Nader*, pp. 166, 103, Pocket Books, New York, 1972

123 'I am responsible': ibid., p. 67

123 'A GM willing to accept': Drucker, *The Concept of the Corporation*, op. cit., p. 309

123 'the twenty largest': see speech of John Mitchell in Savannah, 6 June 1969

123 'In this society of ours': see Anthony Sampson, *The Sovereign State*, p. 135, Hodder & Stoughton, London, 1973

124 'Work expands so as to fill': *Parkinson's Law*, John Murray, London, 1958

124 Laurence J. Peter and Raymond Hull, *The Peter Principle*, William Morrow, New York, 1969

124 'If you have a good company': Robert Townsend, *Up the Organisation*, p. 104, Coronet, London, 1971

124 'If the chief executive': ibid., p. 181

124 'You couldn't save a company': Sampson, *The Sovereign State*, op. cit., pp. 76–7

125 'Theory Y': Douglas McGregor, *The Human Side of Enterprise*, McGraw-Hill, New York, 1960

125 'Theory Z': Abraham Maslow, *Motivation and Personality*, Harper & Row, New York, 1954

125 'Being the customer': Andrzej Huczynski, *Management Gurus*, p. 147, Routledge, London and New York, 1993

126 'The people recognise': Herbert Marcuse, *One-Dimensional Man*, p. 9, Routledge, London, 1964

127 'The real threat': Robert McNamara, *The Essence of Security*, pp. 109–10, Harper & Row, New York, 1968

127 'It is to level life down': Theodore Roszak, *The Making of a Counter Culture*, p. 12, Faber & Faber, London, 1970

128 'After twenty years': Eric Hobsbawm, *Age of Extremes*, p. 285, Michael Joseph, 1994

128 'for the workers': Danny Cohn-Bendit, quoted in Anthony Sampson, *The New Europeans*, p. 130, Hodder & Stoughton, London, 1968

129 'in the most highly motorised': *Vision* Magazine, Paris, May 1972

130 'served as a warning' Hobsbawm, op. cit., p. 285

131 'the search of the youth today': William O. Douglas, *Points of Rebellion*, p. 96, Vintage Books, New York, 1970

131 'the individual is liberated': Charles

Reich, *The Greening of America*,
Penguin, London, 1971

132 'Given our socioeconomic system':
Michael Maccoby, *The Gamesman:
The New Corporate Leaders*, p. 120,
Secker & Warburg, London, 1977

132 'put to use': Ronald Fraser, *1968:
A Student Generation in Revolt*, p. 313,
Chatto & Windus, London, 1988

133 'SDS was absolutely': ibid., pp. 268,
242

134 'to compete seriously': Donald
Burr, quoted in Anthony Sampson,
Empires of the Sky, p. 216, Hodder
& Stoughton, London, 1984

135 'being an entrepreneur': Mick
Brown, *Richard Branson: The Inside
Story*, p. 425, Headline, London,
1992

135 'typically exists naturally': see
Economist Seminar, quoted in
Financial Times, 25 May 1994

CHAPTER TEN

139 'the world's political structures':
Richard J. Barnet and Ronald E.
Muller, *Global Reach*, p. 19, Simon
& Schuster, New York, 1974

139 'the political boundaries'. ibid.,
p18–19

139 'an international corporation' ibid.,
p. 56

139 'I have long dreamed': ibid., pp. 16,
56

139 'the same way all over': Ralph Nader
and William Taylor, *The Big Boys*,
p. 154, Pantheon, New York, 1986

140 'is the most powerful agent': Barnet
and Muller, op. cit., p. 13

140 'the first in history': ibid.

141 'because nobody believes': Nader
and Taylor, op. cit., p. 161

141 'I wonder if': Stanley Adams, *Roche
versus Adams*, p. 226, Jonathan
Cape, London, 1984

141 'As the role and influence':
Christopher Tugendhat, *The
Multinationals*, p. 208, Eyre &
Spottiswoode, London, 1971

141 'when the history': Hugh
Stephenson, *The Coming Clash*,
p. 176, Weidenfeld & Nicolson,
London, 1972

143 'has created a': Sampson, *The
Sovereign State*, op. cit., p. 150.

144 'I want no surprises': ibid., p. 92

144 'Don't you think': Robert Sobel,
ITT, p. 334, Times Books, New
York, 1982

146 'We must re-examine': Anthony
Sampson, *The Seven Sisters*, p. 273,
Hodder & Stoughton, London,
1975

148 'AVIS UNILEVERENSIS': quoted
in Anthony Sampson, *Anatomy of
Britain*, p. 438, Hodder &
Stoughton, London, 1962

149 'Now we are beginning':
Jean-Jacques Servan-Schreiber, *The
American Challenge*, Athenaeum,
New York and Hamish Hamilton,
London, 1968

150 'In the closing years': Richard
Barnet and John Cavanagh, *Global
Dreams*, p. 440, Simon & Schuster,
New York, 1994

151 'Everyone woke up to it': Thomas
Wolfe, *Bonfire of the Vanities*, p. 59,
Jonathan Cape, London, 1988

152 'As the top becomes': Robert Reich,
The Work of Nations, p. 301, Vintage
Books, New York, 1992

CHAPTER ELEVEN

153 'the earthquake of 1923': Shigeto
Tsuru, *Japan's Capitalism*, p. 67,
Cambridge University Press, 1993

153 'The business world in Japan':
Morishima, *Democracy and
Economic Growth*, op. cit.

154 'the most dynamic': MIT, *The
Machine that Changed the World*,
op. cit., p. 195.

154 'They were built': Ronald P. Dore
and Mari Sako, *How the Japanese
Learn to Work*, p. 25, Routledge,
London and New York, 1989

154 'They could quickly': Morishima,

Banking and Industry in Japan, op. cit.

154 'But in a consumer industry': Morita, interview with the author, Tokyo, 20 September 1988

155 'All warfare is based on deception': Sun Tzu, *The Art of War* (edited by James Clavell), pp. 11ff, Delacorte Press, New York, 1983

156 'Two American consultants': James C. Abbeglen and George Stalk Jr, *Kaisha: The Japanese Corporation*, Charles E. Tuttle, Tokyo, 1987

157 'It is middle management': quoted in Charles Hampden-Turner and Fons Trompenaars, *The Seven Cultures of Capitalism*, p. 157, op. cit.

157 'The company resembles': ibid., p. 132

158 'We are going to win': quoted in Hamish Macrae, *The World in 2020*, p. 286, HarperCollins, London, 1994

159 'Although there was no increase': *Taiichi Ohno: Toyota Production System* , p. 18, Tokyo Diamond, 1978

160 'the factory of despair': Tsuru, op. cit., p. 191

162 'Nothing like it': MIT, *The Machine that Changed the World*, op. cit., p. 241

163 'number of Japanese managers': Bill Emmott, *Japan's Global Reach*, pp. 5, 68ff, Arrow Books, London, 1992

163 'Britain was by far': ibid., p. 17

164 'nobody could be more surprised': Akio Morita, *Made in Japan*, p. 126, Fontana, London, 1987

164 'British workers were cheaper': Emmott, op. cit., p. 19

164 'Thanks to Japan': Sir Christopher Hogg, interview with the author, 17 December 1993

165 'Japan is not a Western': Michael Crichton, *Rising Sun*, p. 393, Ballantine, New York, 1993

166 'Oriental multinationals': William

Gibson, *Burning Chrome*, Gollancz, London, 1986

CHAPTER TWELVE

168 'The heroic role': Veblen, *The Theory of Business Enterprise*, op. cit., p. 49

168 'The prevailing theory': George Gilder, *The Spirit of Enterprise*, p. 15, Penguin, London, 1984

168 'Capitalism, as an institutional arrangement': Peter Berger, *The Capitalist Revolution*, p. 195, Basic Books, New York, 1986

169 'Capitalism transforms': Gilder, op. cit., p. 34

170 'We, and all other animals': Richard Dawkins, *The Selfish Gene*, pp. 2, 9, Oxford University Press, Oxford and New York, 1989

170 'In all human societies': W.G. Runciman (Lord Runciman of Doxford), 'Competition for What?', Economic and Social Research Council annual lecture, London, 1993

170 'nature is red in tooth and claw': ibid.

171 'to buy oil on Wall Street': T. Boone Pickens, *Boone*, Houghton Mifflin, Boston, 1988

171 'It's the empire syndrome': ibid., p. 138

173 'I haven't seen you so aroused': Louis Auchinloss, *Honorable Men*, Houghton Mifflin, Boston, 1985

173 'abandoned property': Louis Auchinloss, *Diary of a Yuppie*, Weidenfeld & Nicolson, London, 1987

173 'Texaco is the quintessence': *Sunday Times*, 5 June 1988

173 'the infrastructure is crumbling': Michel Albert (trans. Paul Haviland), *Capitalism Against Capitalism*, p. 55, Whurr Publishers, London, 1993

174 'Anyone observing the raids': ibid., p. 66

174 'they had underperformed': Sir James Goldsmith, International Mergers and Acquisitions Conference, reported in *International Herald-Tribune*, 16 November 1989

175 'Like many brilliant men': F. Scott Fitzgerald, *The Last Tycoon*, p. 117, Penguin Books, London, 1941

175 'you can't shoot': Anthony Sampson, *The Midas Touch*, p. 84, Coronet, London, 1990

176 'the life-giving link': ibid., p. 85

176 'I can think of no other': ibid.

176 'There were still too many': ibid., p. 87

177 'No matter how brilliant': Sir James Goldsmith, Lecture to Adam Smith Institute, London, 19 October 1989

177 'you can be greedy': Sampson, *The Midas Touch*, op. cit., p. 44

177 'mergers reached a new intensity': Margaret Blair (ed.), *The Deal Decade*, p. 289, Brookings Institution, Washington, 1993

178 'a new kind of non-company man': Bryan Burrough and John Helyar, *Barbarians at the Gate*, p. 28, Arrow Books, London, 1990

178 'I don't feel': ibid., p. 622

179 'I love the notoriety': Bryan Burrough, *Barbarians in Retreat*, *Vanity Fair*, March 1993

179 'Jungle red in tooth and claw': Lord Attlee in the House of Lords, 1961

181 'If people ask': interview with Lord Hanson, 13 May 1994

182 'A system which favours': Stanley Wright, *Two Cheers for the Institutions*, p. 33, Social Market Foundation, London, 19??

183 'the largest and longest': William F. Long and David J. Ravenscraft in Blair, *The Deal Decade*, op. cit., p. 205

183 'The improved returns': ibid., p. 5

184 'However much we want': Sampson, *The Midas Touch*, op. cit., p. 59

184 'which earned the loyalty': Albert, *Capitalism Against Capitalism*, op. cit., p. 146

184 'they have become personalities': ibid., p. 196

185 'Things have come a long way': ibid., p. 75

CHAPTER THIRTEEN

186 'Whether we entrust': Norbert Wiener, *The Human Use of Human Beings*, p. 213, Eyre & Spottiswoode, London, 1950

187 'after reading in *Reader's Digest*': Ken Gross, *Ross Perot: The Man Behind the Myth*, pp. 75, 76, 95, Random House, New York, 1992

187 'They had discovered': Tracy Kidder, *The Soul of a New Machine*, pp. 136ff, Avon, New York, 1982

188 'It's a binary world': ibid., p. 146

188 'Kidder concluded': ibid., pp. 240-4.

189 'A barrel of money': see Lacey, *Ford*, op. cit., p. 41

190 'But Xerox could not': For the problems of PARC see Robert X. Cringley, *Accidental Empires*, pp. 82-92, HarperBusiness, New York, 1993

190 'PARC lost out': see Howard Rheingold in *Wired* Magazine, February 1994

191 'It's more fun': John Sculley with John A. Byrne, *Odyssey: From Pepsi to Apple*, pp. 219, 352, 523, William Collins, London, 1988

191 'We built a device': ibid., p. 199

192 'This came just': ibid., p. 265

192 'But by 1980': ibid., p. 438

193 'It doesn't matter': Kidder, op. cit., p. 146

194 'I was just going': Sculley and Byrne, op. cit., p. 59

194 'When I look into': ibid., p. 35

195 'like Rudolf Bing': ibid., p. 254

196 'The belief that men and women': *The HP Way*, Hewlett-Packard, Palo Alto, 1977

197 'Two well-informed critics':
Richard Florida and Martin
Kenney, *The Breakthrough Illusion*,
p. 94, Basic Books, New York,
1990

198 'A comparison of the two regions':
see AnnaLee Saxenian, 'Silicon
Valley Versus Route 128', *Inc*
Magazine, February 1994. See also
Saxenian, *Regional Advantage*,
Harvard University Press,
Cambridge Mass., 1994

200 'Seven octopuses': conference at
San Jose Convention Center,
February 1994

200 'Once business is using
multimedia': *Financial Times*, 8
March 1994

200 William Gibson: 'it was more like a
shopping mall': *Financial Times*, 6
September 1994

200 'Instead of information': John
Browning, *There Will be No Info
Highway*, *Wired* Magazine, February
1994

201 'Norbert Wiener had warned':
Wiener, op. cit., p. 189

201 'In the decade to 1992': see William
Bulkeley in The *Wall Street
Journal*, 1 March 1993

202 'A survey by *Fortune* magazine': 25
February 1991

202 'As an MIT': MIT, *Made in
America*, op. cit., p. 96

202 'Computer buffs': see Allen Myeson
in *International Herald-Tribune*, 28
July 1993

203 'Andersen Consulting': see Tim
Kelsey, 'The Great Computer
Catastrophe', *Independent*, 9 June
1993

203 'There has been a tremendous
reversal': *Wall Street Journal*, 1
March 1993

203 'Roach found that': *The Economist*,
22 January 1994

203 'Technologies like image painting':
Wall Street Journal, 1 March
1993

CHAPTER FOURTEEN

205 'a broad managerial failure': Robert
H. Hayes and William J. Abernathy,
'Managing Our Way to Economic
Decline', *Harvard Business Review*,
July–August 1980

205 'The keys to long-term success':
ibid.

206 'a world in which people': Henry M.
Strage (ed.), *Milestones in
Management*, p. 368, Blackwell
Business, Oxford, 1992

206 'If America is to regain': Peters and
Waterman, *In Search of Excellence*,
op. cit., p. 54

206 'an enormous error': Thomas J.
Peters, *Liberation Management*,
p. xxxi, Macmillan, London,
1992

207 'The international business
environment': MIT, *Made in
America*, op. cit., p. 8

207 'In the immediate': ibid.,
p. 77

207 'Under the new economic': ibid.,
p. 13

208 'Management ceases to be' Charles
Handy, *The Age of Unreason*, p. 122,
Arrow Books, London, 1990

209 'A citizen of the world': Robert
Reich, *The Work of Nations*, op. cit.,
p. 310

211 'Suddenly, employees': MIT, *The
Machine*, op. cit.

211 'brilliance unimpeded by humanity':
Nader and Taylor, op. cit., p. 142

211 'if you can't run': Drucker, *The
Concept of the Corporation*, op. cit.,
p. xii

212 'I could never understand': Gross,
Perot, op. cit., p. 198

212 'It was the first time': MIT, *The
Machine*, op. cit., p. 238

212 'It was a question': interview with
the author, Toyota City, December
1993

214 'offloaded 40 per cent': Yergin, *The
Prize*, op. cit., p. 741

214 'Whither the Chevron Way?':
Chevron Focus, San Francisco,
February/March 1993

214 'a strong culture': Terence Deal and
Alan Kennedy, *Corporate Culture*,
Penguin, London, 1988

216 'made clear the nature': Vonnegut,
Player Piano, op. cit., p34

217 'I'm just a grungy': Nader and
Taylor, op. cit., p. xv

217 'It's really the heart': ibid.,
p. 141

217 'The most competitive': Noel M.
Tichy and Stratford Sherman,
*Control Your Destiny or Someone Else
Will*, p. 168, Doubleday, New
York, 1993

217 'a paternal, feudal': ibid., p. 232

218 'one of the biggest': ibid., p. 197

219 'learn how to dance': Rosabeth
Moss Kanter, *When Giants Learn to
Dance,*, p. 20, Routledge, London,
1990

219 'The corporation is': ibid., pp. 368–9

CHAPTER SIXTEEN

230 'a favourite hobby': *Sunday
Telegraph*, 4 September 1994

231 'creeping stealthily': Richard
Donkin, *Financial Times*, 25 May
1994

231 'Whoever heard of': *Guardian*, 15
June 1994

231 'It's bizarre': *Independent on Sunday*,
12 June 1994

231 'Employees in Britain': ibid.

232 'these touchy-feely': Tichy and
Sherman, op.cit., p. 65

234 'there's only one': *Fortune*
Magazine, 23 September 1991

236 'the elephants' ballet': Sir John
Harvey-Jones, *Making it Happen*,
William Collins, London, 1988

238 'I think diversification': Anthony
Sampson, *The Changing Anatomy of
Britain*, p. 318, Hodder &
Stoughton, London, 1982

238 'Shell was considering': Peter
Schwartz, *The Art of the Long View*,

pp. 56–9, Doubleday Currency,
New York, 1991

239 'growing its own timber': *Fortune*
Magazine, 26 August 1991

239 'We have to choose between':
Broukman, interview with author,
17 February 1993

241 'The concept of federalism':
Harvard Business Review,
November–December 1992

242 'I believe you can go': interview with
William Taylor, *Harvard Business
Review*, March–April 1991

CHAPTER SEVENTEEN

248 'earning $105 million': see Ivan
Fallon, *The Player*, pp. 193, 352,
Hodder & Stoughton, London,
1994

248 'He had flown up': F. Scott
Fitzgerald, *The Last Tycoon*,
Chapter 1

251 'We are witnessing' John Naisbitt,
Reinventing the Future, pp. 12, 87,
1985

251 'Companies have been labouring':
Ronald Henkoff, 'Cost Cutting:
How to do it Right', *Fortune*
Magazine, 9 April 1990

252 'no political home': Drucker, *The
Concept of the Corporation*, op. cit.,
p. xx

252 'he was still very much': Leinberger
and Tucker, *The New Individualists*,
op. cit., p. 395

252 'middling rich' ibid., p. 393

253 'they were likely to': ibid., p. 2

253 'they looked towards
self-expression': ibid., pp. 11–15

253 'For what the successor': ibid.,
p. 403

253 'Maccoby ... conducted': Michael
Maccoby, 'American Character
and the Organizational Man', *The
World and I*, May 1990. See also
Maccoby, *Why Work? Motivating
and Leading the New Generation*,
Touchstone, New York, 1989

253 'foresaw all Europe': report from

Drake Beam Morin, New York,
September 1993

254 'Most writers portray': Sue Dopson
and Rosemary Stewart, Templeton
College, Oxford, 1989

254 'delayering posed no threat':
Malcolm Wheatley, *The Future of
Middle Management*, British Institute
of Management, 1992

255 'Far from being': *The Economist*, 3
September 1994

255 'As the number of layers': interview
with Roger Young, 21 July 1993

255 'delayering has meant': *Are
Managers Getting the Message?*,
Institute of Management, London,
1993

256 'There's no such thing': *Financial
Times*, 8 June 1993

256 'In the future': Harvey-Jones,
Making it Happen, op. cit., p. 70

257 'The dilemma of employers':
Financial Times, 1 June 1994

258 'By 1994 a poll': Will Hutton,
Guardian, 2 August 1994

259 'living laboratories': Huczynski,
Management Gurus, op. cit., p. 56

259 'IBM had even tried': ibid., p. 57

259 'As cells grow': Sculley and Byrne,
op. cit., p. 430

260 'he looked forward': Charles
Handy, *The Age of Unreason*, pp. 20,
132, Arrow Books, London, 1990

260 'Handy saw company': interview
with the author, 15 February 1993

261 'with total conformity':
Hampden-Turner and
Trompenaars, *The Seven Cultures of
Capitalism*, op. cit., pp. 42-3

262 'persuaded the county prosecutor':
Alecia Swasy, *Soap Opera: The
Inside Story of Procter & Gamble*,
pp. 291-305, New York Times
Books, 1993

CHAPTER EIGHTEEN

264 'The richness of life': Peters,
Liberation Management, op.cit.,
p. 375

265 'I decided that': Jonathan
Gathorne-Hardy, *The Office*,
Hodder & Stoughton, London,
1970

265 'as pleasant a way': Keith
Waterhouse, *Office Life*, Michael
Joseph, London, 1978

266 'During most of this period':
Francis Duffy, 'Findings in a
Context', paper by DEGW, London

267 'Our cities are still': Jeremy
Myerson, *Guardian*, 3 December
1993

269 '*Business Week* held a conference':
Sunday Telegraph, 29 July 1994

269 'The phone has become': *Financial
Times*, 28 January 1994.

270 'No walls': *Sunday Times*, 3 April
1994

270 'It advised clients': Voice Message
Educational Committee, *Making the
Most of Voice Mail*, Vanguard
Communications Corporation, 1-
201-605-8000

271 'we were intimate': John Seabrook,
E-Mail from Bill, *New Yorker*, 10
January 1994

271 'Only about 7.6 million': *Independent
on Sunday*, 20 February 1994

272 'A study of home teleworkers':
Leslie Haddon and Roger
Silverstone, *Guardian*, 22 March
1994

275 'the whole of downtown Seattle':
Joel Garreau, *Edge City*, p. 27,
Doubleday, New York, 1991

276 'Maybe it worked': ibid., p. 412

CHAPTER NINETEEN

277 'emotional economy': Michael
Roper, *Masculinity and the British
Organization Man Since 1945*, p. 6,
Oxford University Press, 1994

277 'Managerial work offered': ibid.,
p. 185, quoting Rosemary Pringle

278 'From the geyser ventilators': John
Betjeman, 'Business Girls', from *A
Few Late Chrysanthemums*, John
Murray, London, 1954

278 'The modern organisation': Mike Savage and Anne Witz (eds), *Gender and Bureaucracy*, pp. 10–11, Blackwell, Oxford, 1992

279 'power is neither': quoted by Michael Crichton in *Disclosure*, Century, London, 1994. Mrs Graham commented to me: 'Crichton said I said it, so I accept that.'

279 'When you married me': Auchinloss, *Honorable Men*, op. cit.

280 'Nien Cheng': Nien Cheng, *Life and Death in Shanghai*, Grafton Books, London, 1986

280 'wives were expected': Hilary Callen and Shirley Ardener (eds), *The Incorporated Wife*, pp. 124–32, Croom Helm, London, 1984

281 'a group of women employees': Swasy, *Soap Opera*, op. cit., pp. 11–12, 113–16

281 'Perhaps companies like Unilever': Political and Economic Planning, *Women in Top Jobs*, p. 77, Allen & Unwin, London, 1971

282 'The emotional style': Arlie Russell Hochschild, *The Managed Heart*, pp. 5, 7, University of California Press, 1985

282 'While managment was being defined': Kanter, *Men and Women . . .*, op. cit., p. 25

282 'The male is the name': quoted in Wright Mills, *White Collar*, op. cit., p. 200

282 'the company is in favor': Heller, *Something Happened*, op. cit., p. 71

283 '60 per cent of publishing assistants': see *Financial Times*, 14 July 1993

284 'Zac, you're so charming': Caryl Churchill, *Serious Money*, p. 104, Methuen, London, 1987

284 'In 1985 8 per cent': Savage and Witz, *Gender and Bureacracy*, op. cit., pp 142, 155. Also private information on Midland Bank.

285 'It is almost as though': Harvey-Jones, *Making it Happen*, op. cit., p. 256

285 'In 1977 only forty-six': Judith H. Dobrzynski in *Business Week*, 22 November 1993

285 'It has come about': *Financial Times*, 6 May 1994

286 'from 10.2 per cent': Institute of Management press release, 3 May 1994

286 'Now that hierarchy': Peters, *Liberation Management*, op. cit., p. 450

286 'the typical director': Arthur Andersen Corporate Register, quoted in *Financial Times*, 7 April 1992

286 'chief executives' secretaries': Reward Group report, 13 August 1992. See *Financial Times*, 14 August 1992

287 'In these more open': Mary Baker, letter to *The Times*, 9 May 1994

287 'Women succeed': see *International Herald-Tribune*, 19 August 1993

287 'People who can juggle': Charles Handy, *The Empty Raincoat*, p. 179, Hutchinson, London, 1994

288 'I don't cook': *Fortune* Magazine, 30 July 1990

288 'The ambition on the part': *Women in Management*, p. 34, Spencer Stuart, London, 1993

288 'Nearly all the women': see Eve MacSweeny, 'The Death of the Career Girl?', *Vogue*, London, April 1994

288 'Women have been succeeding': interview in *Daily Mail*, 7 July 1994

289 'A marriage within': Ezra Vogel, *Japan's New Middle Class*, p. 107, University of California Press, 1963

290 'twelve women': Takie Sugiyama Lebra: 'Gender and Culture in the Japanese Political Economy: Self-Portrayals of Prominent Businesswomen', in Kumon and Rosovsky (eds), *The Political Economy*

of Japan, Vol. 3, pp. 362–419, Stanford University Press, 1992

290 'You could say women': speech to School of Oriental and African Studies, London, 17 March 1993

CHAPTER TWENTY

294 'In some cases': Yashiro, speech to Foreign Press Center of Japan. See *Mainichi Daily News*, 8 December 1993

295 'Sony's white-collar staff': see Emiko Terazono in *Financial Times*, 23 May 1994

295 'Honda was trying': see *Financial Times*, 30 March 1994

298 'They're not going to change': *Business Week*, 6 June 1994

299 'A leader is best': *Business Week*, 1 November 1 1993

299 'The three of us': *Time*, 13 December 1993

300 'In this new world':Berger, in *McKinsey Quarterly*, 1994, Vol. 1

300 'For you, the essence of management': see Chapter 11

301 'a much more organic': see Hampden-Turner and Trompenaars, *The Seven Cultures of Capitalism*, op. cit., p. 132

302 'It was not till': MIT, *The Machine*, op. cit., p. 235

303 'same bed, different dreams': see *Insight Japan*, London, March 1994

303 'We're not selling watches': Perrin, quoted in *International Management*, London, December 1987

304 'Britain had 120,000 accountants': Management Services Commission, *The Making of Managers*, p. 12, Management Services Commission, London, 1987

304 'Companies have asked': ibid., pp. 13,16

305 'Moving from a classic':Peter Davis, *Independent on Sunday*, 3 July 1994

305 'I didn't want to keep living': Peter Davis, *Business Week*, 11 July 1994

306 'The core corporation': Reich, *The Work of Nations*, op. cit., pp. 81, 243

306 'As Christopher Lorenz': *Financial Times*, 27 April 27 1994

CHAPTER TWENTY-ONE

308 'It has pitilessly': Karl Marx, *The Communist Manifesto*, 1848

309 'The engine turns': *London Review of Books*, 7 April 1994

310 'The coming political battle': Robert Reich, quoted in *Financial Times*, 7 June 1994

310 'The social and cultural effects': John Gray, *The Undoing of Conservatism*, p. 22, Social Market Foundation, London, 1994

312 'ABB is not as decentralised': *Business Week*, 7 February 1994

313 'the corporate bureaucracy': Mochizuku, lecture to Royal Society of Arts, London, 1994

314 'The French caste system': British Council Conference on Production and Reproduction of Elites in France and Britain, Paris, 26 November 1993

315 'Four thousand gardeners': Albert, *Capitalism Against Capitalism*, op. cit., p. 81

315 'Escalation of fees': Wright, *Two Cheers for the Institutions*, op;. cit., p. 42

315 'You ain't seen nothin' yet': Graef Crystal, *Sunday Telegraph*, 2 October 1994

317 'Frankly, some payoffs': ibid.

317 'The funds can't manage': interview with the author, 19 November 1993

Index

339